very! very!
sweet

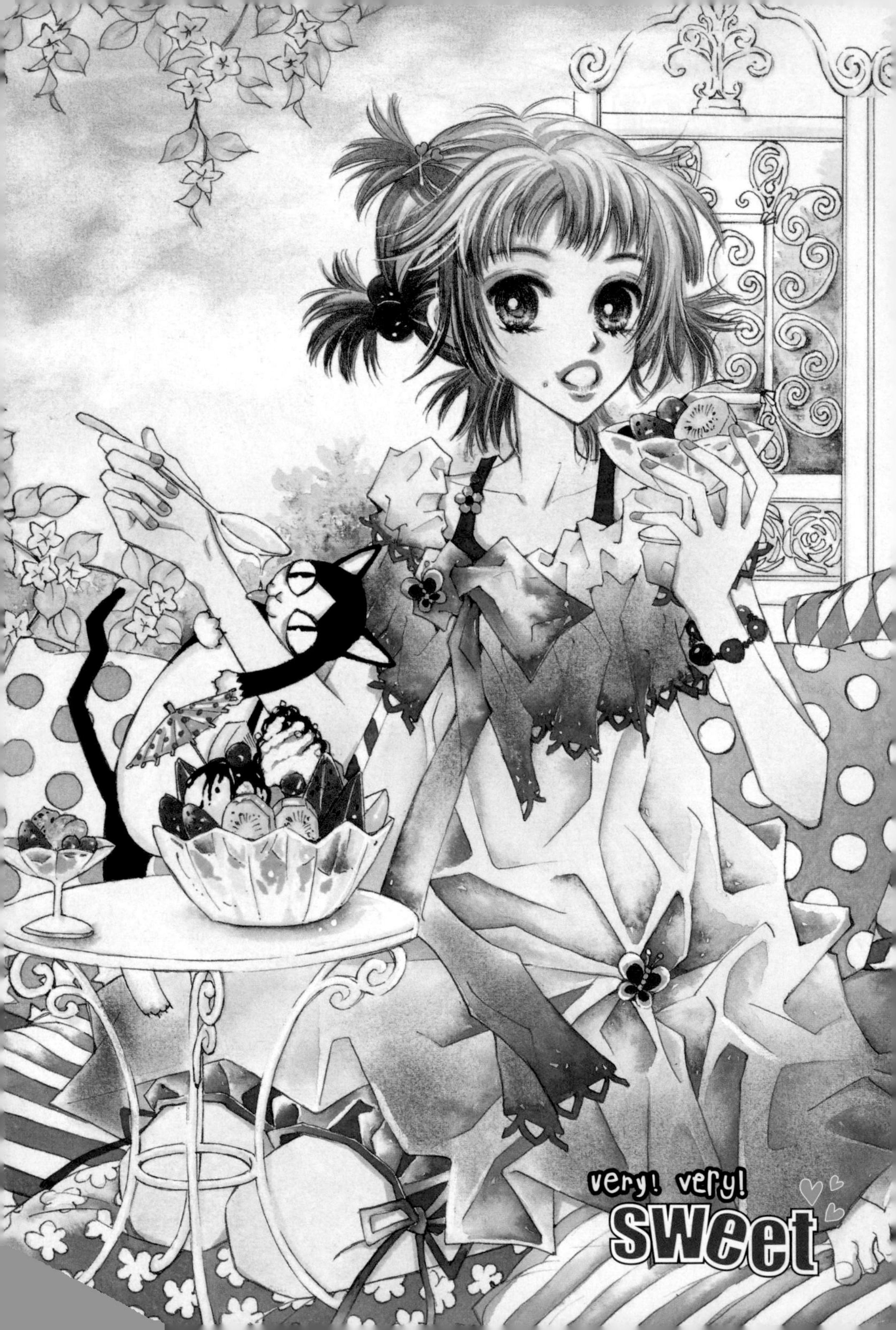
very! very!
sweet

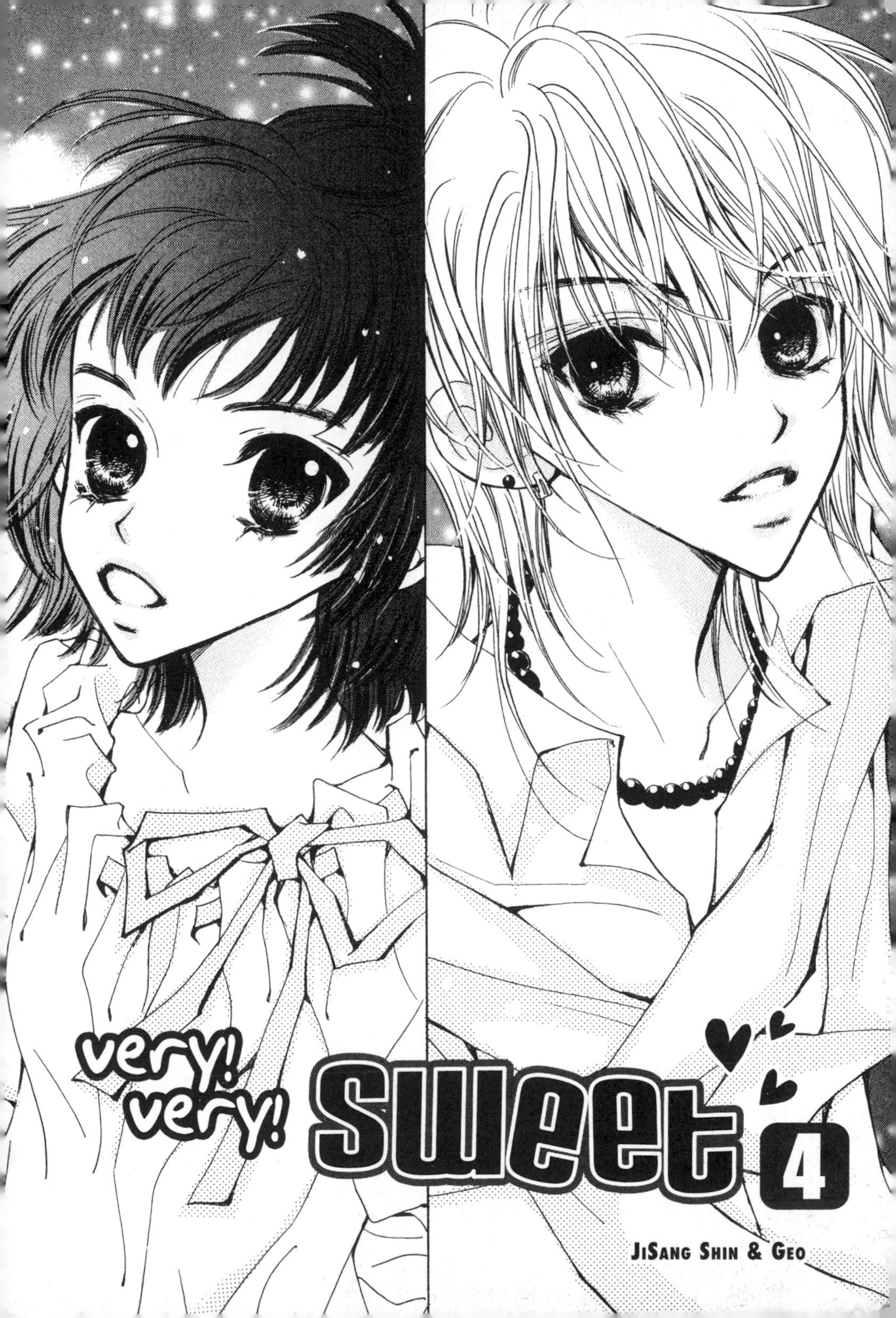
very! very! sweet 4
JiSang Shin & Geo

There's a certain place in my house where, if I face in that direction when I sleep, I always have nightmares. However, even knowing this, half the time I still end up sleeping facing that direction. Only after having a nightmare—and waking up disoriented—do I regret sleeping that way. I must be a birdbrain. I keep forgetting and forgetting and forgetting...

Perhaps it's because I've gotten old...??? But I can't even use that as an excuse. My forgetfulness has almost become a habit. Ever since I was young, I don't remember remembering anything for more than ten minutes. Even during elementary school, I'd always forget to bring my required materials for the day, and there were more days that I went to school without them than with them. What a difficult life it was for a girl at such a young age... T.T Even as a kid, worried over my future self, telling myself, "I mustn't be so forgetful when I'm an adult."

The reason I'm telling this story is because my old habits are still with me in "Very! Very! Sweet." Even here in volume 4, I made a huge mistake. Sniffle... There was a specific word I wanted to fix, and I totally forgot about it. So in this volume, there will be a certain part that won't make sense. ^^;;; What is it? Shall I give a present to the one who can guess it right? But in looking for that one mistake, I hope that there aren't a bunch of other mistakes being found... ^^;;

Anyway.
"Very! Very! Sweet!" has a lot of mistakes here and there, but, thanks to all you readers who still support us with lots of love and care, today as always this little birdbrain will pedal hard in creating a fun and mistake-free "Very! Very! Sweet"!!!

*Note: To preserve the jokes related to the character names, we have opted to keep Korean name order—family name first, given name last.

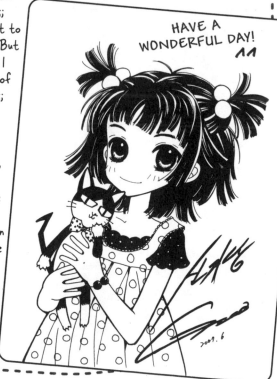

HAVE A WONDERFUL DAY! ^^
2007. 6

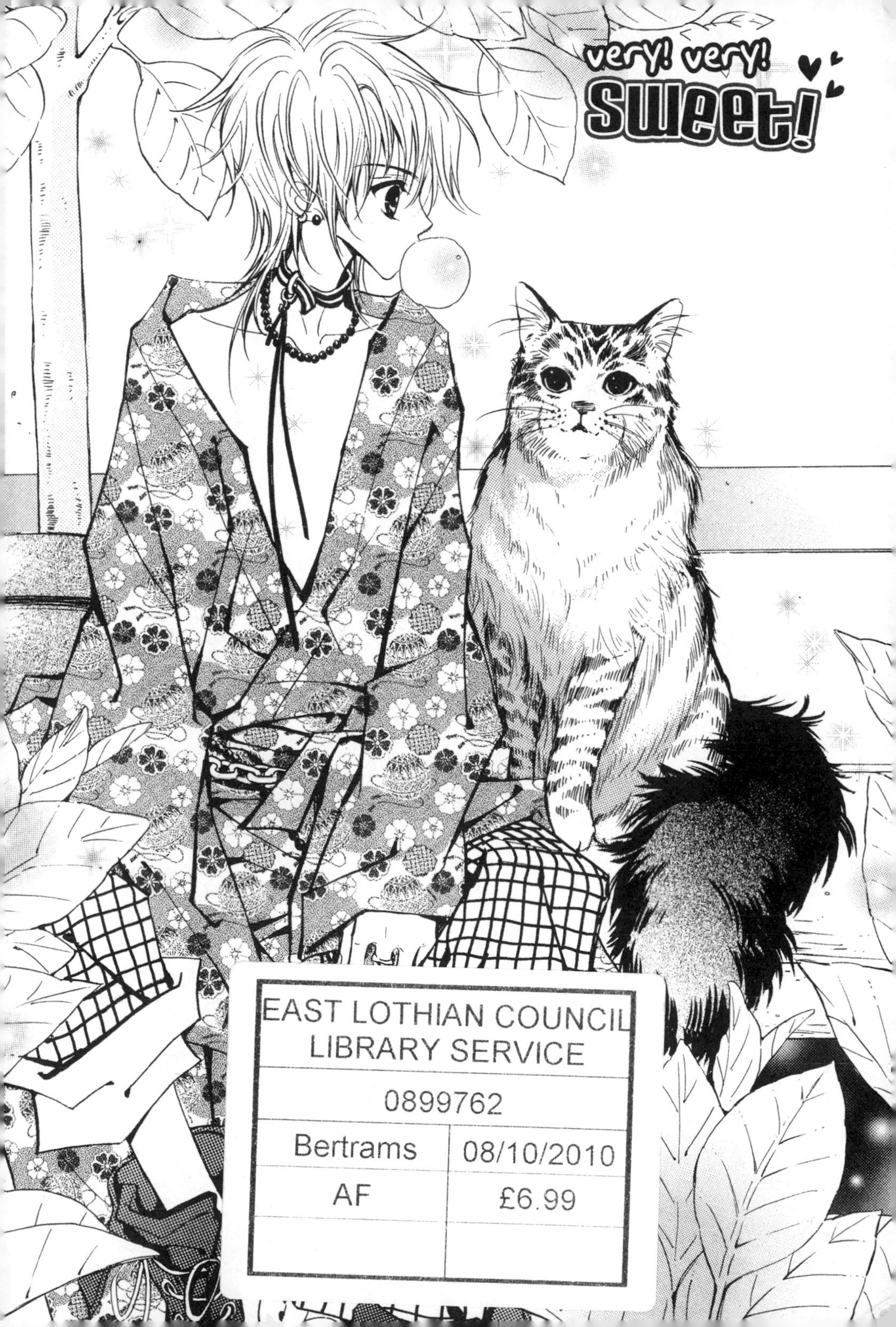
very! very!
sweet!

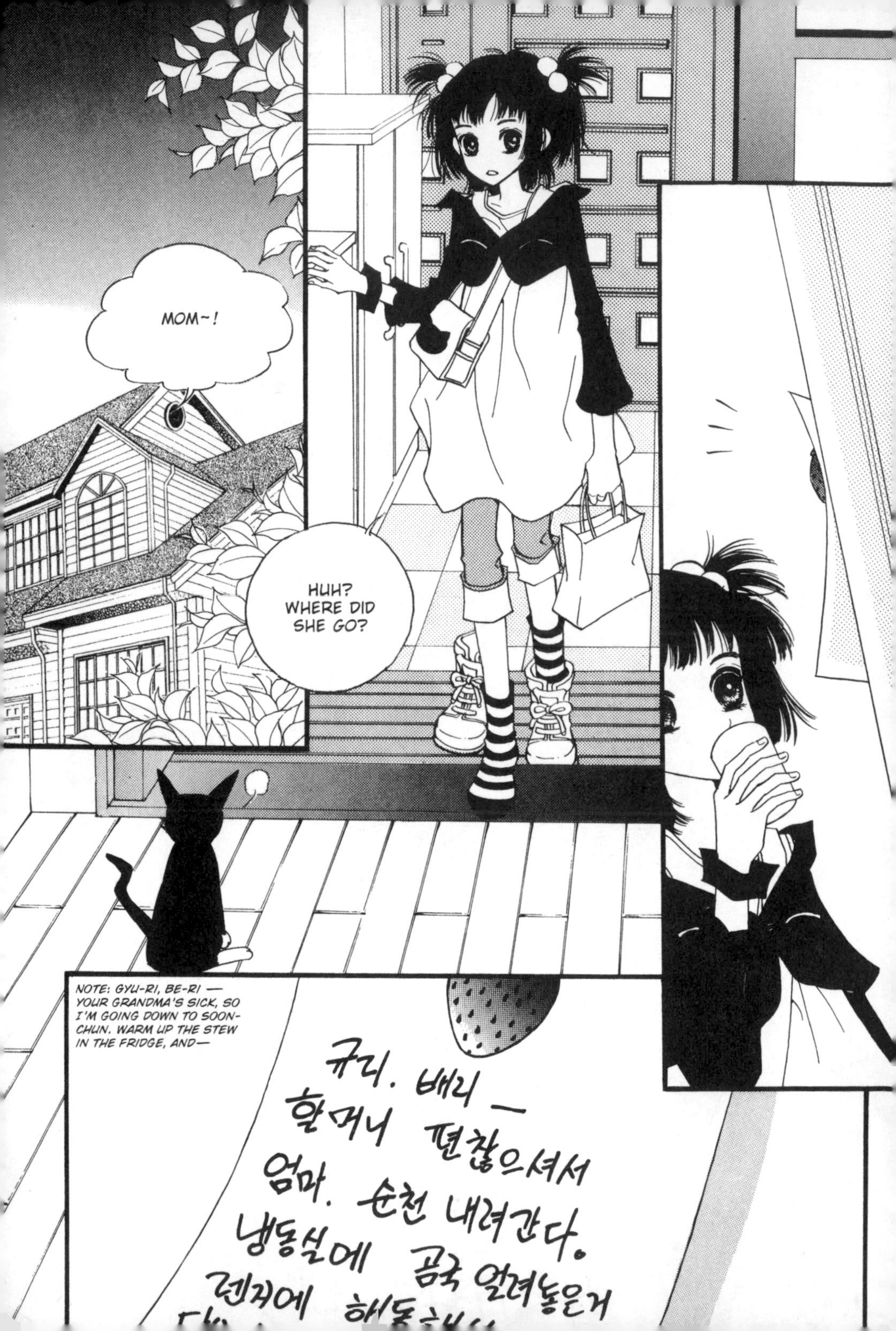
MOM~!
HUH? WHERE DID SHE GO?
NOTE: GYU-RI, BE-RI — YOUR GRANDMA'S SICK, SO I'M GOING DOWN TO SOON-CHUN. WARM UP THE STEW IN THE FRIDGE, AND—
규리. 배리 —
할머니 편찮으셔서
엄마. 순천 내려간다.
냉동실에 곰국 얼려놓은거
렌지에 해동해서

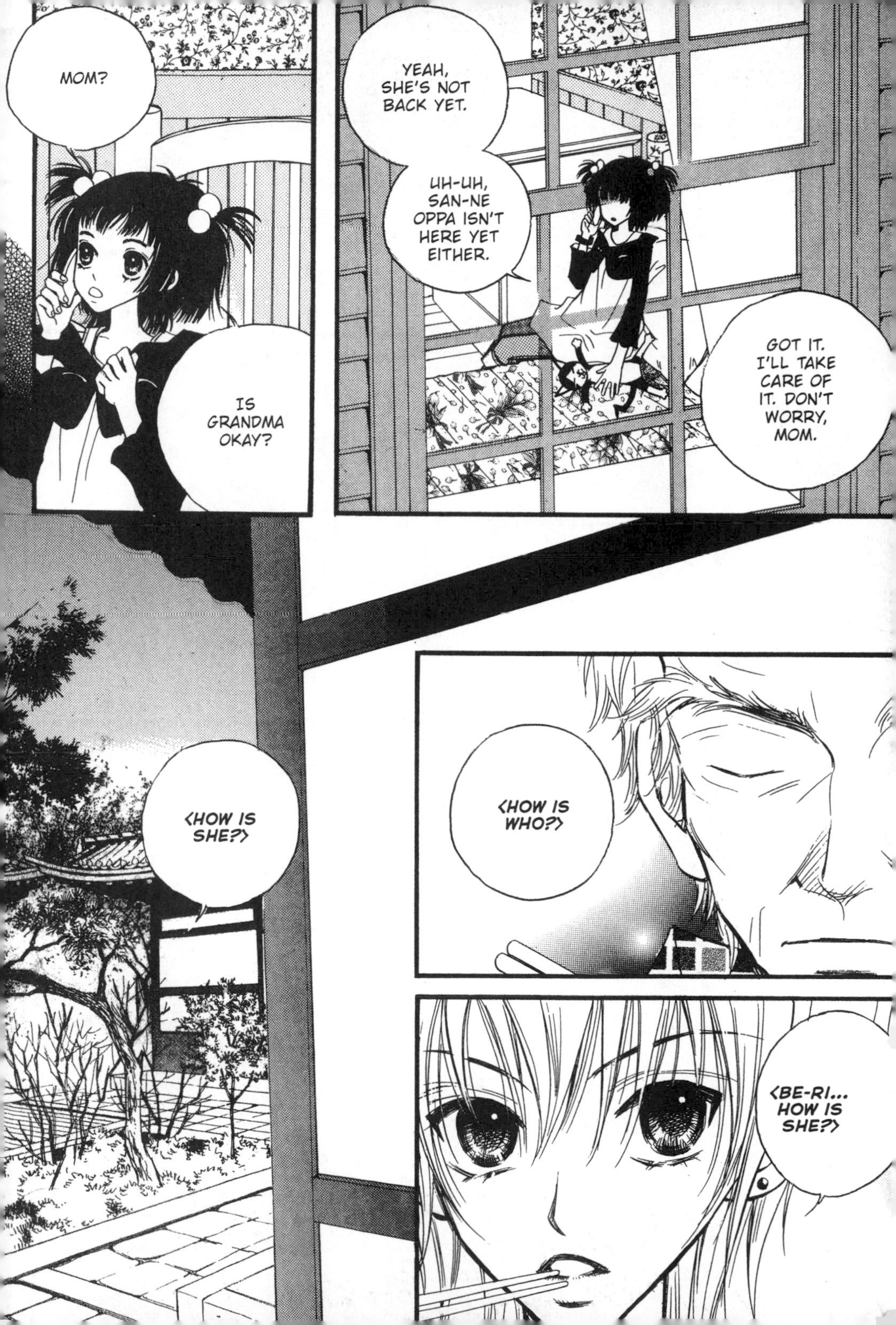
MOM?
IS GRANDMA OKAY?
YEAH, SHE'S NOT BACK YET.
UH-UH, SAN-NE OPPA ISN'T HERE YET EITHER.
GOT IT. I'LL TAKE CARE OF IT. DON'T WORRY, MOM.
<HOW IS SHE?>
<HOW IS WHO?>
<BE-RI... HOW IS SHE?>

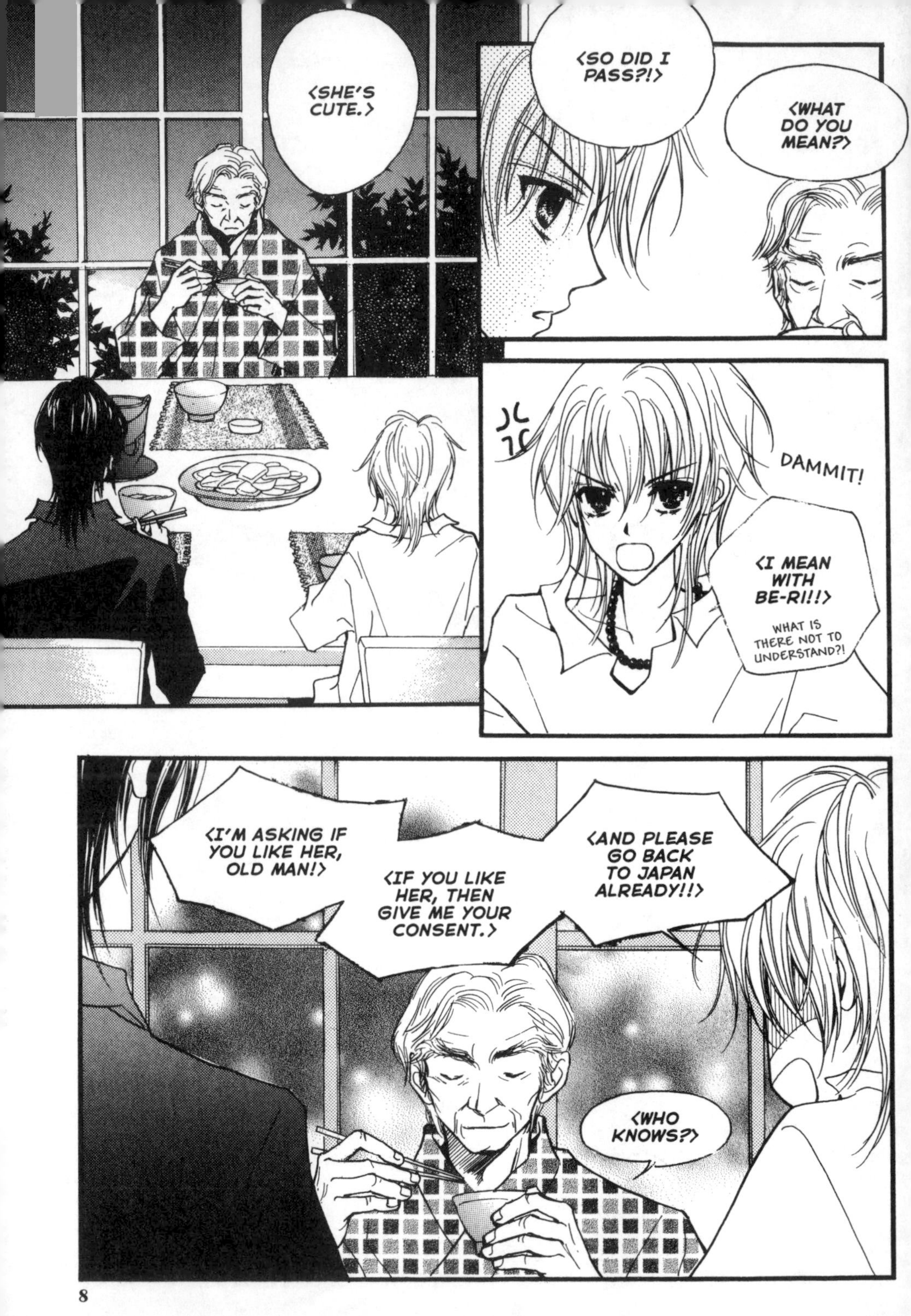
<SHE'S CUTE.>
<SO DID I PASS?!>
<WHAT DO YOU MEAN?>
DAMMIT!
<I MEAN WITH BE-RI!!>
WHAT IS THERE NOT TO UNDERSTAND?!
<I'M ASKING IF YOU LIKE HER, OLD MAN!>
<IF YOU LIKE HER, THEN GIVE ME YOUR CONSENT.>
<AND PLEASE GO BACK TO JAPAN ALREADY!!>
<WHO KNOWS?>

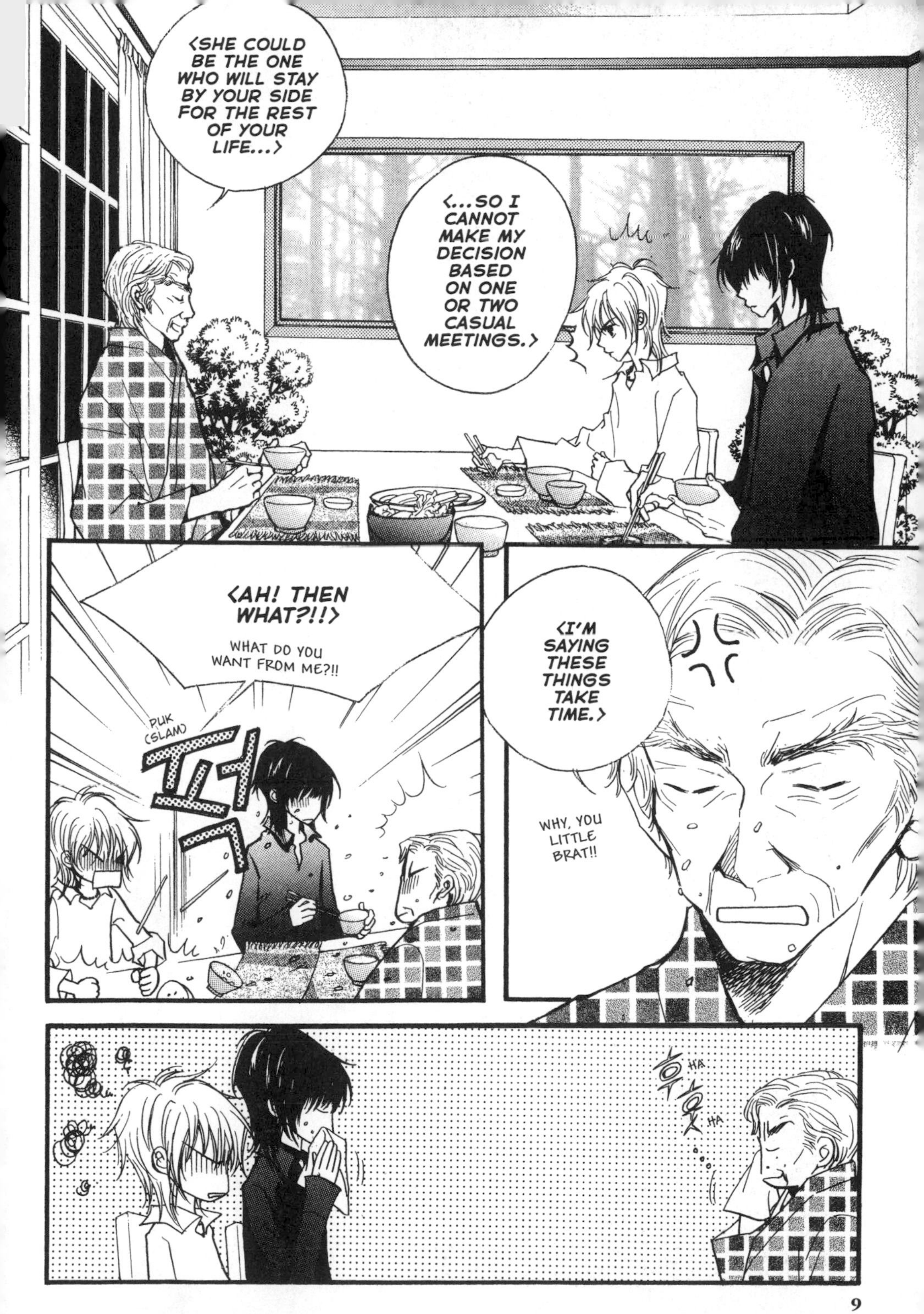

<SHE COULD BE THE ONE WHO WILL STAY BY YOUR SIDE FOR THE REST OF YOUR LIFE...>
<...SO I CANNOT MAKE MY DECISION BASED ON ONE OR TWO CASUAL MEETINGS.>
<AH! THEN WHAT?!!>
WHAT DO YOU WANT FROM ME?!!
PUK (SLAM)
<I'M SAYING THESE THINGS TAKE TIME.>
WHY, YOU LITTLE BRAT!!
HA
HA

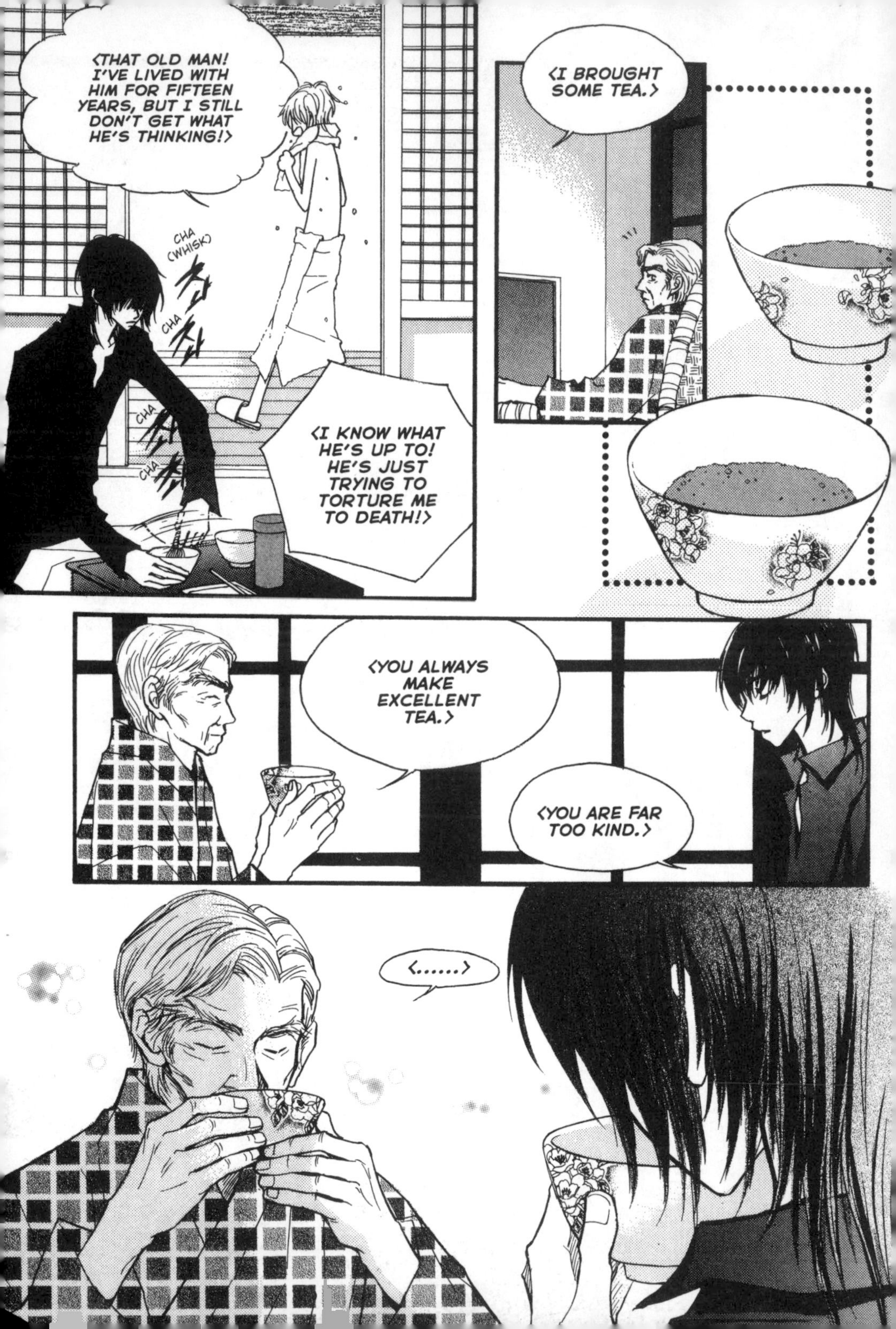

<THAT OLD MAN! I'VE LIVED WITH HIM FOR FIFTEEN YEARS, BUT I STILL DON'T GET WHAT HE'S THINKING!>
CHA (WHISK)
CHA
CHA
CHA
<I KNOW WHAT HE'S UP TO! HE'S JUST TRYING TO TORTURE ME TO DEATH!>
<I BROUGHT SOME TEA.>
<YOU ALWAYS MAKE EXCELLENT TEA.>
<YOU ARE FAR TOO KIND.>
<......>

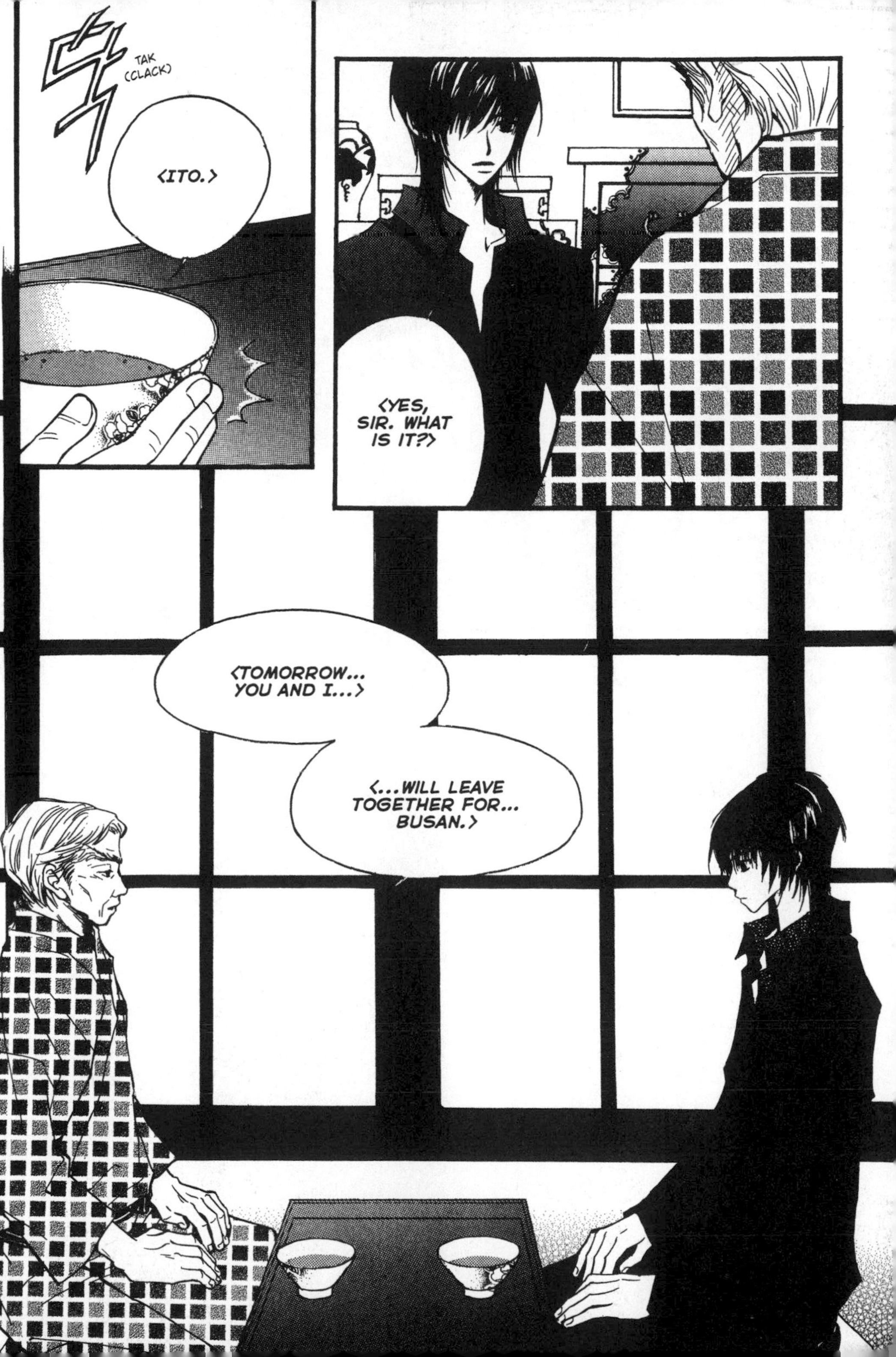
TAK (CLACK)
<ITO.>
<YES, SIR. WHAT IS IT?>
<TOMORROW... YOU AND I...>
<...WILL LEAVE TOGETHER FOR... BUSAN.>

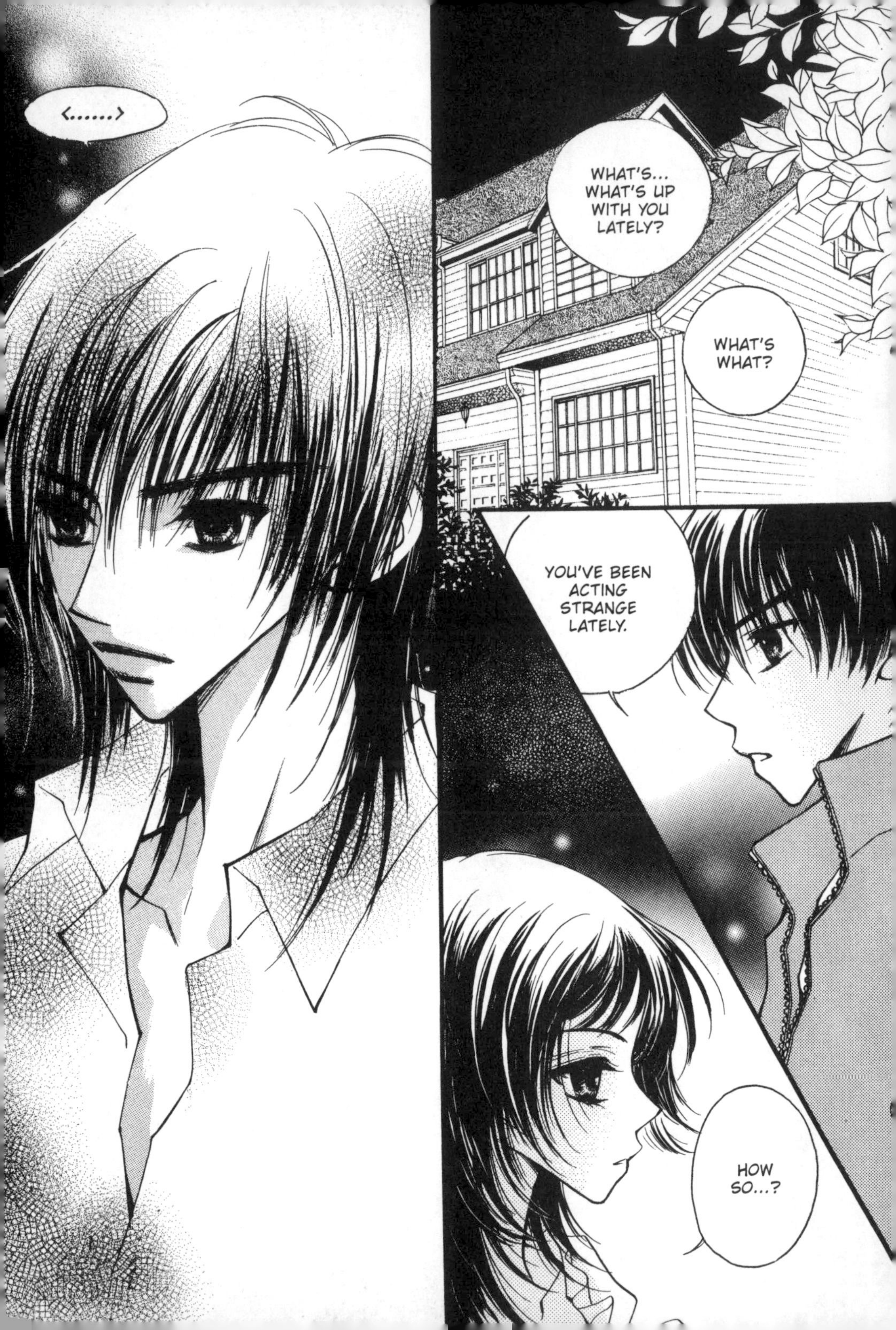
<......>
WHAT'S... WHAT'S UP WITH YOU LATELY?
WHAT'S WHAT?
YOU'VE BEEN ACTING STRANGE LATELY.
HOW SO...?

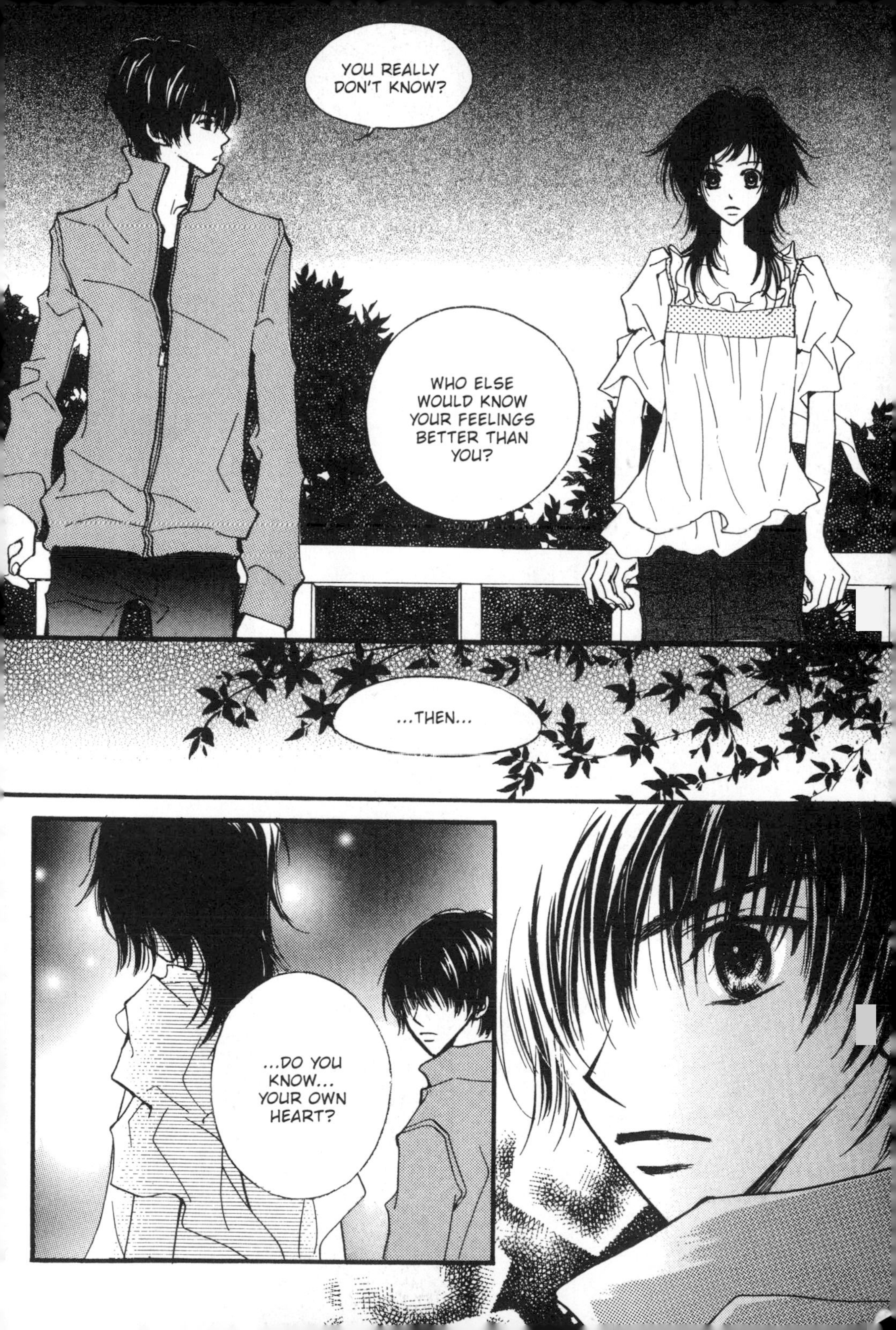
YOU REALLY DON'T KNOW?
WHO ELSE WOULD KNOW YOUR FEELINGS BETTER THAN YOU?
...THEN...
...DO YOU KNOW... YOUR OWN HEART?

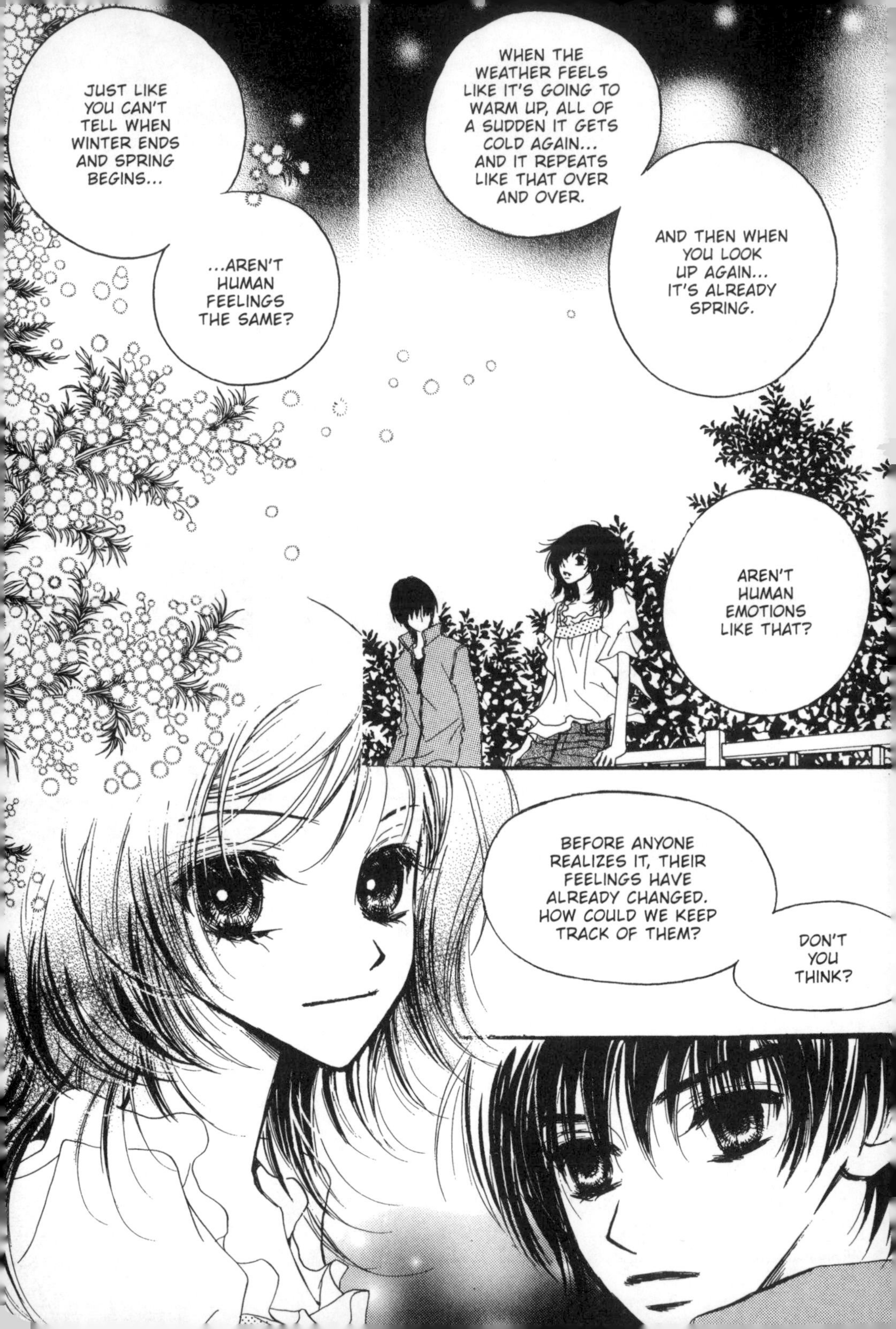
JUST LIKE YOU CAN'T TELL WHEN WINTER ENDS AND SPRING BEGINS...
...AREN'T HUMAN FEELINGS THE SAME?
WHEN THE WEATHER FEELS LIKE IT'S GOING TO WARM UP, ALL OF A SUDDEN IT GETS COLD AGAIN... AND IT REPEATS LIKE THAT OVER AND OVER.
AND THEN WHEN YOU LOOK UP AGAIN... IT'S ALREADY SPRING.
AREN'T HUMAN EMOTIONS LIKE THAT?
BEFORE ANYONE REALIZES IT, THEIR FEELINGS HAVE ALREADY CHANGED. HOW COULD WE KEEP TRACK OF THEM?
DON'T YOU THINK?

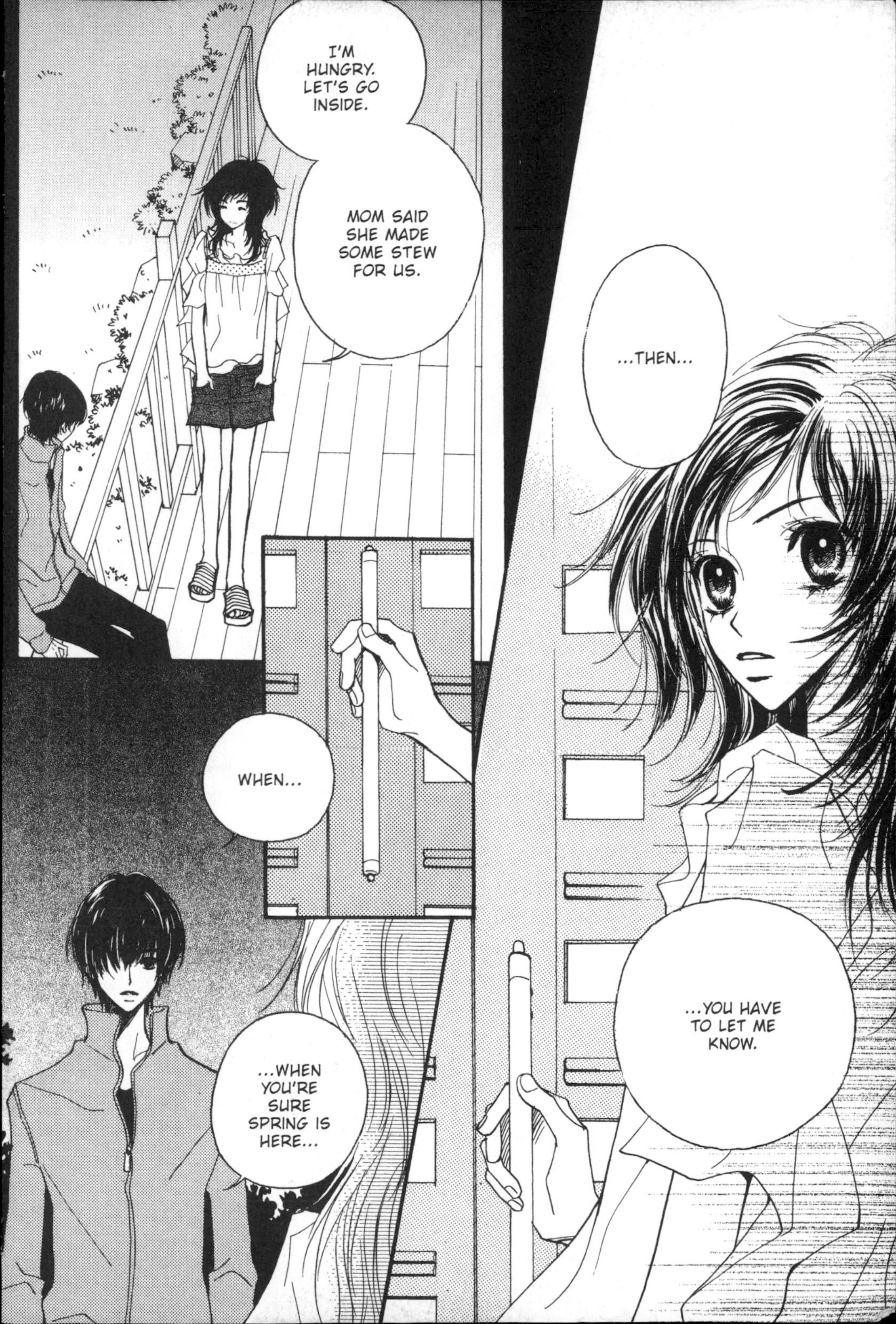
I'M HUNGRY. LET'S GO INSIDE.
MOM SAID SHE MADE SOME STEW FOR US.
WHEN...
...WHEN YOU'RE SURE SPRING IS HERE...
...THEN...
...YOU HAVE TO LET ME KNOW.

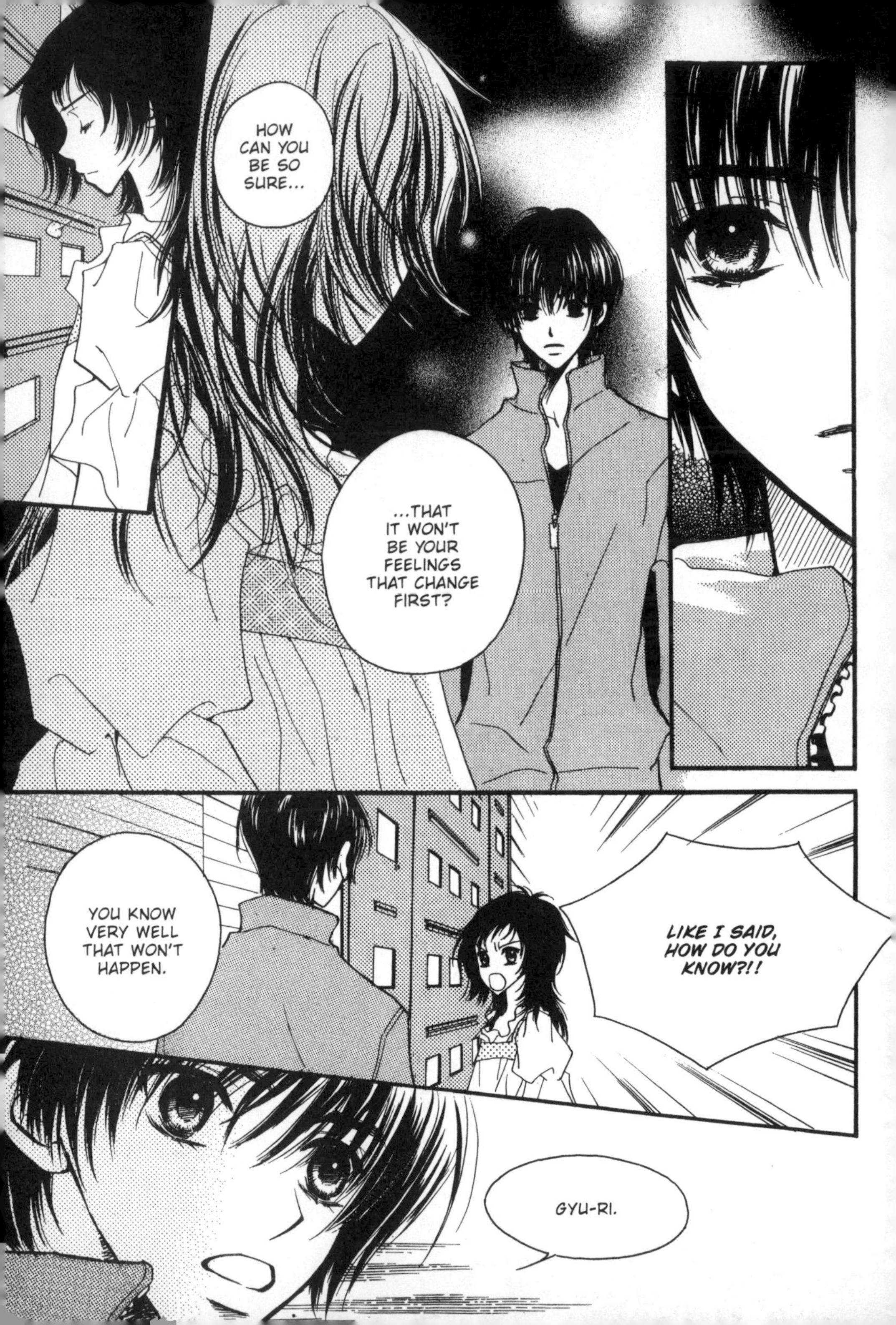
HOW CAN YOU BE SO SURE...
...THAT IT WON'T BE YOUR FEELINGS THAT CHANGE FIRST?
YOU KNOW VERY WELL THAT WON'T HAPPEN.
LIKE I SAID, HOW DO YOU KNOW?!!
GYU-RI.

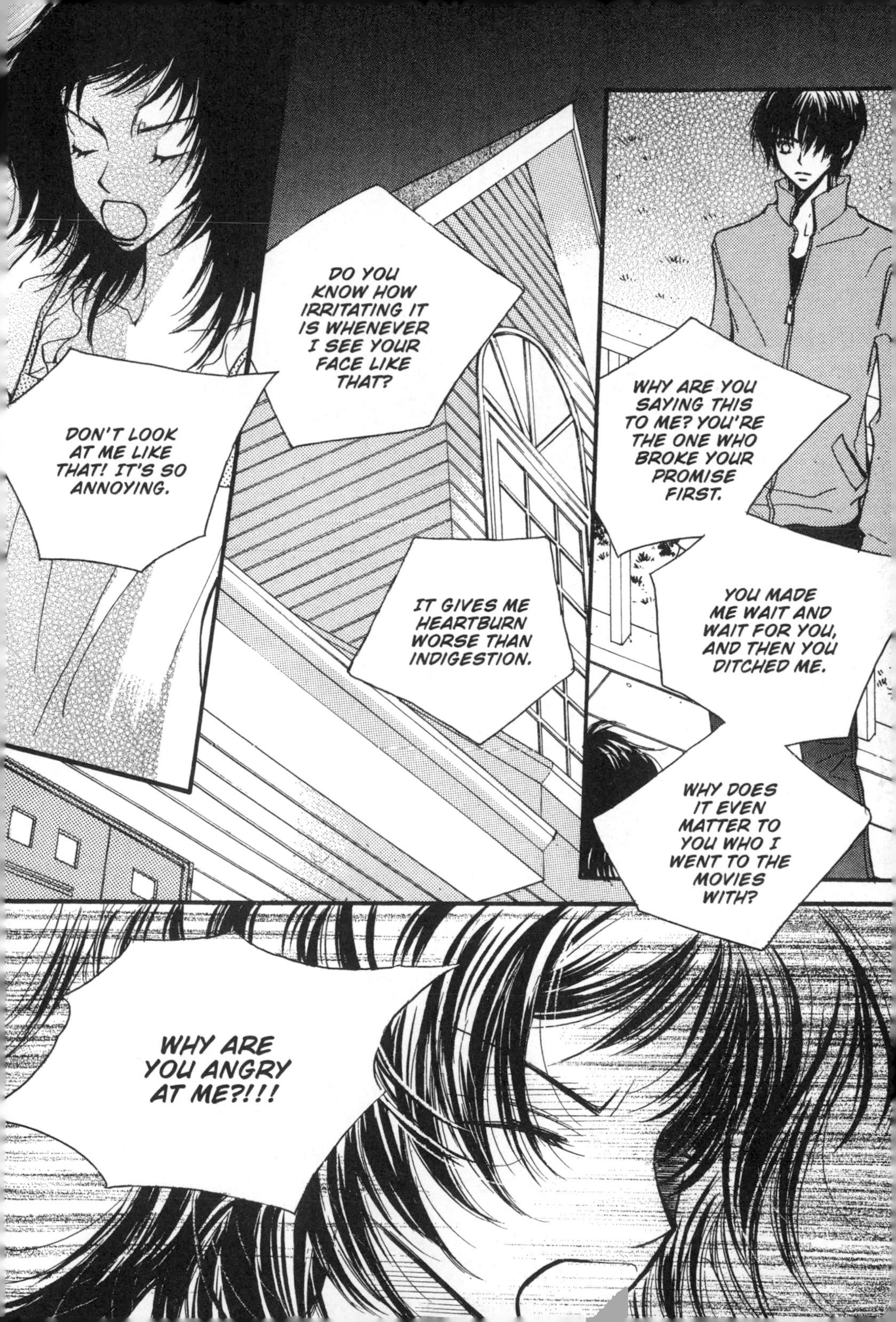
DON'T LOOK AT ME LIKE THAT! IT'S SO ANNOYING.
DO YOU KNOW HOW IRRITATING IT IS WHENEVER I SEE YOUR FACE LIKE THAT?
IT GIVES ME HEARTBURN WORSE THAN INDIGESTION.
WHY ARE YOU SAYING THIS TO ME? YOU'RE THE ONE WHO BROKE YOUR PROMISE FIRST.
YOU MADE ME WAIT AND WAIT FOR YOU, AND THEN YOU DITCHED ME.
WHY DOES IT EVEN MATTER TO YOU WHO I WENT TO THE MOVIES WITH?
WHY ARE YOU ANGRY AT ME?!!!

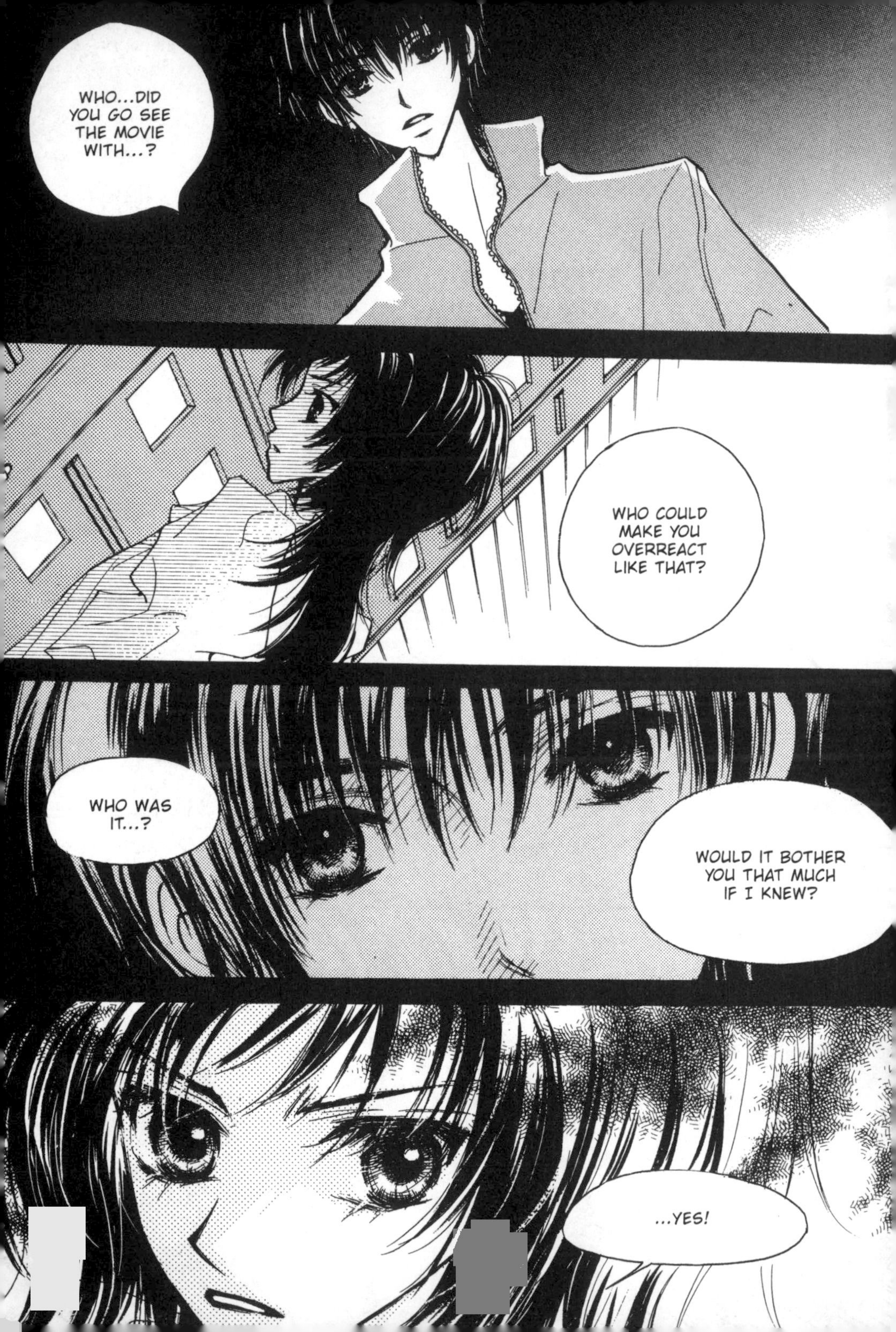
WHO...DID YOU GO SEE THE MOVIE WITH...?
WHO COULD MAKE YOU OVERREACT LIKE THAT?
WHO WAS IT...?
WOULD IT BOTHER YOU THAT MUCH IF I KNEW?
...YES!

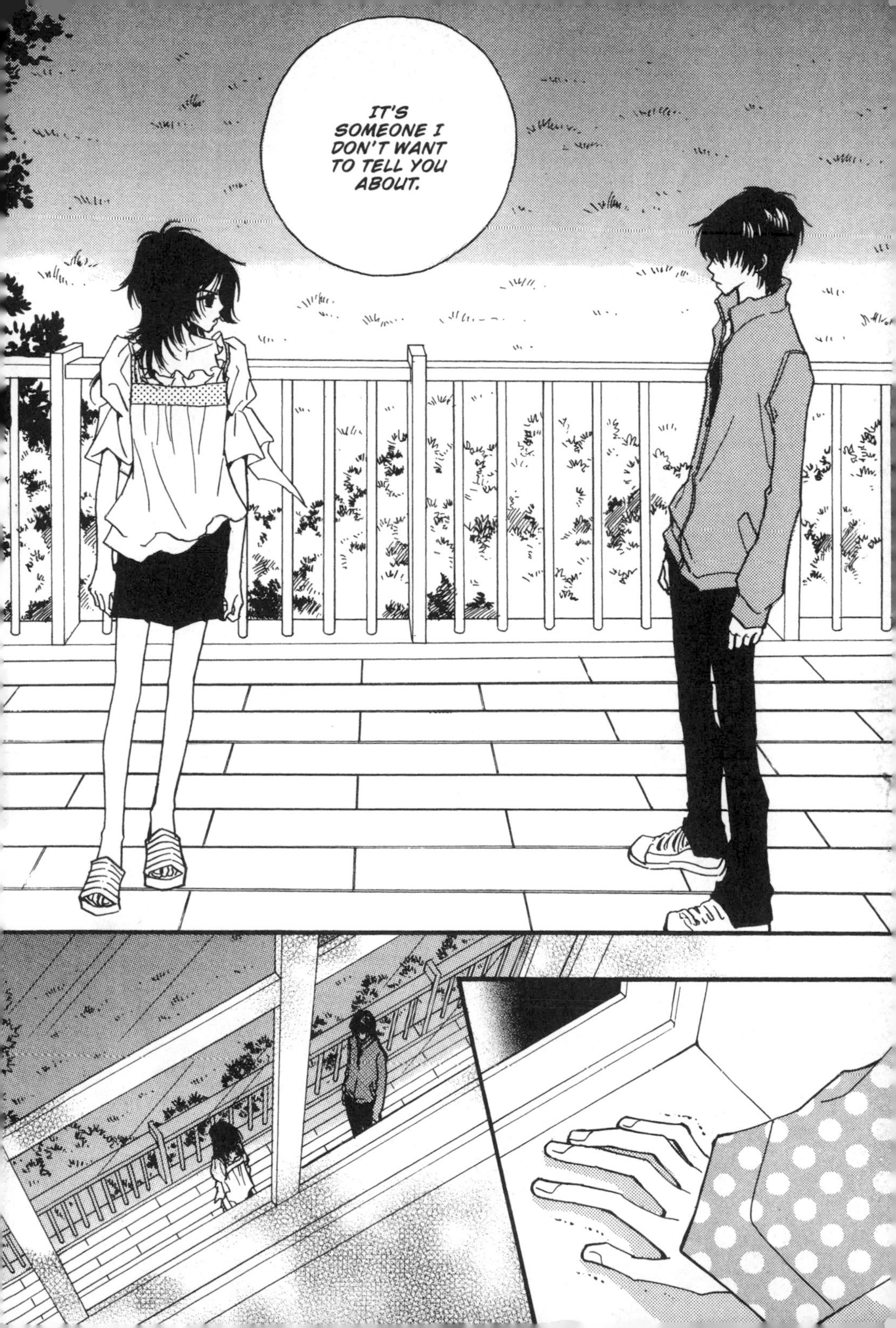
IT'S SOMEONE I DON'T WANT TO TELL YOU ABOUT.

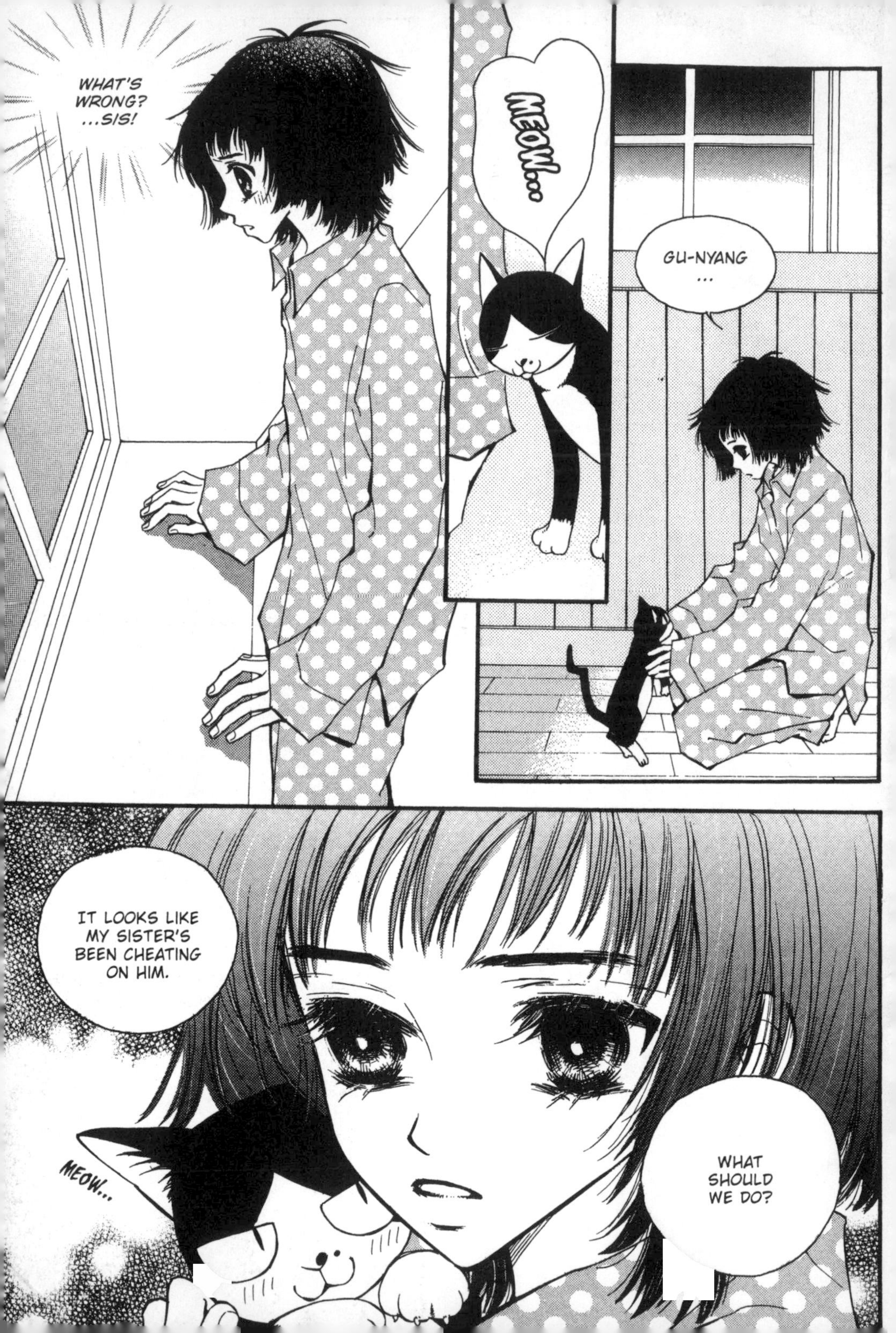
WHAT'S WRONG? ...SIS!
MEOW...
GU-NYANG ...
IT LOOKS LIKE MY SISTER'S BEEN CHEATING ON HIM.
MEOW...
WHAT SHOULD WE DO?

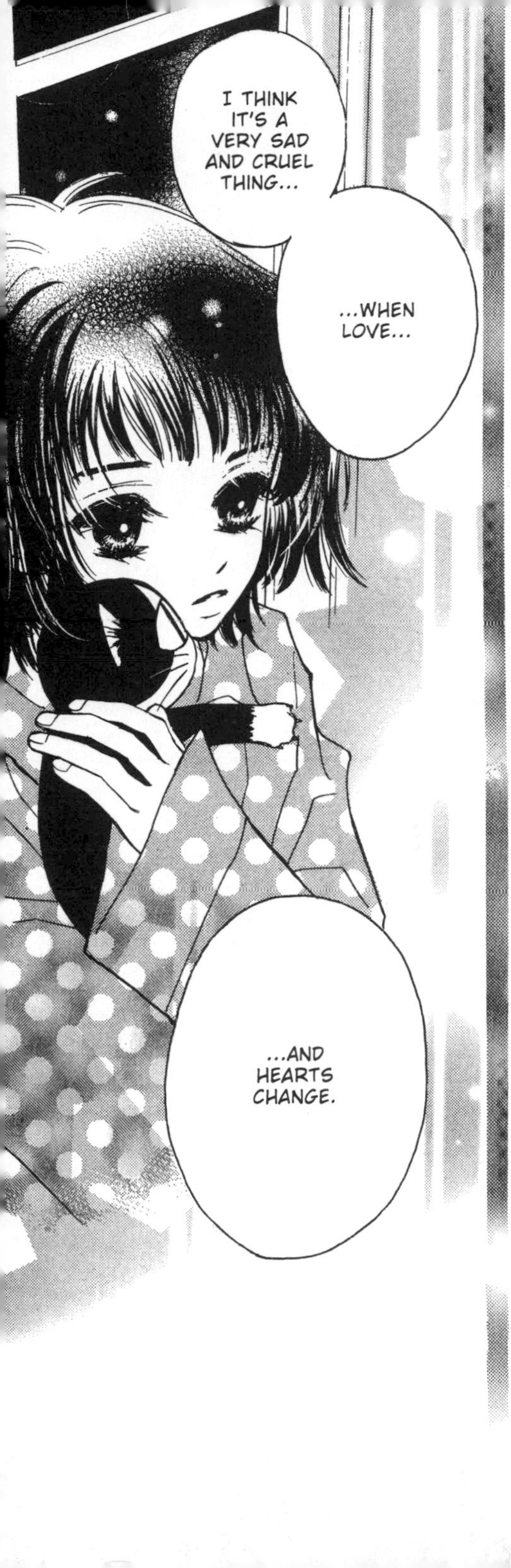
I THINK IT'S A VERY SAD AND CRUEL THING...
...WHEN LOVE...
...AND HEARTS CHANGE.
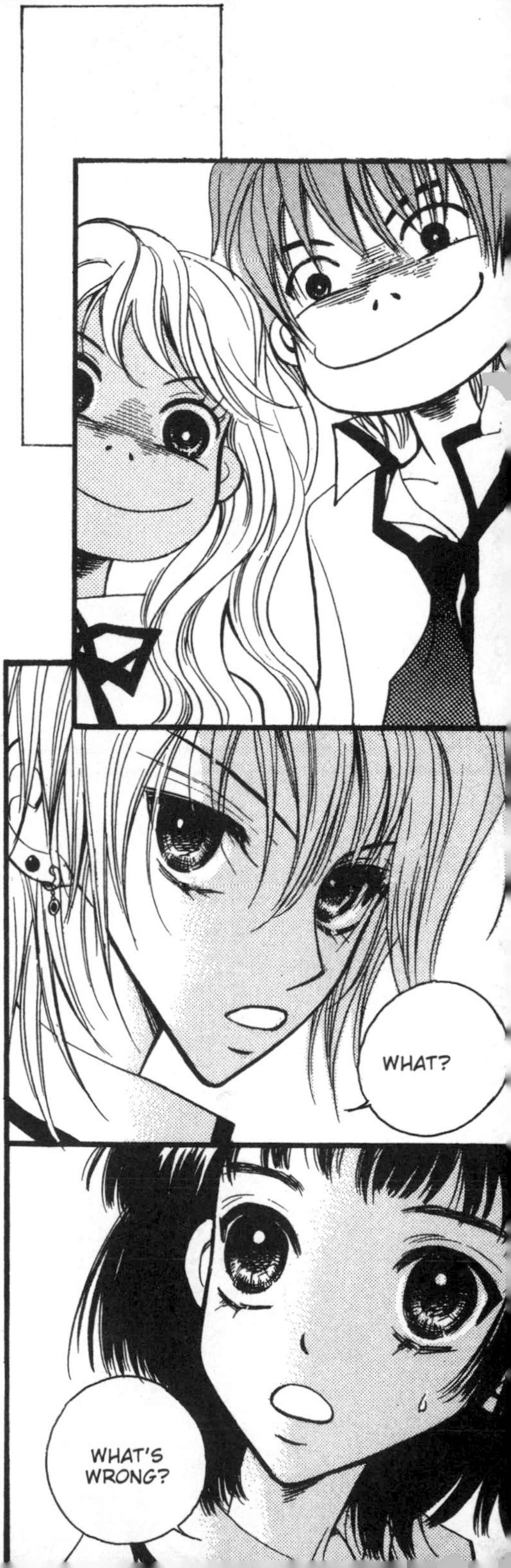
WHAT?
WHAT'S WRONG?

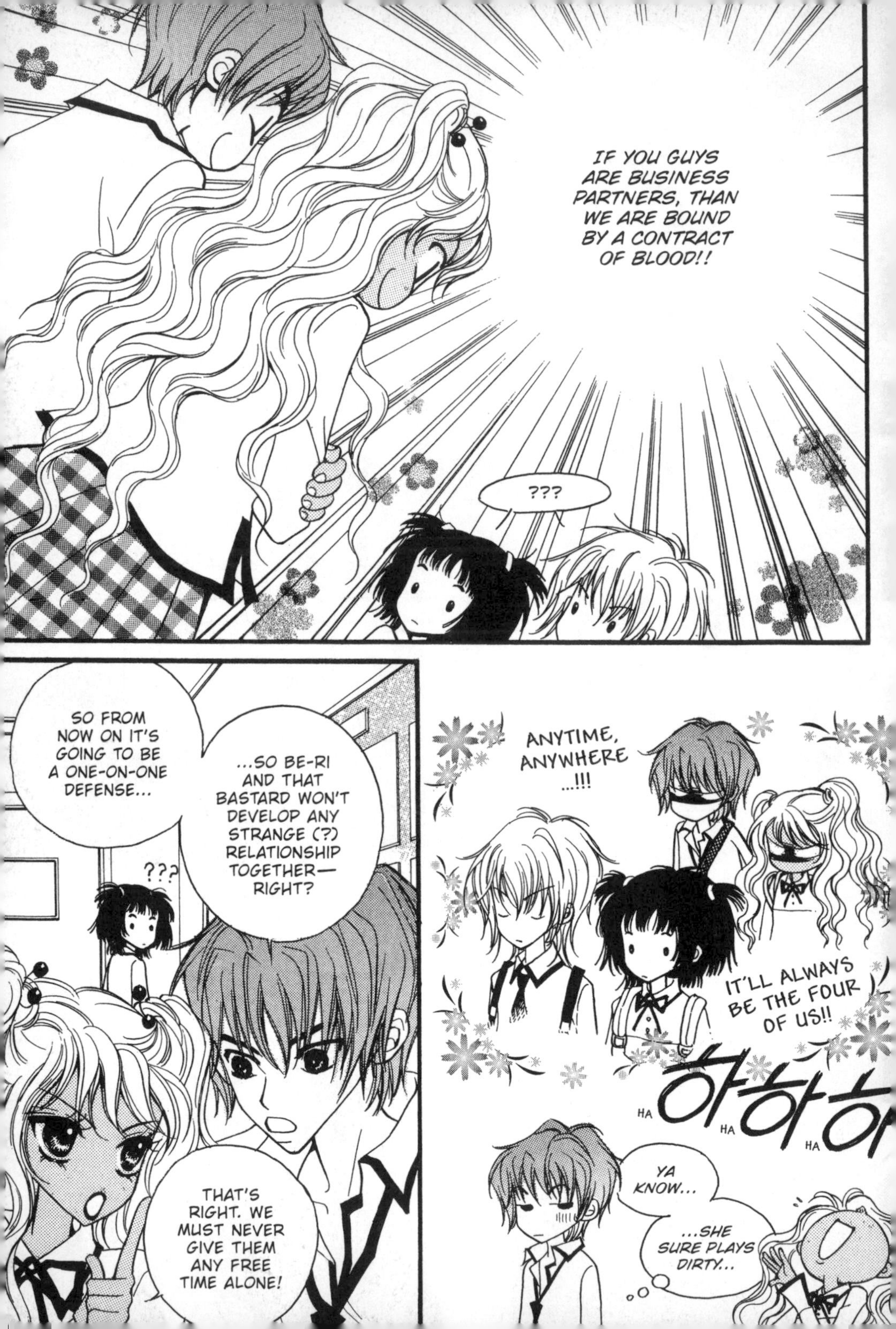
IF YOU GUYS ARE BUSINESS PARTNERS, THAN WE ARE BOUND BY A CONTRACT OF BLOOD!!
???
SO FROM NOW ON IT'S GOING TO BE A ONE-ON-ONE DEFENSE...
...SO BE-RI AND THAT BASTARD WON'T DEVELOP ANY STRANGE (?) RELATIONSHIP TOGETHER— RIGHT?
???
THAT'S RIGHT. WE MUST NEVER GIVE THEM ANY FREE TIME ALONE!
ANYTIME, ANYWHERE ...!!!
IT'LL ALWAYS BE THE FOUR OF US!!
HA 하 HA 하 HA
YA KNOW...
...SHE SURE PLAYS DIRTY...

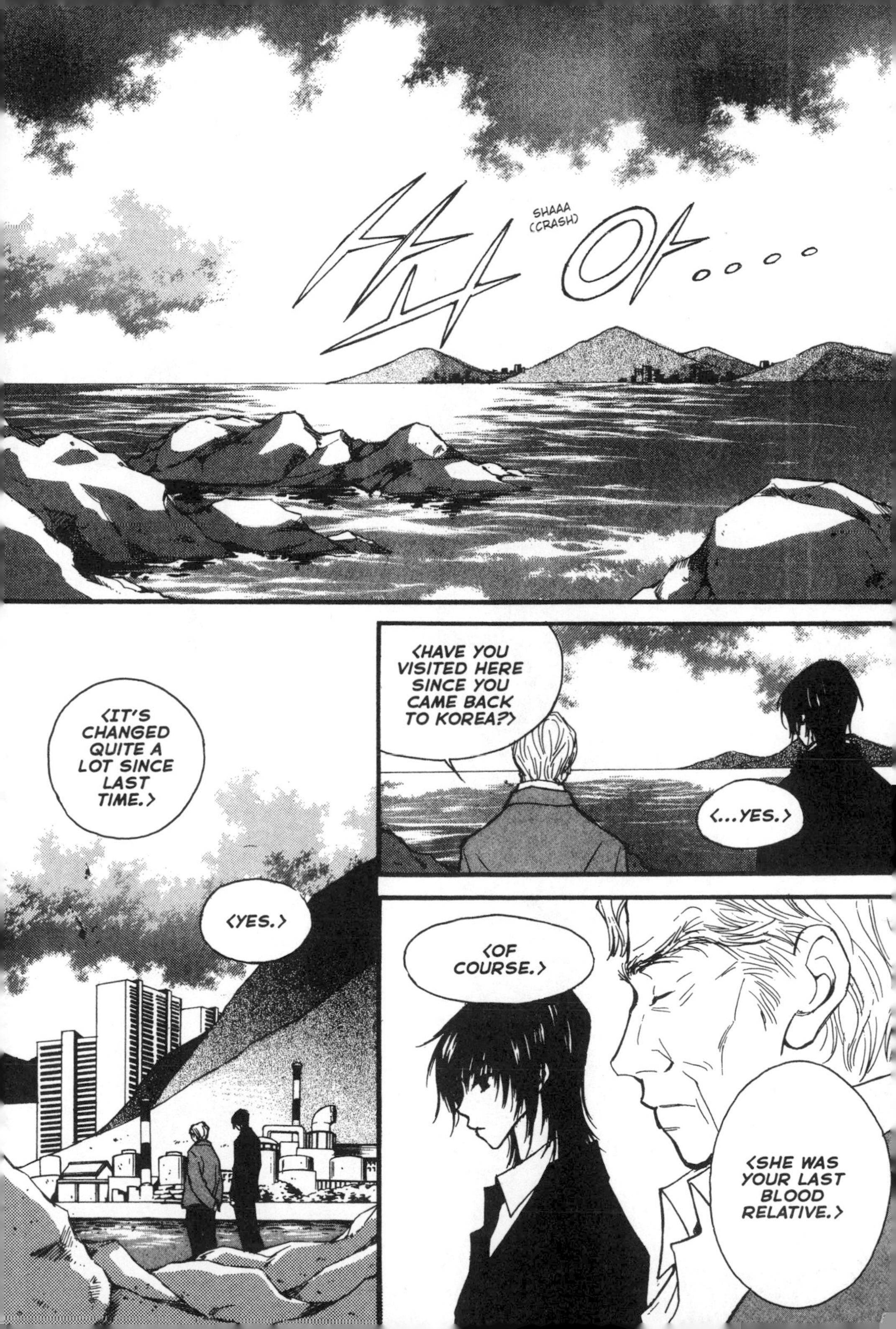
SHAAA (CRASH)
<IT'S CHANGED QUITE A LOT SINCE LAST TIME.>
<YES.>
<HAVE YOU VISITED HERE SINCE YOU CAME BACK TO KOREA?>
<...YES.>
<OF COURSE.>
<SHE WAS YOUR LAST BLOOD RELATIVE.>

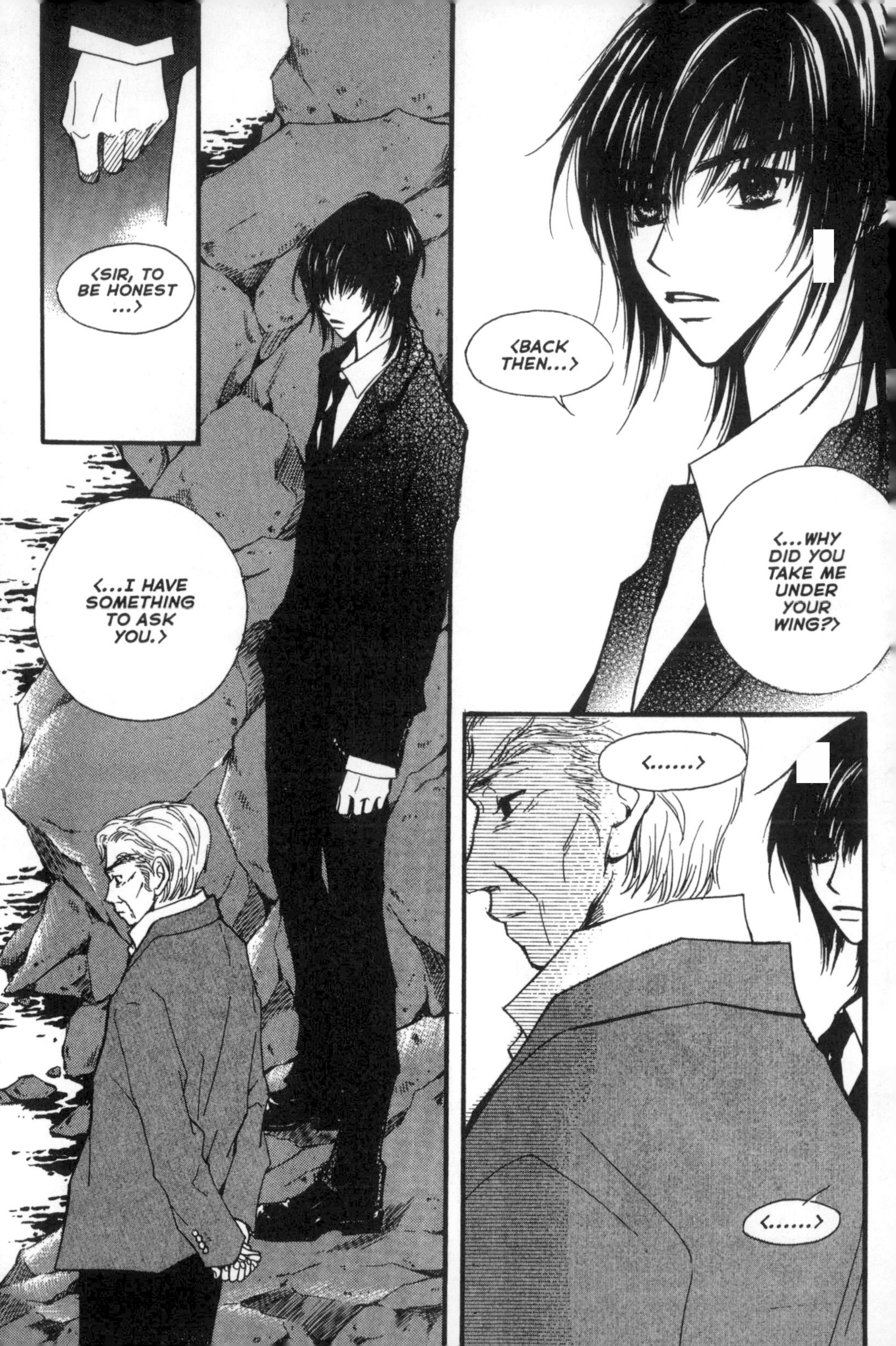
<SIR, TO BE HONEST ...>
<...I HAVE SOMETHING TO ASK YOU.>
<BACK THEN...>
<...WHY DID YOU TAKE ME UNDER YOUR WING?>
<......>
<......>

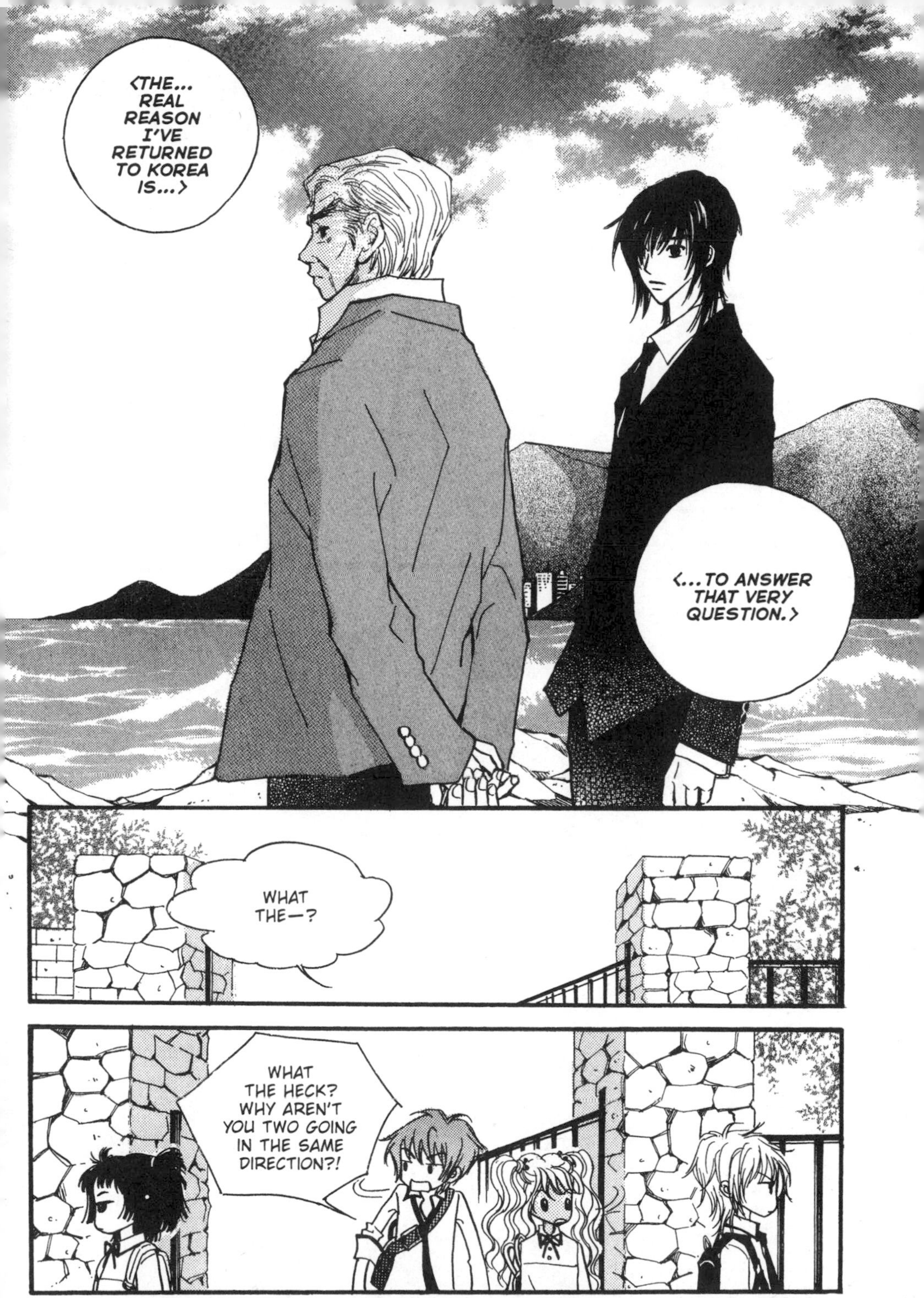
<THE... REAL REASON I'VE RETURNED TO KOREA IS...>
<...TO ANSWER THAT VERY QUESTION.>
WHAT THE—?
WHAT THE HECK? WHY AREN'T YOU TWO GOING IN THE SAME DIRECTION?!

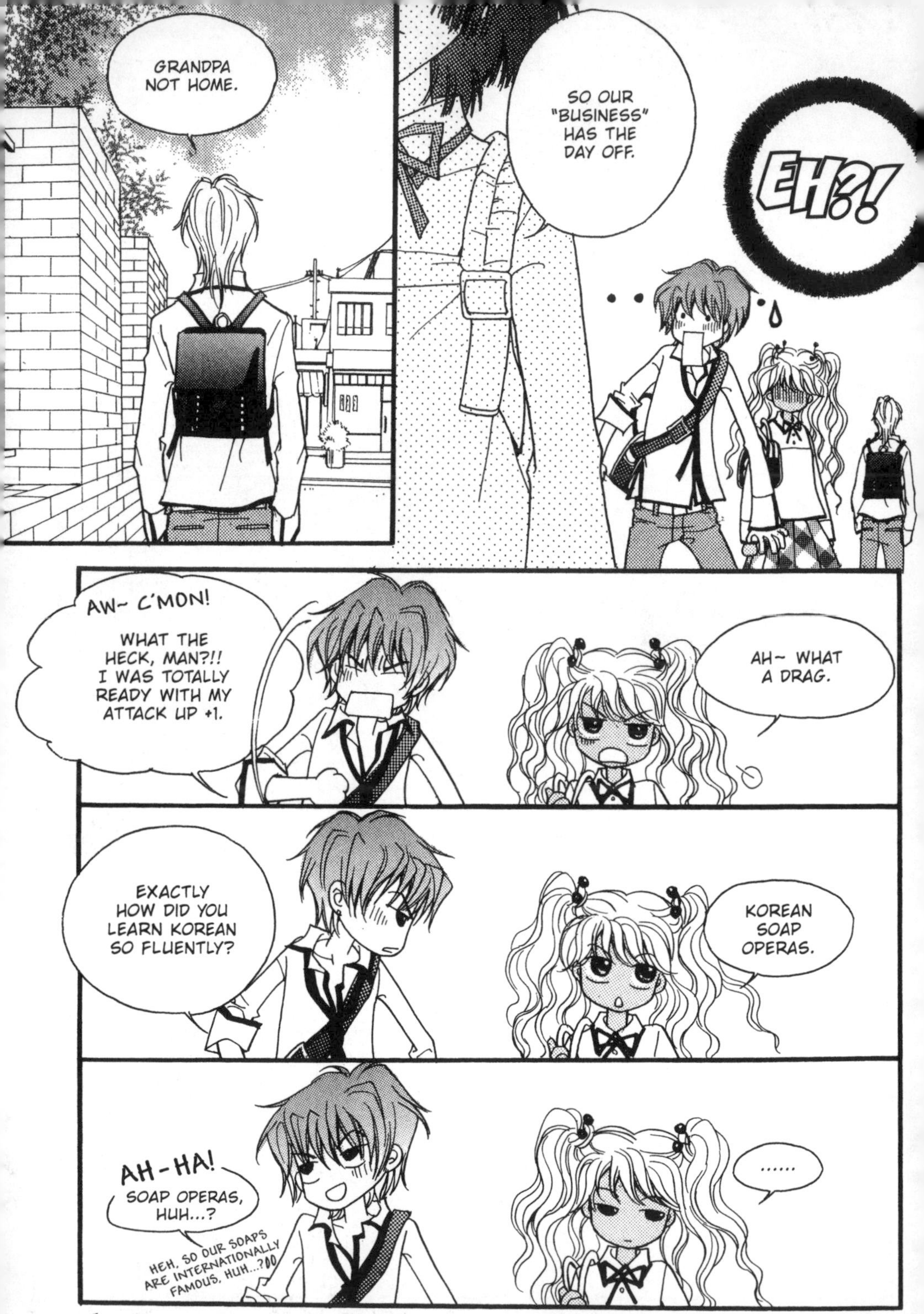
GRANDPA NOT HOME.
SO OUR "BUSINESS" HAS THE DAY OFF.
EH?!
AW~ C'MON!
WHAT THE HECK, MAN?!! I WAS TOTALLY READY WITH MY ATTACK UP +1.
AH~ WHAT A DRAG.
EXACTLY HOW DID YOU LEARN KOREAN SO FLUENTLY?
KOREAN SOAP OPERAS.
AH-HA!
SOAP OPERAS, HUH...?
HEH, SO OUR SOAPS ARE INTERNATIONALLY FAMOUS, HUH...?
......

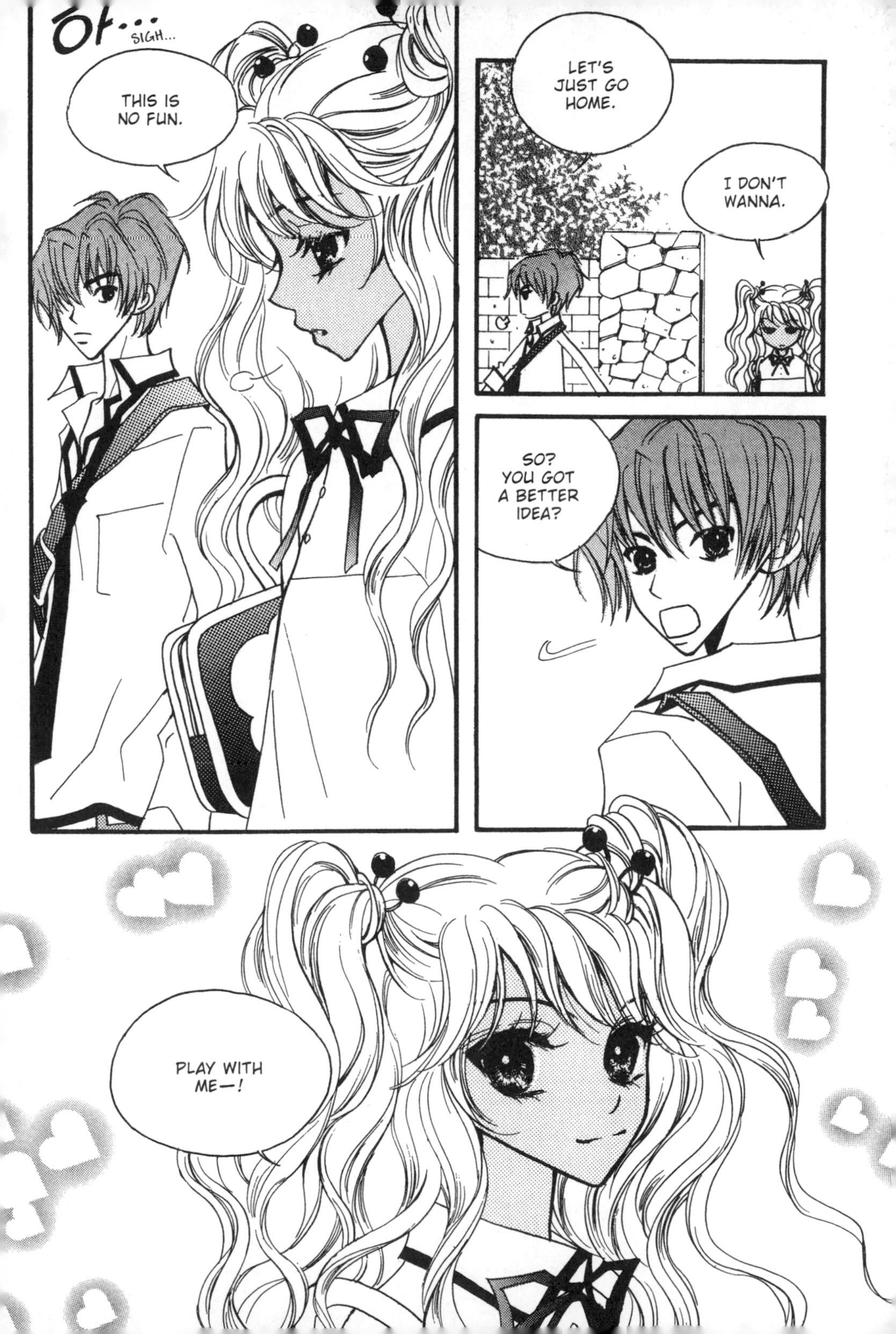

하...
SIGH...
THIS IS NO FUN.
LET'S JUST GO HOME.
I DON'T WANNA.
SO? YOU GOT A BETTER IDEA?
PLAY WITH ME—!

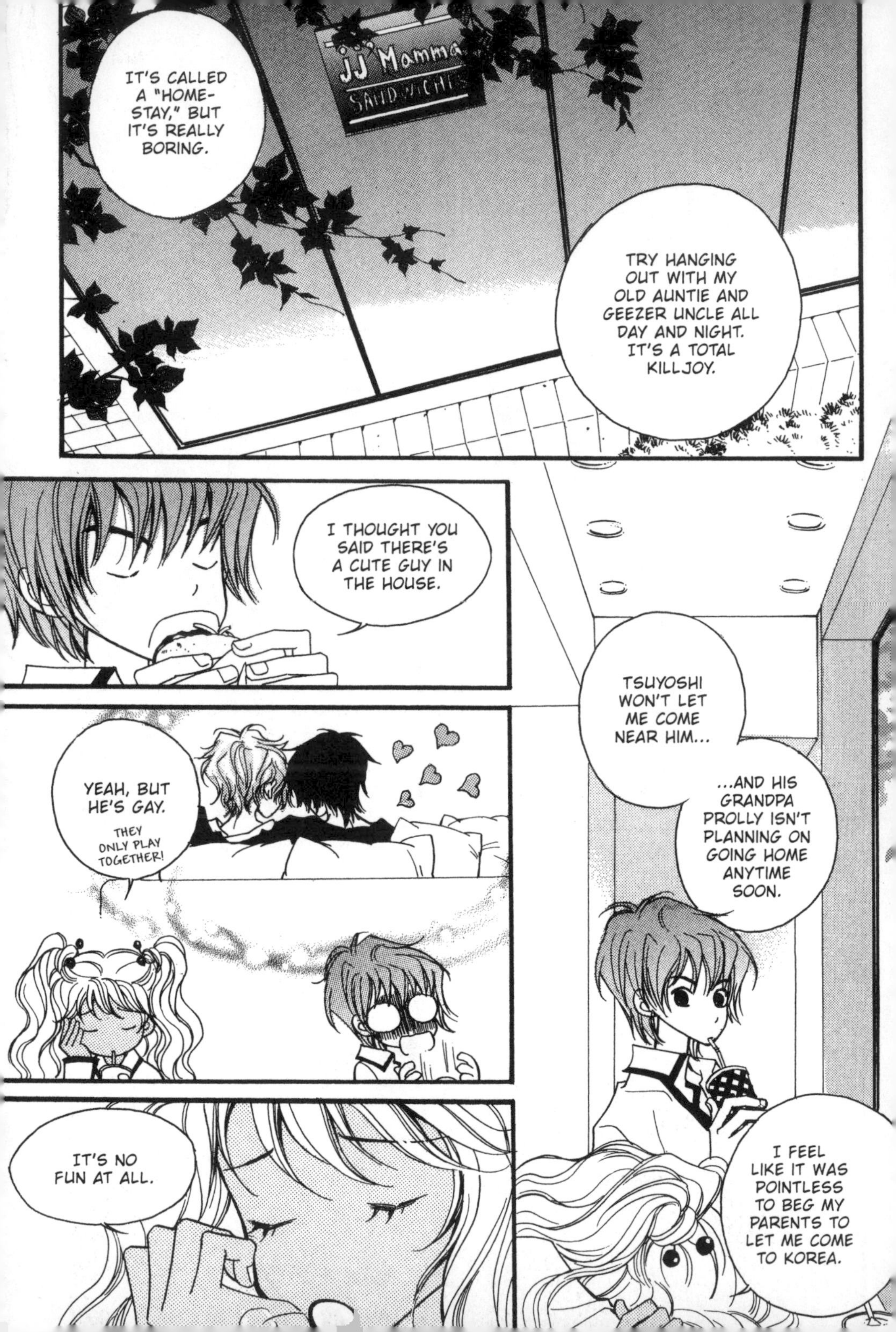
JJ Mamma
SANDWICHES
IT'S CALLED A "HOME-STAY," BUT IT'S REALLY BORING.
TRY HANGING OUT WITH MY OLD AUNTIE AND GEEZER UNCLE ALL DAY AND NIGHT. IT'S A TOTAL KILLJOY.
I THOUGHT YOU SAID THERE'S A CUTE GUY IN THE HOUSE.
YEAH, BUT HE'S GAY.
THEY ONLY PLAY TOGETHER!
IT'S NO FUN AT ALL.
TSUYOSHI WON'T LET ME COME NEAR HIM...
...AND HIS GRANDPA PROLLY ISN'T PLANNING ON GOING HOME ANYTIME SOON.
I FEEL LIKE IT WAS POINTLESS TO BEG MY PARENTS TO LET ME COME TO KOREA.

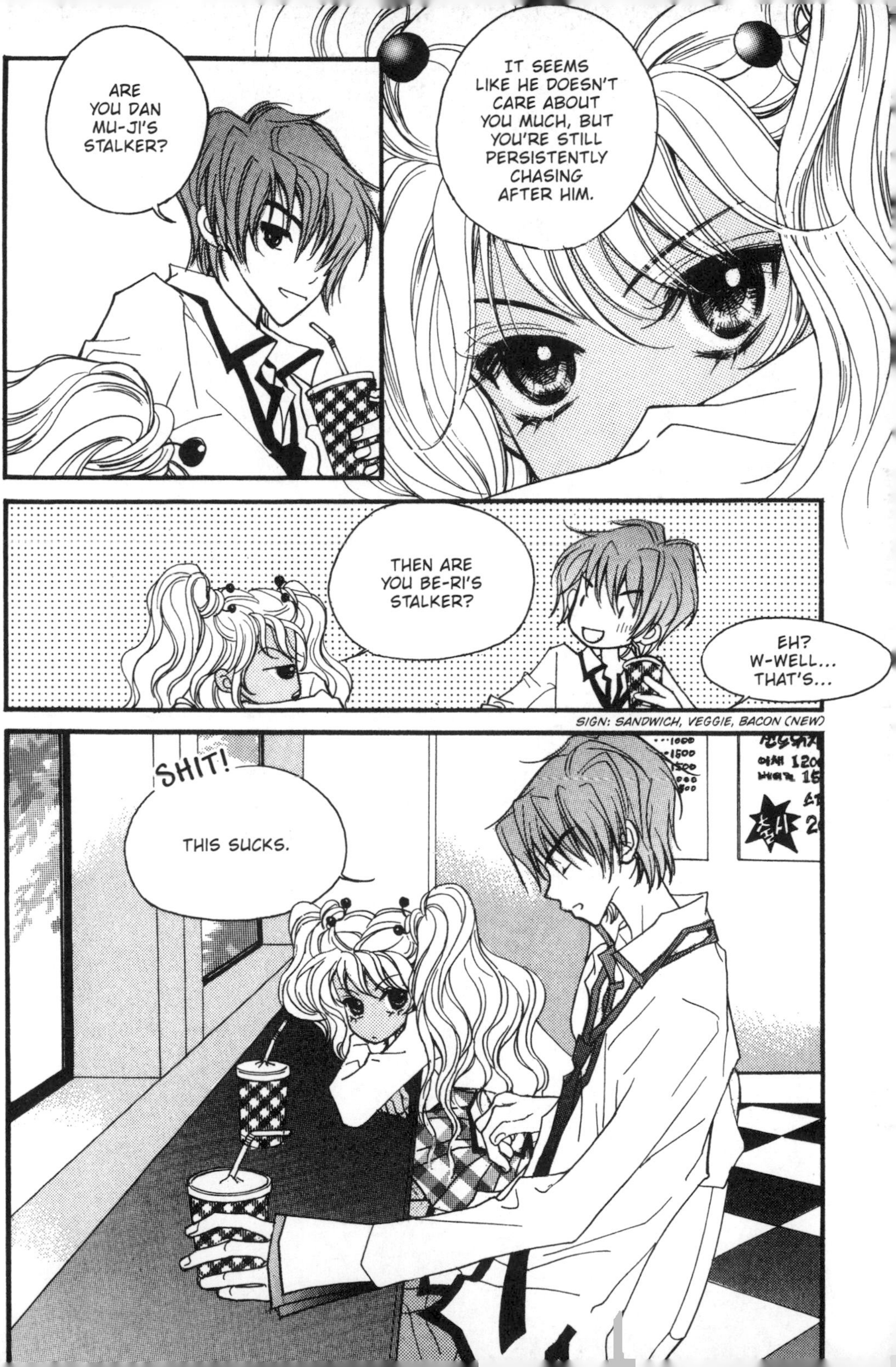
ARE YOU DAN MU-JI'S STALKER?
IT SEEMS LIKE HE DOESN'T CARE ABOUT YOU MUCH, BUT YOU'RE STILL PERSISTENTLY CHASING AFTER HIM.
THEN ARE YOU BE-RI'S STALKER?
EH? W-WELL... THAT'S...
SIGN: SANDWICH, VEGGIE, BACON (NEW)
SHIT!
THIS SUCKS.

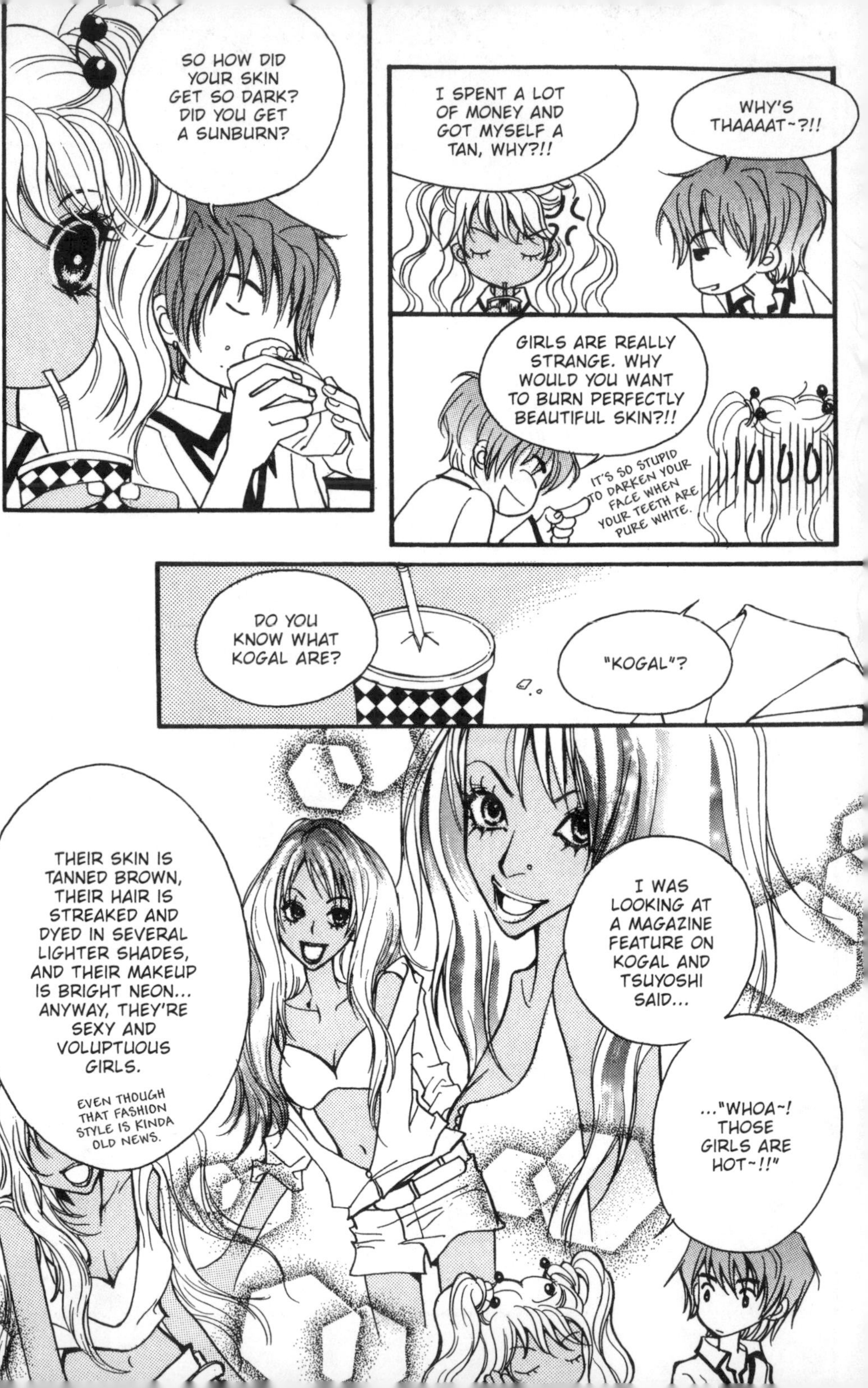
SO HOW DID YOUR SKIN GET SO DARK? DID YOU GET A SUNBURN?
I SPENT A LOT OF MONEY AND GOT MYSELF A TAN, WHY?!!
WHY'S THAAAAT~?!!
GIRLS ARE REALLY STRANGE. WHY WOULD YOU WANT TO BURN PERFECTLY BEAUTIFUL SKIN?!!
IT'S SO STUPID TO DARKEN YOUR FACE WHEN YOUR TEETH ARE PURE WHITE.
DO YOU KNOW WHAT KOGAL ARE?
"KOGAL"?
THEIR SKIN IS TANNED BROWN, THEIR HAIR IS STREAKED AND DYED IN SEVERAL LIGHTER SHADES, AND THEIR MAKEUP IS BRIGHT NEON... ANYWAY, THEY'RE SEXY AND VOLUPTUOUS GIRLS.
EVEN THOUGH THAT FASHION STYLE IS KINDA OLD NEWS.
I WAS LOOKING AT A MAGAZINE FEATURE ON KOGAL AND TSUYOSHI SAID...
..."WHOA~! THOSE GIRLS ARE HOT~!!"

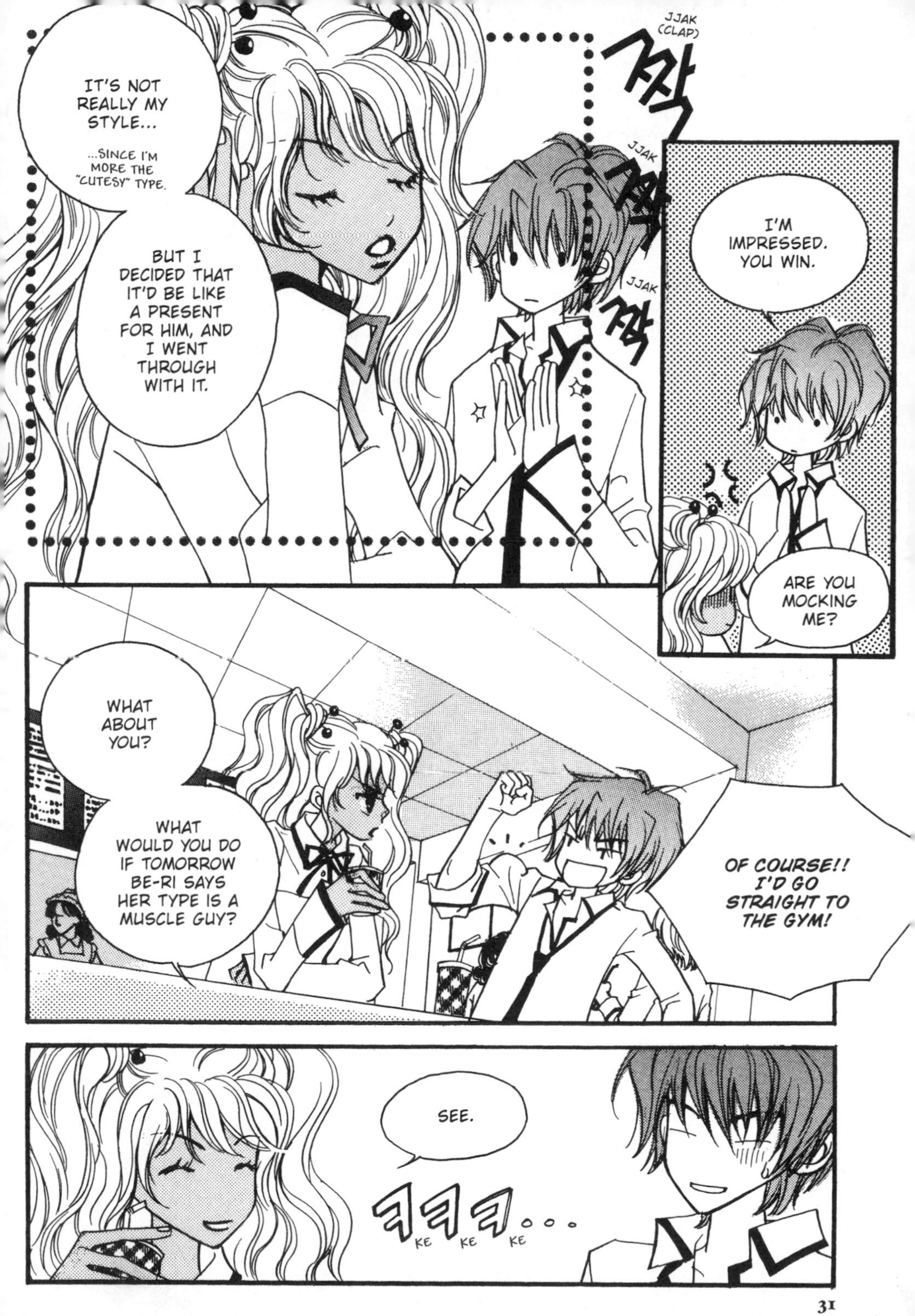
IT'S NOT REALLY MY STYLE...
...SINCE I'M MORE THE "CUTESY" TYPE.
BUT I DECIDED THAT IT'D BE LIKE A PRESENT FOR HIM, AND I WENT THROUGH WITH IT.
JJAK (CLAP)
JJAK
JJAK
I'M IMPRESSED. YOU WIN.
ARE YOU MOCKING ME?
WHAT ABOUT YOU?
WHAT WOULD YOU DO IF TOMORROW BE-RI SAYS HER TYPE IS A MUSCLE GUY?
OF COURSE!! I'D GO STRAIGHT TO THE GYM!
SEE.
KE KE KE

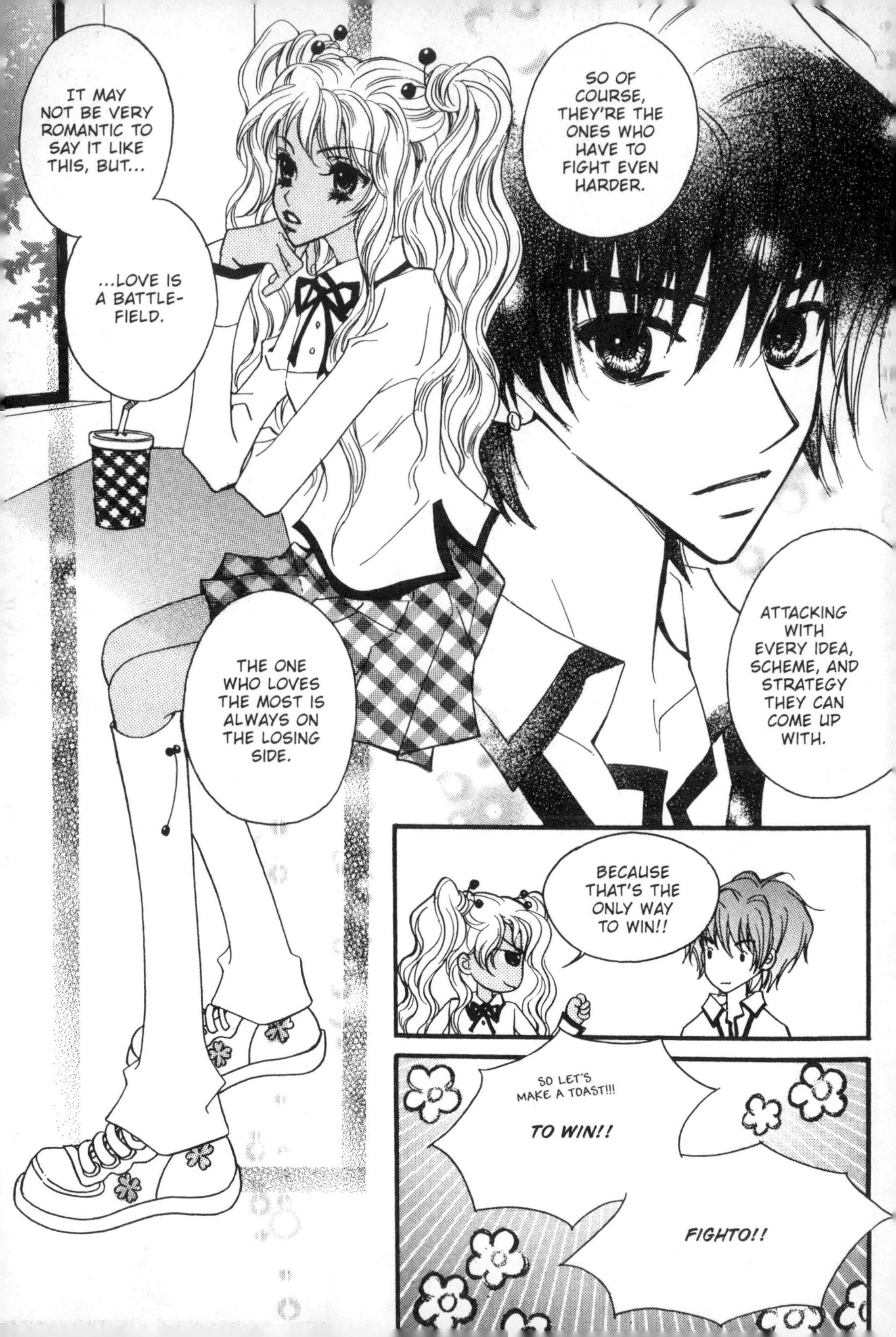
IT MAY NOT BE VERY ROMANTIC TO SAY IT LIKE THIS, BUT...
...LOVE IS A BATTLE-FIELD.
SO OF COURSE, THEY'RE THE ONES WHO HAVE TO FIGHT EVEN HARDER.
THE ONE WHO LOVES THE MOST IS ALWAYS ON THE LOSING SIDE.
ATTACKING WITH EVERY IDEA, SCHEME, AND STRATEGY THEY CAN COME UP WITH.
BECAUSE THAT'S THE ONLY WAY TO WIN!!
SO LET'S MAKE A TOAST!!!
TO WIN!!
FIGHTO!!

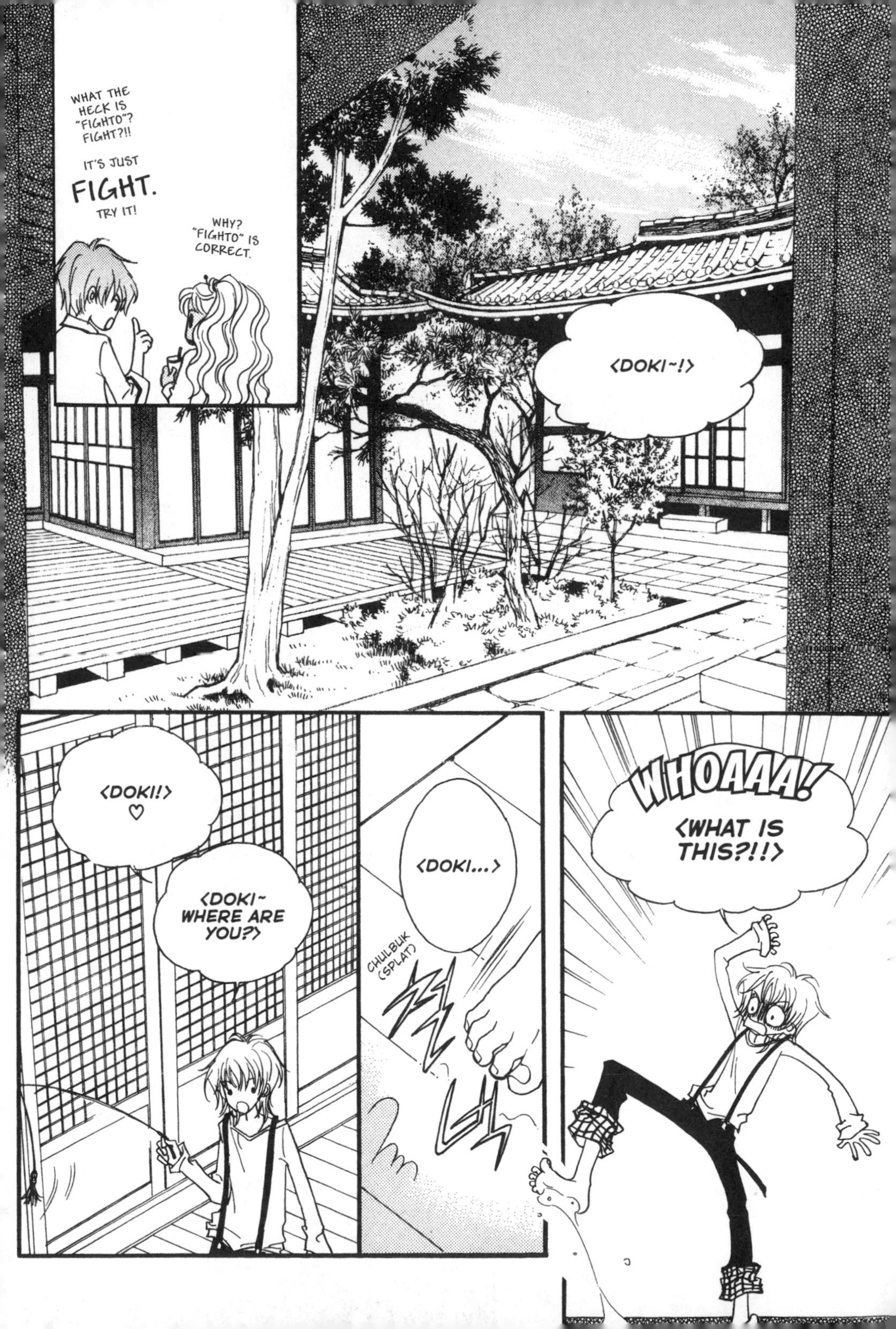
WHAT THE HECK IS "FIGHTO"? FIGHT?!!
IT'S JUST FIGHT. TRY IT!
WHY? "FIGHTO" IS CORRECT.
<DOKI~!>
<DOKI!> ♡
<DOKI~ WHERE ARE YOU?>
<DOKI...>
CHULBUK (SPLAT)
WHOAAA!
<WHAT IS THIS?!!>

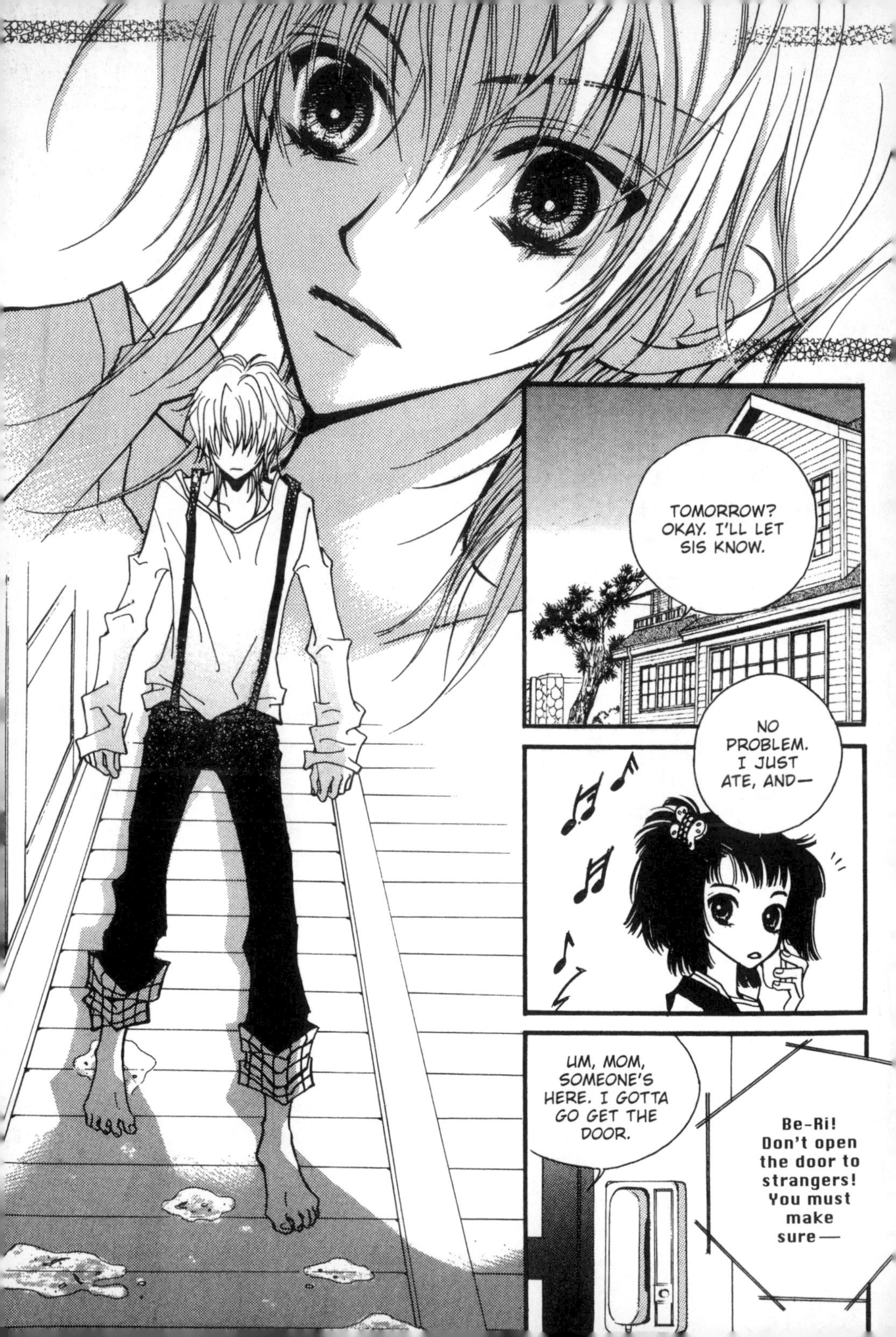
TOMORROW? OKAY. I'LL LET SIS KNOW.
NO PROBLEM. I JUST ATE, AND—
UM, MOM, SOMEONE'S HERE. I GOTTA GO GET THE DOOR.
Be-Ri! Don't open the door to strangers! You must make sure—

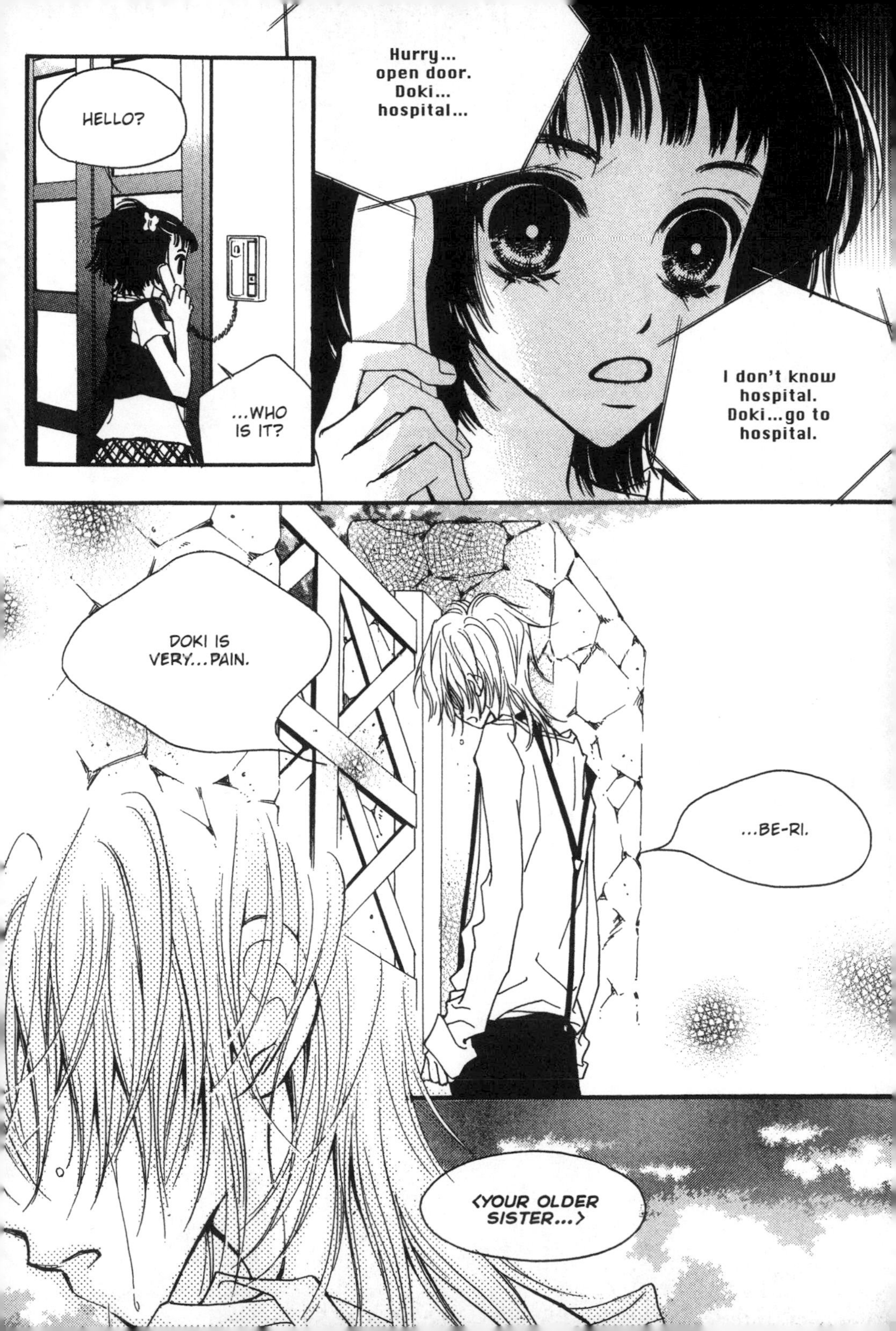
HELLO?
...WHO IS IT?
Hurry... open door. Doki... hospital...
I don't know hospital. Doki...go to hospital.
DOKI IS VERY...PAIN.
...BE-RI.
<YOUR OLDER SISTER...>

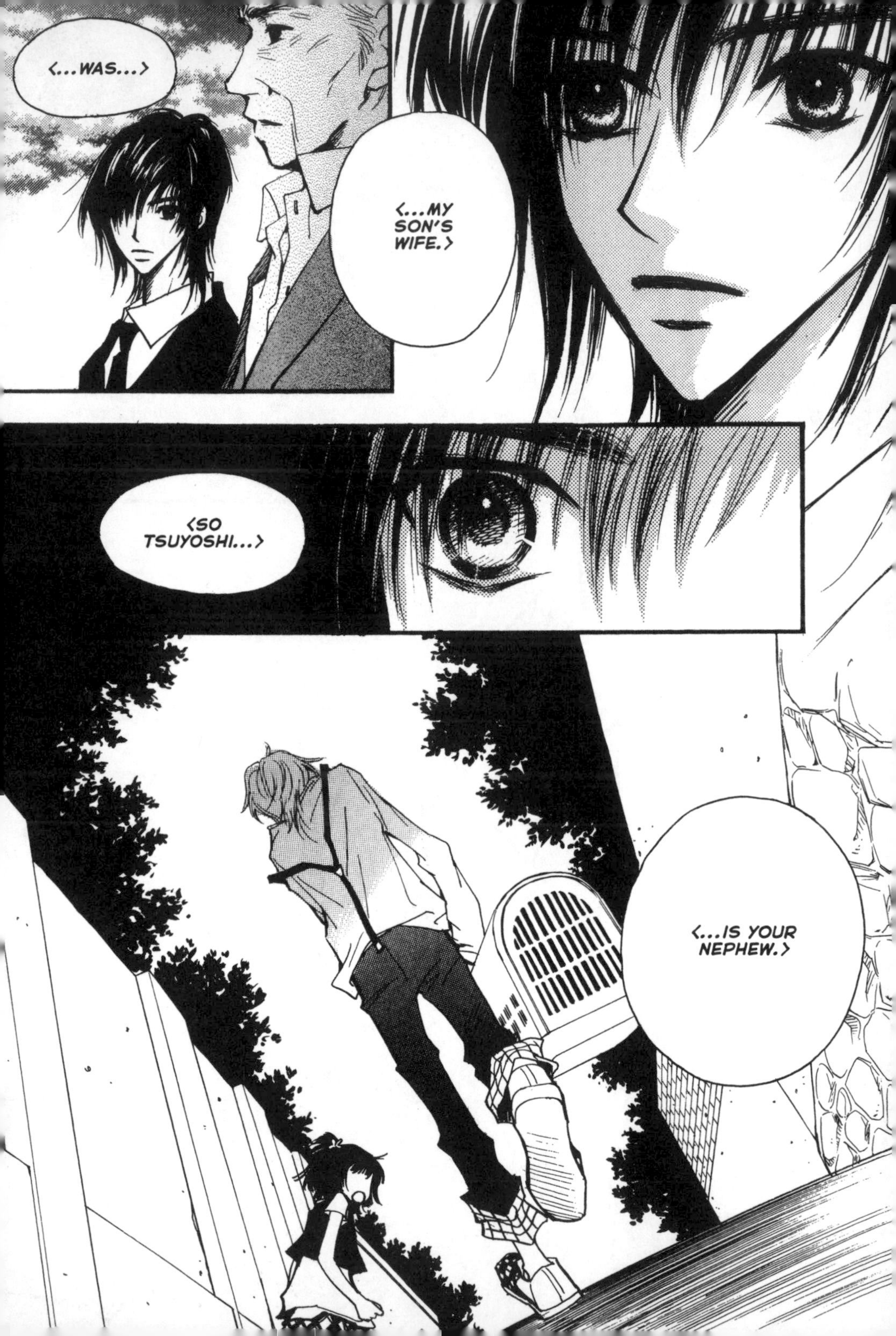
<...WAS...>
<...MY SON'S WIFE.>
<SO TSUYOSHI...>
<...IS YOUR NEPHEW.>

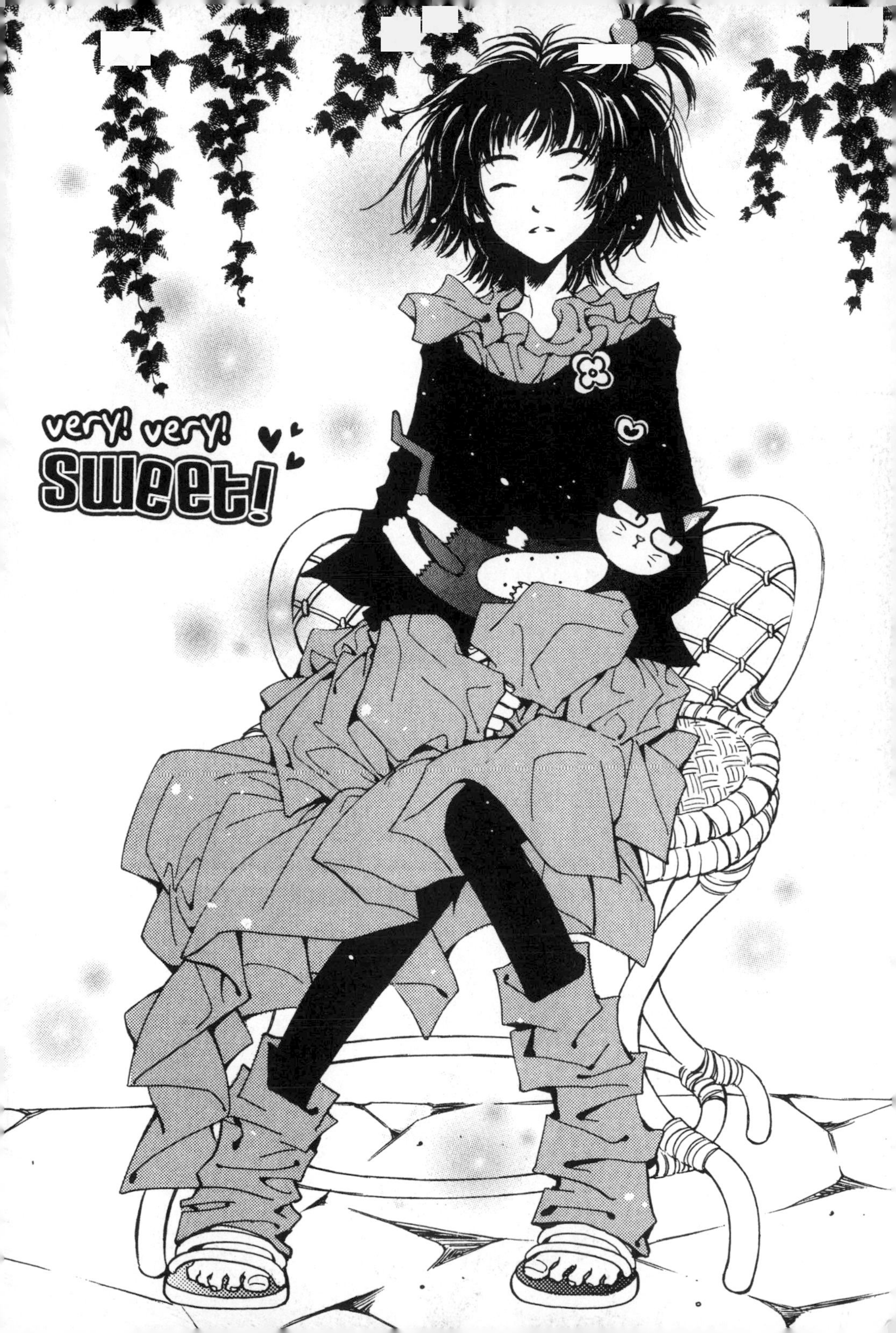
very! very! sweet!

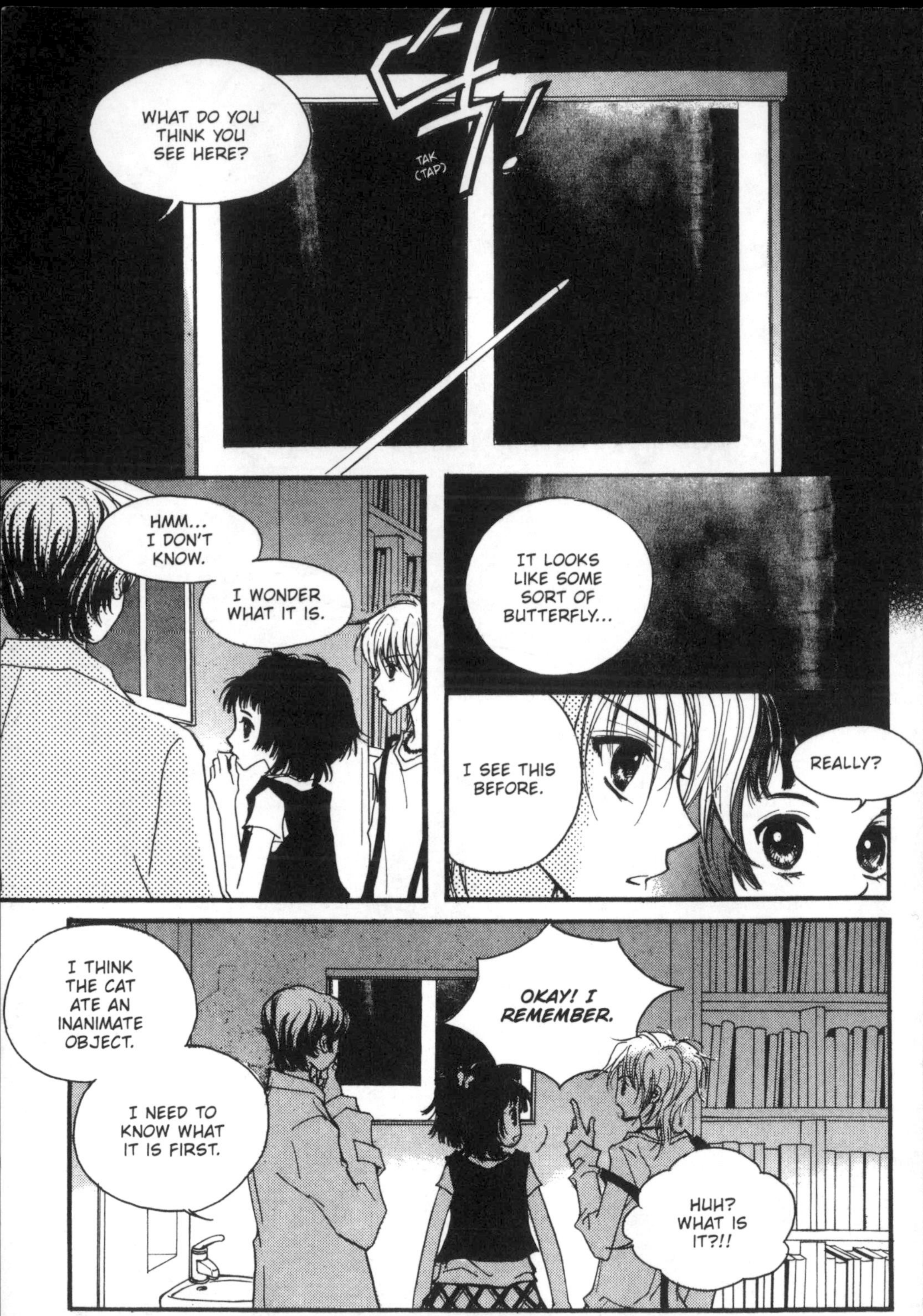
WHAT DO YOU THINK YOU SEE HERE?
TAK (TAP)
HMM... I DON'T KNOW.
I WONDER WHAT IT IS.
IT LOOKS LIKE SOME SORT OF BUTTERFLY...
I SEE THIS BEFORE.
REALLY?
I THINK THE CAT ATE AN INANIMATE OBJECT.
I NEED TO KNOW WHAT IT IS FIRST.
OKAY! I REMEMBER.
HUH? WHAT IS IT?!!

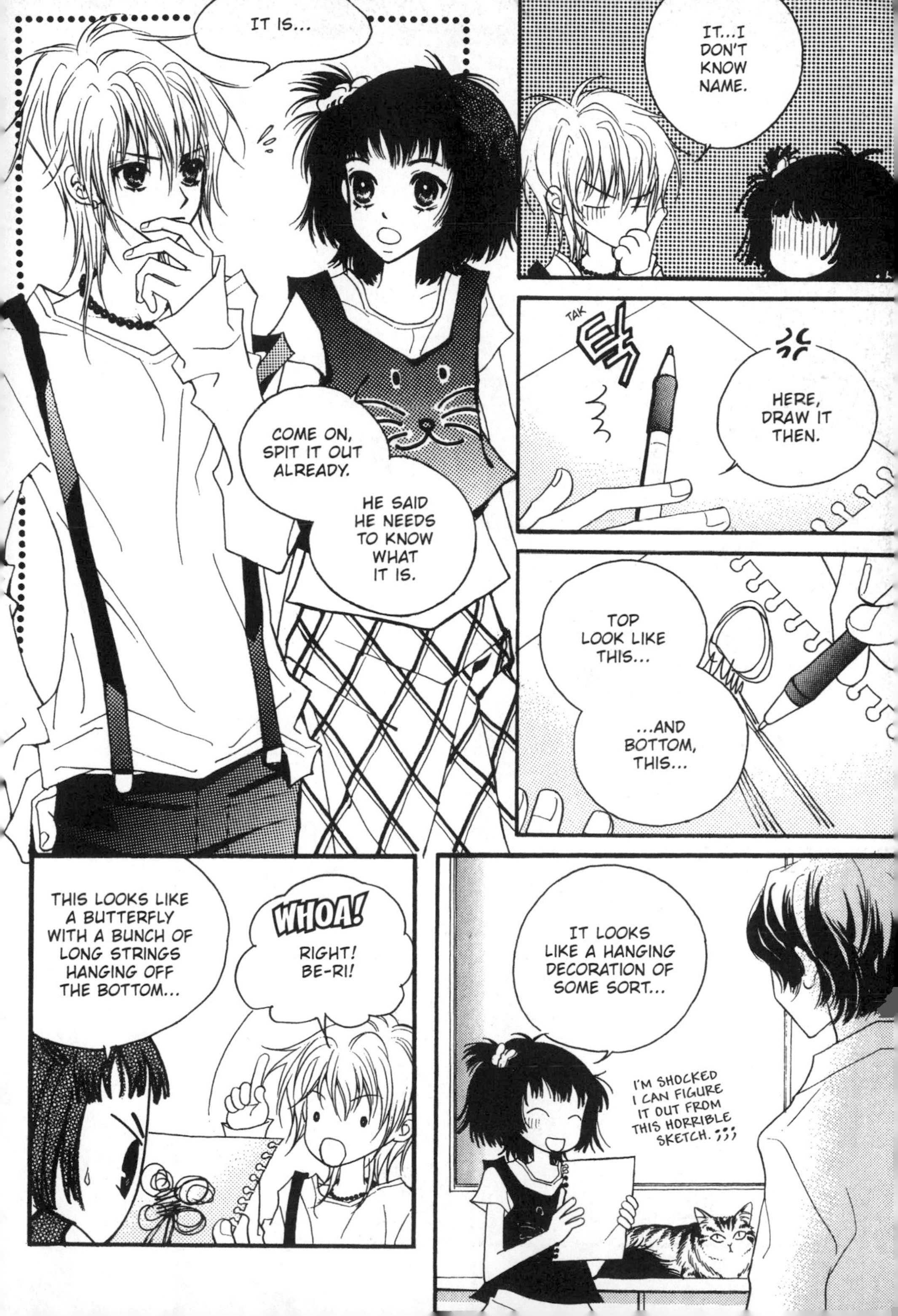
IT IS...
COME ON, SPIT IT OUT ALREADY.
HE SAID HE NEEDS TO KNOW WHAT IT IS.
IT...I DON'T KNOW NAME.
TAK
HERE, DRAW IT THEN.
TOP LOOK LIKE THIS...
...AND BOTTOM, THIS...
THIS LOOKS LIKE A BUTTERFLY WITH A BUNCH OF LONG STRINGS HANGING OFF THE BOTTOM...
WHOA!
RIGHT! BE-RI!
IT LOOKS LIKE A HANGING DECORATION OF SOME SORT...
I'M SHOCKED I CAN FIGURE IT OUT FROM THIS HORRIBLE SKETCH.

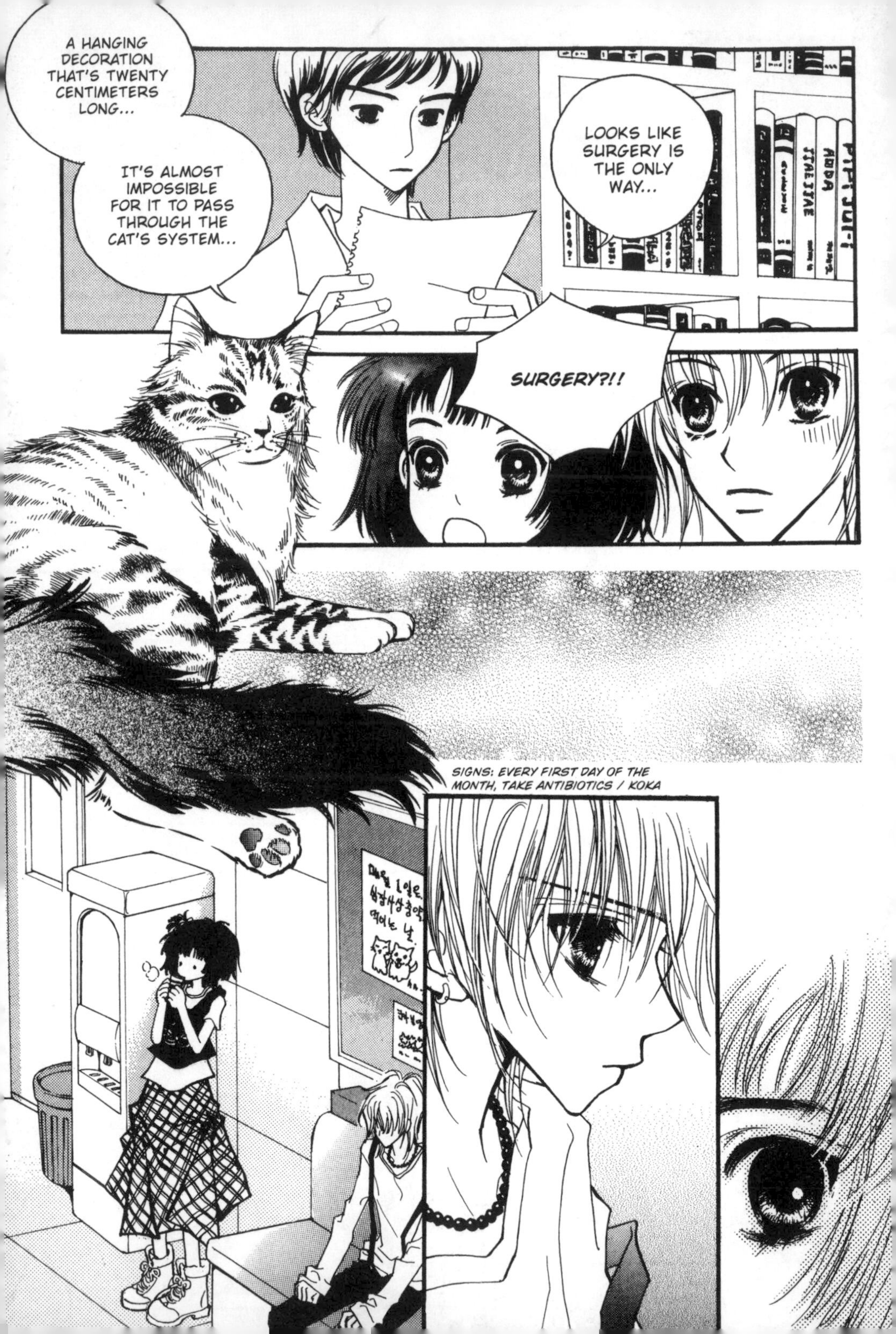
A HANGING DECORATION THAT'S TWENTY CENTIMETERS LONG...
IT'S ALMOST IMPOSSIBLE FOR IT TO PASS THROUGH THE CAT'S SYSTEM...
LOOKS LIKE SURGERY IS THE ONLY WAY...
SURGERY?!!
SIGNS: EVERY FIRST DAY OF THE MONTH, TAKE ANTIBIOTICS / KOKA

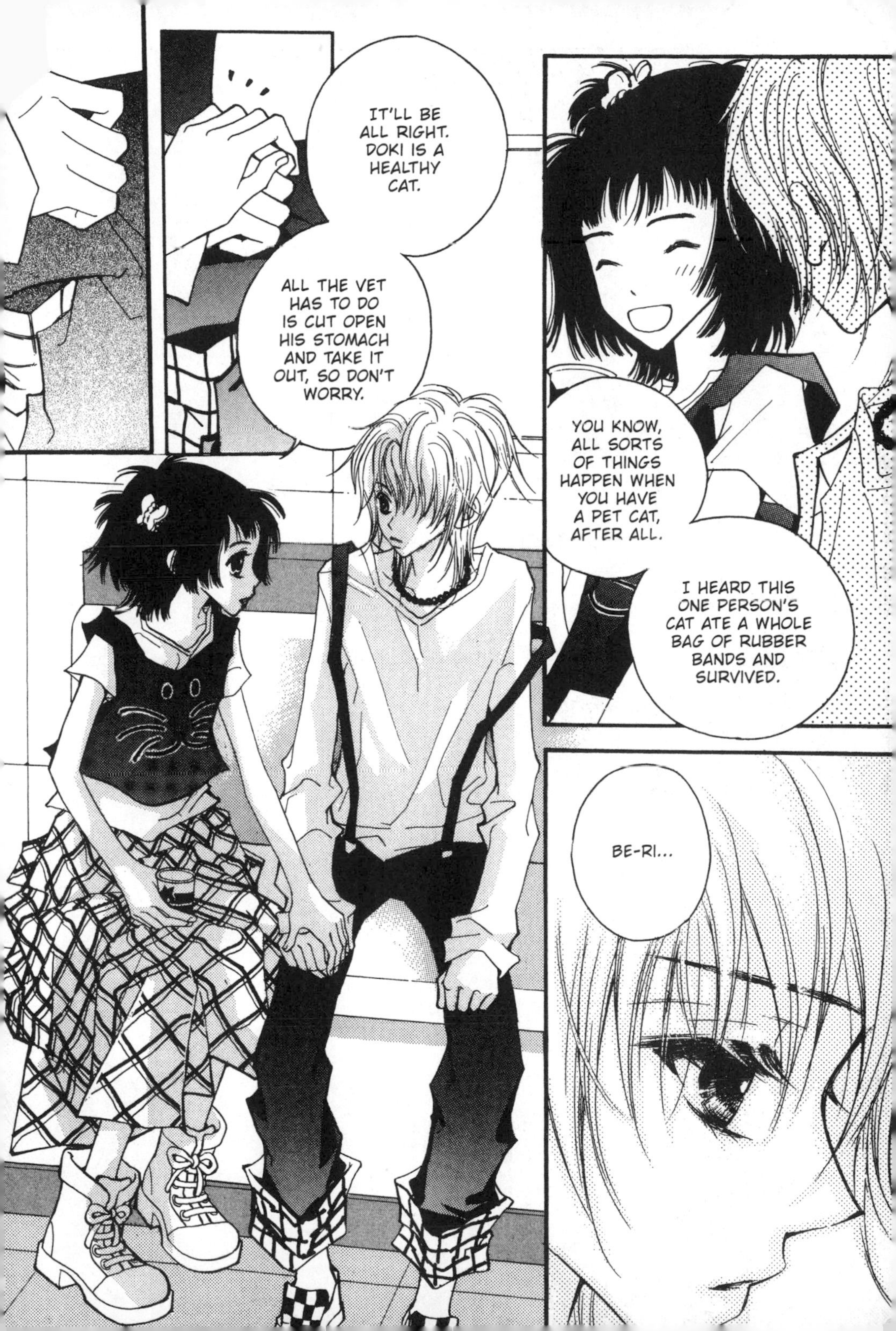
...
IT'LL BE ALL RIGHT. DOKI IS A HEALTHY CAT.
ALL THE VET HAS TO DO IS CUT OPEN HIS STOMACH AND TAKE IT OUT, SO DON'T WORRY.
YOU KNOW, ALL SORTS OF THINGS HAPPEN WHEN YOU HAVE A PET CAT, AFTER ALL.
I HEARD THIS ONE PERSON'S CAT ATE A WHOLE BAG OF RUBBER BANDS AND SURVIVED.
BE-RI...

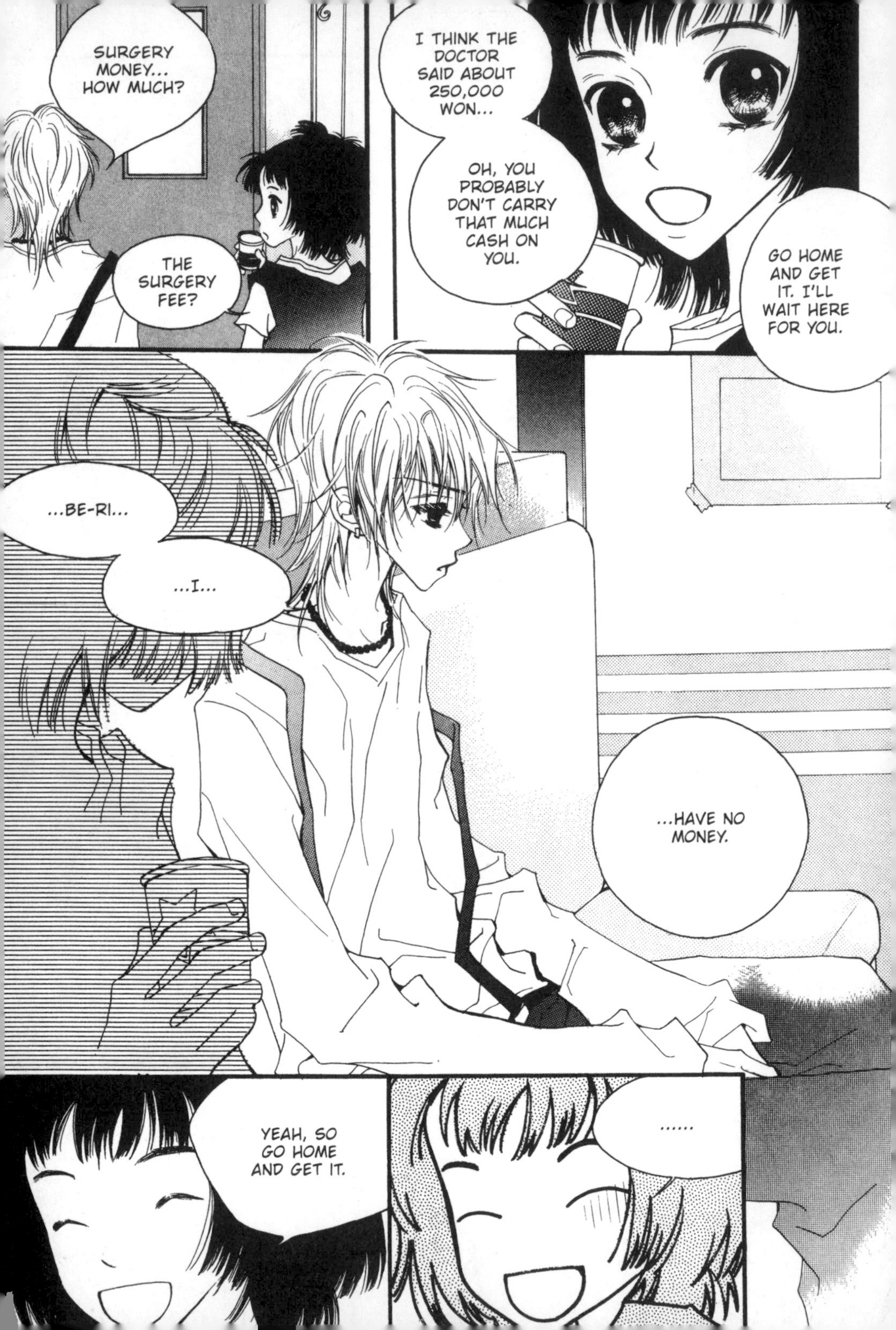
SURGERY MONEY... HOW MUCH?
THE SURGERY FEE?
I THINK THE DOCTOR SAID ABOUT 250,000 WON...
OH, YOU PROBABLY DON'T CARRY THAT MUCH CASH ON YOU.
GO HOME AND GET IT. I'LL WAIT HERE FOR YOU.
...BE-RI...
...I...
...HAVE NO MONEY.
YEAH, SO GO HOME AND GET IT.
......

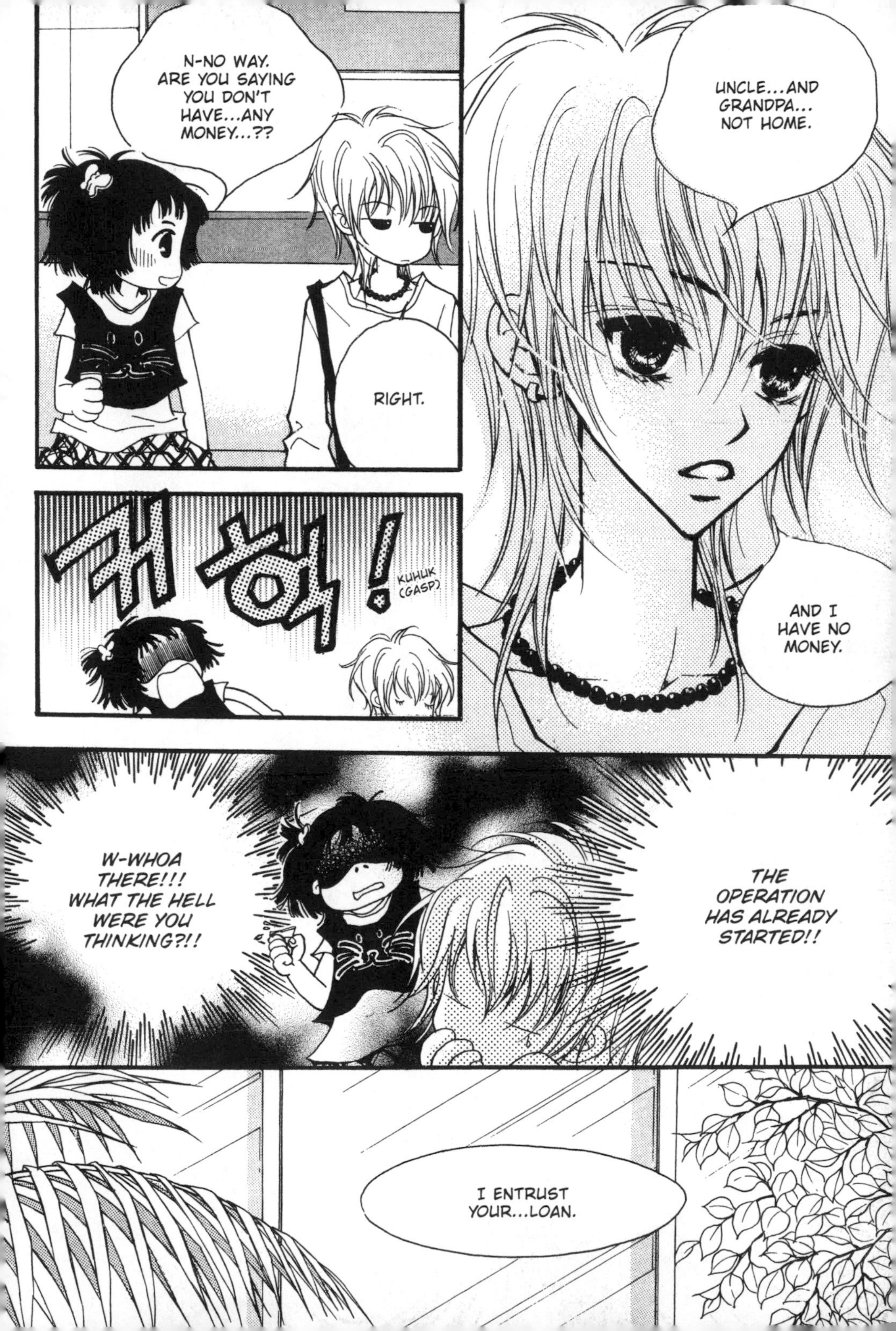
N-NO WAY. ARE YOU SAYING YOU DON'T HAVE...ANY MONEY...??
RIGHT.
커헉!
KUHUK (GASP)
UNCLE...AND GRANDPA... NOT HOME.
AND I HAVE NO MONEY.
W-WHOA THERE!!! WHAT THE HELL WERE YOU THINKING?!!
THE OPERATION HAS ALREADY STARTED!!
I ENTRUST YOUR...LOAN.

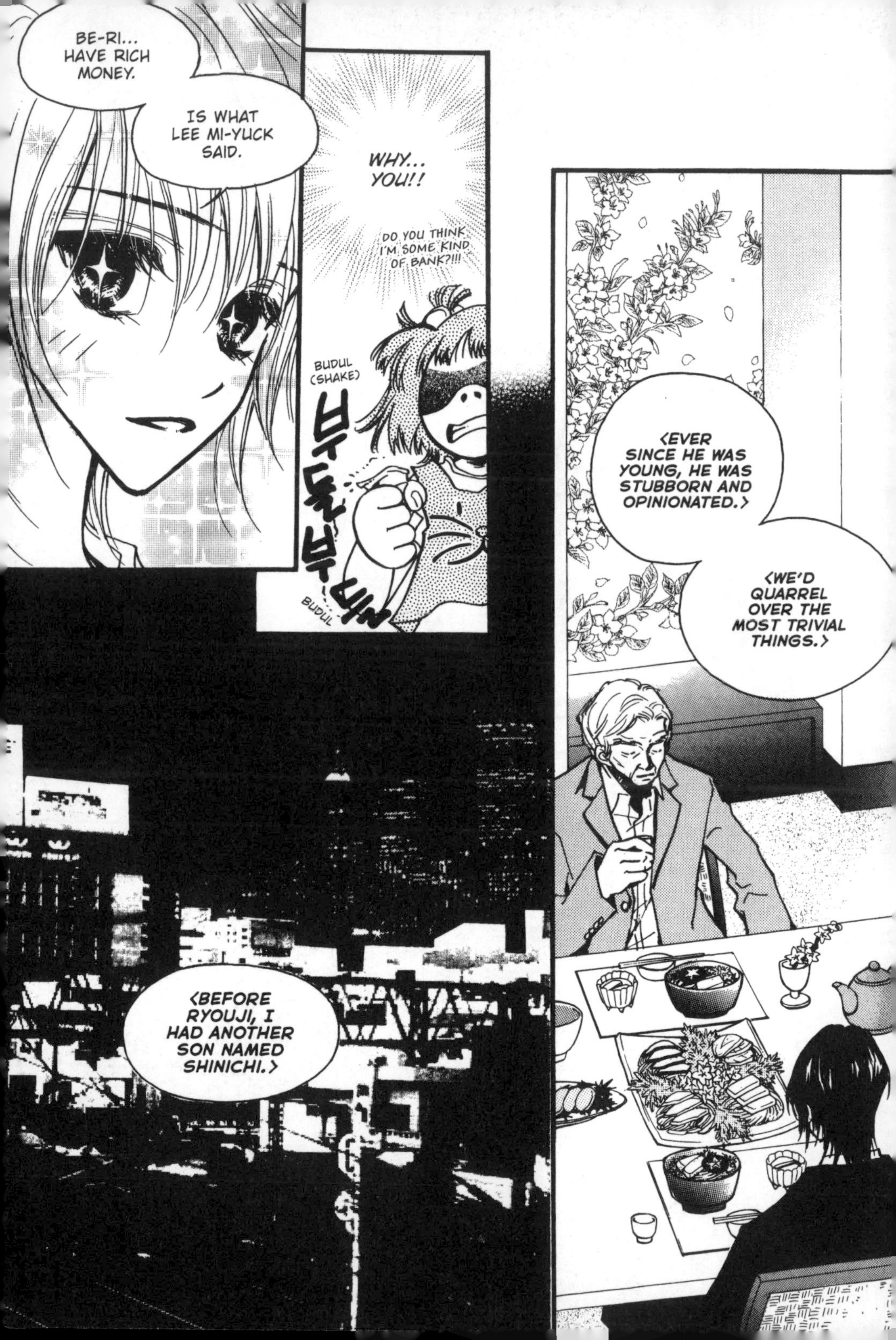
BE-RI... HAVE RICH MONEY.
IS WHAT LEE MI-YUCK SAID.
WHY... YOU!!
DO YOU THINK I'M SOME KIND OF BANK?!!!
BUDUL (SHAKE)
부들부들
BUDUL
<BEFORE RYOUJI, I HAD ANOTHER SON NAMED SHINICHI.>
<EVER SINCE HE WAS YOUNG, HE WAS STUBBORN AND OPINIONATED.>
<WE'D QUARREL OVER THE MOST TRIVIAL THINGS.>

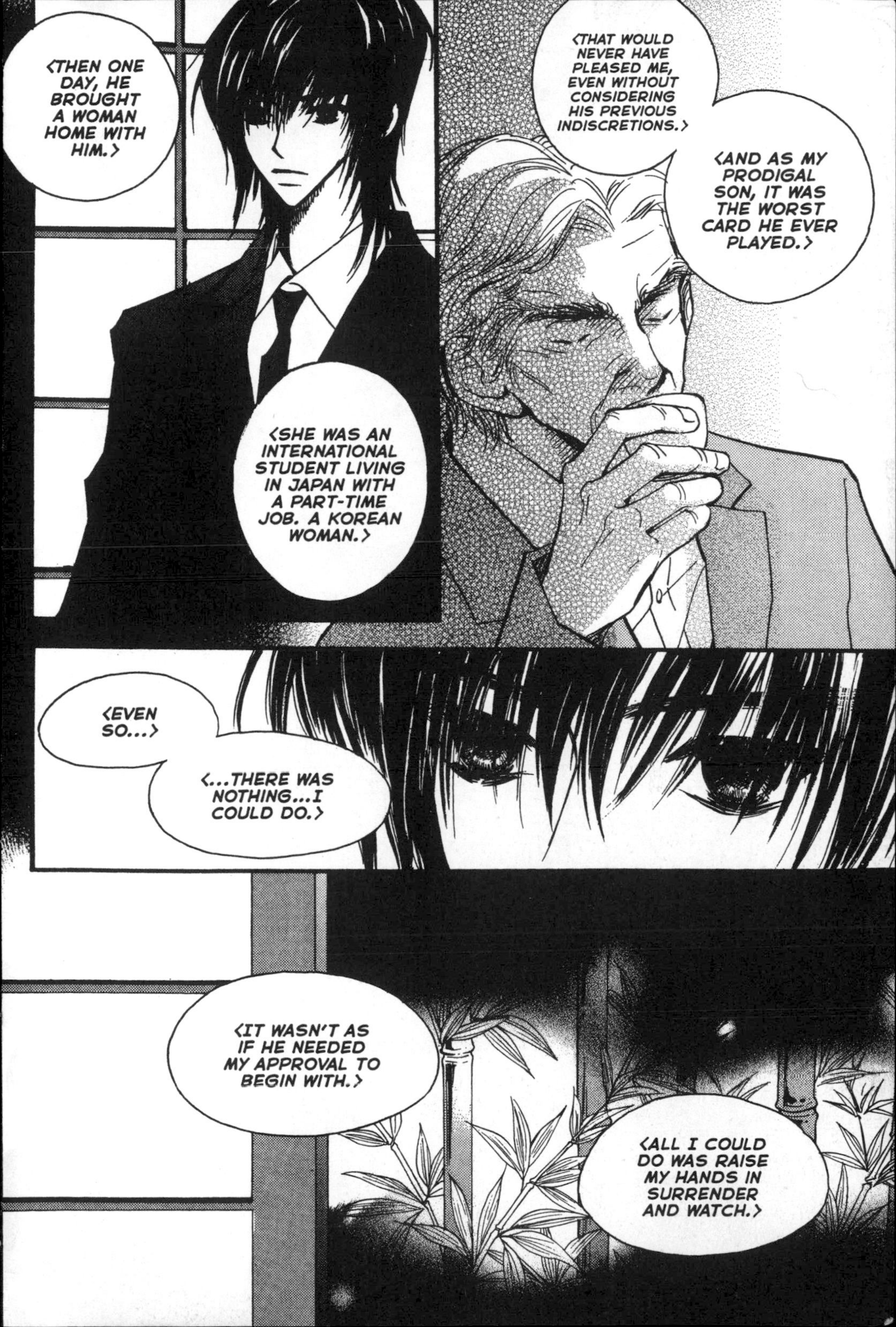
<THEN ONE DAY, HE BROUGHT A WOMAN HOME WITH HIM.>
<THAT WOULD NEVER HAVE PLEASED ME, EVEN WITHOUT CONSIDERING HIS PREVIOUS INDISCRETIONS.>
<AND AS MY PRODIGAL SON, IT WAS THE WORST CARD HE EVER PLAYED.>
<SHE WAS AN INTERNATIONAL STUDENT LIVING IN JAPAN WITH A PART-TIME JOB. A KOREAN WOMAN.>
<EVEN SO...>
<...THERE WAS NOTHING...I COULD DO.>
<IT WASN'T AS IF HE NEEDED MY APPROVAL TO BEGIN WITH.>
<ALL I COULD DO WAS RAISE MY HANDS IN SURRENDER AND WATCH.>

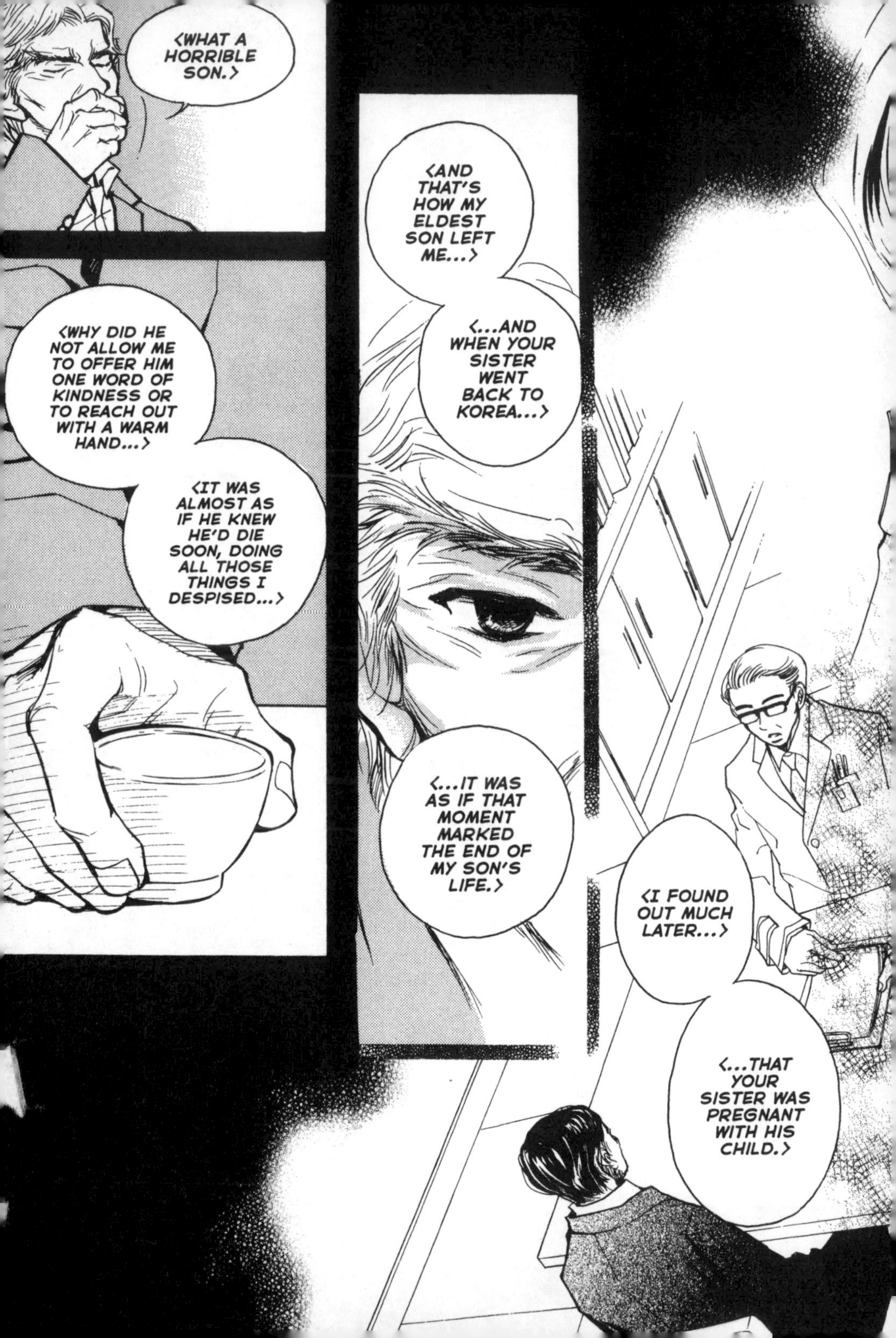
<WHAT A HORRIBLE SON.>
<WHY DID HE NOT ALLOW ME TO OFFER HIM ONE WORD OF KINDNESS OR TO REACH OUT WITH A WARM HAND...>
<IT WAS ALMOST AS IF HE KNEW HE'D DIE SOON, DOING ALL THOSE THINGS I DESPISED...>
<AND THAT'S HOW MY ELDEST SON LEFT ME...>
<...AND WHEN YOUR SISTER WENT BACK TO KOREA...>
<...IT WAS AS IF THAT MOMENT MARKED THE END OF MY SON'S LIFE.>
<I FOUND OUT MUCH LATER...>
<...THAT YOUR SISTER WAS PREGNANT WITH HIS CHILD.>

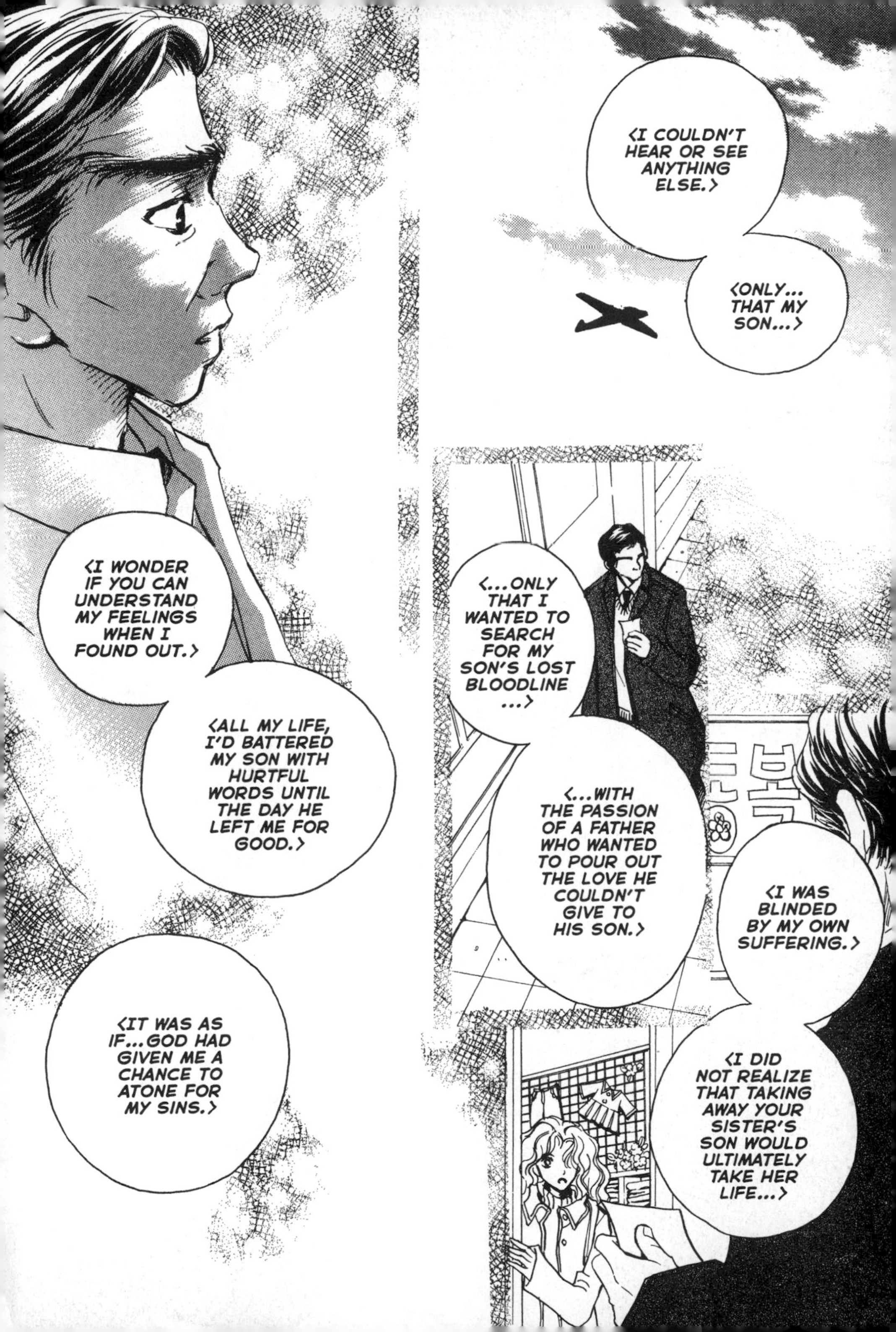
<I WONDER IF YOU CAN UNDERSTAND MY FEELINGS WHEN I FOUND OUT.>
<ALL MY LIFE, I'D BATTERED MY SON WITH HURTFUL WORDS UNTIL THE DAY HE LEFT ME FOR GOOD.>
<IT WAS AS IF...GOD HAD GIVEN ME A CHANCE TO ATONE FOR MY SINS.>
<I COULDN'T HEAR OR SEE ANYTHING ELSE.>
<ONLY... THAT MY SON...>
<...ONLY THAT I WANTED TO SEARCH FOR MY SON'S LOST BLOODLINE ...>
<...WITH THE PASSION OF A FATHER WHO WANTED TO POUR OUT THE LOVE HE COULDN'T GIVE TO HIS SON.>
<I WAS BLINDED BY MY OWN SUFFERING.>
<I DID NOT REALIZE THAT TAKING AWAY YOUR SISTER'S SON WOULD ULTIMATELY TAKE HER LIFE...>

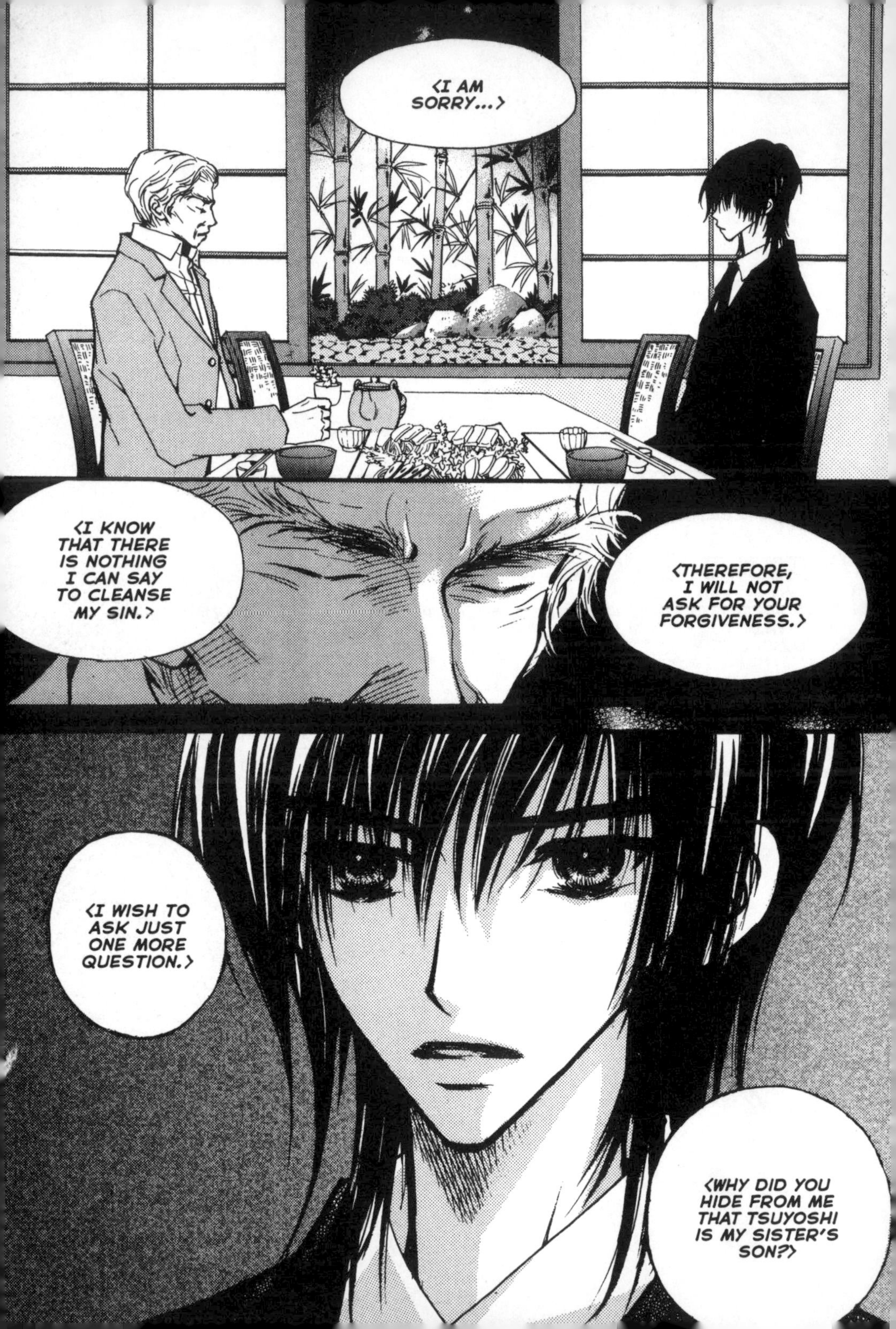
<I AM SORRY...>
<I KNOW THAT THERE IS NOTHING I CAN SAY TO CLEANSE MY SIN.>
<THEREFORE, I WILL NOT ASK FOR YOUR FORGIVENESS.>
<I WISH TO ASK JUST ONE MORE QUESTION.>
<WHY DID YOU HIDE FROM ME THAT TSUYOSHI IS MY SISTER'S SON?>

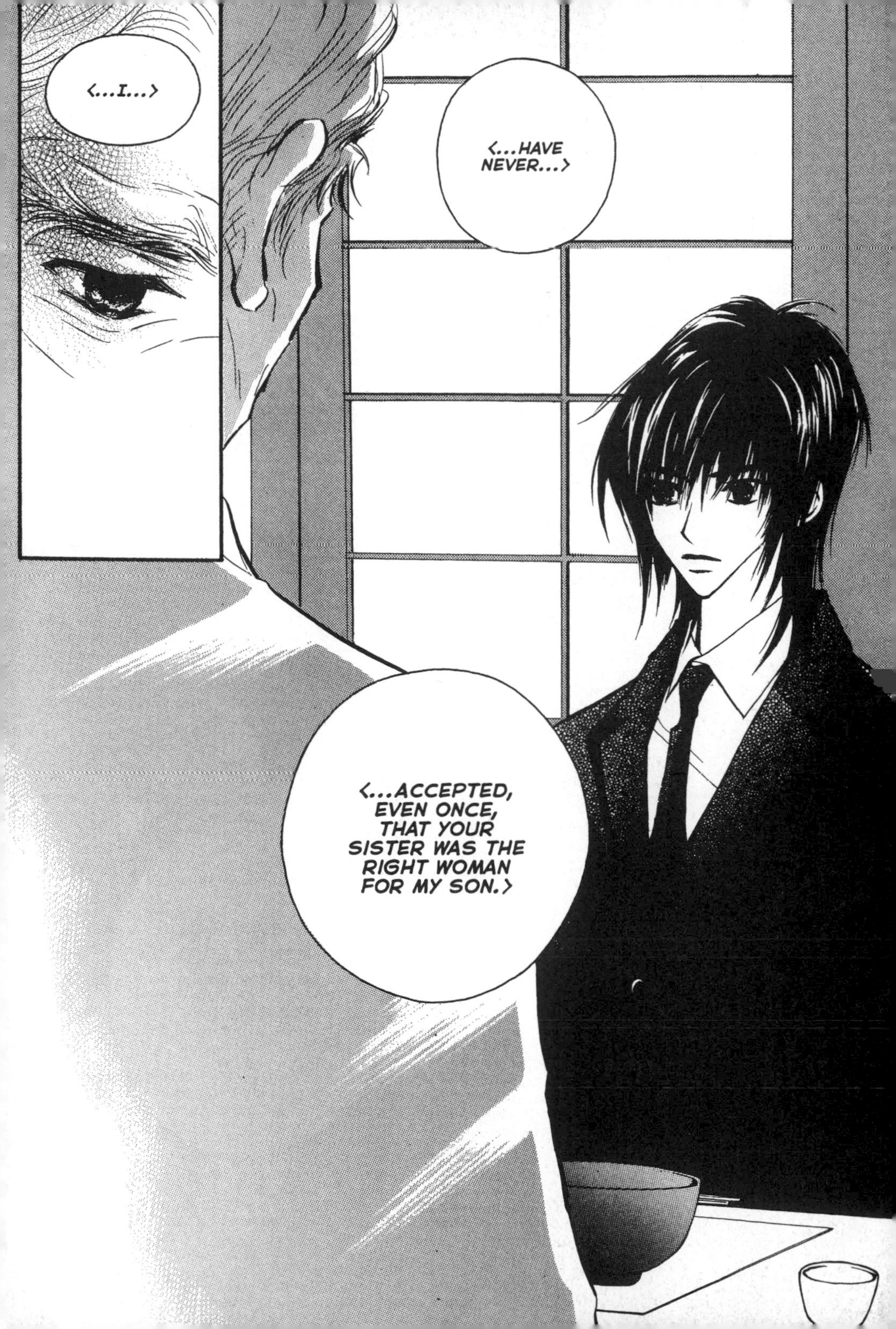
<...I...>
<...HAVE NEVER...>
<...ACCEPTED, EVEN ONCE, THAT YOUR SISTER WAS THE RIGHT WOMAN FOR MY SON.>

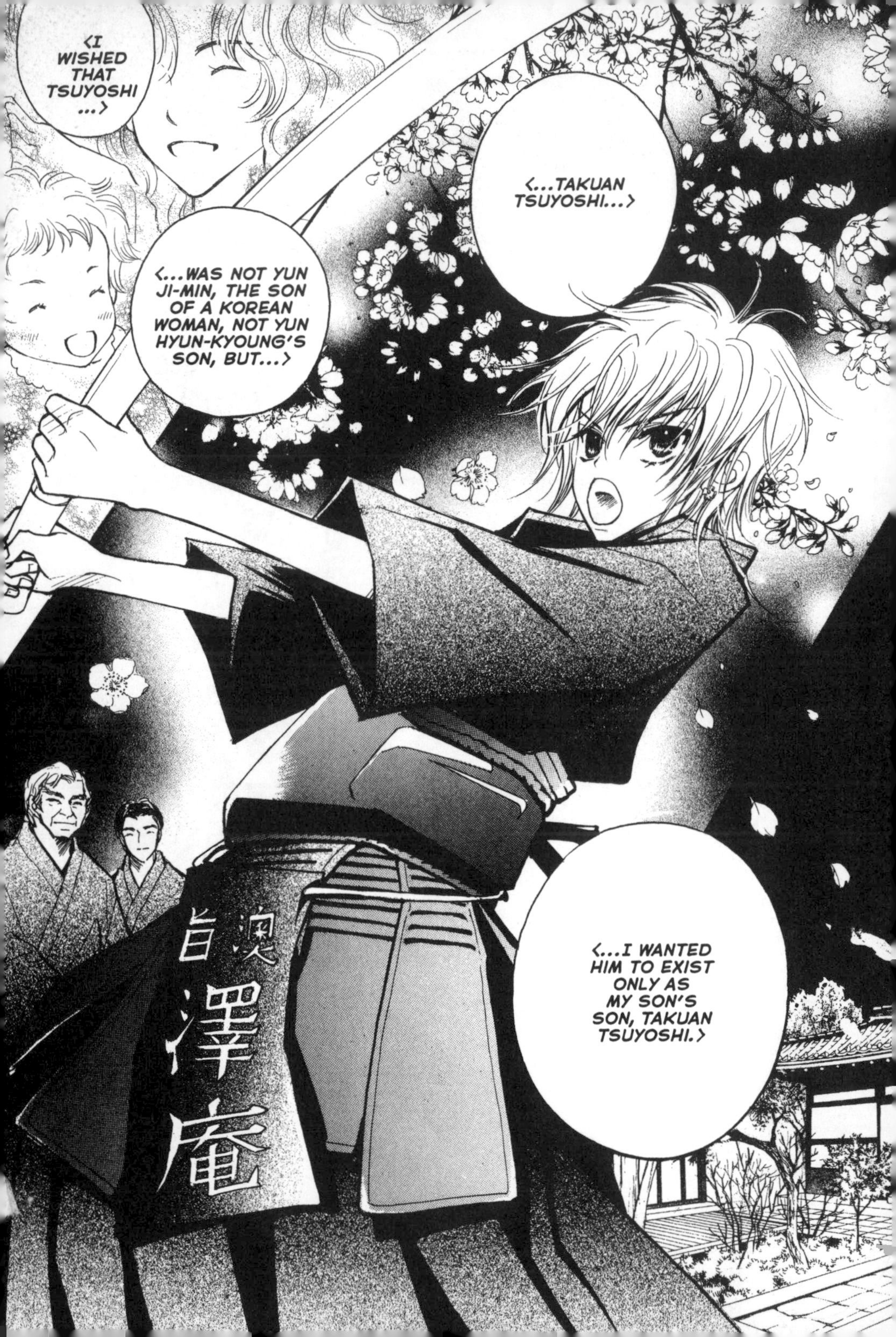
‹I WISHED THAT TSUYOSHI ...›
‹...WAS NOT YUN JI-MIN, THE SON OF A KOREAN WOMAN, NOT YUN HYUN-KYOUNG'S SON, BUT...›
‹...TAKUAN TSUYOSHI...›
澤庵
‹...I WANTED HIM TO EXIST ONLY AS MY SON'S SON, TAKUAN TSUYOSHI.›

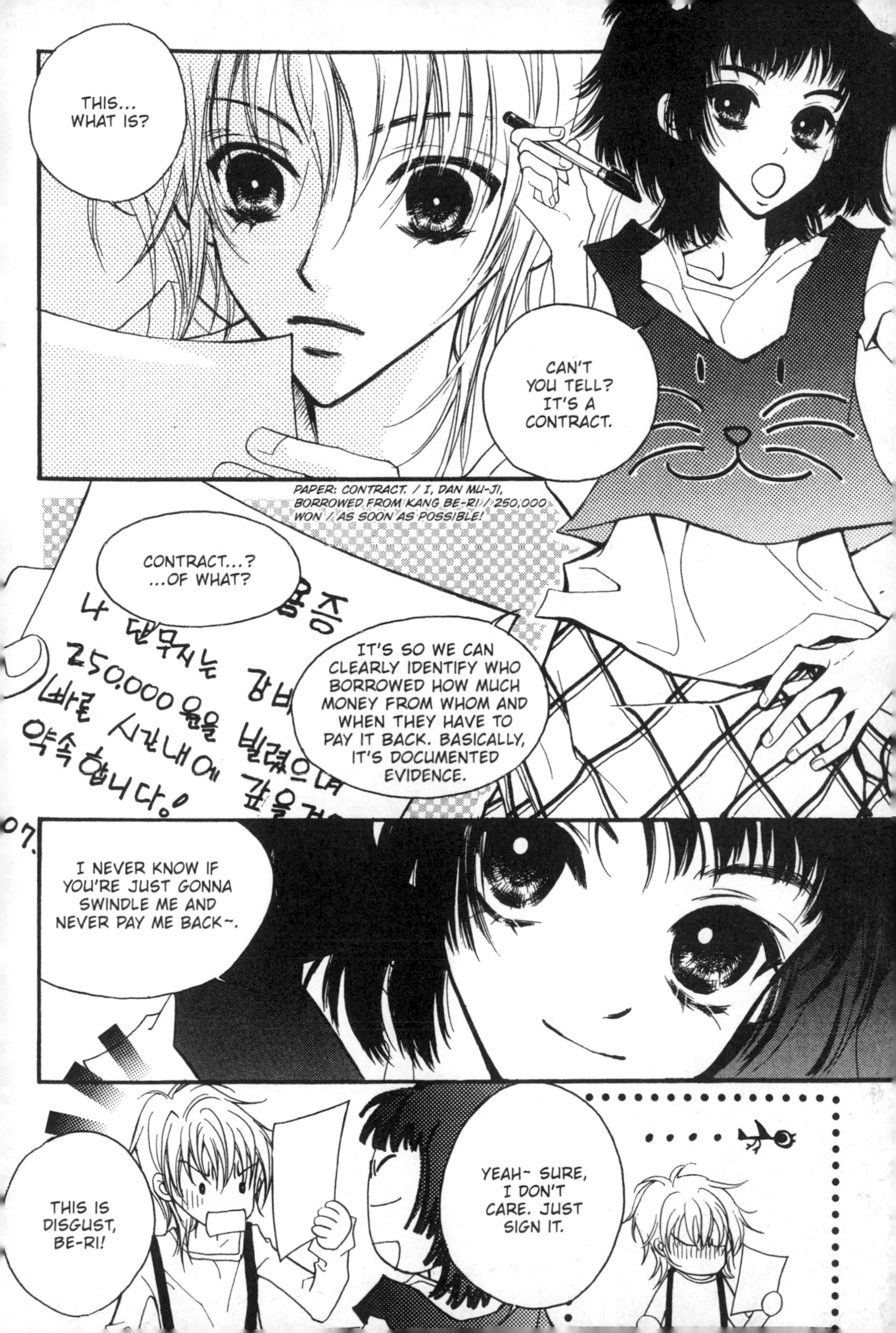
THIS... WHAT IS?
CAN'T YOU TELL? IT'S A CONTRACT.
PAPER: CONTRACT. / I, DAN MU-JI, BORROWED FROM KANG BE-RI / 250,000 WON / AS SOON AS POSSIBLE!
CONTRACT...? ...OF WHAT?
나 단무지는
250,000원을
빠른 시간내에
약속합니다!
IT'S SO WE CAN CLEARLY IDENTIFY WHO BORROWED HOW MUCH MONEY FROM WHOM AND WHEN THEY HAVE TO PAY IT BACK. BASICALLY, IT'S DOCUMENTED EVIDENCE.
I NEVER KNOW IF YOU'RE JUST GONNA SWINDLE ME AND NEVER PAY ME BACK~.
THIS IS DISGUST, BE-RI!
YEAH~ SURE, I DON'T CARE. JUST SIGN IT.

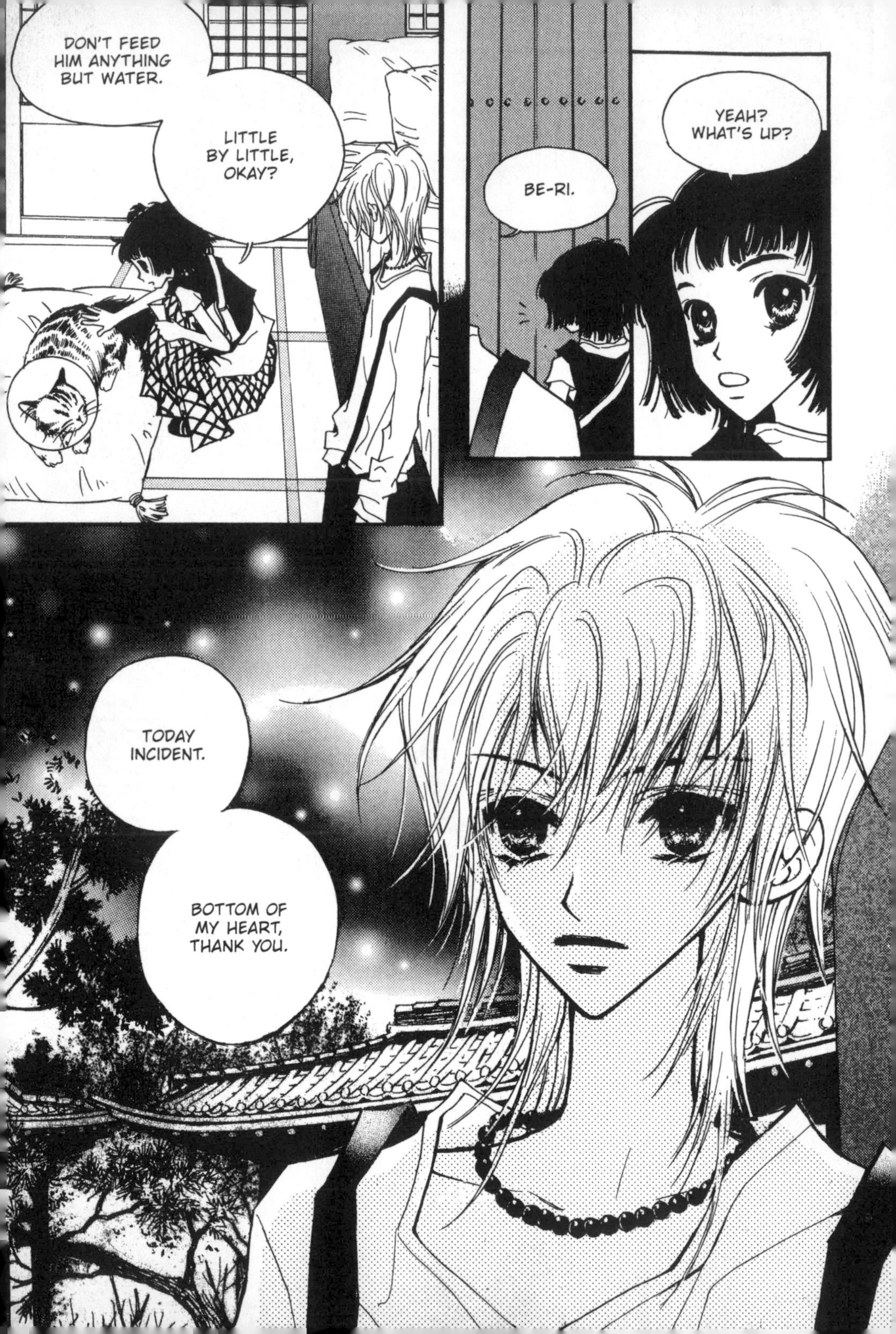
DON'T FEED HIM ANYTHING BUT WATER.
LITTLE BY LITTLE, OKAY?
BE-RI.
YEAH? WHAT'S UP?
TODAY INCIDENT.
BOTTOM OF MY HEART, THANK YOU.

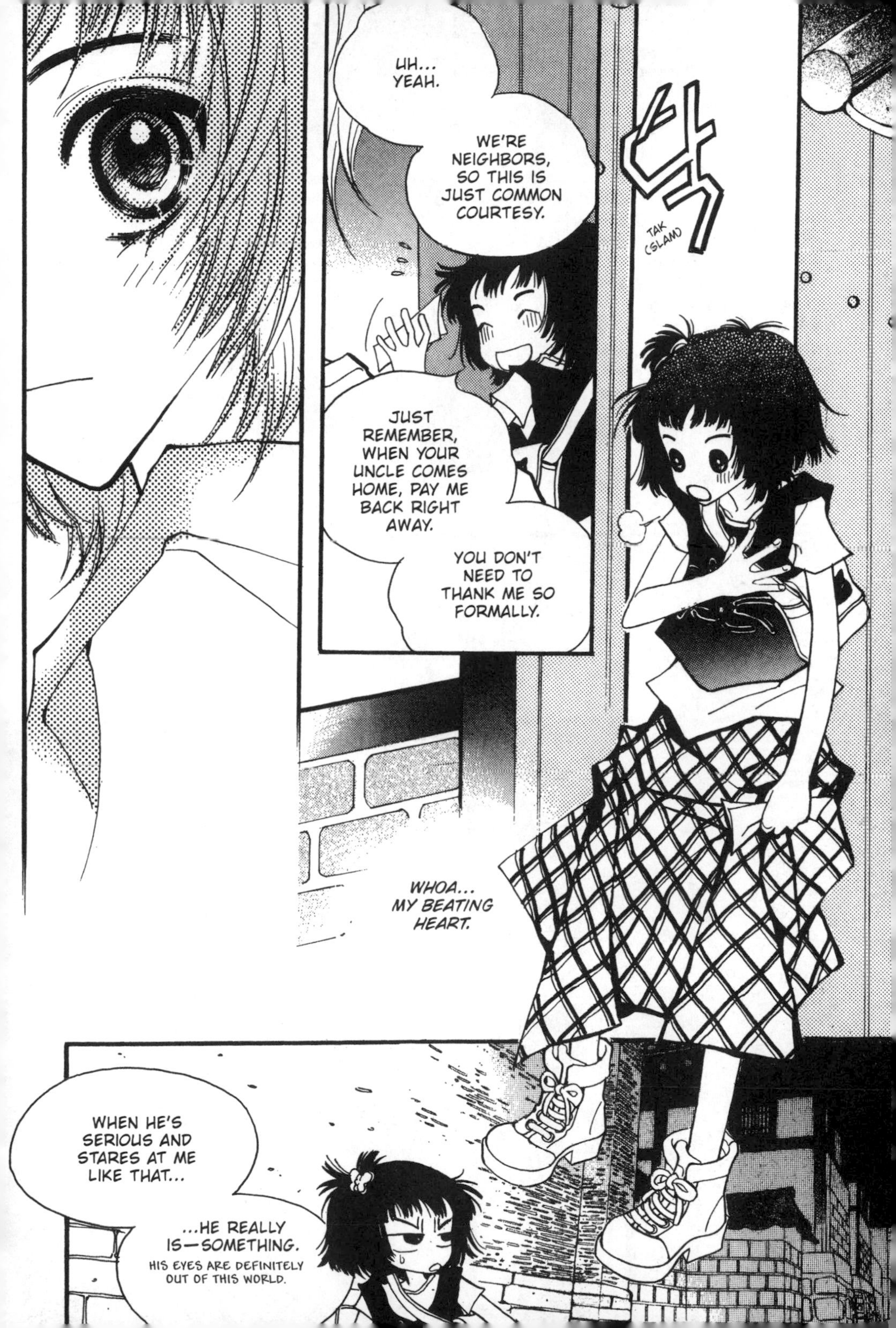
UH... YEAH.
WE'RE NEIGHBORS, SO THIS IS JUST COMMON COURTESY.
JUST REMEMBER, WHEN YOUR UNCLE COMES HOME, PAY ME BACK RIGHT AWAY.
YOU DON'T NEED TO THANK ME SO FORMALLY.
탁
TAK (SLAM)
WHOA... MY BEATING HEART.
WHEN HE'S SERIOUS AND STARES AT ME LIKE THAT...
...HE REALLY IS—SOMETHING.
HIS EYES ARE DEFINITELY OUT OF THIS WORLD.

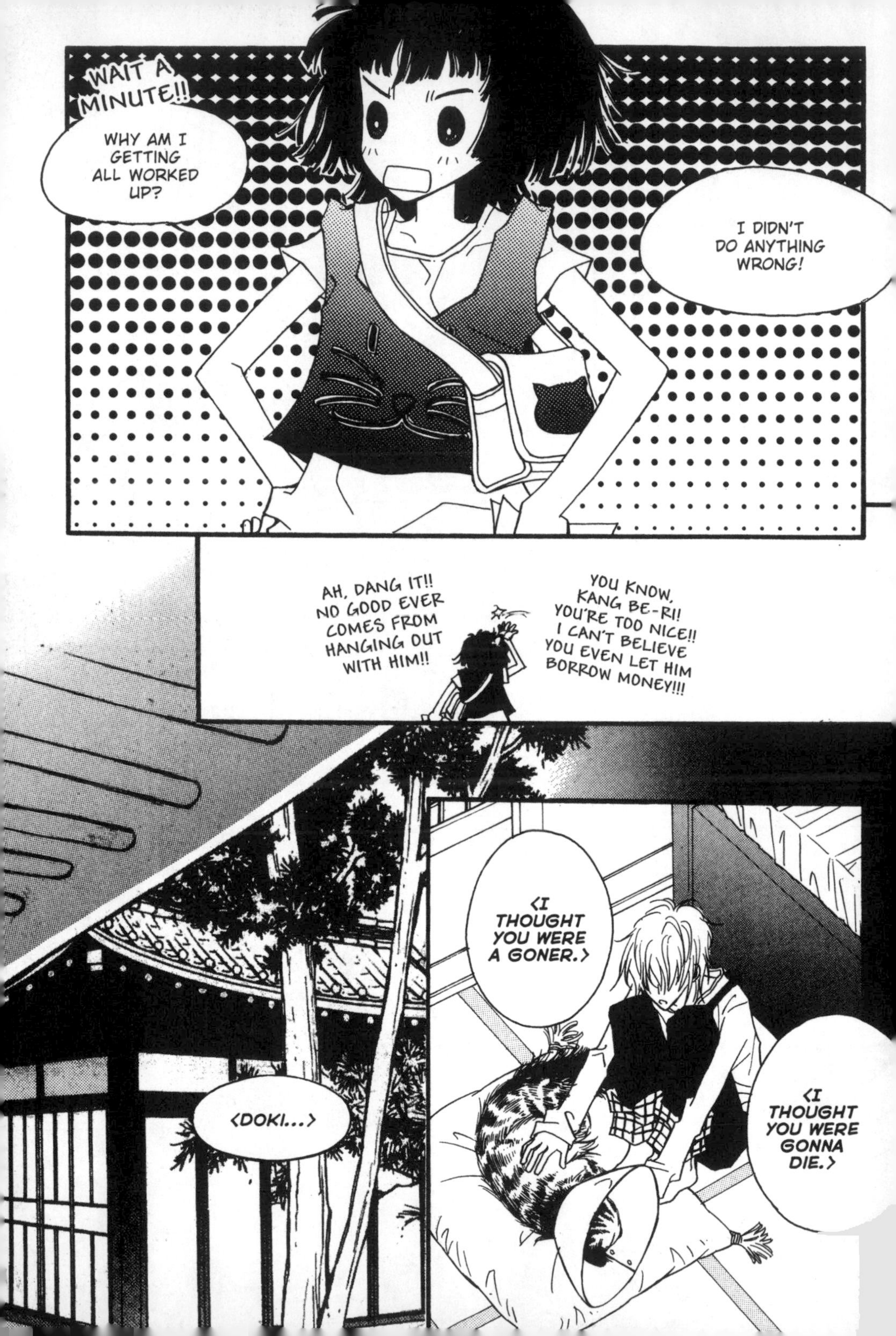
WAIT A MINUTE!!
WHY AM I GETTING ALL WORKED UP?
I DIDN'T DO ANYTHING WRONG!
AH, DANG IT!! NO GOOD EVER COMES FROM HANGING OUT WITH HIM!!
YOU KNOW, KANG BE-RI! YOU'RE TOO NICE!! I CAN'T BELIEVE YOU EVEN LET HIM BORROW MONEY!!!
<DOKI...>
<I THOUGHT YOU WERE A GONER.>
<I THOUGHT YOU WERE GONNA DIE.>

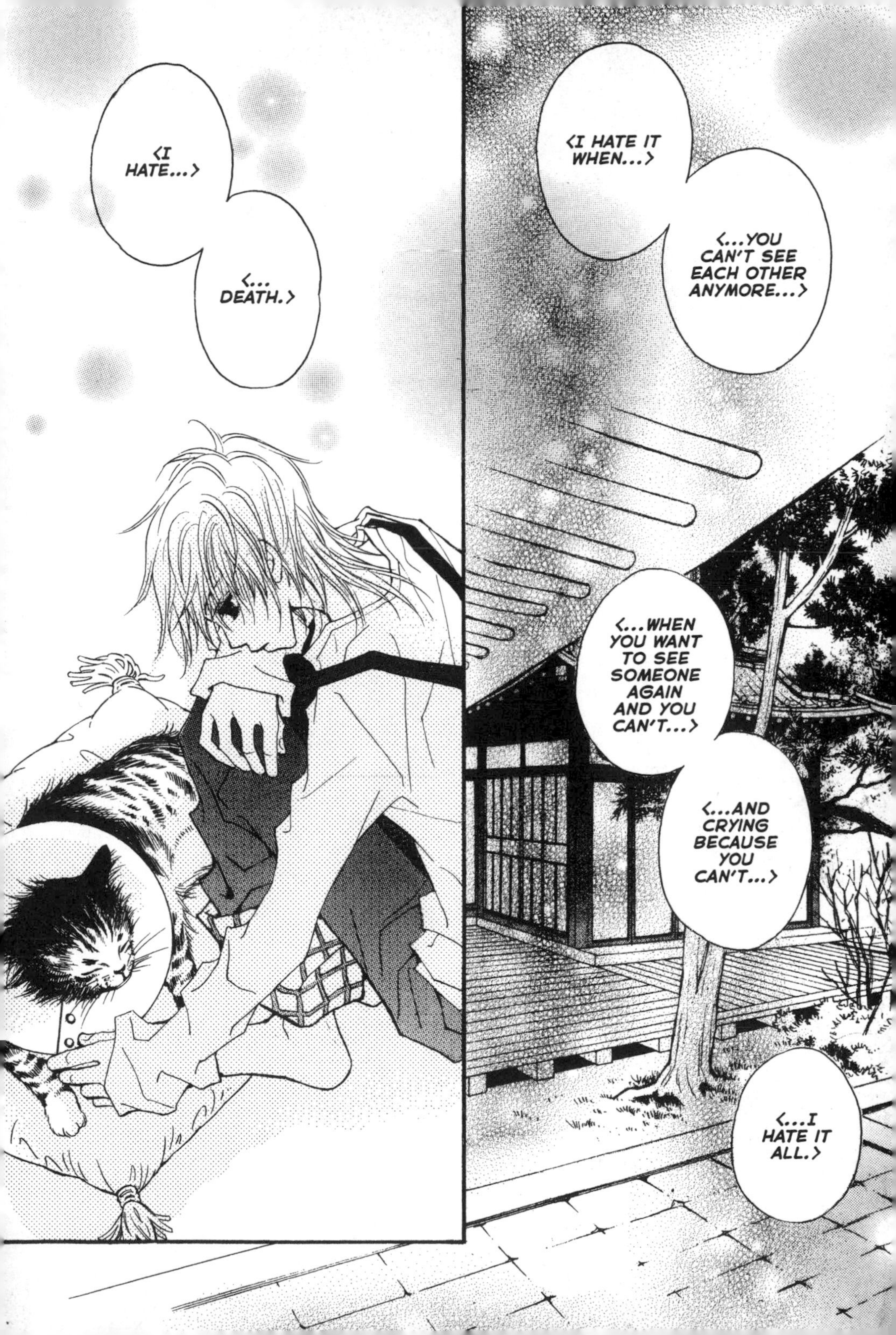
<I HATE...>
<...DEATH.>
<I HATE IT WHEN...>
<...YOU CAN'T SEE EACH OTHER ANYMORE...>
<...WHEN YOU WANT TO SEE SOMEONE AGAIN AND YOU CAN'T...>
<...AND CRYING BECAUSE YOU CAN'T...>
<...I HATE IT ALL.>

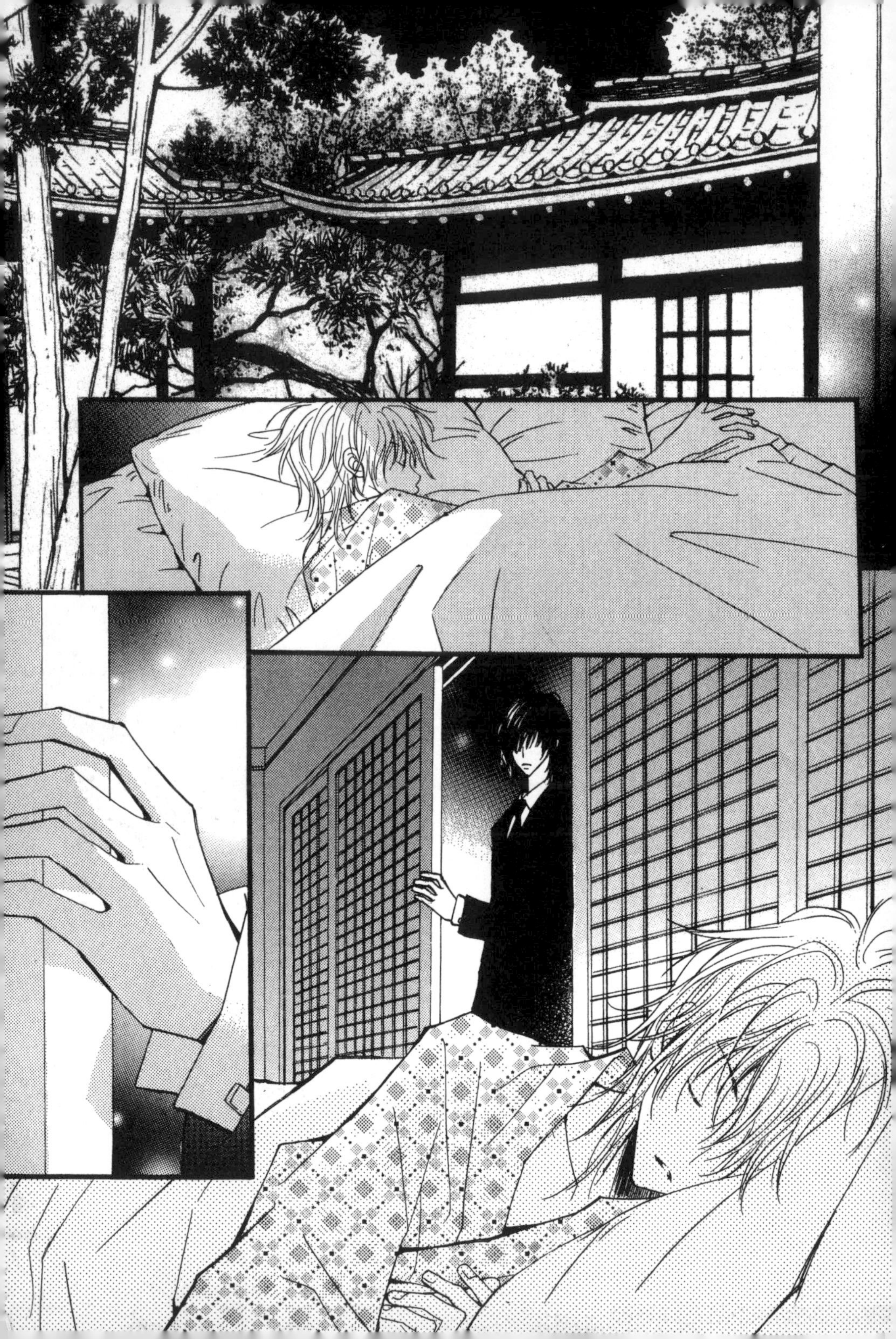

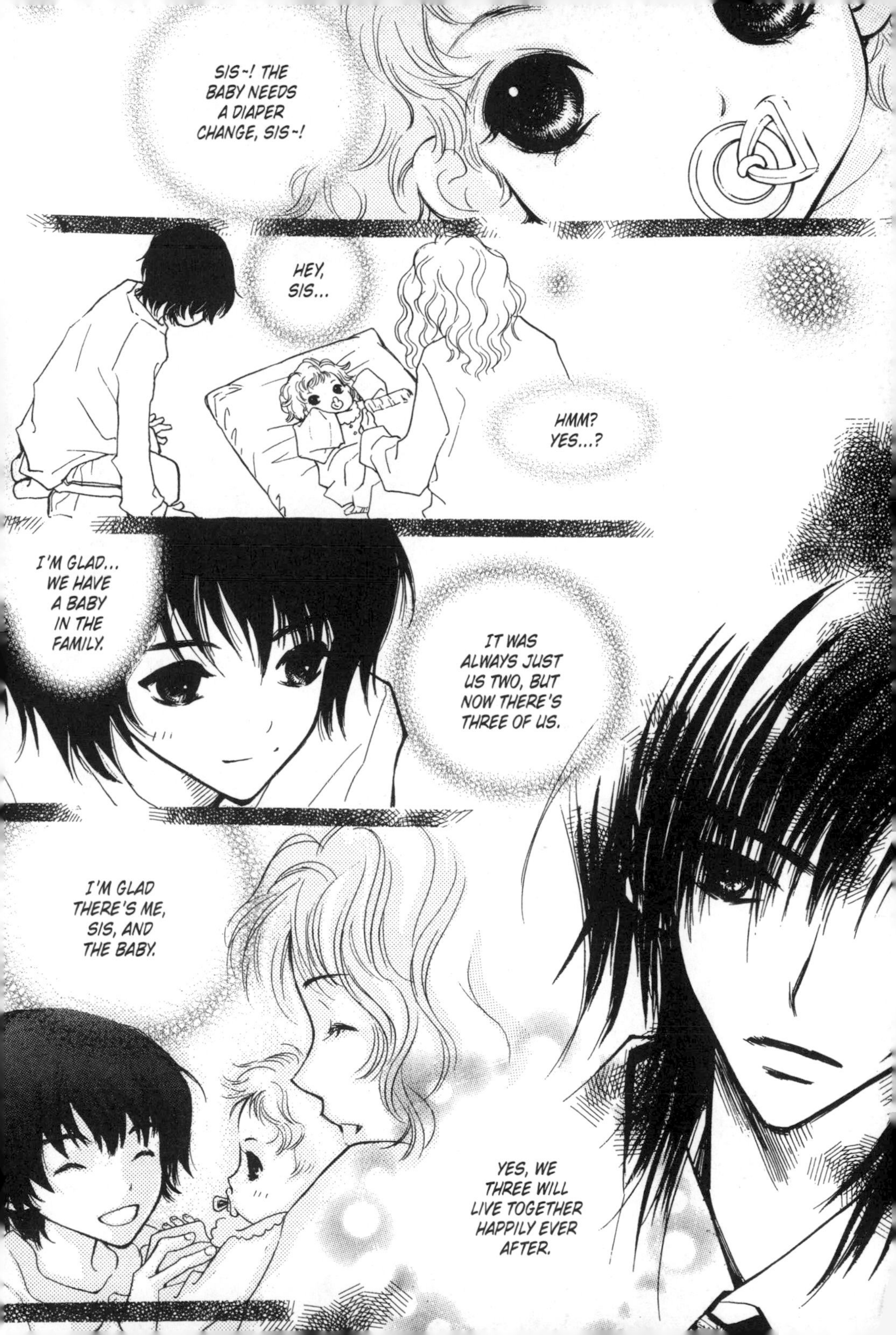
SIS~! THE BABY NEEDS A DIAPER CHANGE, SIS~!
HEY, SIS...
HMM? YES...?
I'M GLAD... WE HAVE A BABY IN THE FAMILY.
IT WAS ALWAYS JUST US TWO, BUT NOW THERE'S THREE OF US.
I'M GLAD THERE'S ME, SIS, AND THE BABY.
YES, WE THREE WILL LIVE TOGETHER HAPPILY EVER AFTER.

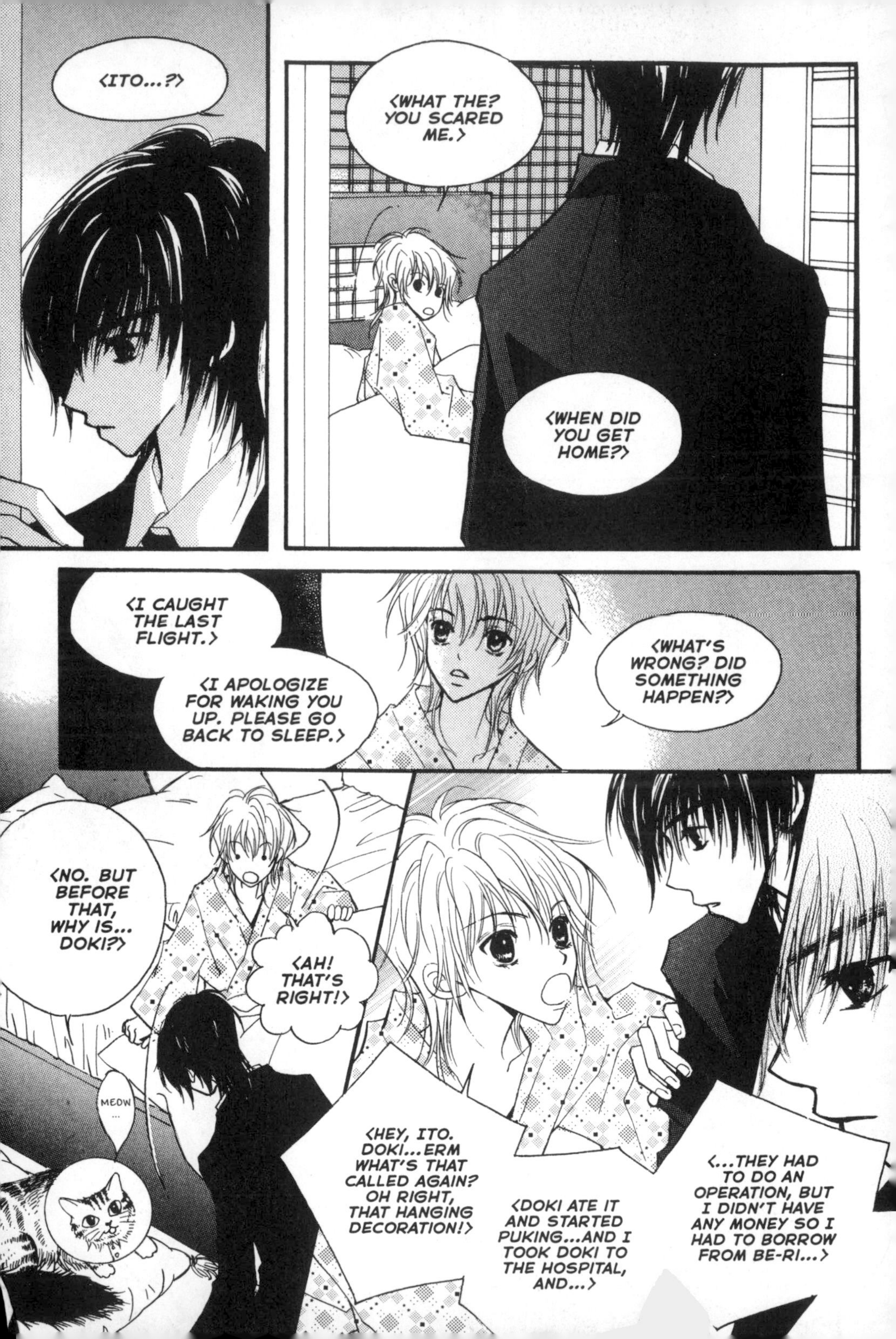
<ITO...?>
<WHAT THE? YOU SCARED ME.>
<WHEN DID YOU GET HOME?>
<I CAUGHT THE LAST FLIGHT.>
<I APOLOGIZE FOR WAKING YOU UP. PLEASE GO BACK TO SLEEP.>
<WHAT'S WRONG? DID SOMETHING HAPPEN?>
<NO. BUT BEFORE THAT, WHY IS... DOKI?>
<AH! THAT'S RIGHT!>
MEOW ...
<HEY, ITO. DOKI...ERM WHAT'S THAT CALLED AGAIN? OH RIGHT, THAT HANGING DECORATION!>
<DOKI ATE IT AND STARTED PUKING...AND I TOOK DOKI TO THE HOSPITAL, AND...>
<...THEY HAD TO DO AN OPERATION, BUT I DIDN'T HAVE ANY MONEY SO I HAD TO BORROW FROM BE-RI...>

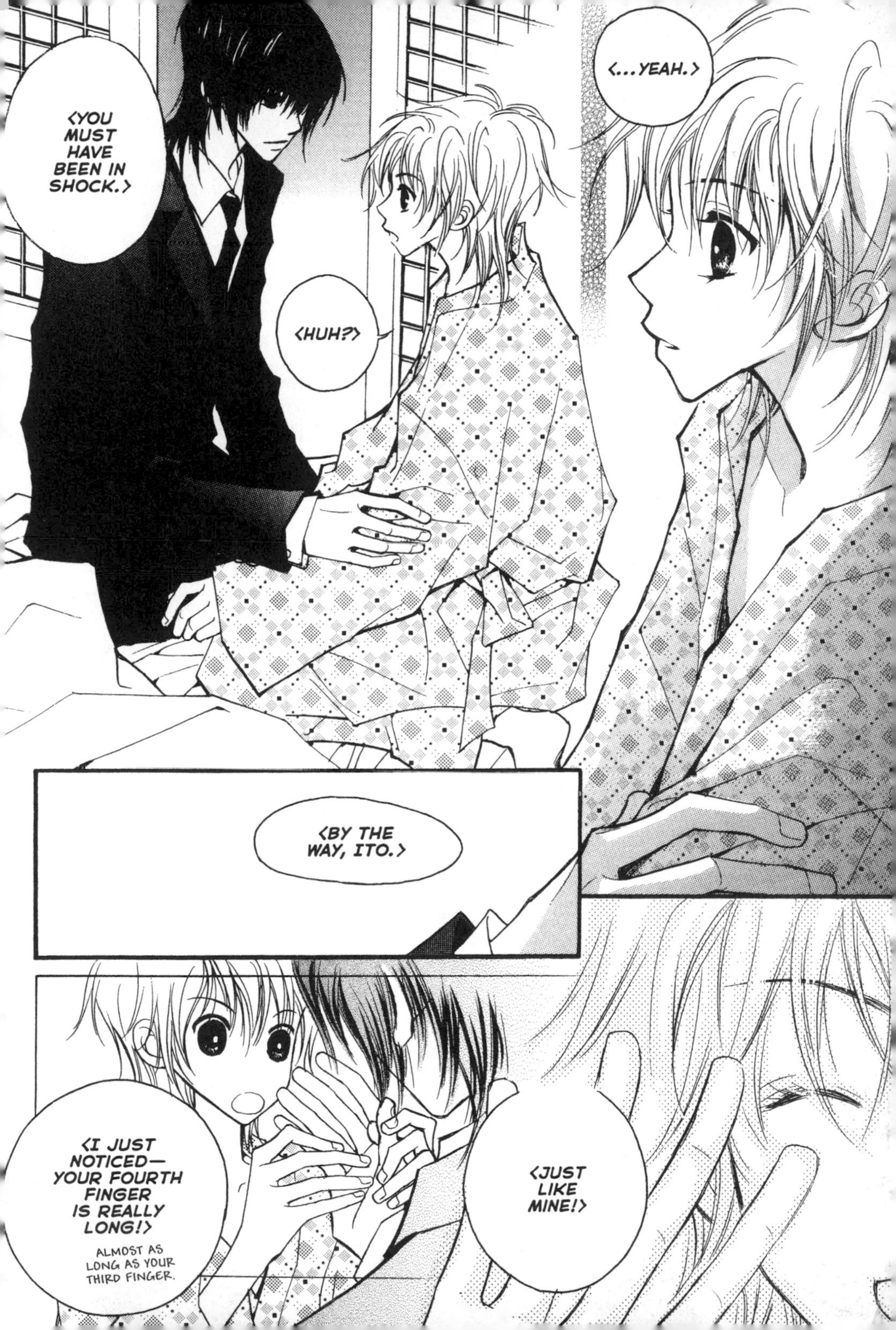
<YOU MUST HAVE BEEN IN SHOCK.>
<HUH?>
<...YEAH.>
<BY THE WAY, ITO.>
<I JUST NOTICED— YOUR FOURTH FINGER IS REALLY LONG!>
ALMOST AS LONG AS YOUR THIRD FINGER.
<JUST LIKE MINE!>

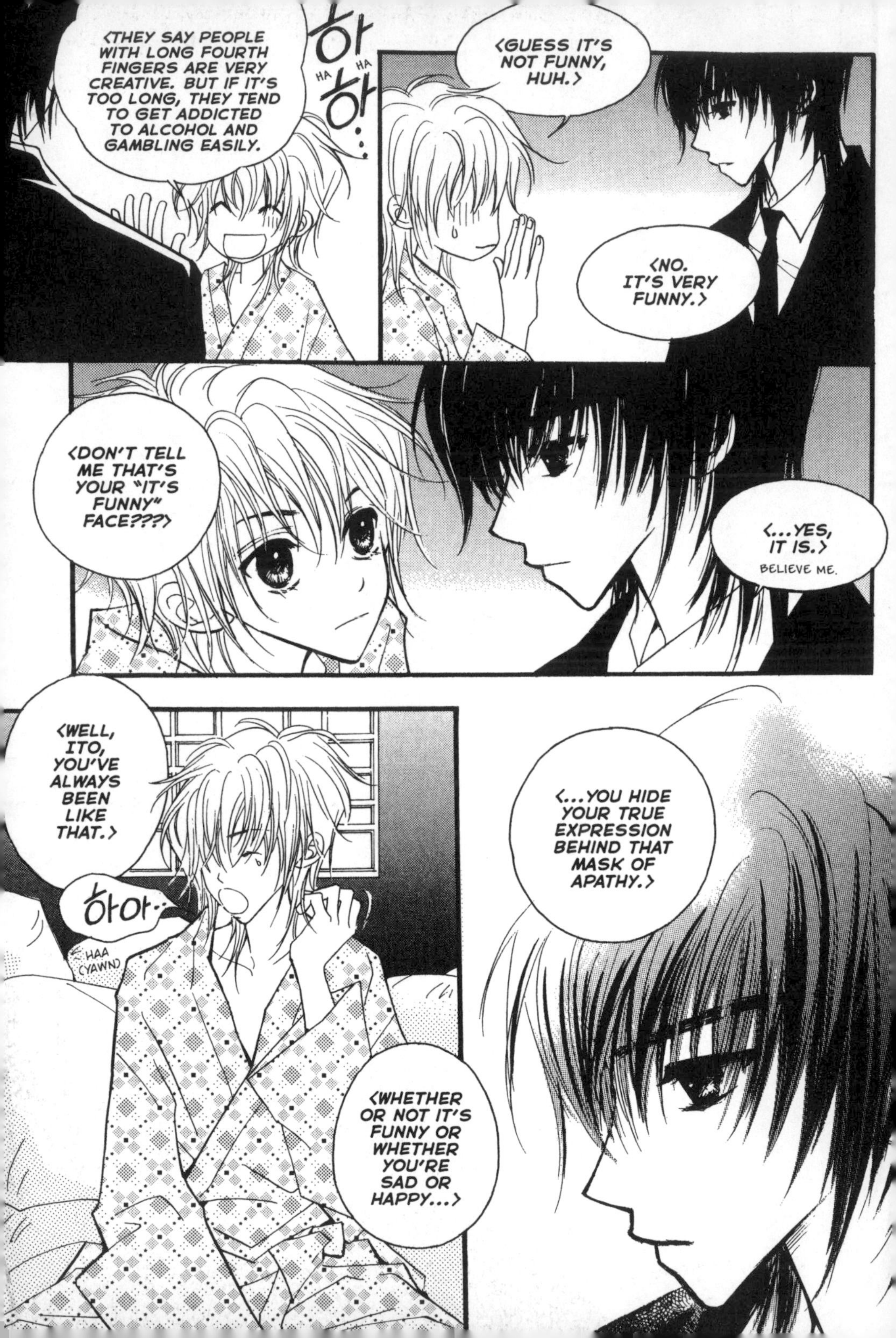
<THEY SAY PEOPLE WITH LONG FOURTH FINGERS ARE VERY CREATIVE. BUT IF IT'S TOO LONG, THEY TEND TO GET ADDICTED TO ALCOHOL AND GAMBLING EASILY.
하하
HA HA
<GUESS IT'S NOT FUNNY, HUH.>
<NO. IT'S VERY FUNNY.>
<DON'T TELL ME THAT'S YOUR "IT'S FUNNY" FACE???>
<...YES, IT IS.>
BELIEVE ME.
<WELL, ITO, YOU'VE ALWAYS BEEN LIKE THAT.>
하아...
HAA (YAWN)
<...YOU HIDE YOUR TRUE EXPRESSION BEHIND THAT MASK OF APATHY.>
<WHETHER OR NOT IT'S FUNNY OR WHETHER YOU'RE SAD OR HAPPY...>

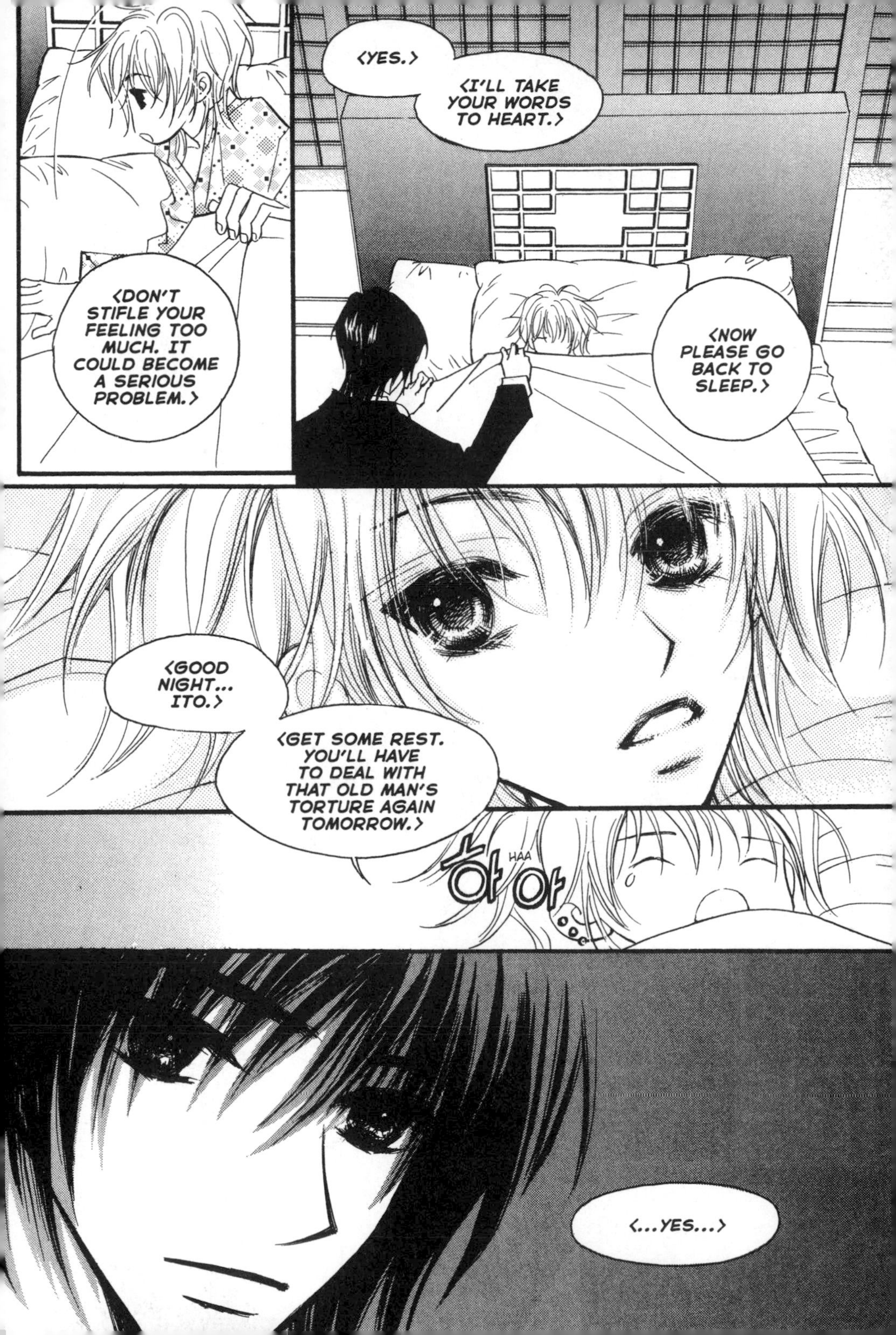
<DON'T STIFLE YOUR FEELING TOO MUCH. IT COULD BECOME A SERIOUS PROBLEM.>
<YES.>
<I'LL TAKE YOUR WORDS TO HEART.>
<NOW PLEASE GO BACK TO SLEEP.>
<GOOD NIGHT... ITO.>
<GET SOME REST. YOU'LL HAVE TO DEAL WITH THAT OLD MAN'S TORTURE AGAIN TOMORROW.>
하아
HAA
<...YES...>

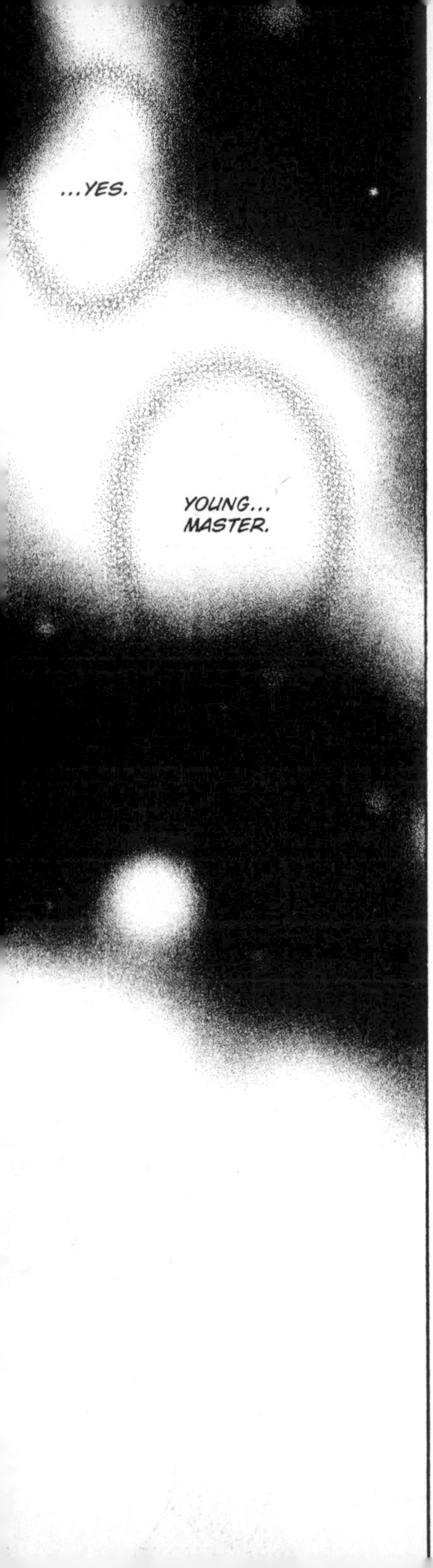
...YES.
YOUNG... MASTER.
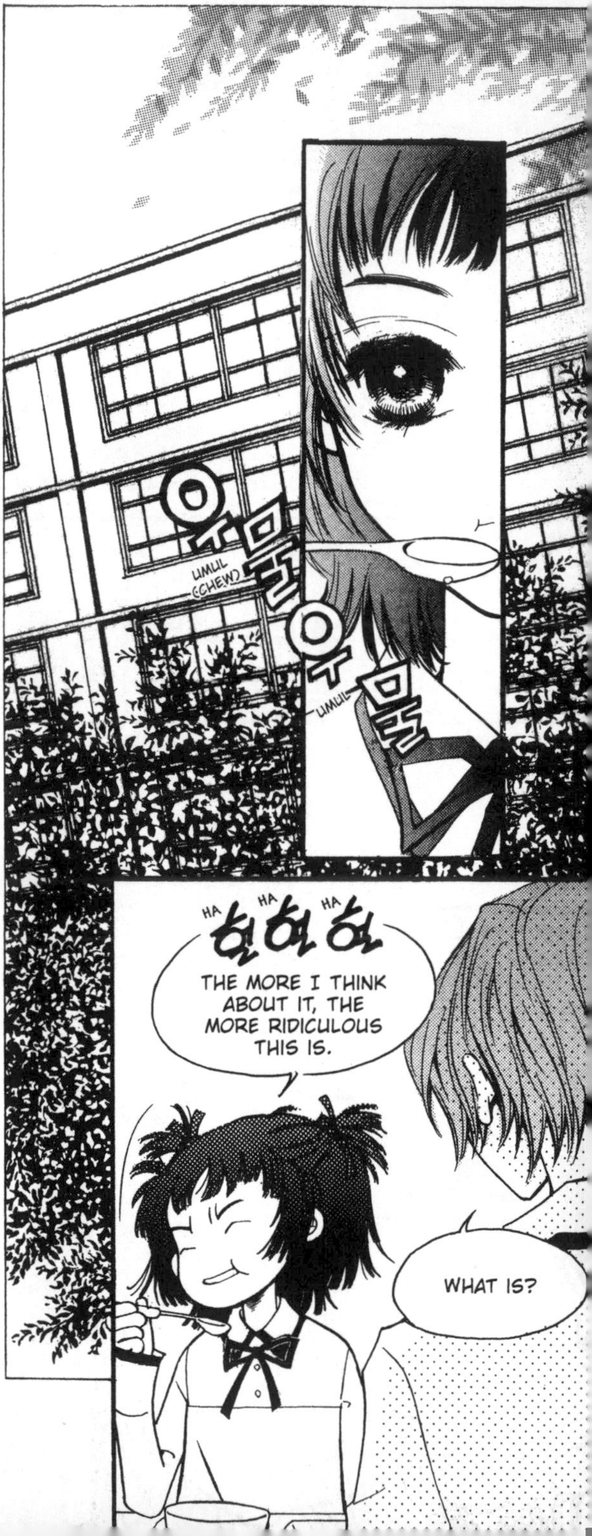
UMUL (CHEW)
UMUL
HA HA HA
THE MORE I THINK ABOUT IT, THE MORE RIDICULOUS THIS IS.
WHAT IS?

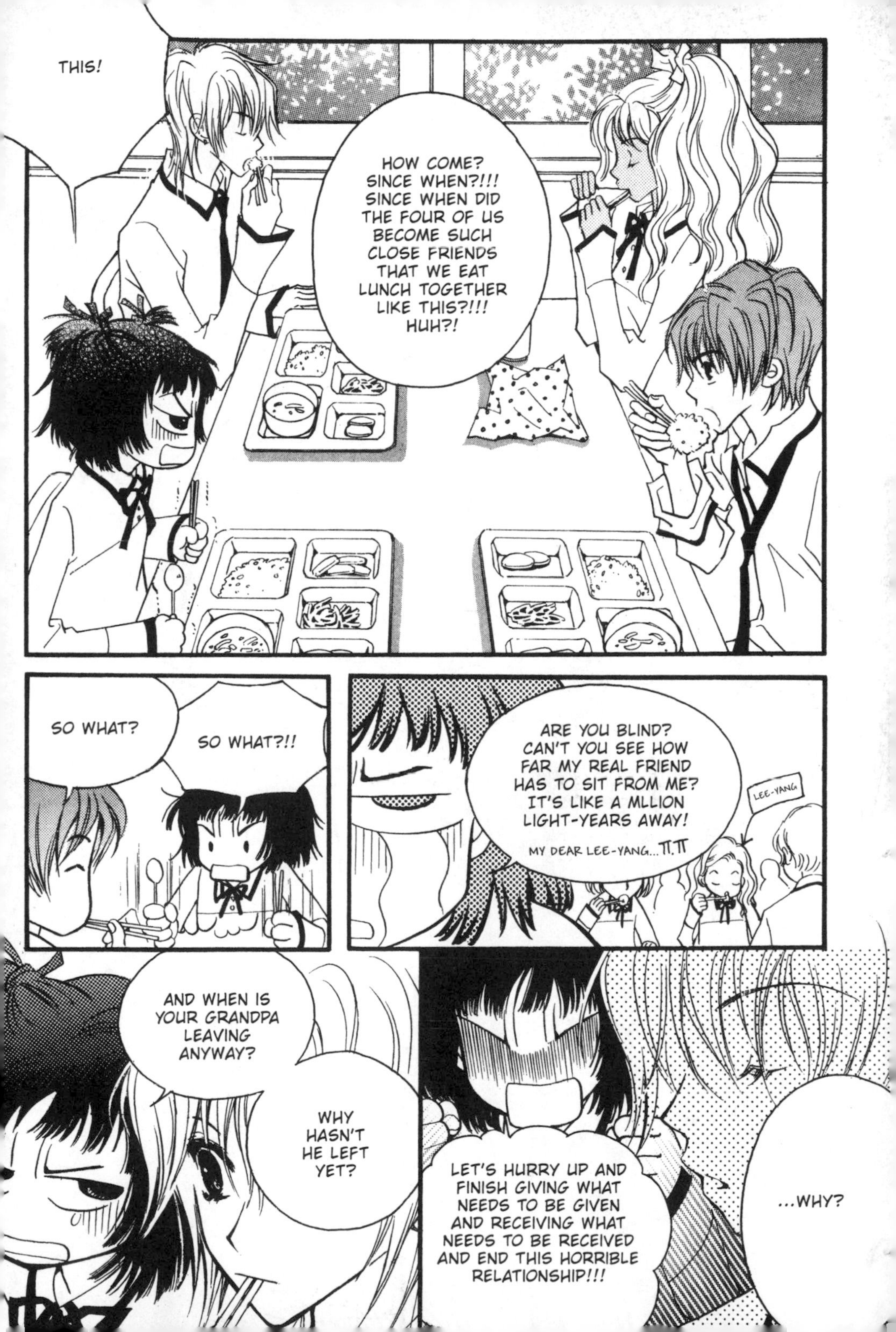
THIS!
HOW COME? SINCE WHEN?!!! SINCE WHEN DID THE FOUR OF US BECOME SUCH CLOSE FRIENDS THAT WE EAT LUNCH TOGETHER LIKE THIS?!!! HUH?!
SO WHAT?
SO WHAT?!!
ARE YOU BLIND? CAN'T YOU SEE HOW FAR MY REAL FRIEND HAS TO SIT FROM ME? IT'S LIKE A MLLION LIGHT-YEARS AWAY!
MY DEAR LEE-YANG... π.π
LEE-YANG
AND WHEN IS YOUR GRANDPA LEAVING ANYWAY?
WHY HASN'T HE LEFT YET?
LET'S HURRY UP AND FINISH GIVING WHAT NEEDS TO BE GIVEN AND RECEIVING WHAT NEEDS TO BE RECEIVED AND END THIS HORRIBLE RELATIONSHIP!!!
...WHY?

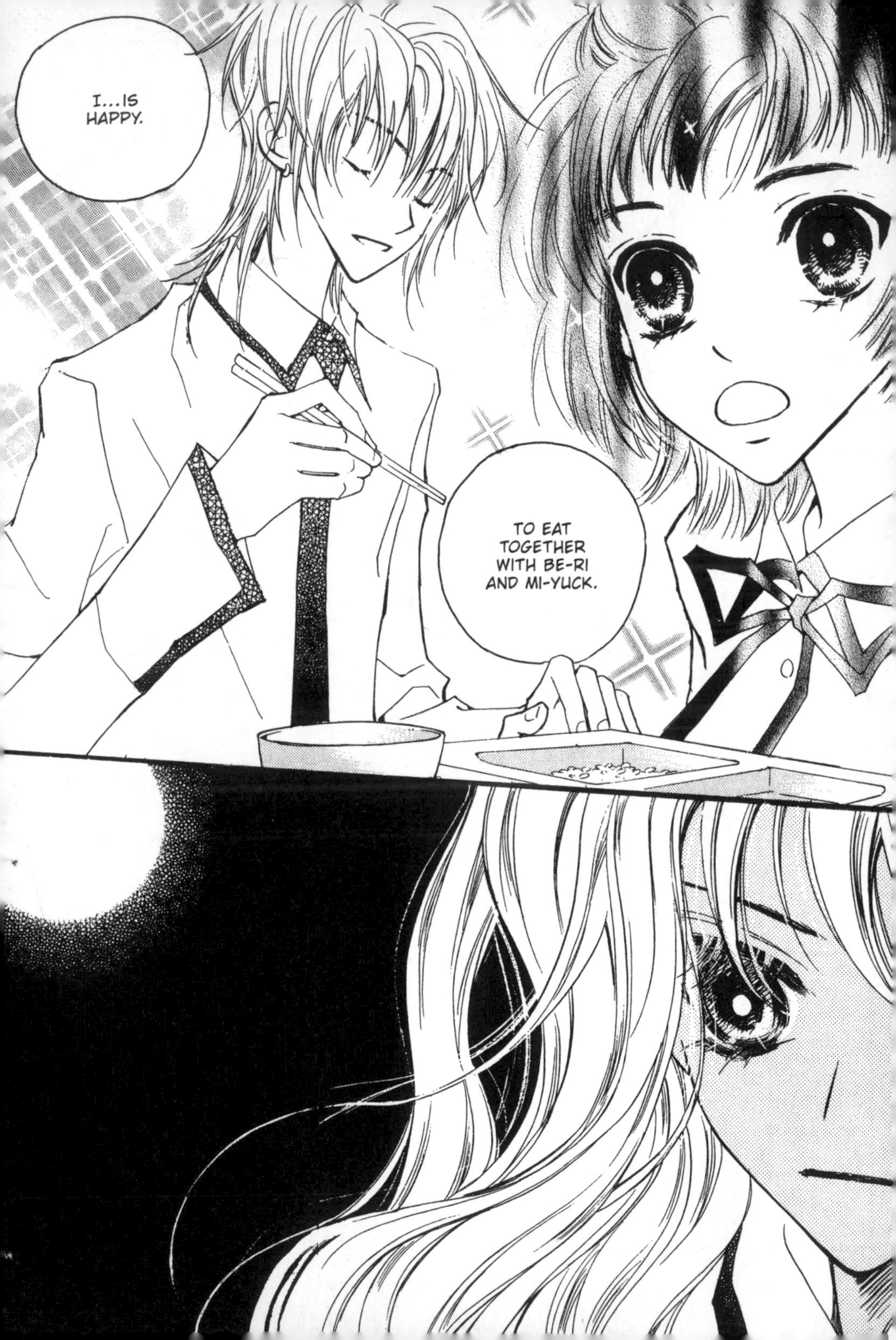
I...IS HAPPY.
TO EAT TOGETHER WITH BE-RI AND MI-YUCK.

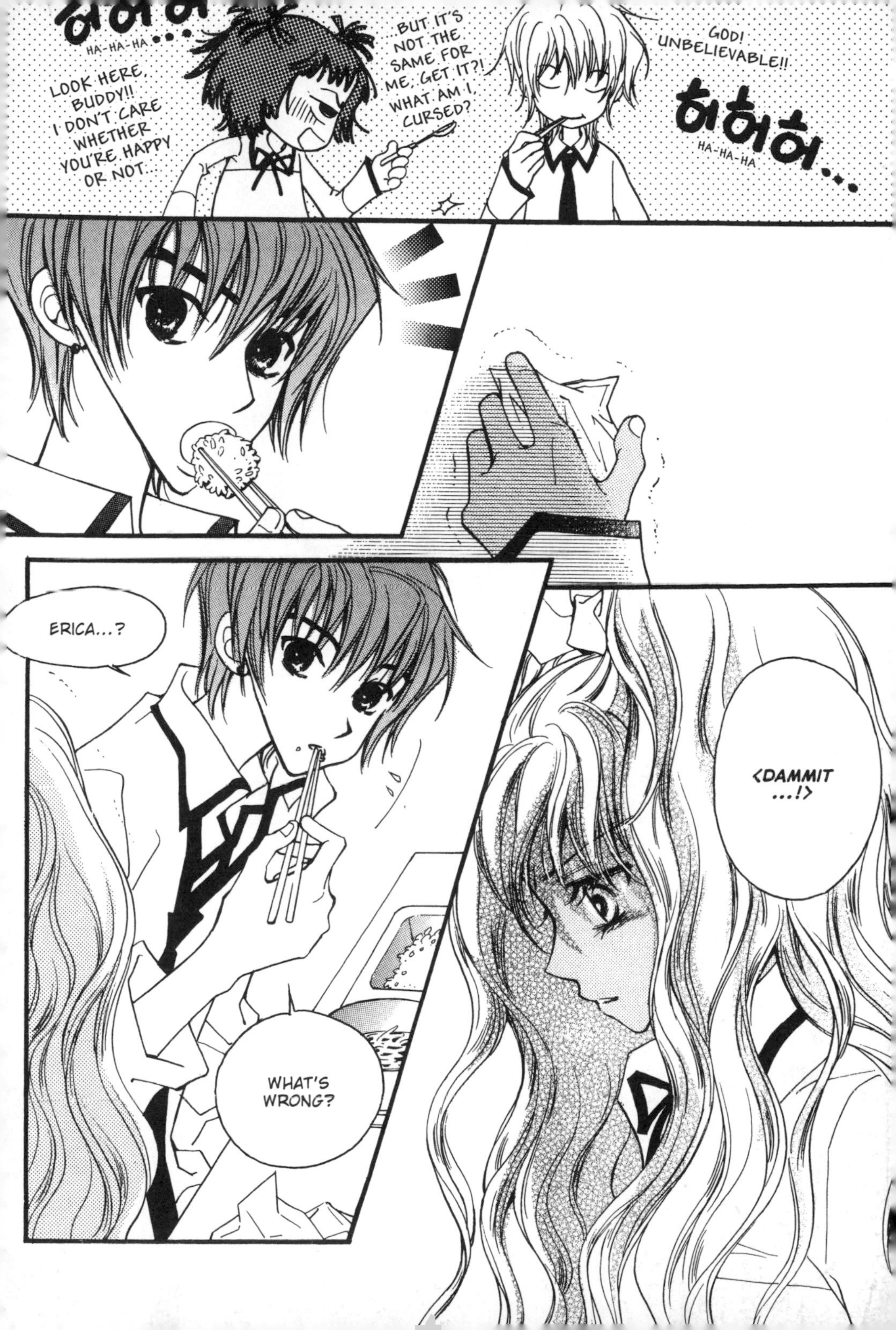
허허허...
HA-HA-HA
LOOK HERE, BUDDY!! I DON'T CARE WHETHER YOU'RE HAPPY OR NOT...
BUT IT'S NOT THE SAME FOR ME, GET IT?! WHAT AM I, CURSED?
GOD! UNBELIEVABLE!!
허허허...
HA-HA-HA
ERICA...?
WHAT'S WRONG?
<DAMMIT ...!>

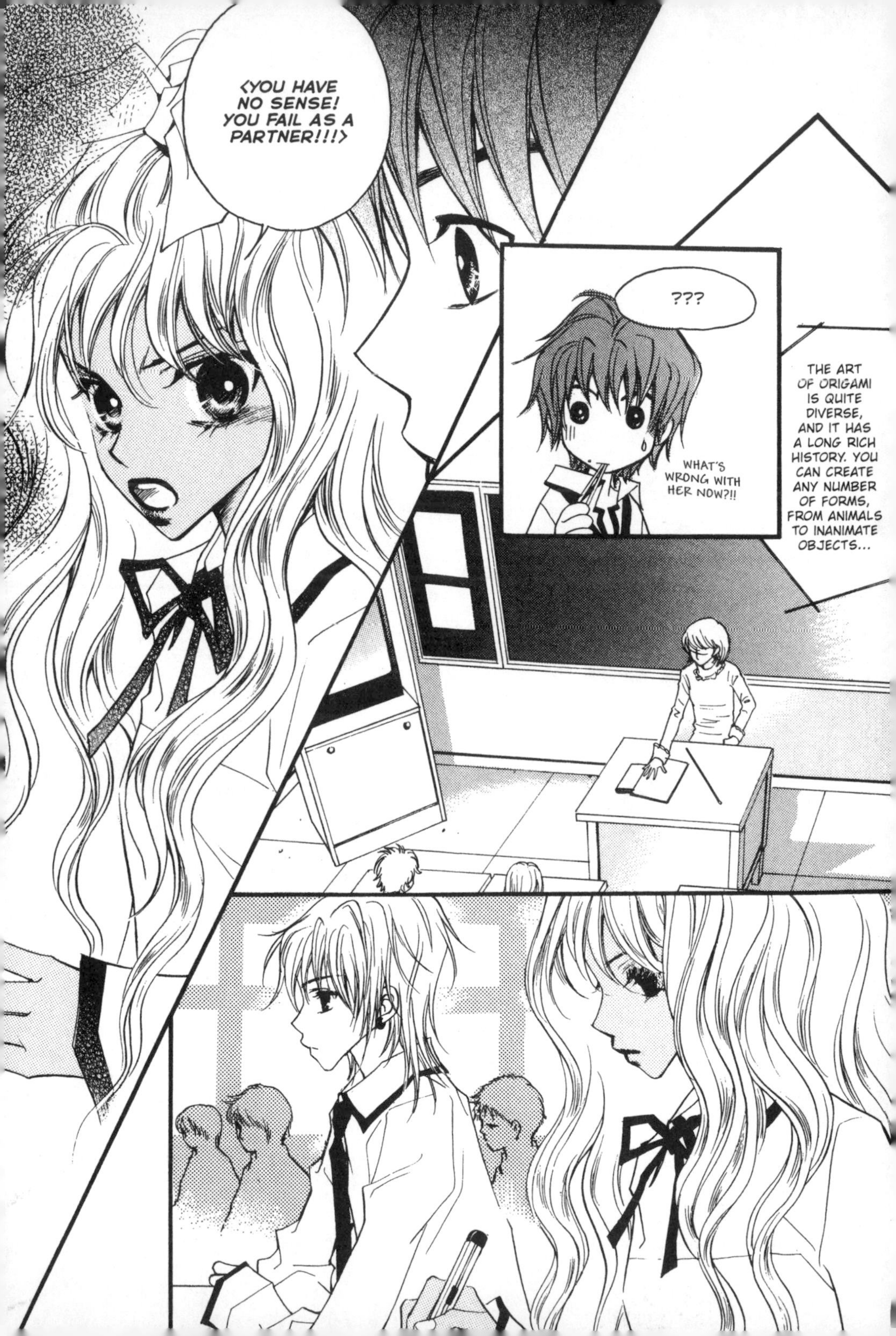
<YOU HAVE NO SENSE! YOU FAIL AS A PARTNER!!!>
???
WHAT'S WRONG WITH HER NOW?!!
THE ART OF ORIGAMI IS QUITE DIVERSE, AND IT HAS A LONG RICH HISTORY. YOU CAN CREATE ANY NUMBER OF FORMS, FROM ANIMALS TO INANIMATE OBJECTS...

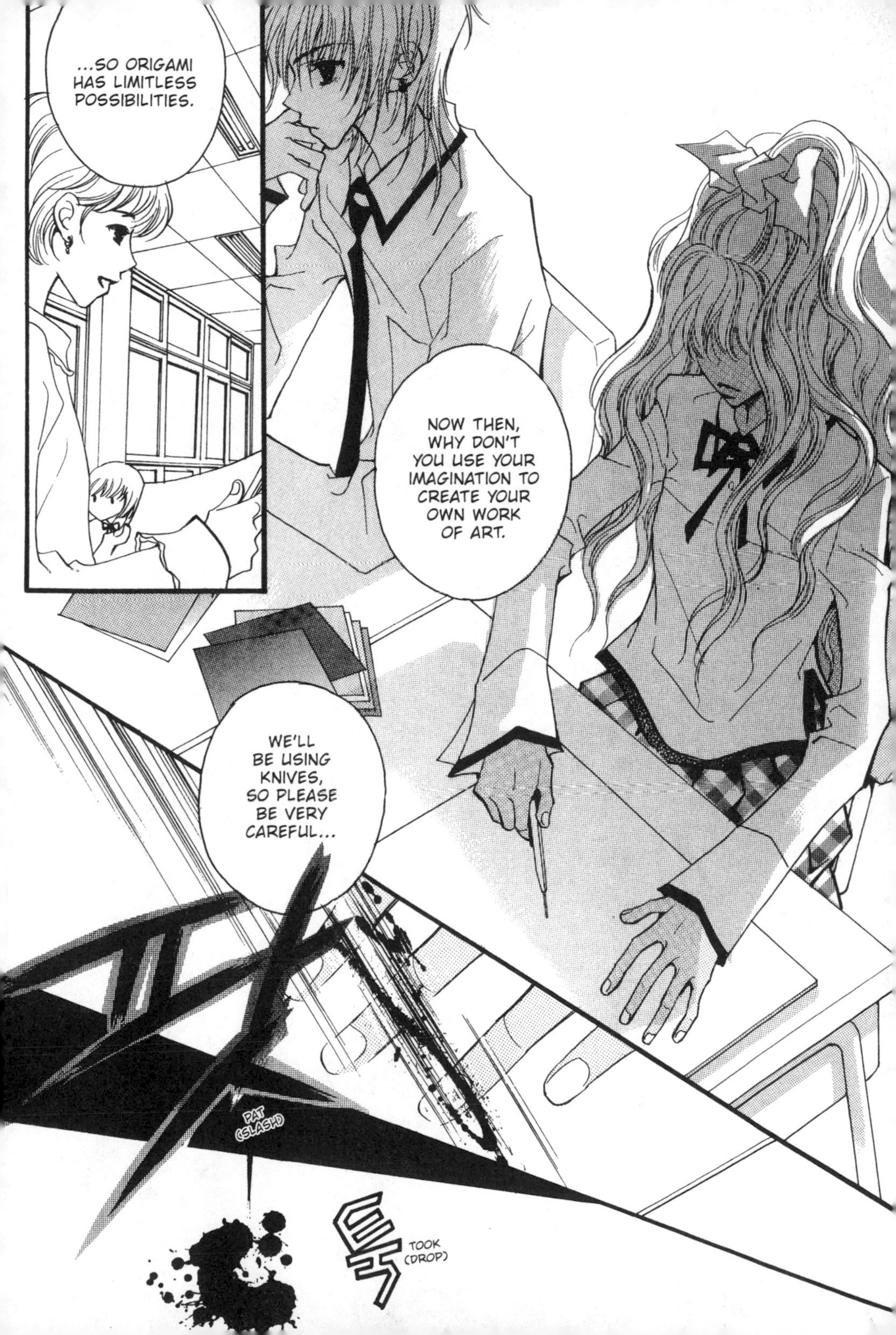
...SO ORIGAMI HAS LIMITLESS POSSIBILITIES.
NOW THEN, WHY DON'T YOU USE YOUR IMAGINATION TO CREATE YOUR OWN WORK OF ART.
WE'LL BE USING KNIVES, SO PLEASE BE VERY CAREFUL...
PAT (SLASH)
TOOK (DROP)

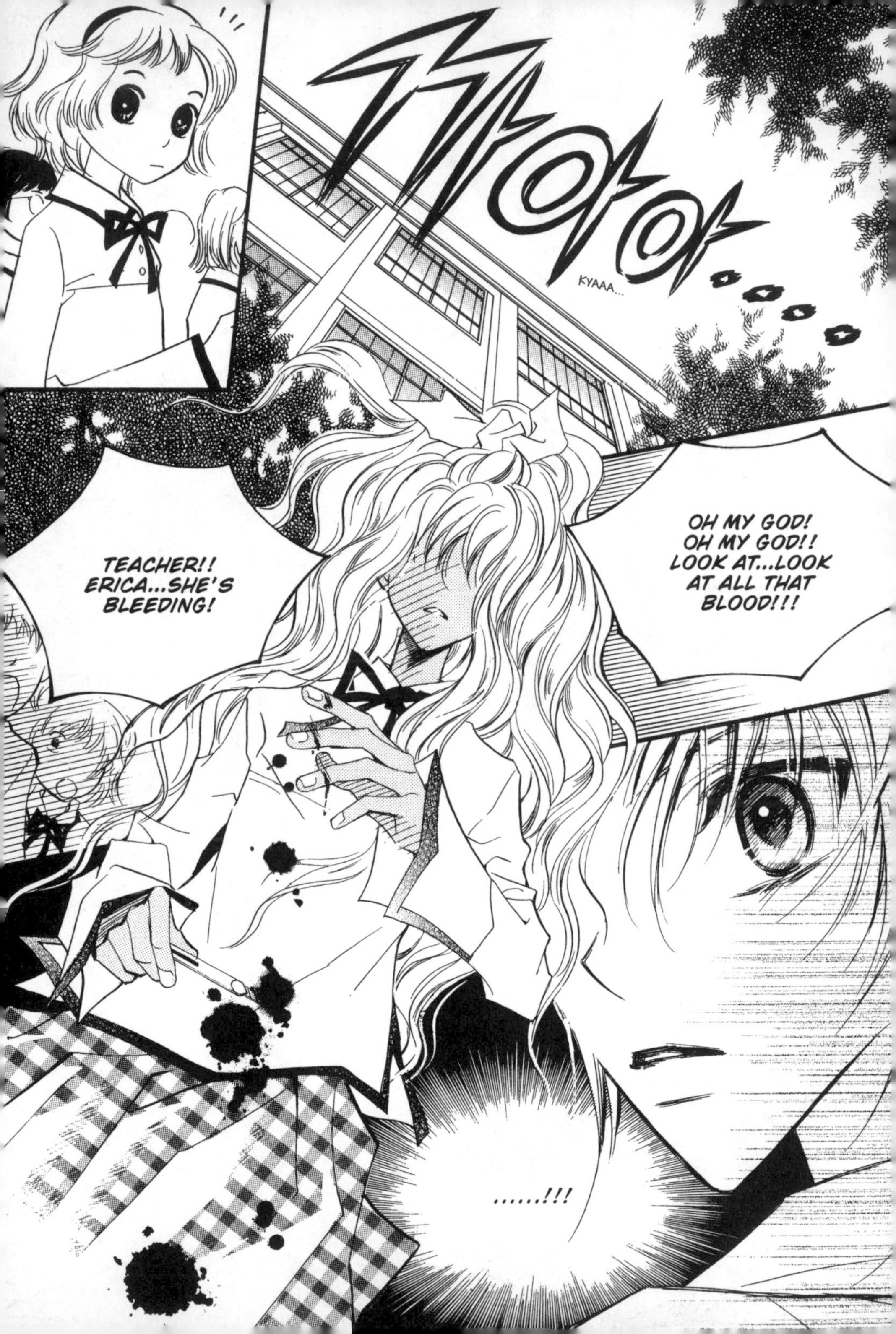
KYAAA...
TEACHER!! ERICA...SHE'S BLEEDING!
OH MY GOD! OH MY GOD!! LOOK AT...LOOK AT ALL THAT BLOOD!!!
......!!!

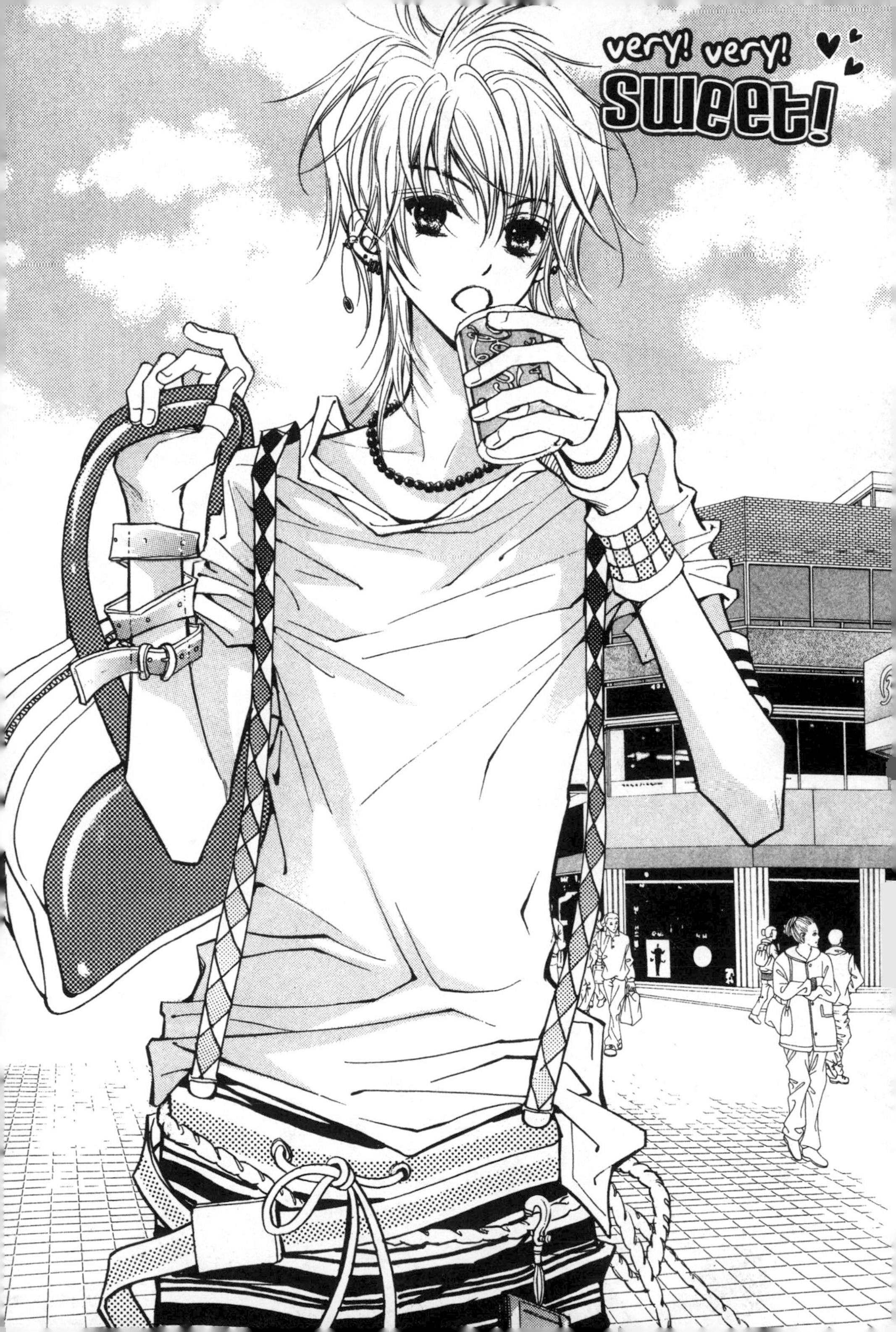
very! very!
Sweet!

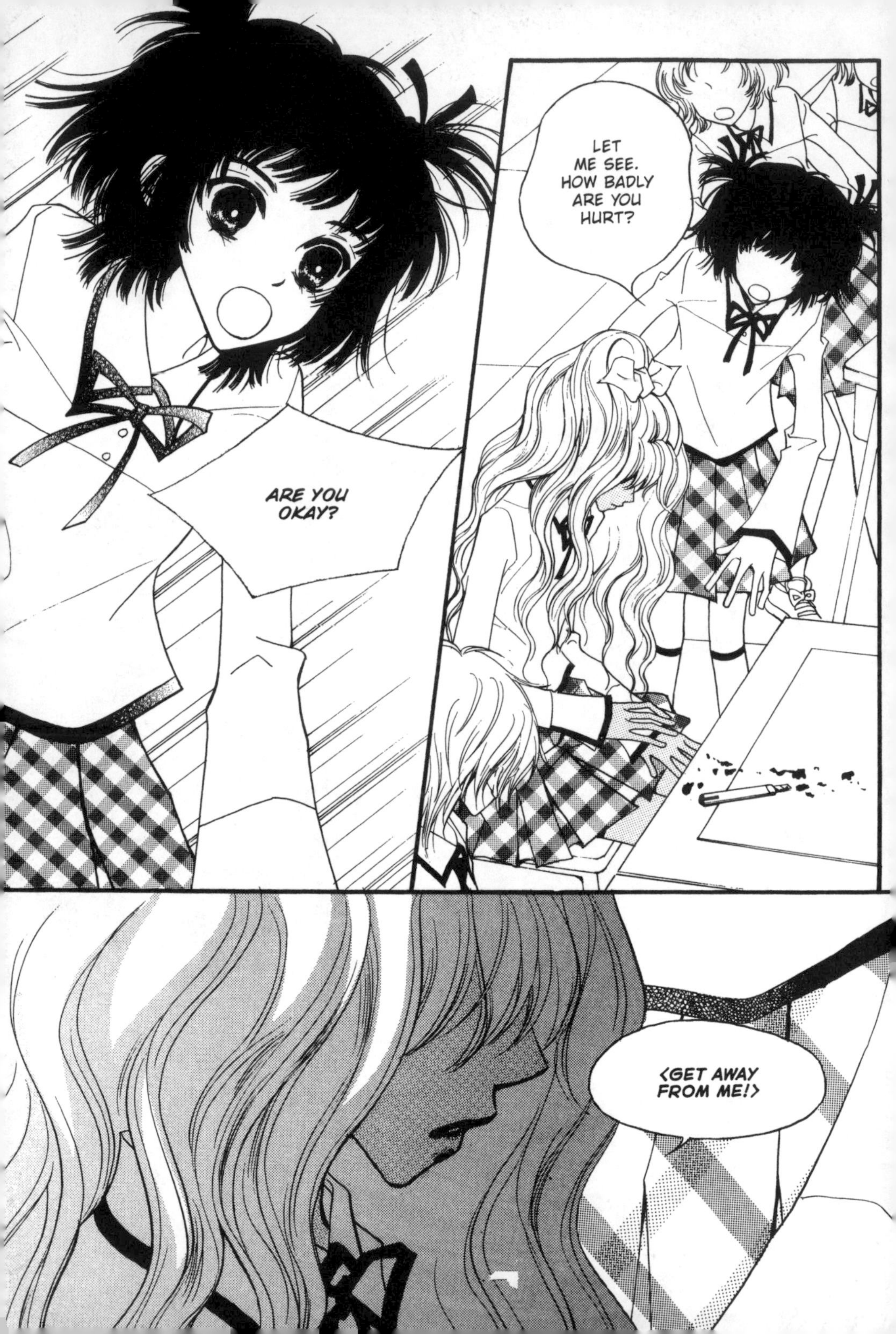
ARE YOU OKAY?
LET ME SEE. HOW BADLY ARE YOU HURT?
<GET AWAY FROM ME!>

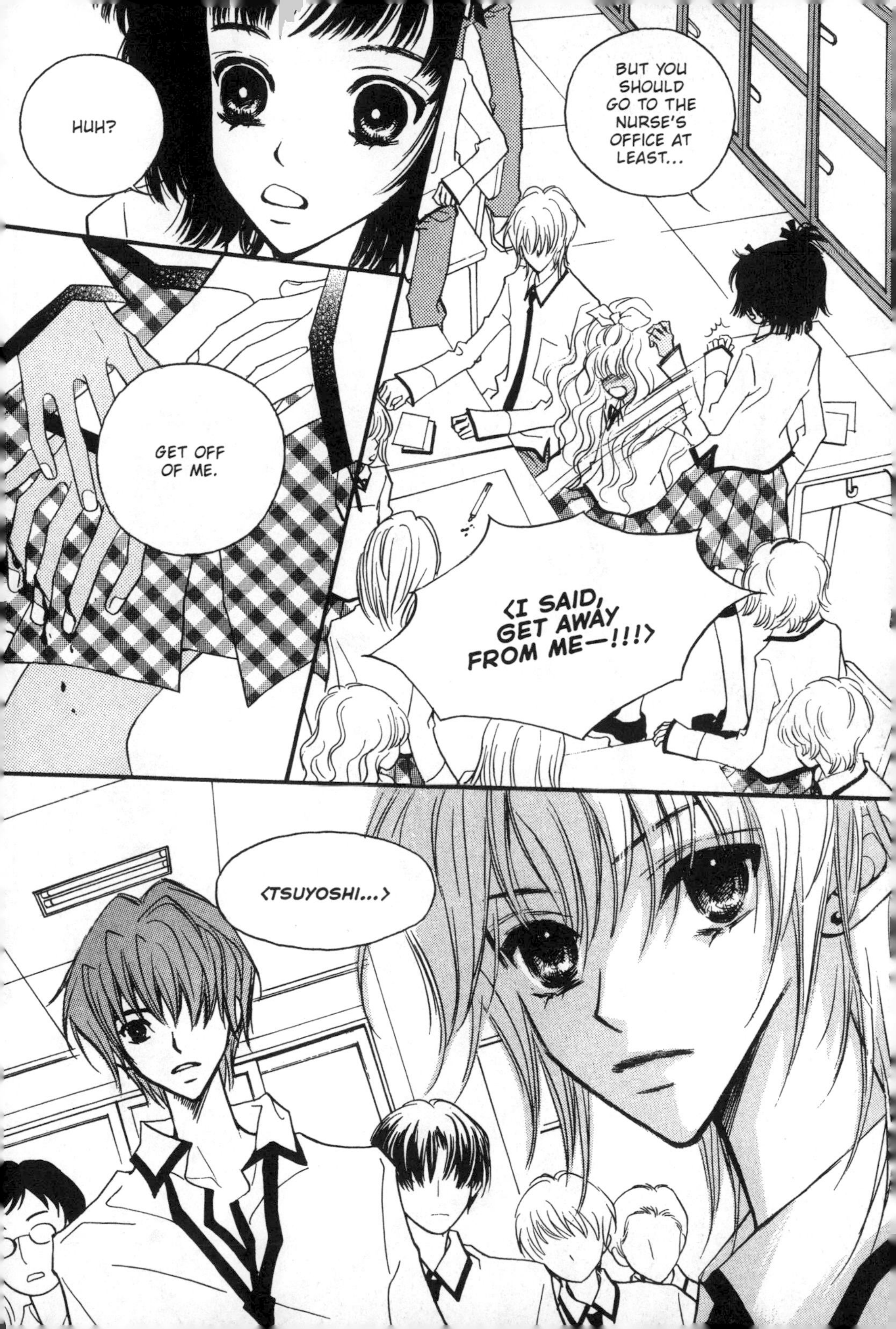
HUH?
GET OFF OF ME.
BUT YOU SHOULD GO TO THE NURSE'S OFFICE AT LEAST...
<I SAID, GET AWAY FROM ME—!!!>
<TSUYOSHI...>

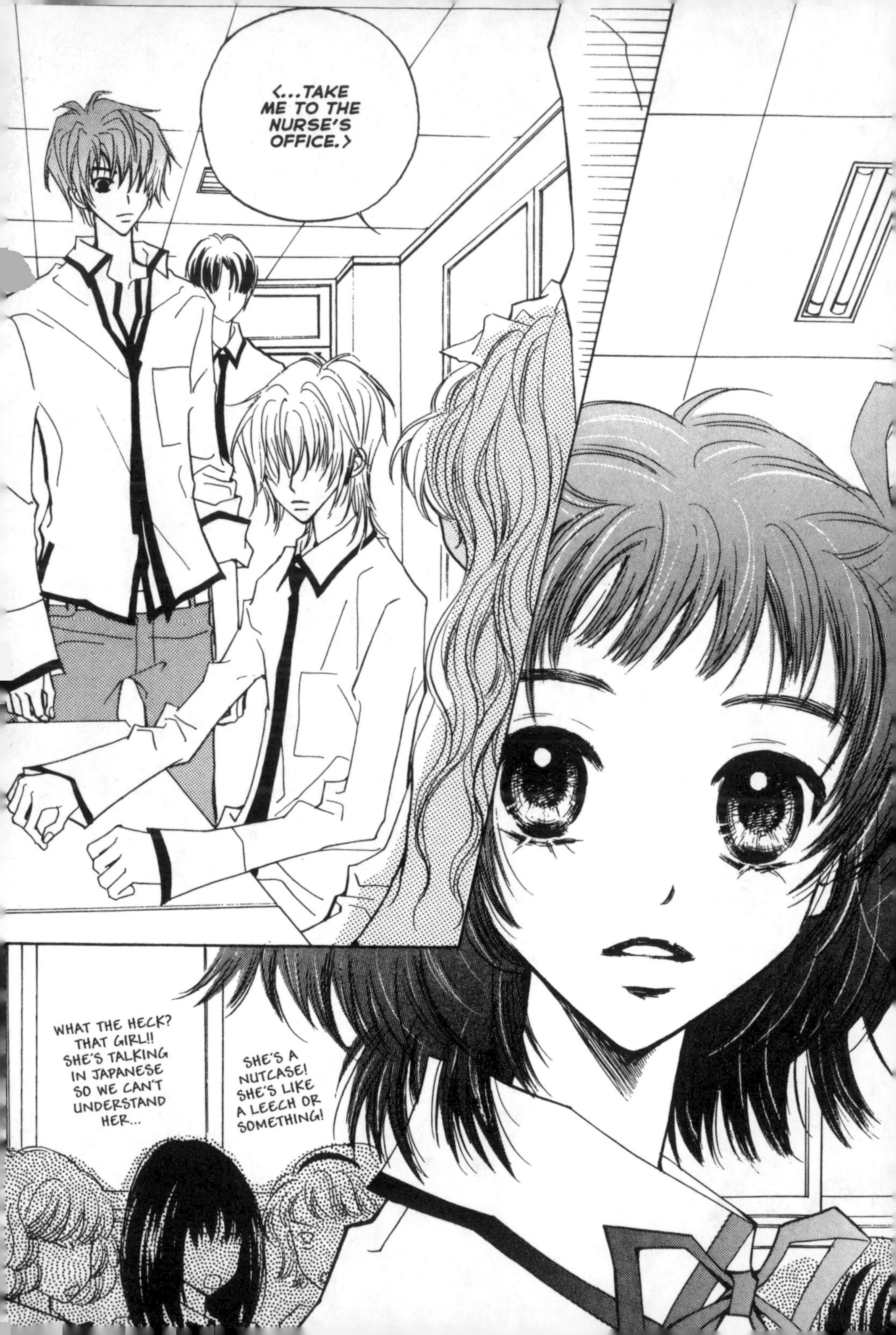
<...TAKE ME TO THE NURSE'S OFFICE.>
WHAT THE HECK? THAT GIRL!! SHE'S TALKING IN JAPANESE SO WE CAN'T UNDERSTAND HER...
SHE'S A NUTCASE! SHE'S LIKE A LEECH OR SOMETHING!

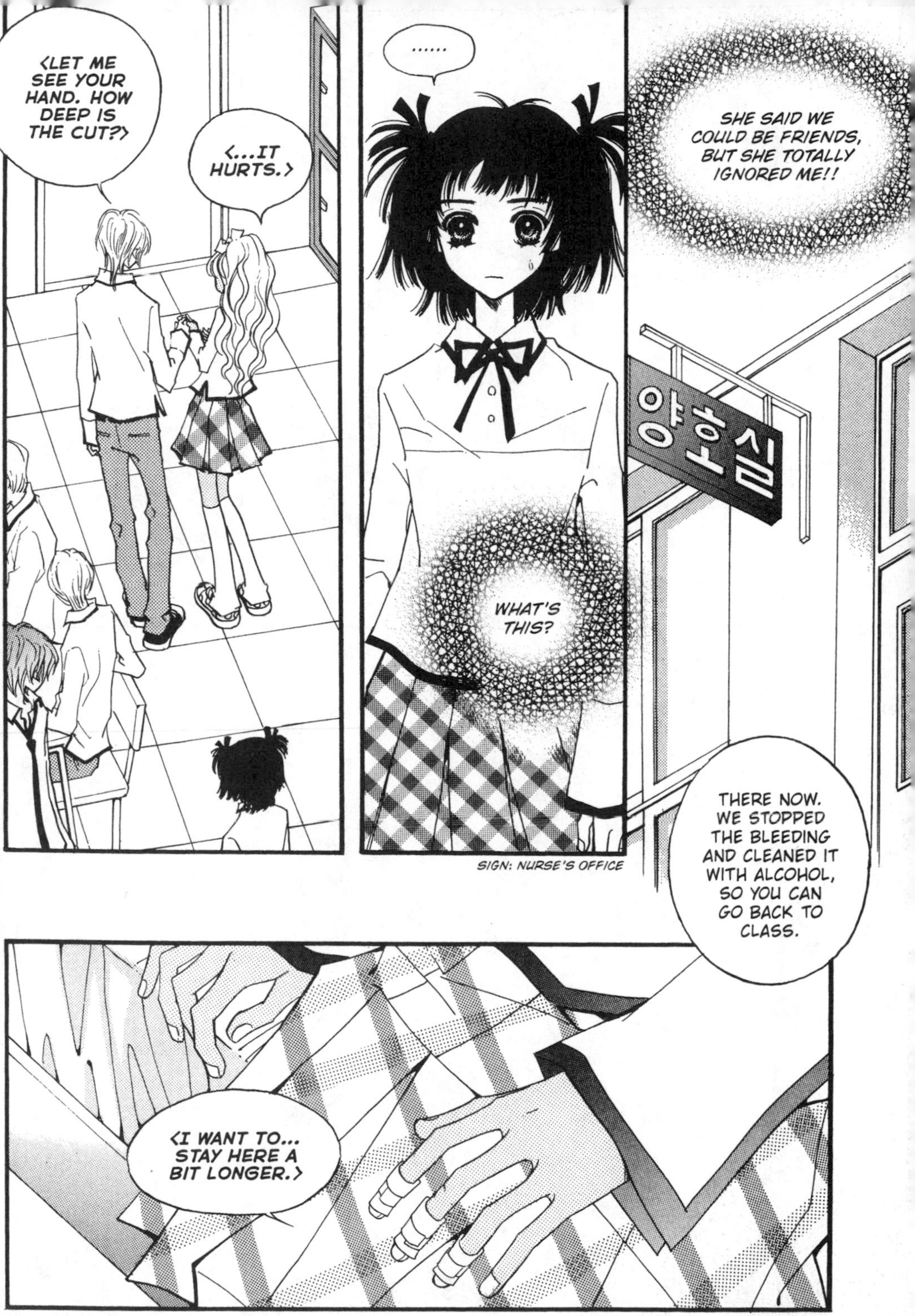

<LET ME SEE YOUR HAND. HOW DEEP IS THE CUT?>
<...IT HURTS.>
......
SHE SAID WE COULD BE FRIENDS, BUT SHE TOTALLY IGNORED ME!!
WHAT'S THIS?
양호실
SIGN: NURSE'S OFFICE
THERE NOW. WE STOPPED THE BLEEDING AND CLEANED IT WITH ALCOHOL, SO YOU CAN GO BACK TO CLASS.
<I WANT TO... STAY HERE A BIT LONGER.>

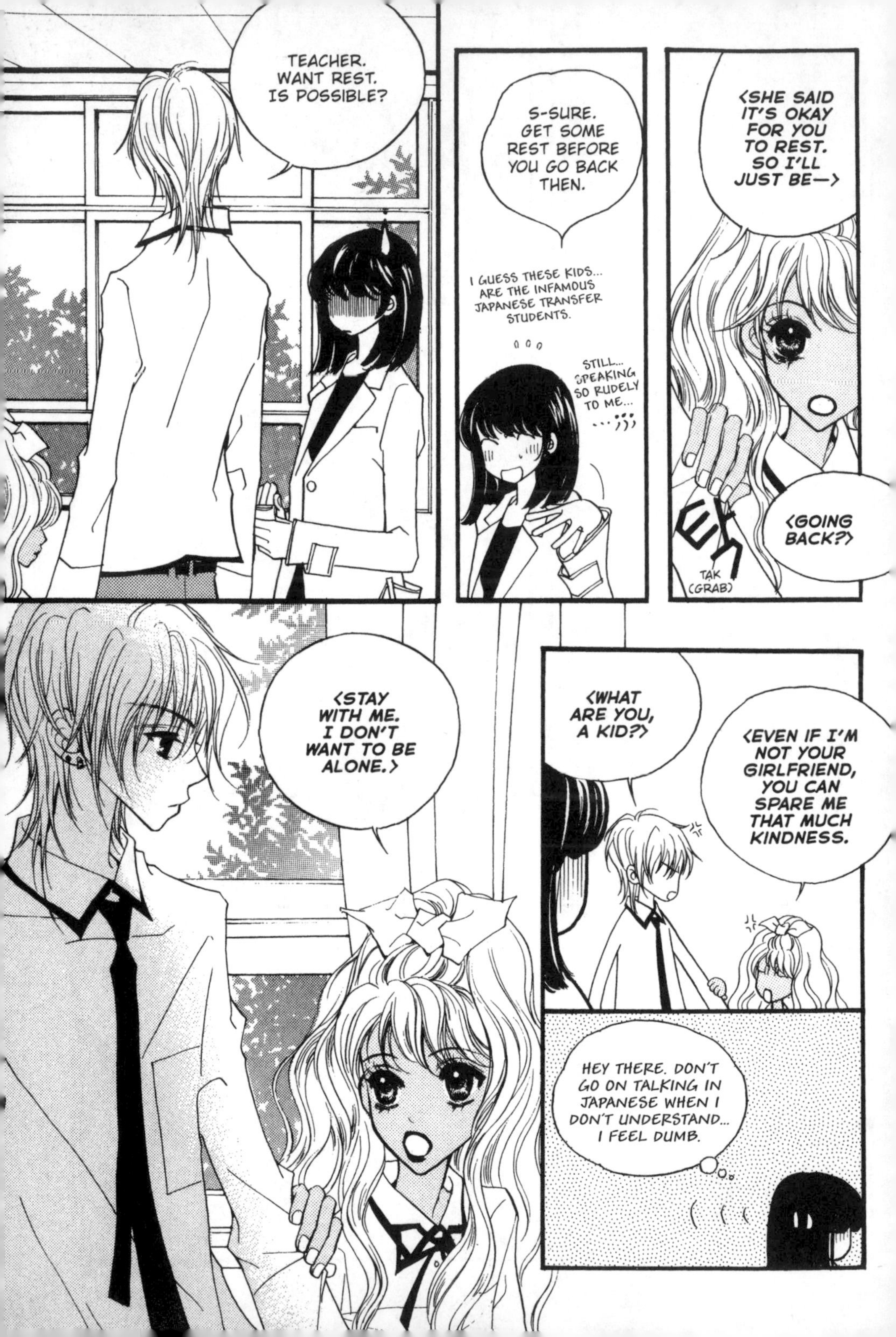
TEACHER. WANT REST. IS POSSIBLE?
S-SURE. GET SOME REST BEFORE YOU GO BACK THEN.
I GUESS THESE KIDS... ARE THE INFAMOUS JAPANESE TRANSFER STUDENTS.
STILL... SPEAKING SO RUDELY TO ME...
<SHE SAID IT'S OKAY FOR YOU TO REST. SO I'LL JUST BE—>
<GOING BACK?>
TAK (GRAB)
<STAY WITH ME. I DON'T WANT TO BE ALONE.>
<WHAT ARE YOU, A KID?>
<EVEN IF I'M NOT YOUR GIRLFRIEND, YOU CAN SPARE ME THAT MUCH KINDNESS.
HEY THERE. DON'T GO ON TALKING IN JAPANESE WHEN I DON'T UNDERSTAND... I FEEL DUMB.

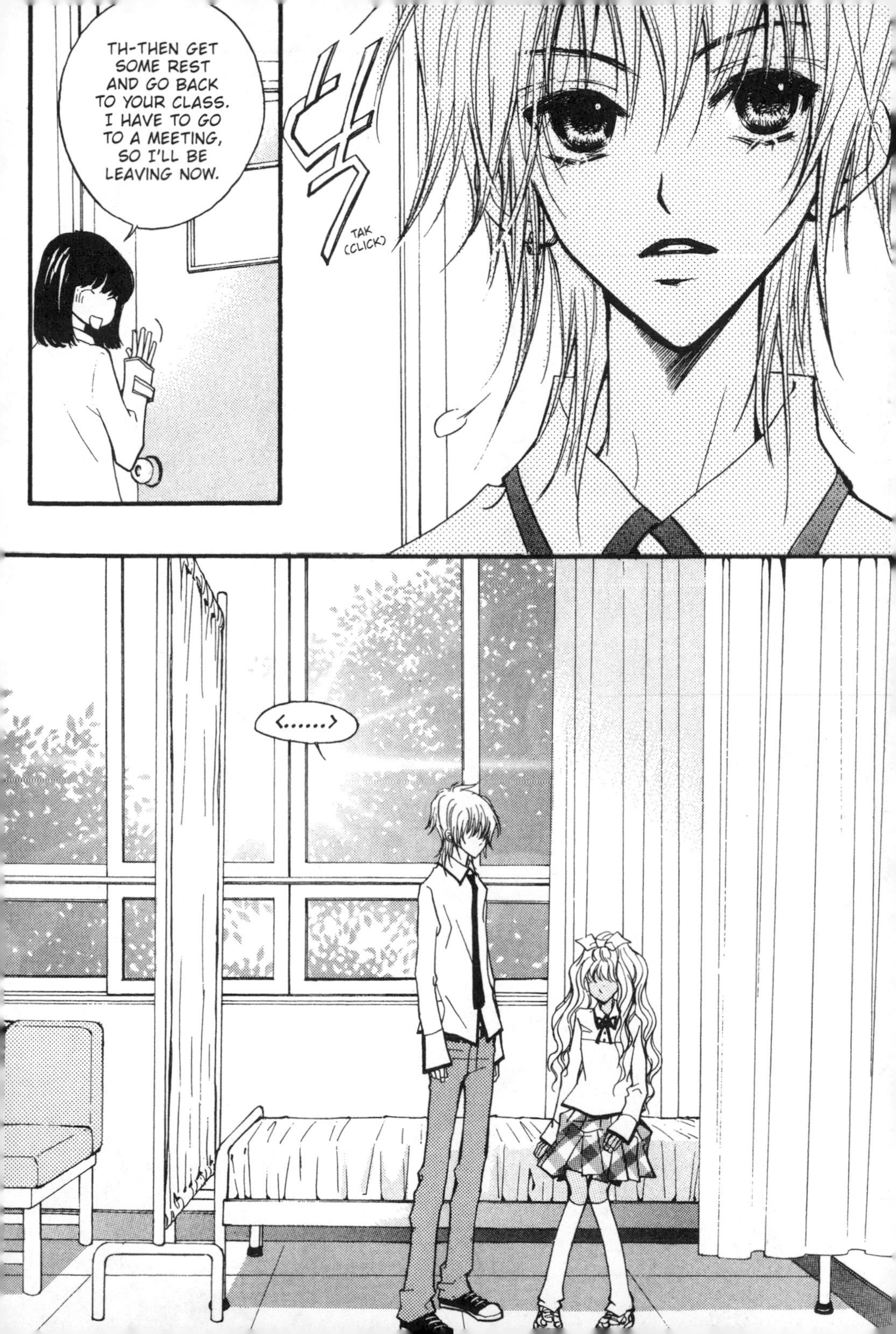
TH-THEN GET SOME REST AND GO BACK TO YOUR CLASS. I HAVE TO GO TO A MEETING, SO I'LL BE LEAVING NOW.
TAK (CLICK)
<......>

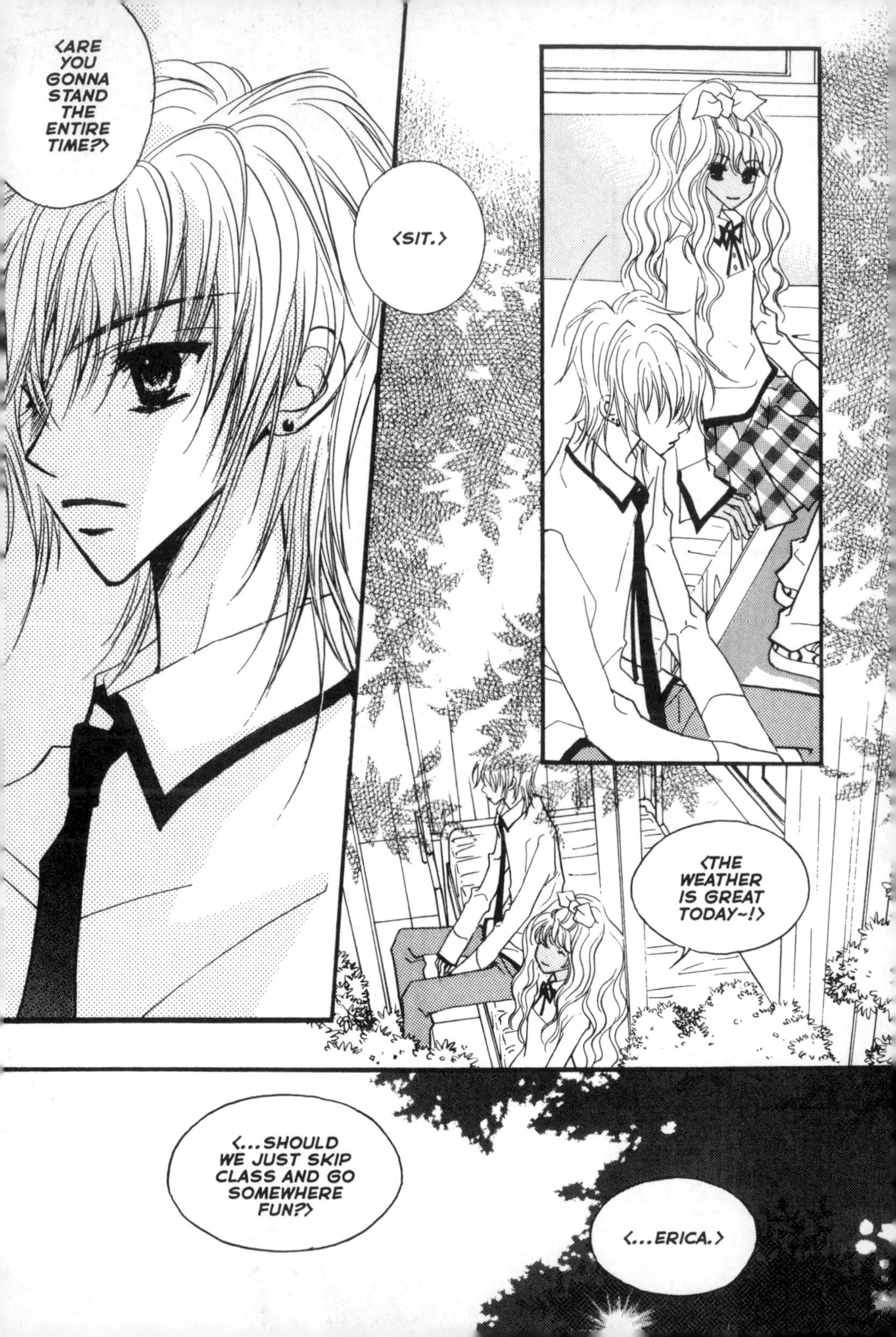
<ARE YOU GONNA STAND THE ENTIRE TIME?>
<SIT.>
<THE WEATHER IS GREAT TODAY~!>
<...SHOULD WE JUST SKIP CLASS AND GO SOMEWHERE FUN?>
<...ERICA.>

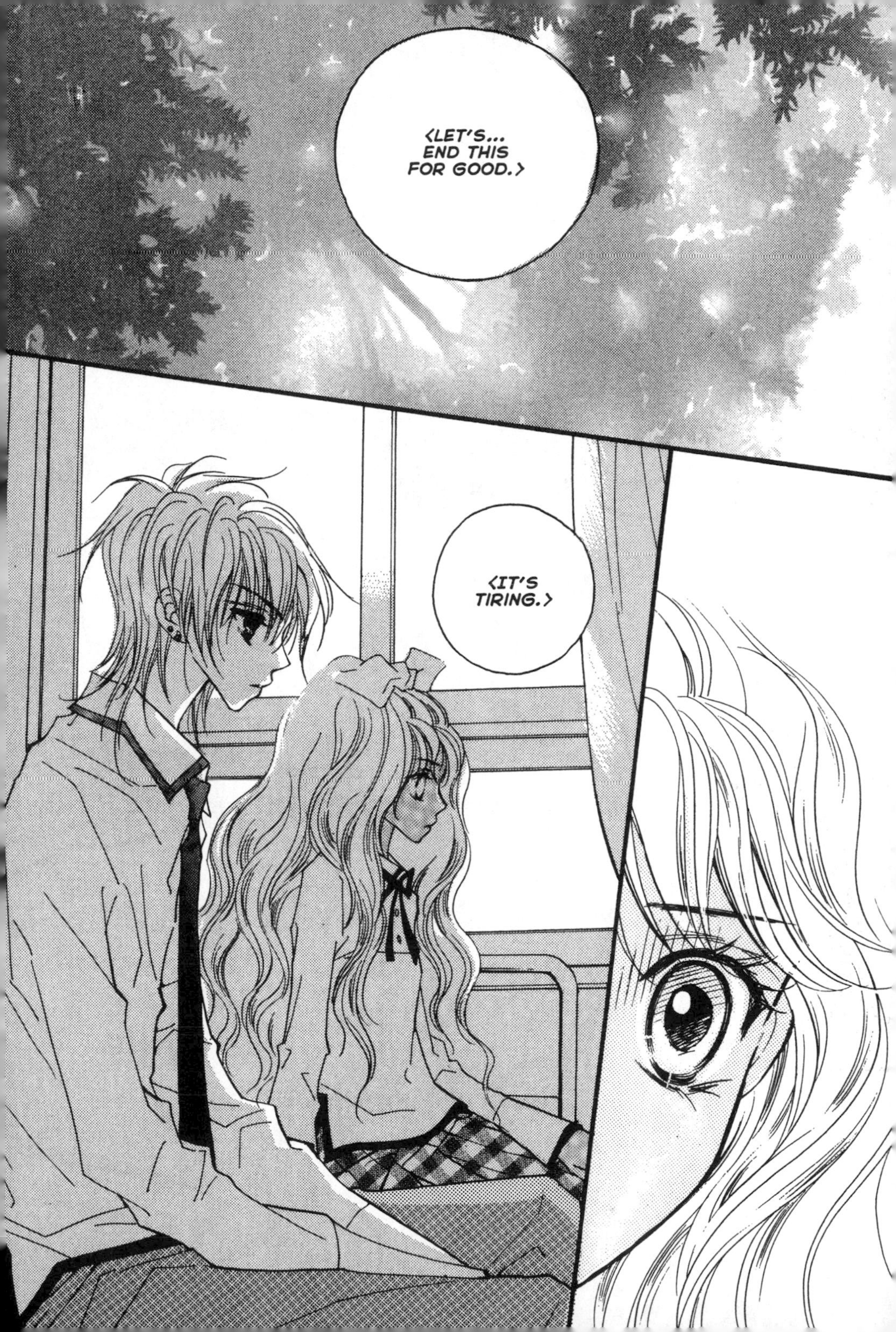
<LET'S... END THIS FOR GOOD.>
<IT'S TIRING.>

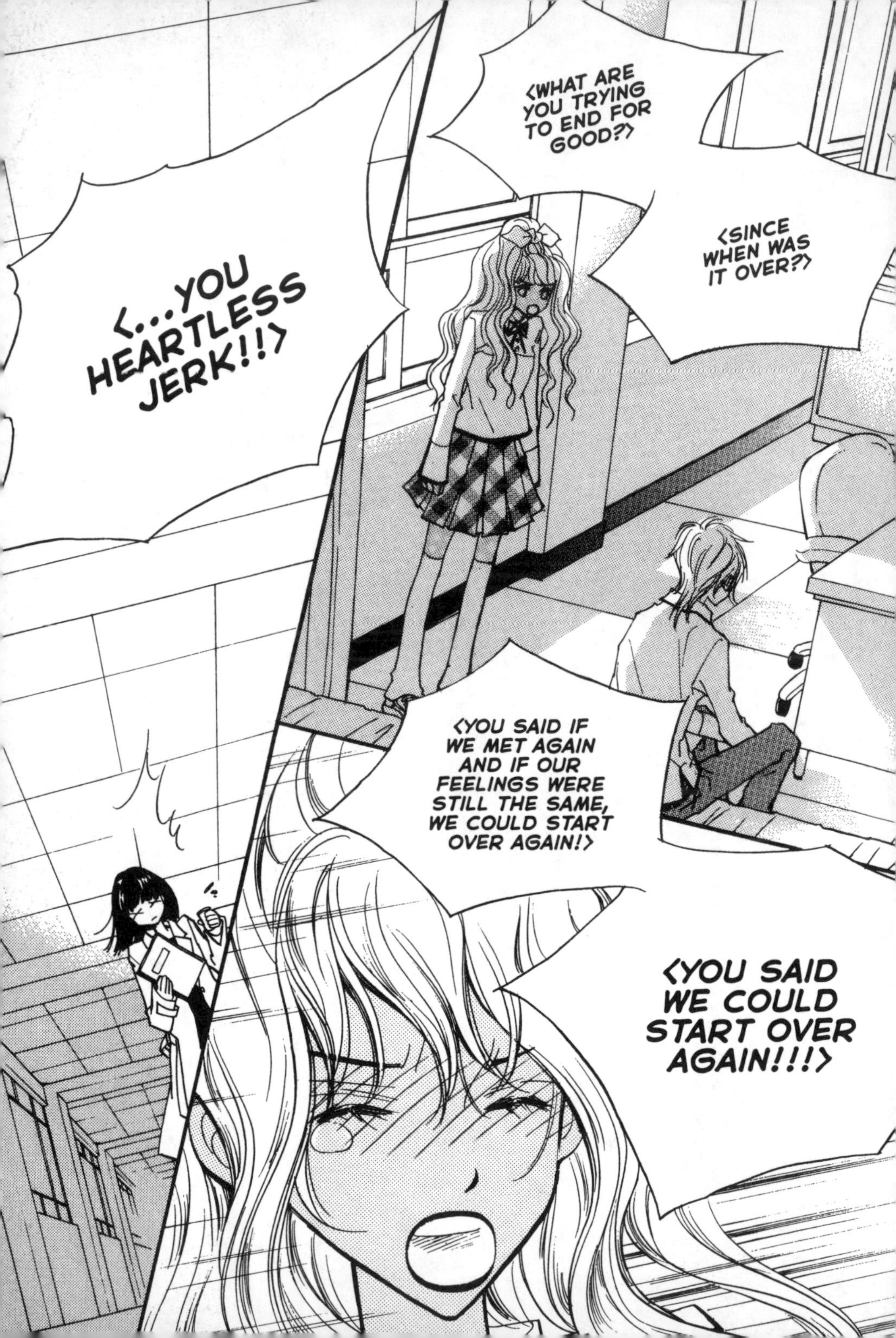
<...YOU HEARTLESS JERK!!>
<WHAT ARE YOU TRYING TO END FOR GOOD?>
<SINCE WHEN WAS IT OVER?>
<YOU SAID IF WE MET AGAIN AND IF OUR FEELINGS WERE STILL THE SAME, WE COULD START OVER AGAIN!>
<YOU SAID WE COULD START OVER AGAIN!!!>

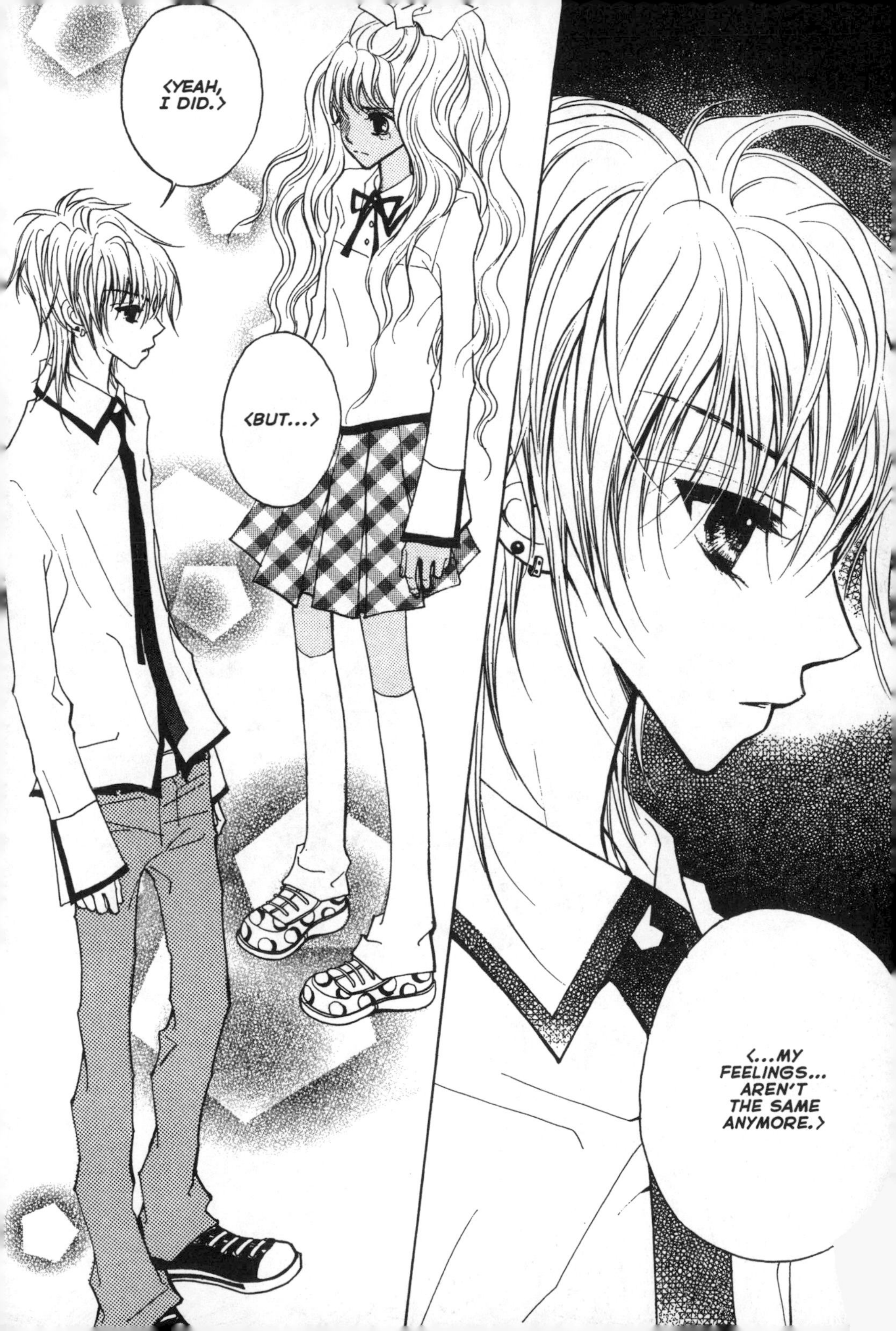
<YEAH, I DID.>
<BUT...>
<...MY FEELINGS... AREN'T THE SAME ANYMORE.>

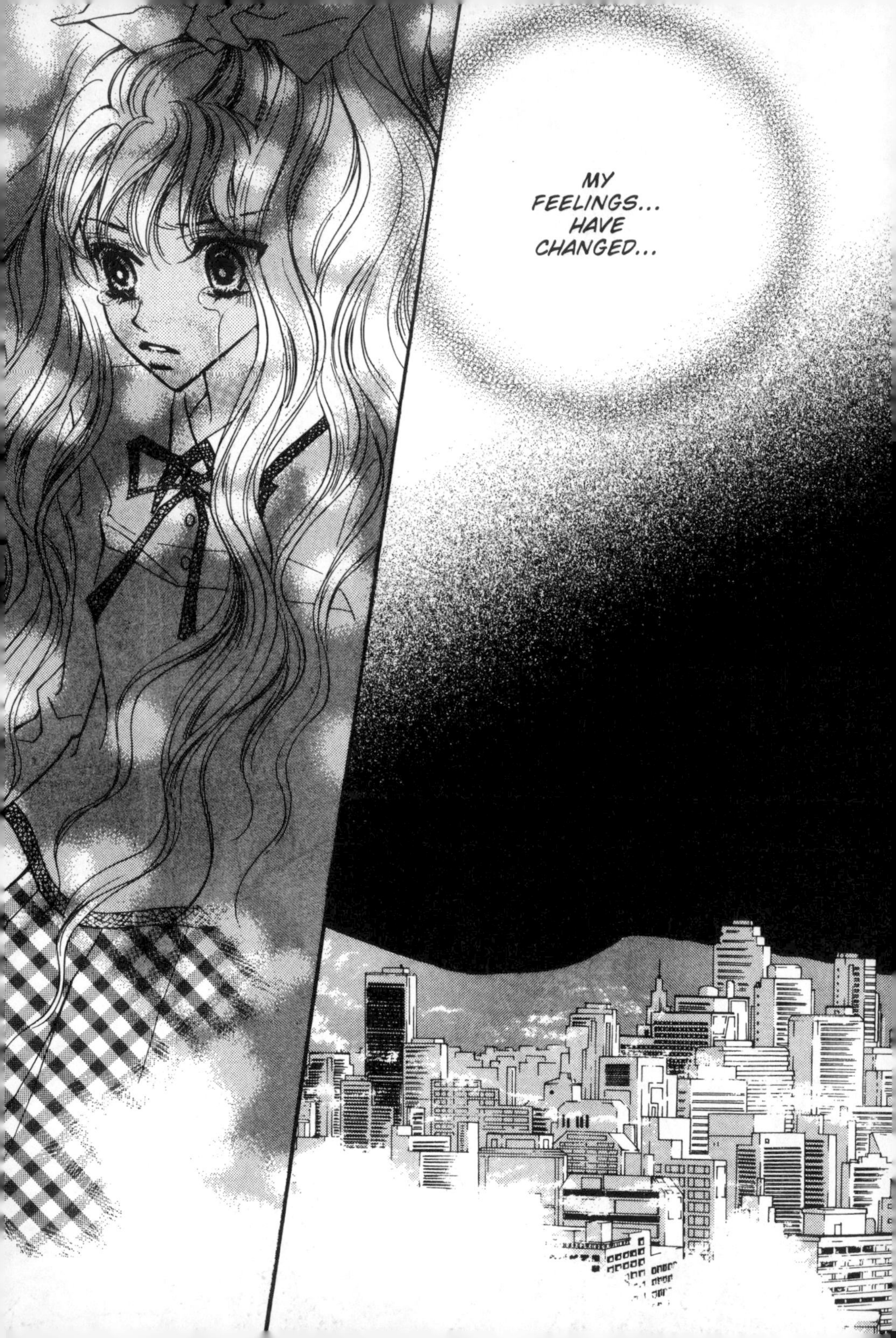
MY FEELINGS... HAVE CHANGED...

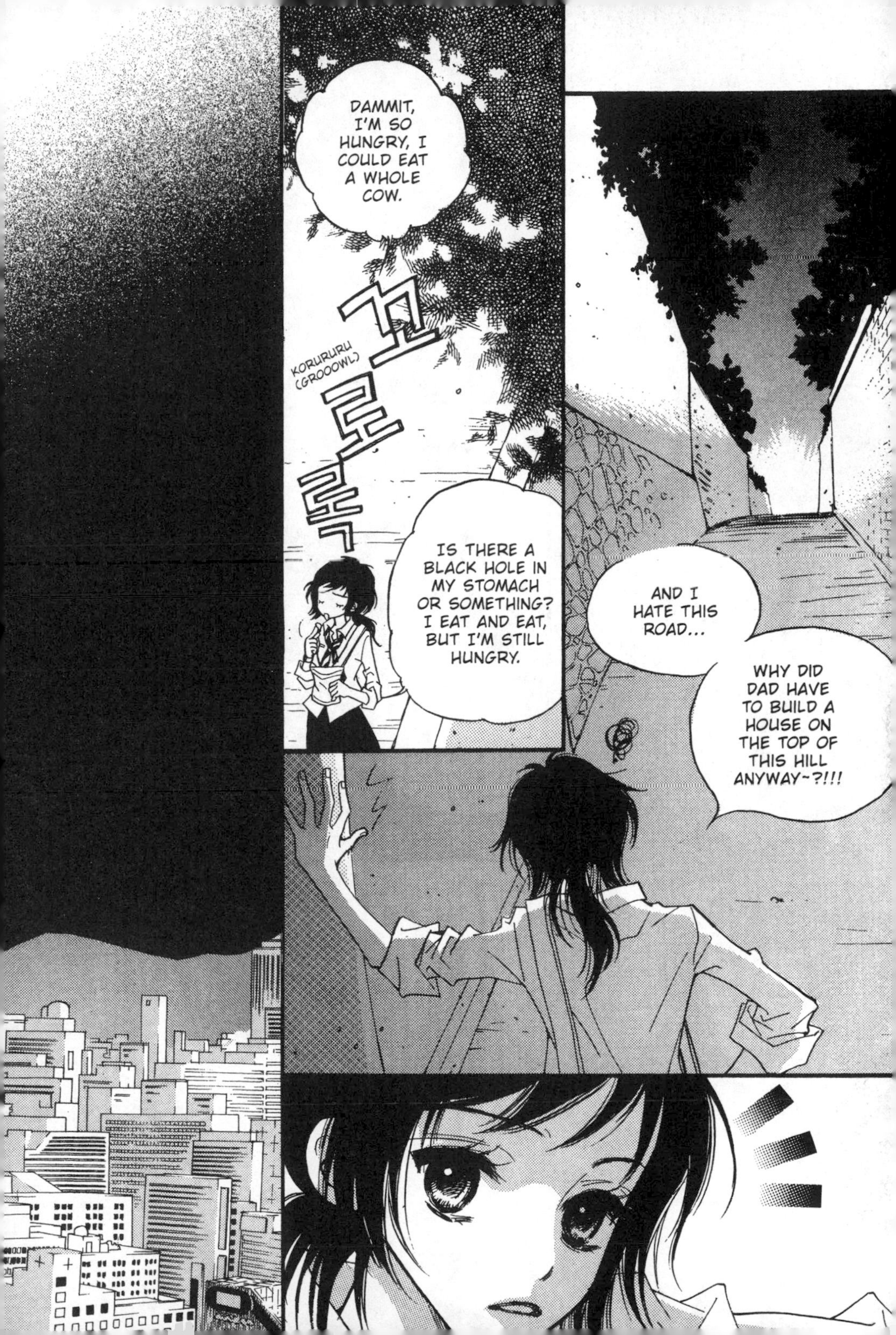

DAMMIT, I'M SO HUNGRY, I COULD EAT A WHOLE COW.
KORURURU (GROOOWL)
IS THERE A BLACK HOLE IN MY STOMACH OR SOMETHING? I EAT AND EAT, BUT I'M STILL HUNGRY.
AND I HATE THIS ROAD...
WHY DID DAD HAVE TO BUILD A HOUSE ON THE TOP OF THIS HILL ANYWAY~?!!!

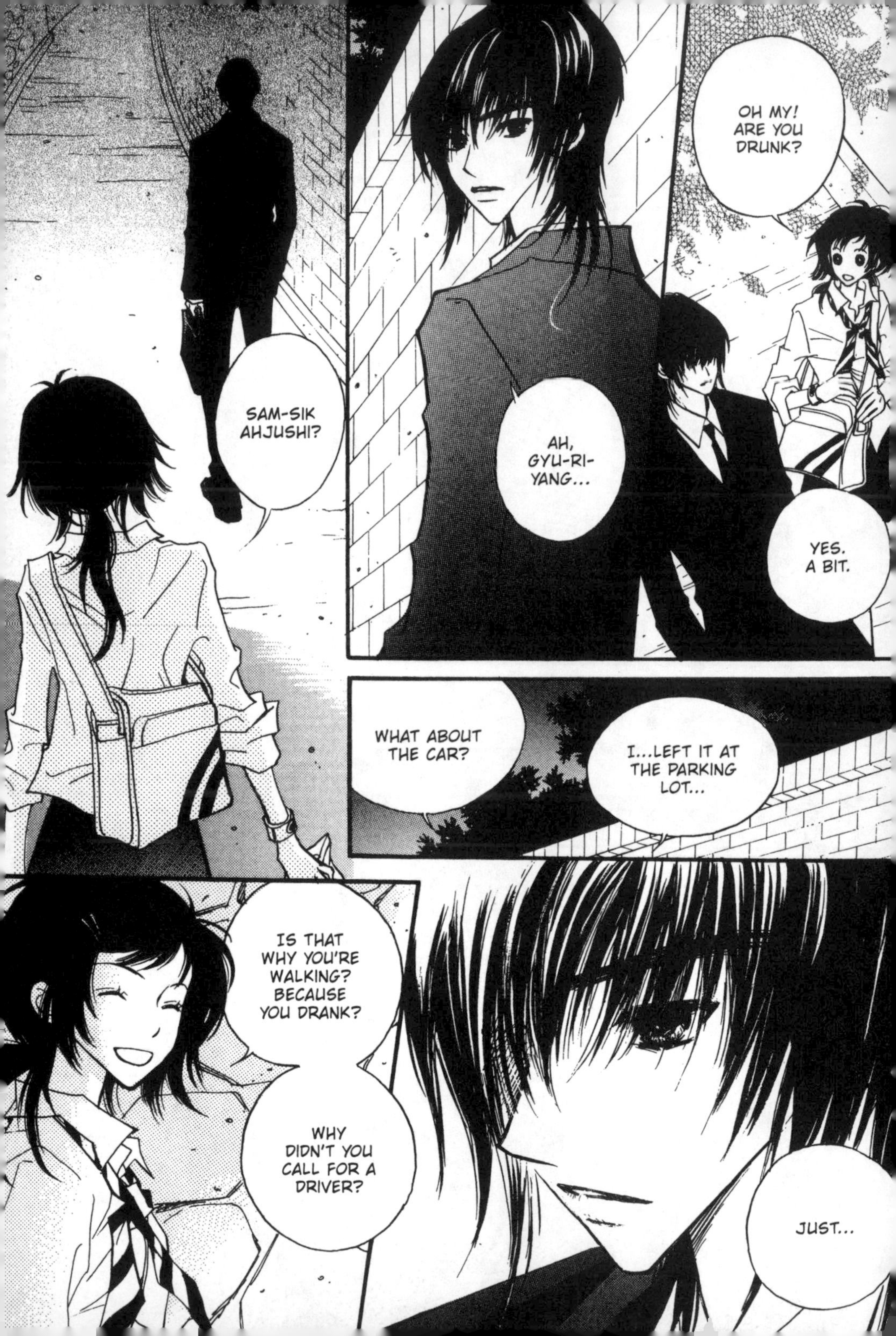
SAM-SIK AHJUSHI?
AH, GYU-RI-YANG...
OH MY! ARE YOU DRUNK?
YES. A BIT.
WHAT ABOUT THE CAR?
I...LEFT IT AT THE PARKING LOT...
IS THAT WHY YOU'RE WALKING? BECAUSE YOU DRANK?
WHY DIDN'T YOU CALL FOR A DRIVER?
JUST...

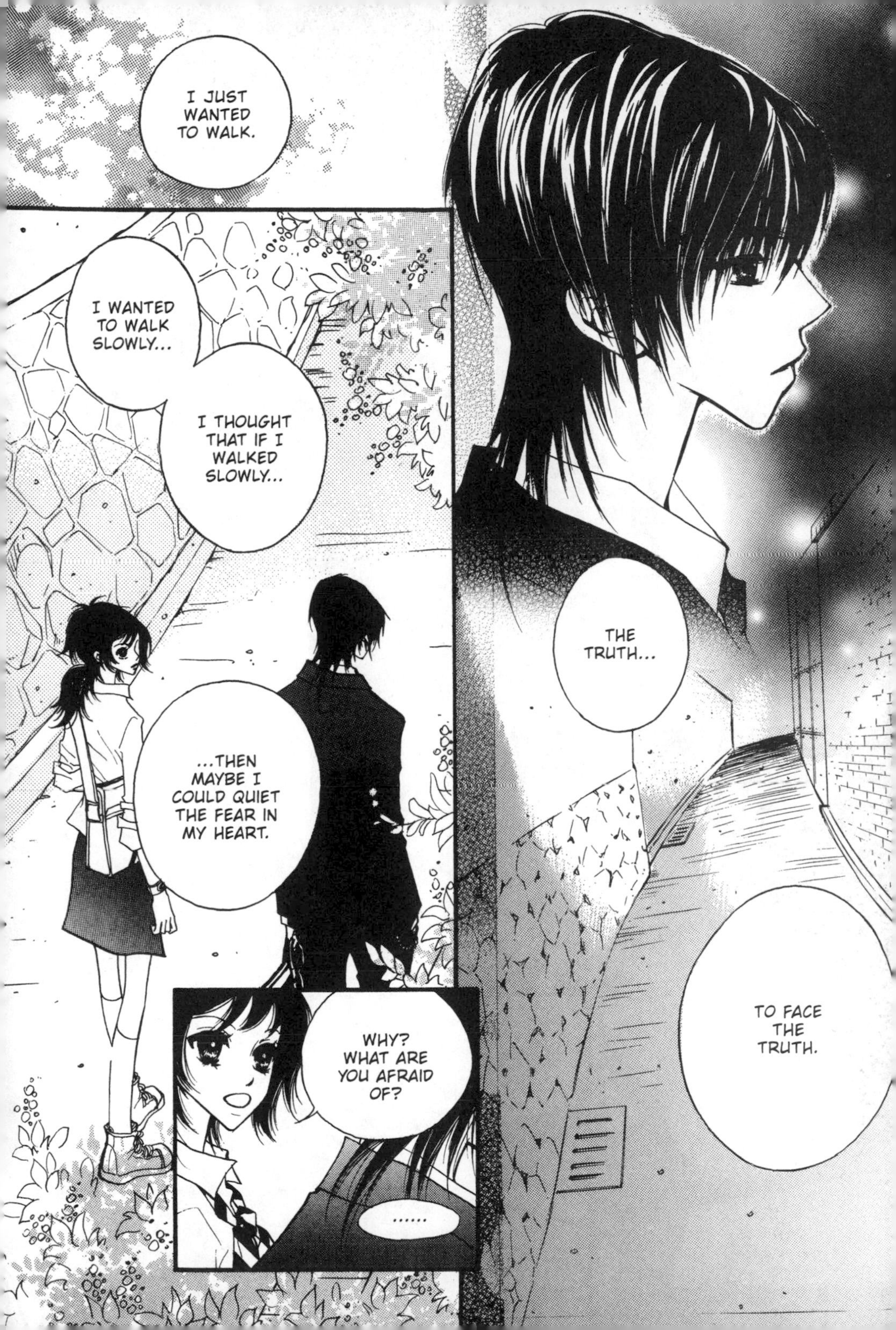

I JUST WANTED TO WALK.
I WANTED TO WALK SLOWLY...
I THOUGHT THAT IF I WALKED SLOWLY...
...THEN MAYBE I COULD QUIET THE FEAR IN MY HEART.
WHY? WHAT ARE YOU AFRAID OF?
......
THE TRUTH...
TO FACE THE TRUTH.

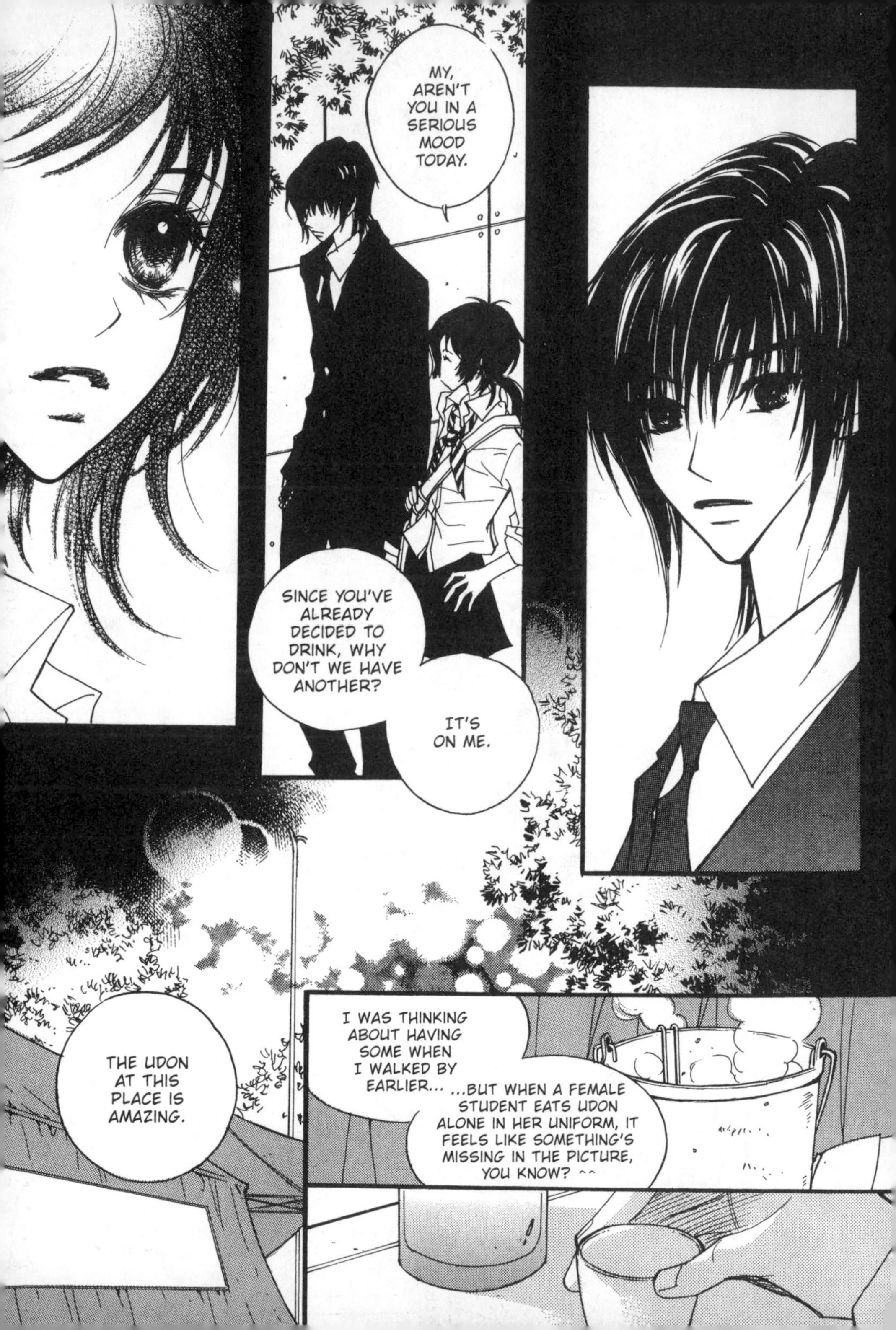
MY, AREN'T YOU IN A SERIOUS MOOD TODAY.
SINCE YOU'VE ALREADY DECIDED TO DRINK, WHY DON'T WE HAVE ANOTHER?
IT'S ON ME.
THE UDON AT THIS PLACE IS AMAZING.
I WAS THINKING ABOUT HAVING SOME WHEN I WALKED BY EARLIER...
...BUT WHEN A FEMALE STUDENT EATS UDON ALONE IN HER UNIFORM, IT FEELS LIKE SOMETHING'S MISSING IN THE PICTURE, YOU KNOW? ^^

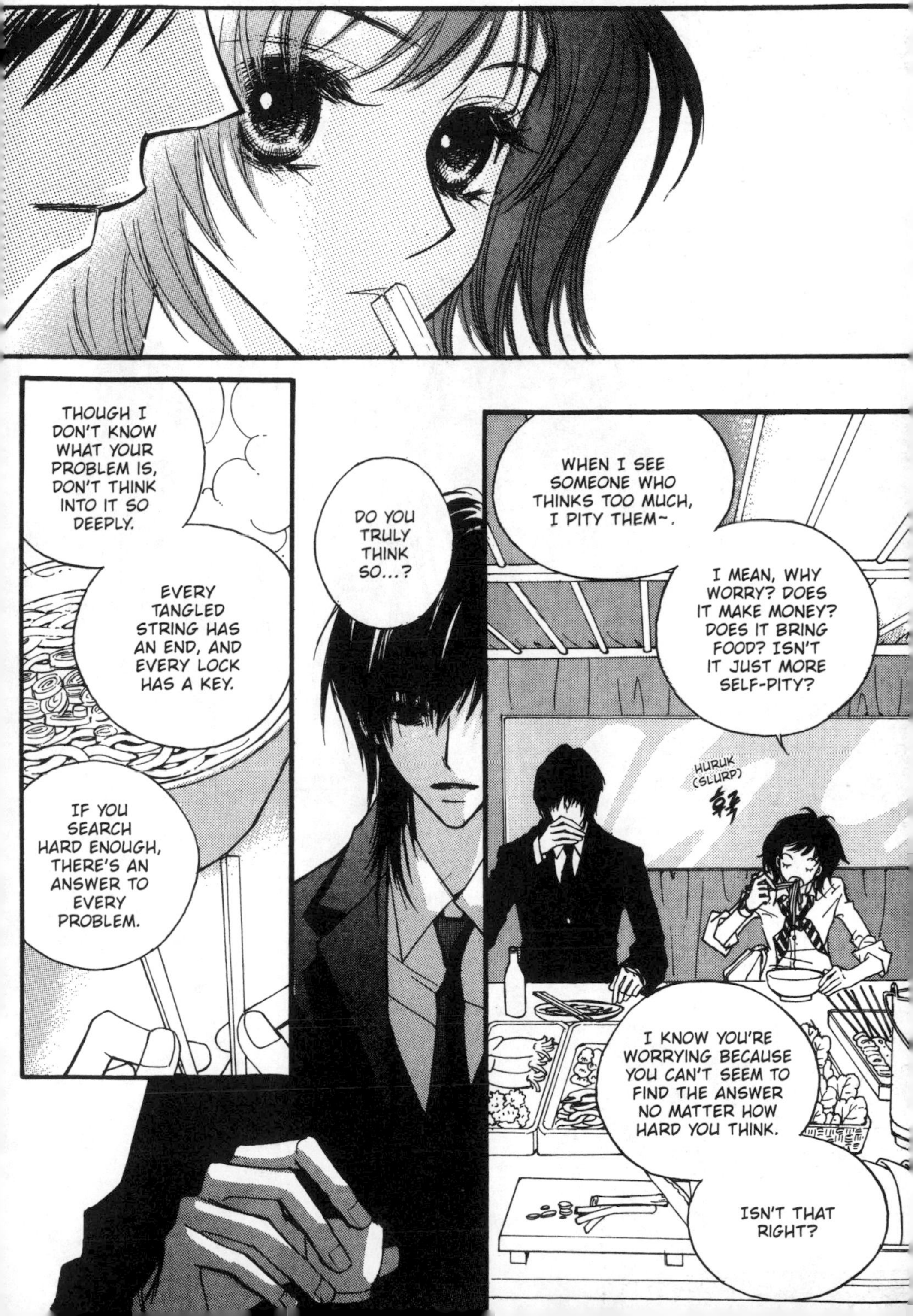
THOUGH I DON'T KNOW WHAT YOUR PROBLEM IS, DON'T THINK INTO IT SO DEEPLY.
EVERY TANGLED STRING HAS AN END, AND EVERY LOCK HAS A KEY.
IF YOU SEARCH HARD ENOUGH, THERE'S AN ANSWER TO EVERY PROBLEM.
DO YOU TRULY THINK SO...?
WHEN I SEE SOMEONE WHO THINKS TOO MUCH, I PITY THEM~.
I MEAN, WHY WORRY? DOES IT MAKE MONEY? DOES IT BRING FOOD? ISN'T IT JUST MORE SELF-PITY?
HURUK (SLURP)
I KNOW YOU'RE WORRYING BECAUSE YOU CAN'T SEEM TO FIND THE ANSWER NO MATTER HOW HARD YOU THINK.
ISN'T THAT RIGHT?

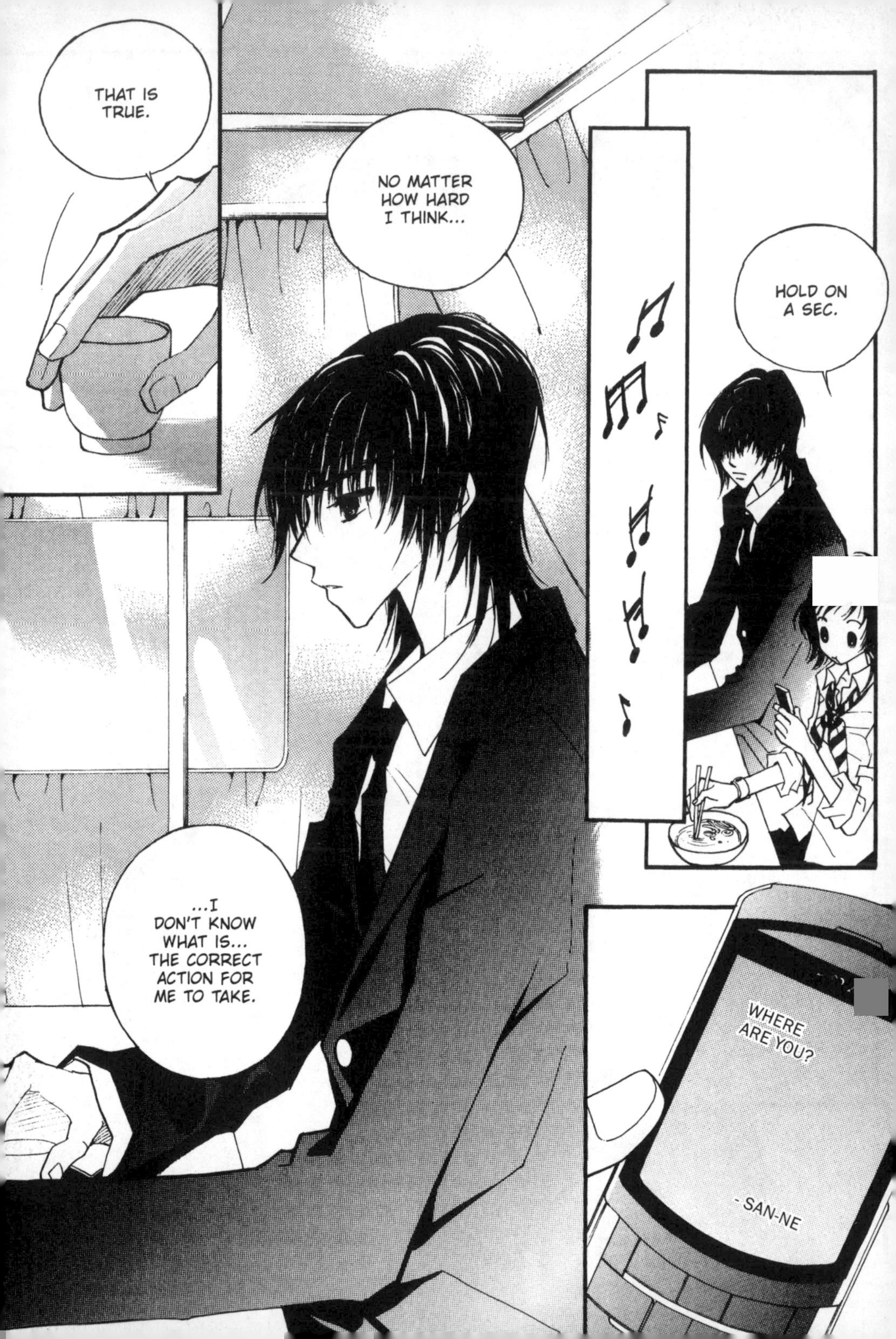
THAT IS TRUE.
NO MATTER HOW HARD I THINK...
...I DON'T KNOW WHAT IS... THE CORRECT ACTION FOR ME TO TAKE.
HOLD ON A SEC.
WHERE ARE YOU?
- SAN-NE

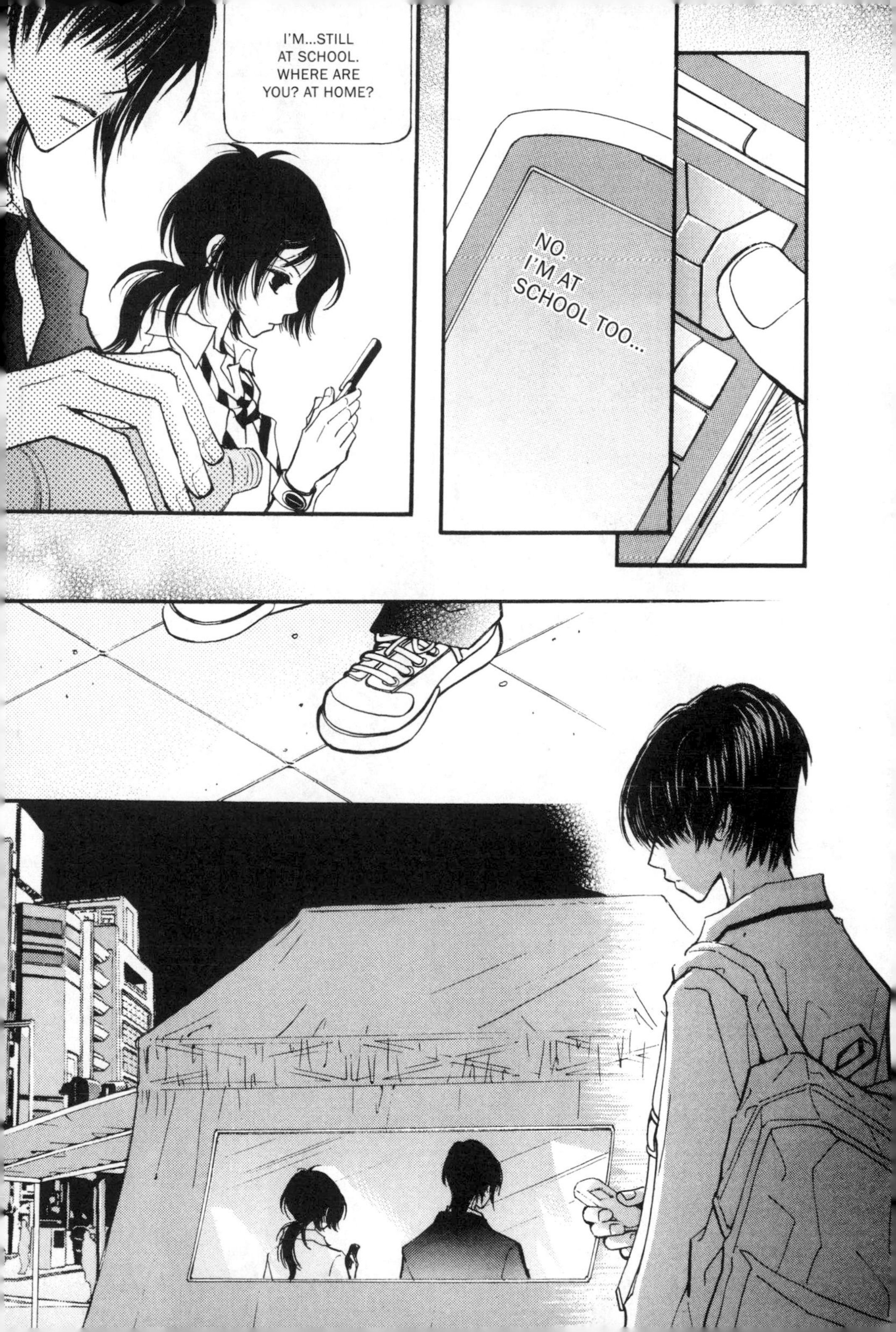
NO. I'M AT SCHOOL TOO...
I'M...STILL AT SCHOOL. WHERE ARE YOU? AT HOME?

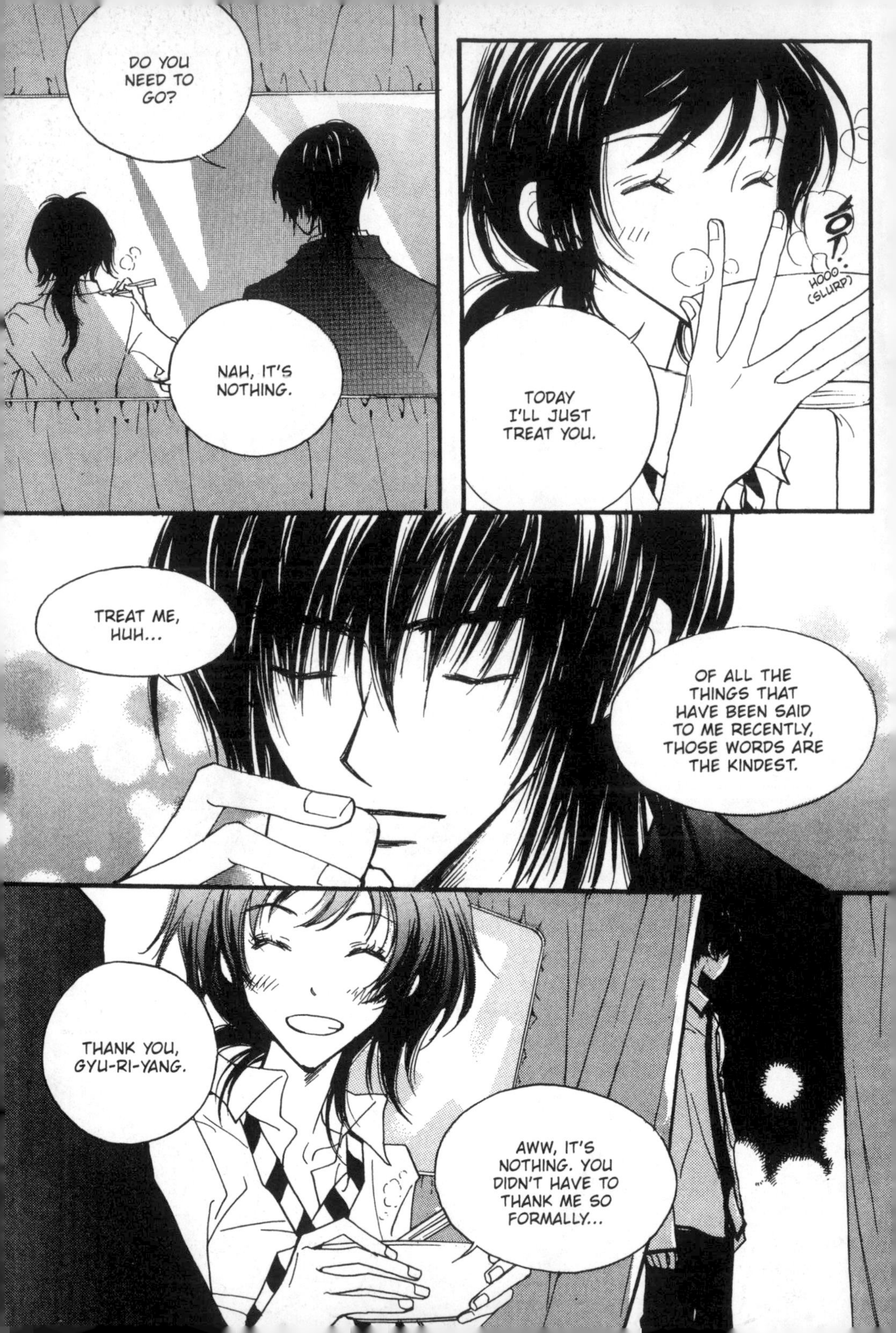
DO YOU NEED TO GO?
NAH, IT'S NOTHING.
TODAY I'LL JUST TREAT YOU.
HOOO (SLURP)
TREAT ME, HUH...
OF ALL THE THINGS THAT HAVE BEEN SAID TO ME RECENTLY, THOSE WORDS ARE THE KINDEST.
THANK YOU, GYU-RI-YANG.
AWW, IT'S NOTHING. YOU DIDN'T HAVE TO THANK ME SO FORMALLY...

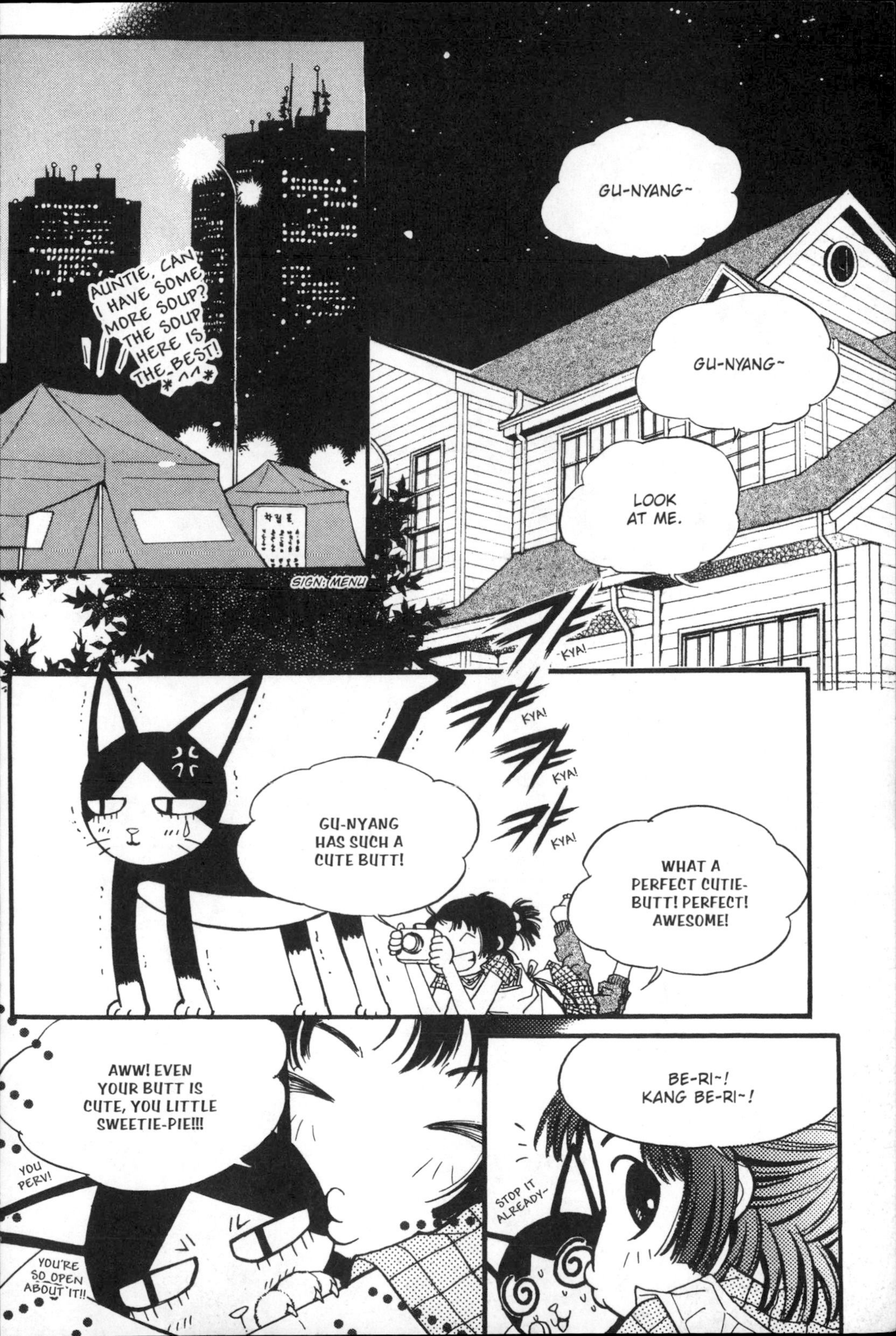
AUNTIE, CAN I HAVE SOME MORE SOUP? THE SOUP HERE IS THE BEST! *^^*
SIGN: MENU
GU-NYANG~
GU-NYANG~
LOOK AT ME.
KYA!
KYA!
KYA!
KYA!
GU-NYANG HAS SUCH A CUTE BUTT!
WHAT A PERFECT CUTIE-BUTT! PERFECT! AWESOME!
AWW! EVEN YOUR BUTT IS CUTE, YOU LITTLE SWEETIE-PIE!!!
YOU PERV!
YOU'RE SO OPEN ABOUT IT!!
BE-RI~! KANG BE-RI~!
STOP IT ALREADY~

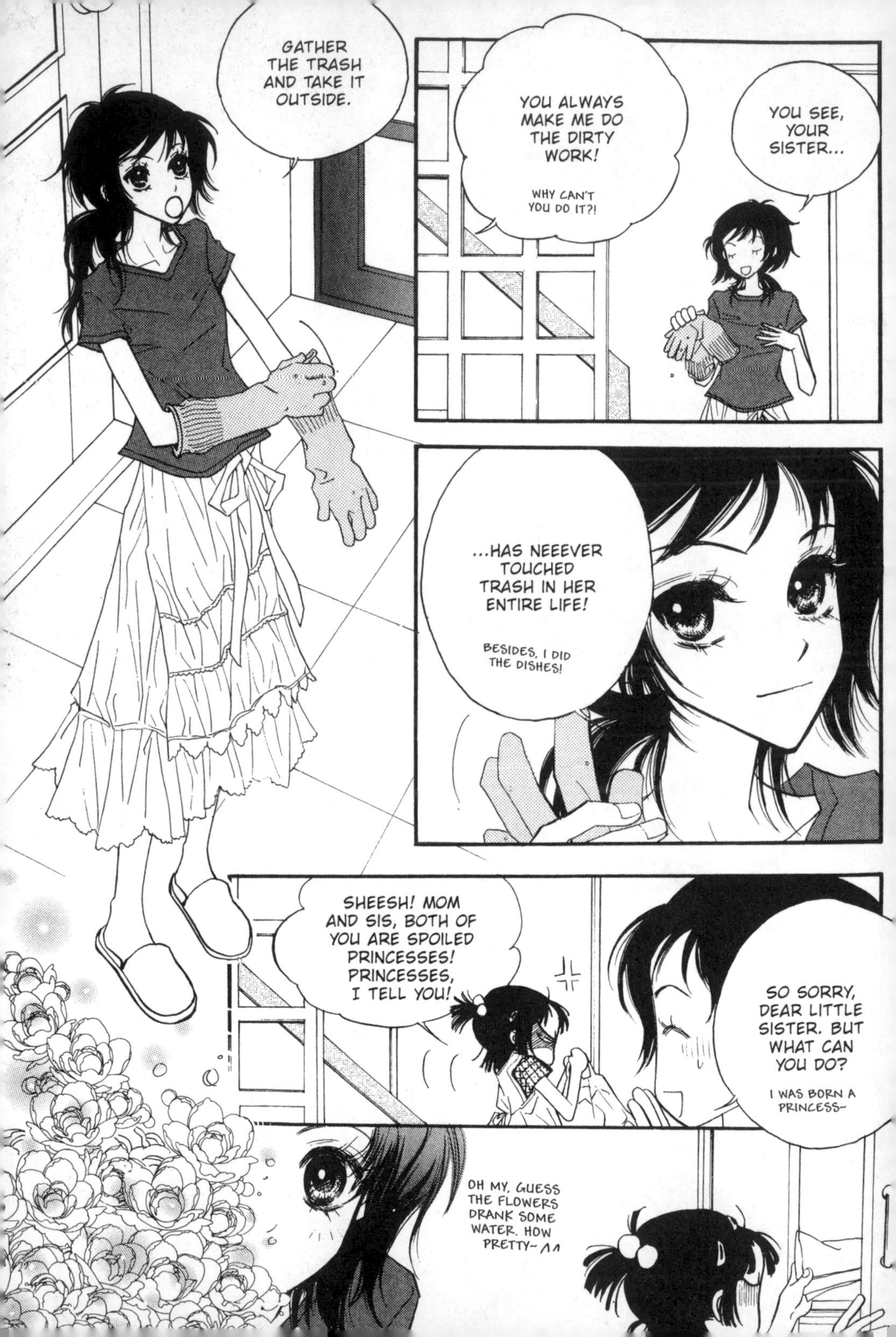
GATHER THE TRASH AND TAKE IT OUTSIDE.
YOU ALWAYS MAKE ME DO THE DIRTY WORK!
WHY CAN'T YOU DO IT?!
YOU SEE, YOUR SISTER...
...HAS NEEEVER TOUCHED TRASH IN HER ENTIRE LIFE!
BESIDES, I DID THE DISHES!
SHEESH! MOM AND SIS, BOTH OF YOU ARE SPOILED PRINCESSES! PRINCESSES, I TELL YOU!
SO SORRY, DEAR LITTLE SISTER. BUT WHAT CAN YOU DO?
I WAS BORN A PRINCESS~
OH MY, GUESS THE FLOWERS DRANK SOME WATER. HOW PRETTY~ ^^

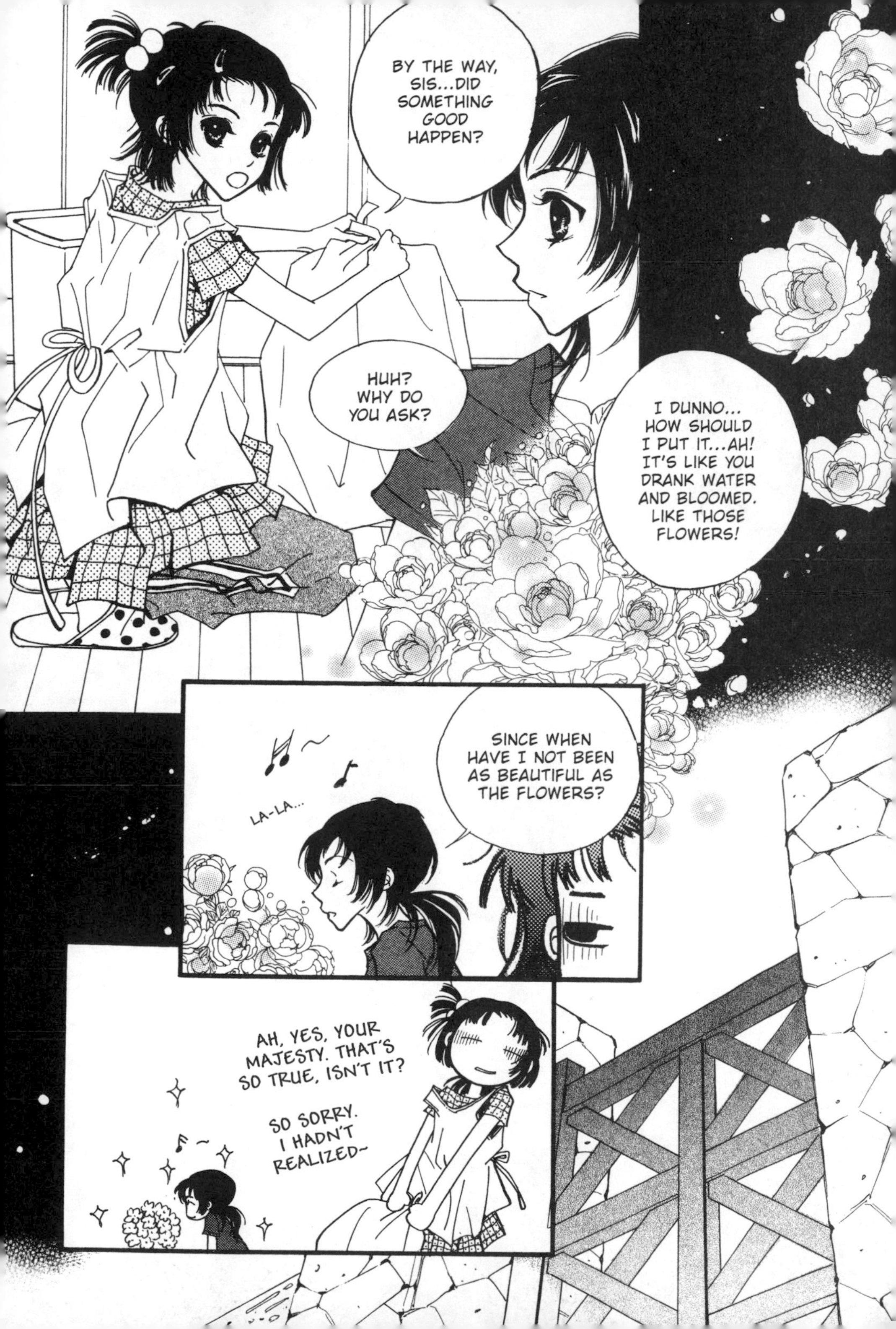
BY THE WAY, SIS...DID SOMETHING GOOD HAPPEN?
HUH? WHY DO YOU ASK?
I DUNNO... HOW SHOULD I PUT IT...AH! IT'S LIKE YOU DRANK WATER AND BLOOMED. LIKE THOSE FLOWERS!
LA-LA...
SINCE WHEN HAVE I NOT BEEN AS BEAUTIFUL AS THE FLOWERS?
AH, YES, YOUR MAJESTY. THAT'S SO TRUE, ISN'T IT?
SO SORRY. I HADN'T REALIZED~

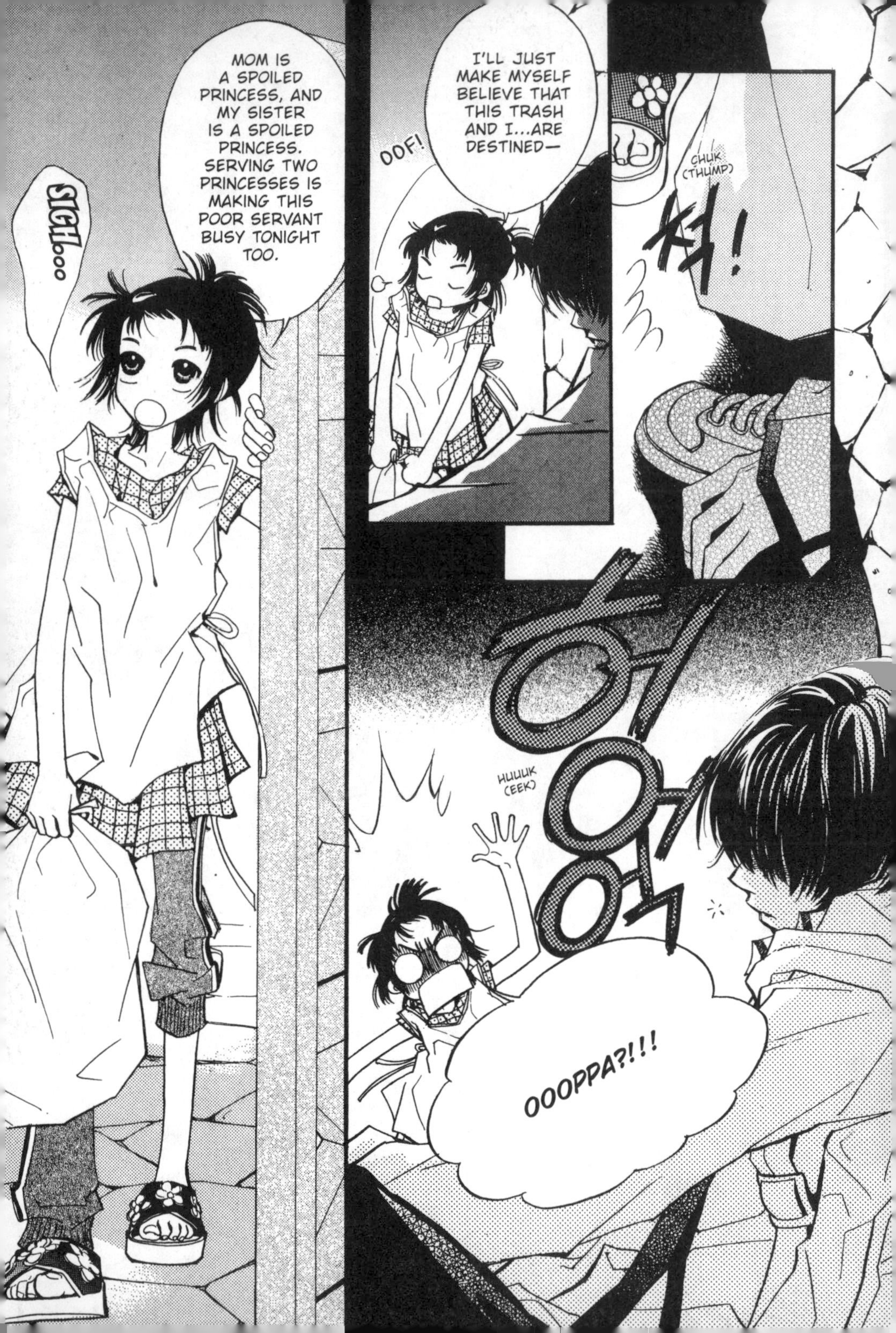
MOM IS A SPOILED PRINCESS, AND MY SISTER IS A SPOILED PRINCESS. SERVING TWO PRINCESSES IS MAKING THIS POOR SERVANT BUSY TONIGHT TOO.
SIGHooo
I'LL JUST MAKE MYSELF BELIEVE THAT THIS TRASH AND I...ARE DESTINED—
OOF!
CHUK (THUMP)
HUUUK (EEK)
OOOPPA?!!!

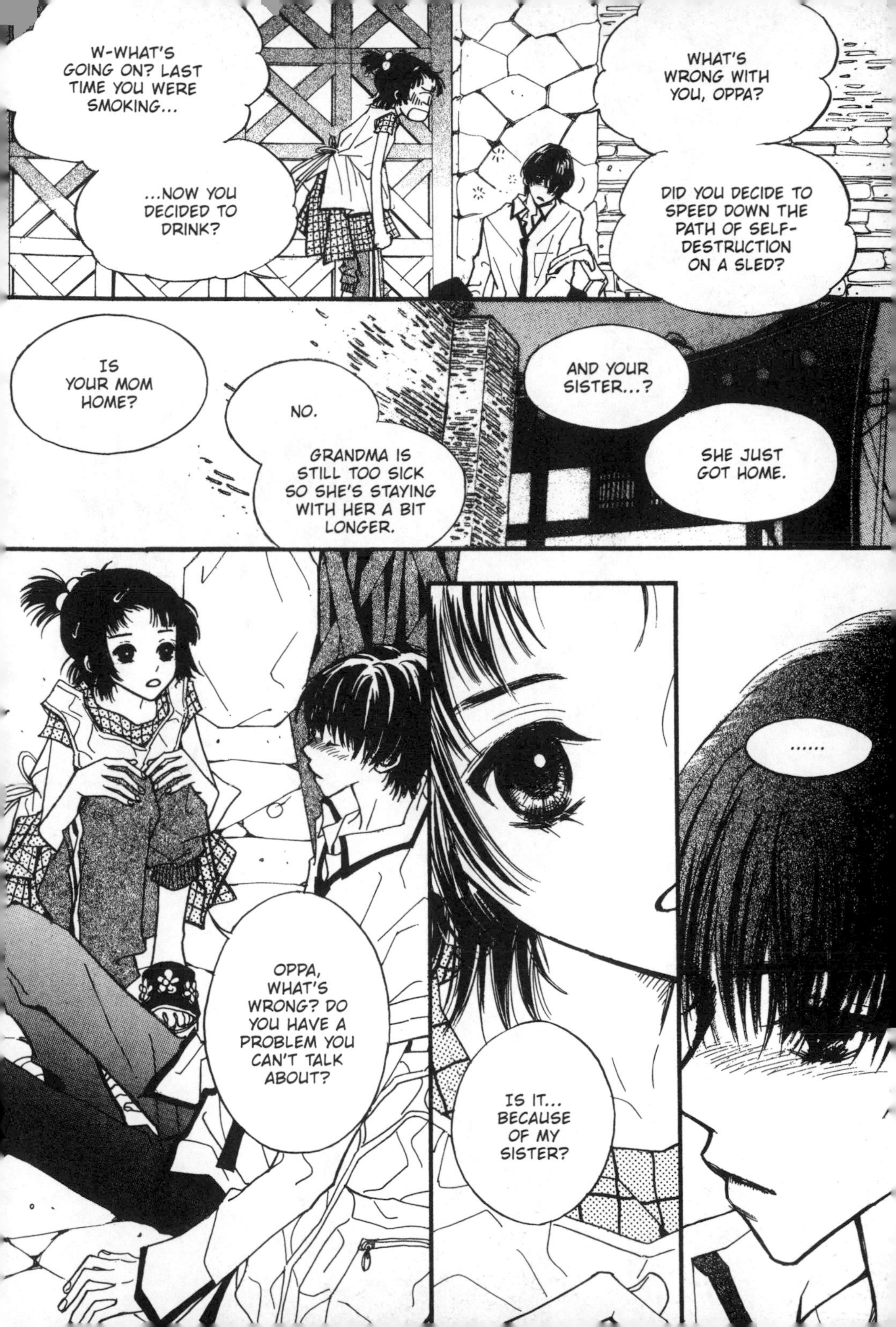
W-WHAT'S GOING ON? LAST TIME YOU WERE SMOKING...
...NOW YOU DECIDED TO DRINK?
WHAT'S WRONG WITH YOU, OPPA?
DID YOU DECIDE TO SPEED DOWN THE PATH OF SELF-DESTRUCTION ON A SLED?
IS YOUR MOM HOME?
NO.
GRANDMA IS STILL TOO SICK SO SHE'S STAYING WITH HER A BIT LONGER.
AND YOUR SISTER...?
SHE JUST GOT HOME.
OPPA, WHAT'S WRONG? DO YOU HAVE A PROBLEM YOU CAN'T TALK ABOUT?
IS IT... BECAUSE OF MY SISTER?
......

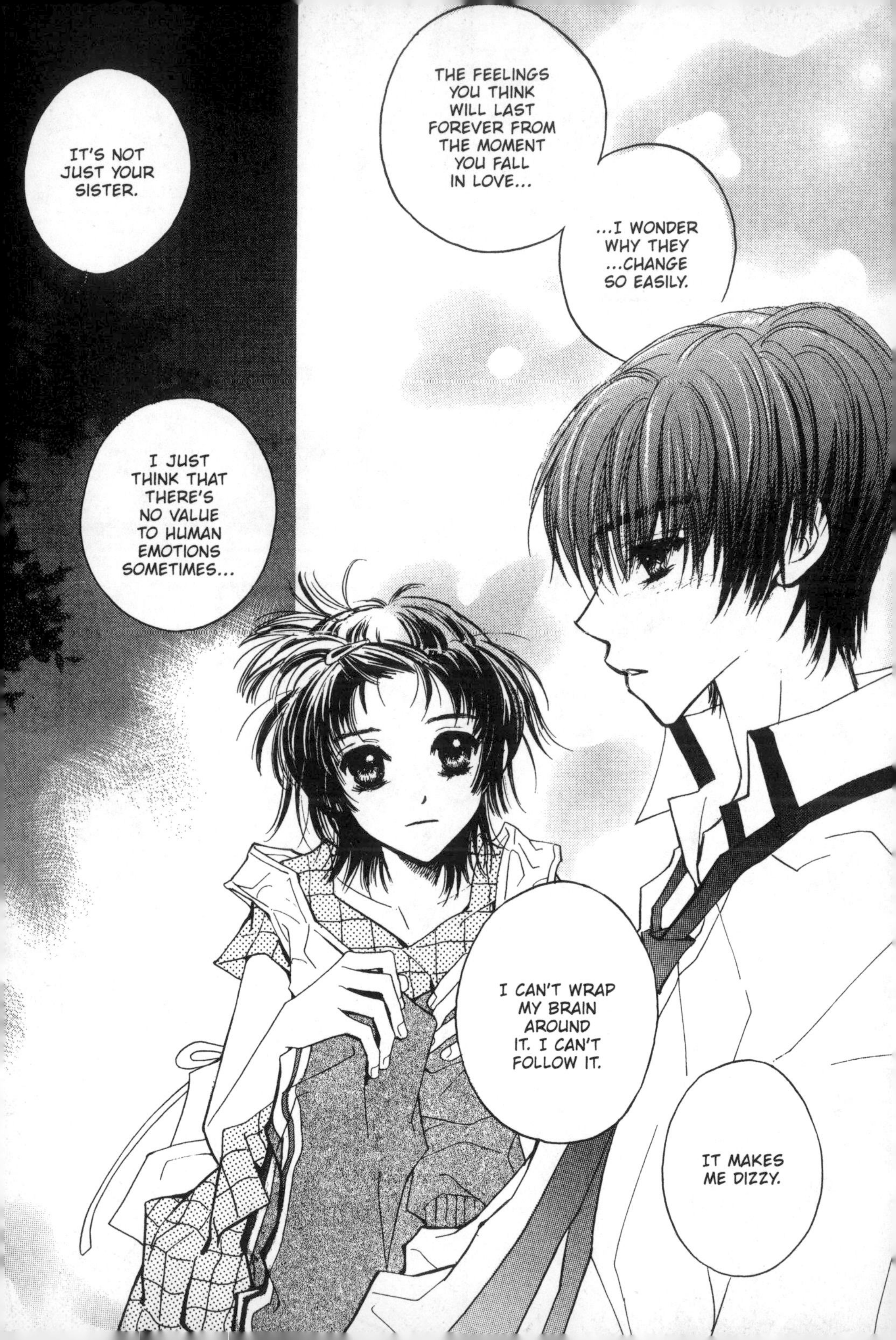
IT'S NOT JUST YOUR SISTER.
THE FEELINGS YOU THINK WILL LAST FOREVER FROM THE MOMENT YOU FALL IN LOVE...
...I WONDER WHY THEY ...CHANGE SO EASILY.
I JUST THINK THAT THERE'S NO VALUE TO HUMAN EMOTIONS SOMETIMES...
I CAN'T WRAP MY BRAIN AROUND IT. I CAN'T FOLLOW IT.
IT MAKES ME DIZZY.

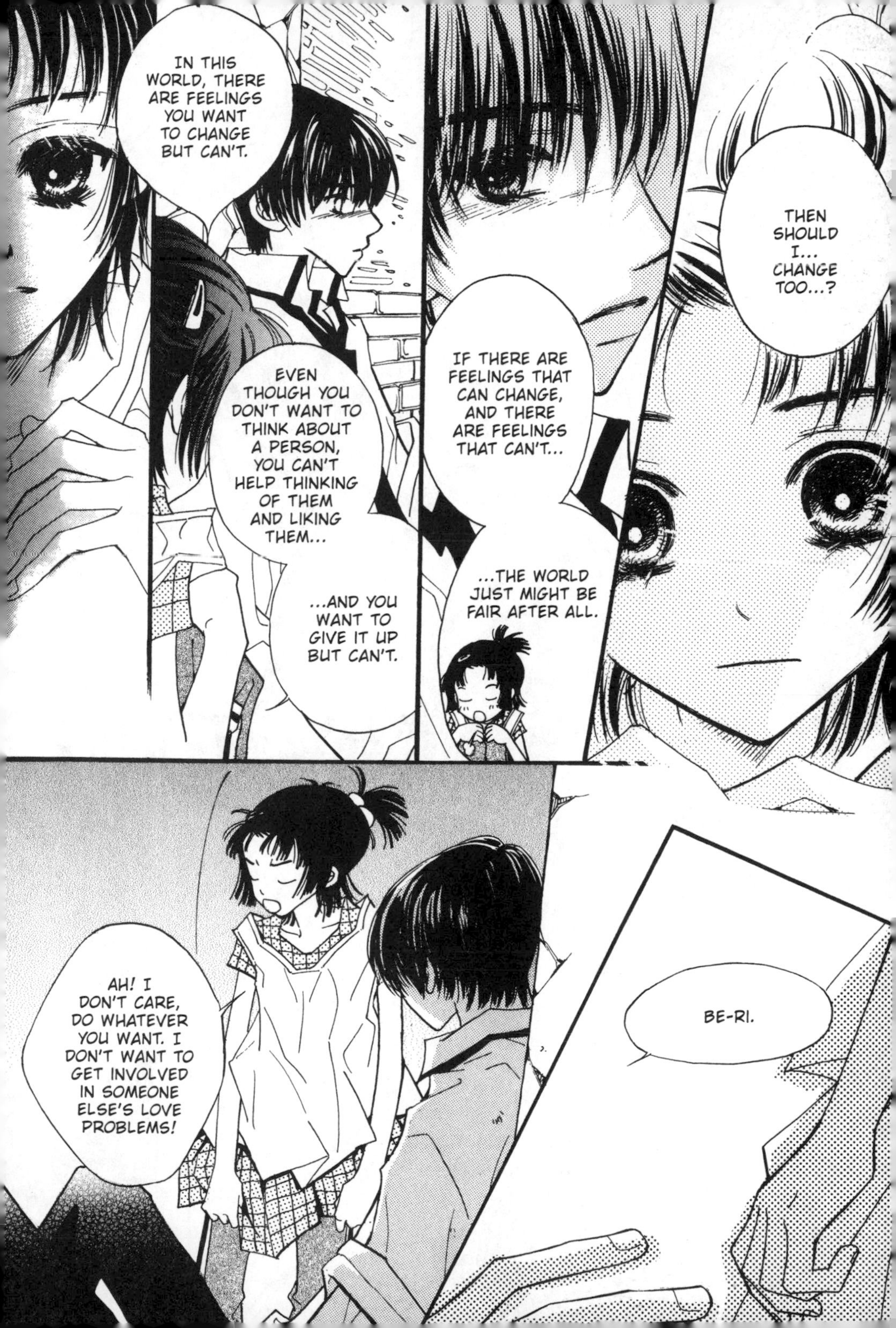
IN THIS WORLD, THERE ARE FEELINGS YOU WANT TO CHANGE BUT CAN'T.
EVEN THOUGH YOU DON'T WANT TO THINK ABOUT A PERSON, YOU CAN'T HELP THINKING OF THEM AND LIKING THEM...
...AND YOU WANT TO GIVE IT UP BUT CAN'T.
IF THERE ARE FEELINGS THAT CAN CHANGE, AND THERE ARE FEELINGS THAT CAN'T...
...THE WORLD JUST MIGHT BE FAIR AFTER ALL.
THEN SHOULD I... CHANGE TOO...?
AH! I DON'T CARE, DO WHATEVER YOU WANT. I DON'T WANT TO GET INVOLVED IN SOMEONE ELSE'S LOVE PROBLEMS!
BE-RI.

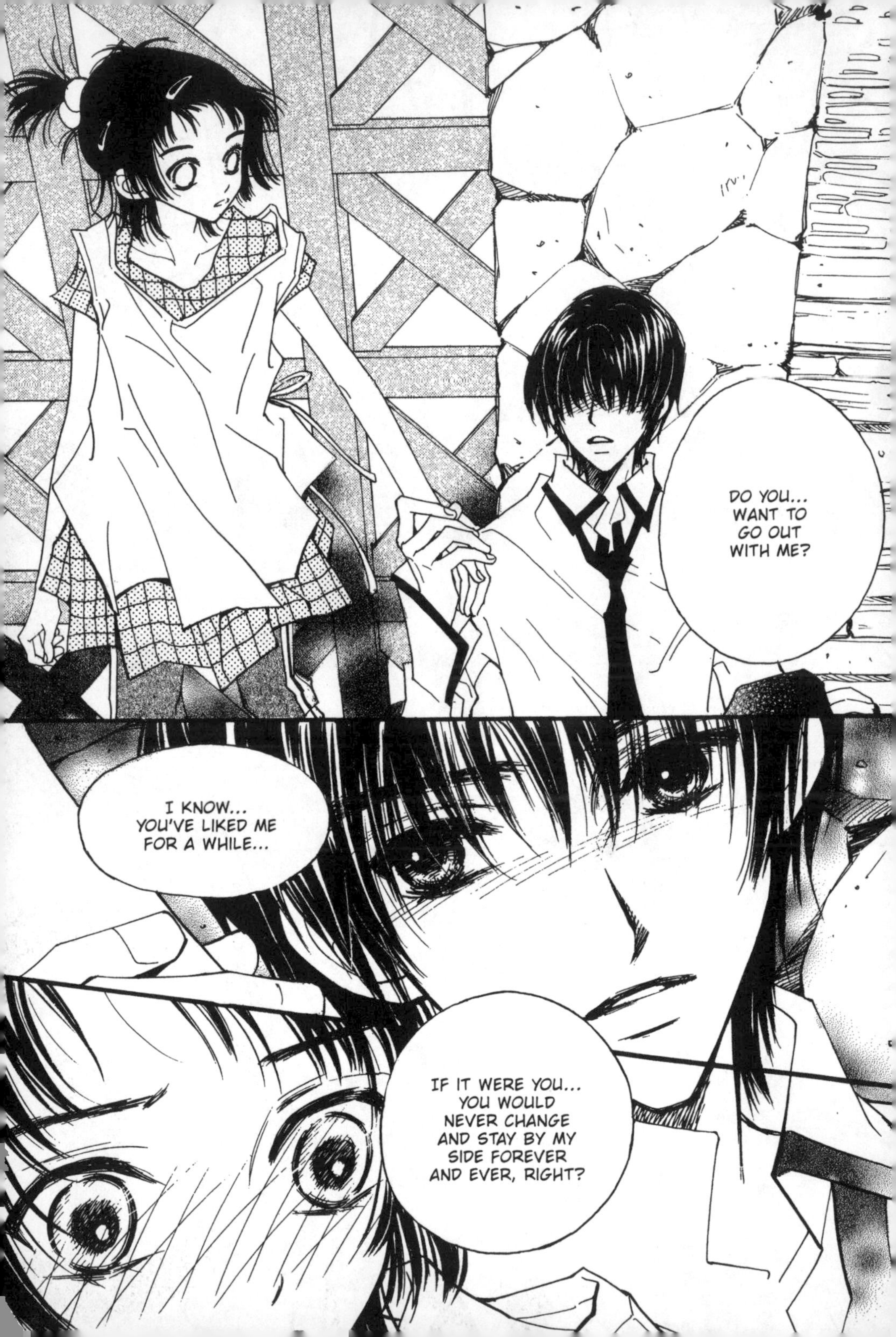
DO YOU... WANT TO GO OUT WITH ME?
I KNOW... YOU'VE LIKED ME FOR A WHILE...
IF IT WERE YOU... YOU WOULD NEVER CHANGE AND STAY BY MY SIDE FOREVER AND EVER, RIGHT?

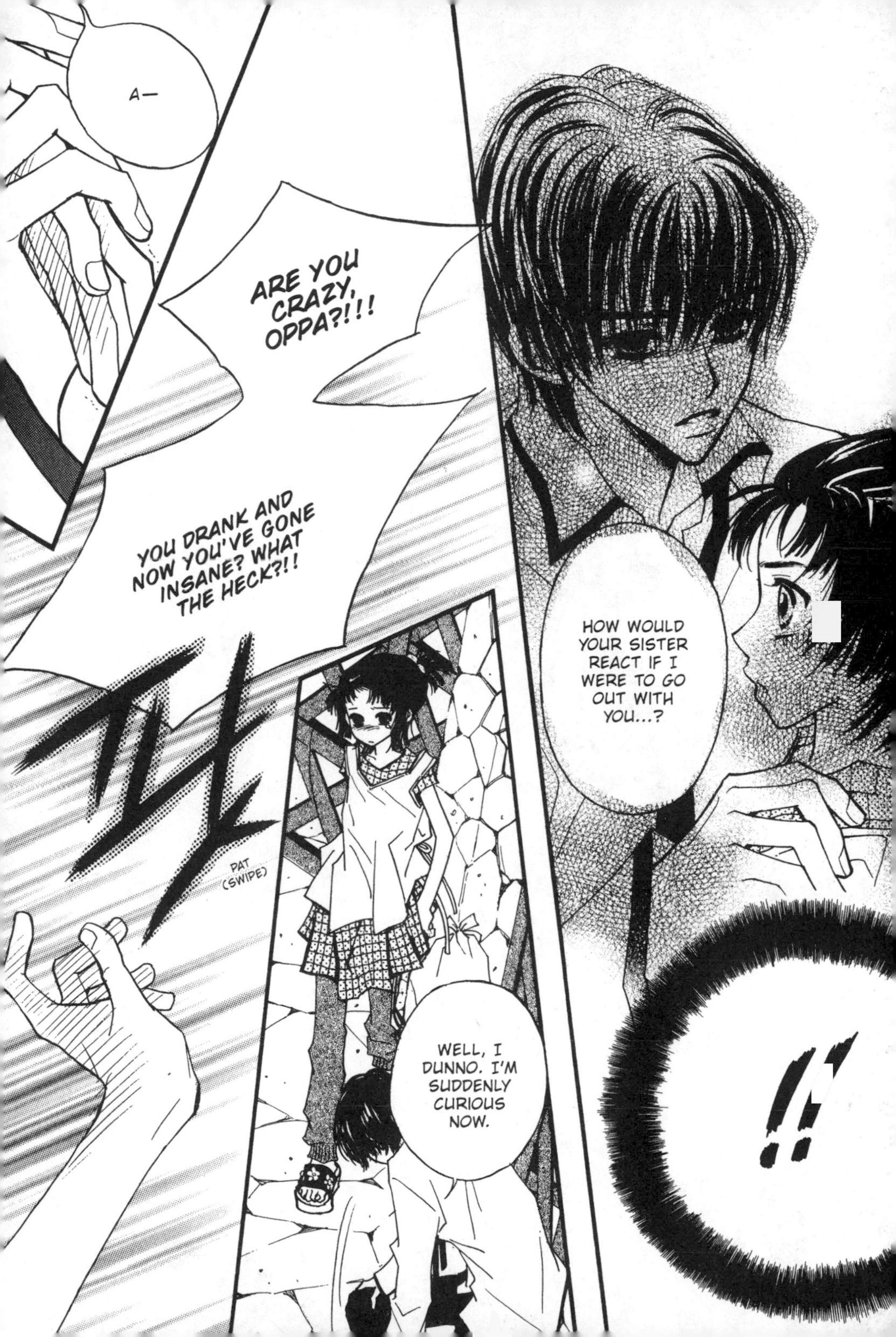
A—
ARE YOU CRAZY, OPPA?!!!
YOU DRANK AND NOW YOU'VE GONE INSANE? WHAT THE HECK?!!
PAT (SWIPE)
WELL, I DUNNO. I'M SUDDENLY CURIOUS NOW.
HOW WOULD YOUR SISTER REACT IF I WERE TO GO OUT WITH YOU...?
!!

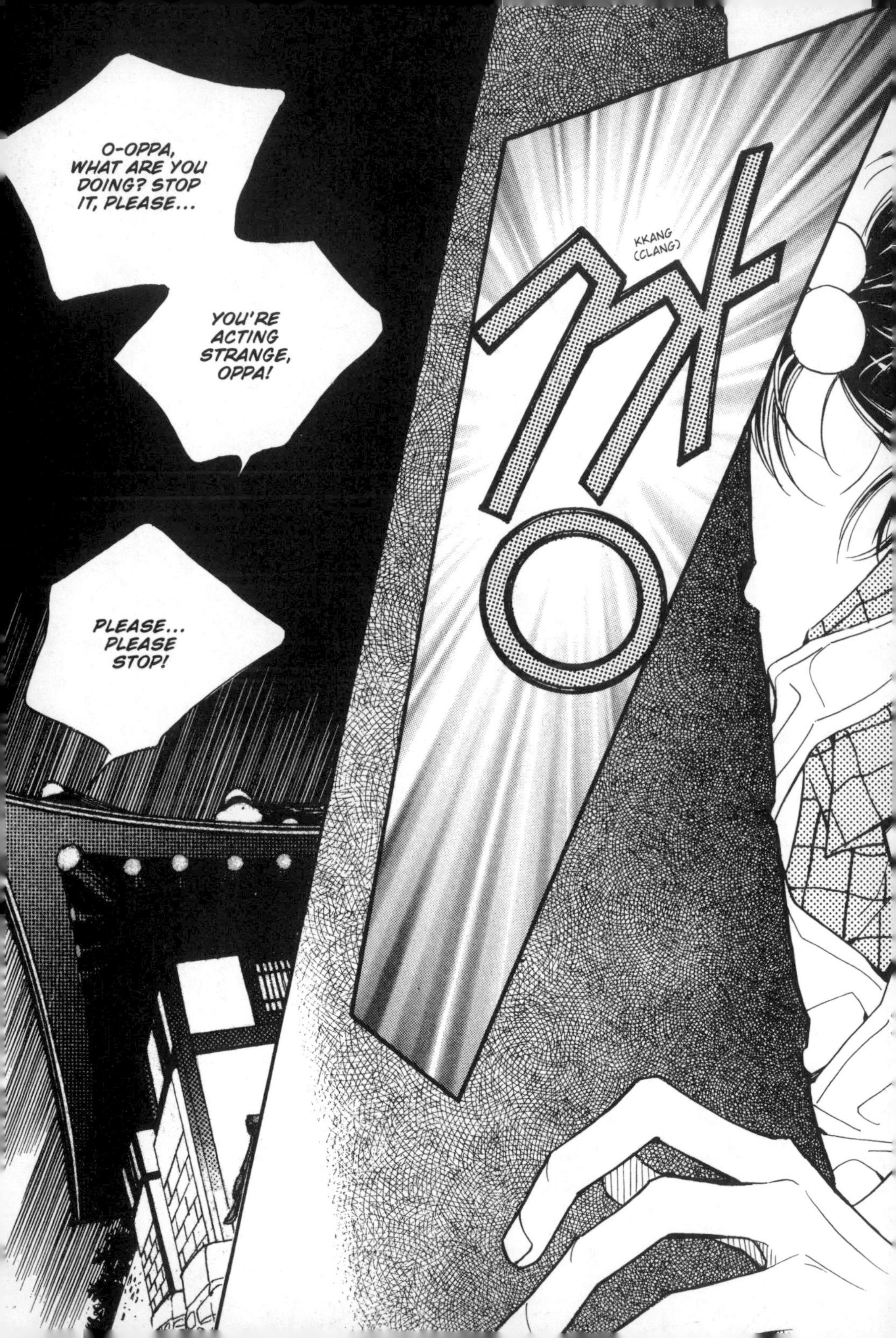
O-OPPA, WHAT ARE YOU DOING? STOP IT, PLEASE...
YOU'RE ACTING STRANGE, OPPA!
PLEASE... PLEASE STOP!
KKANG (CLANG)

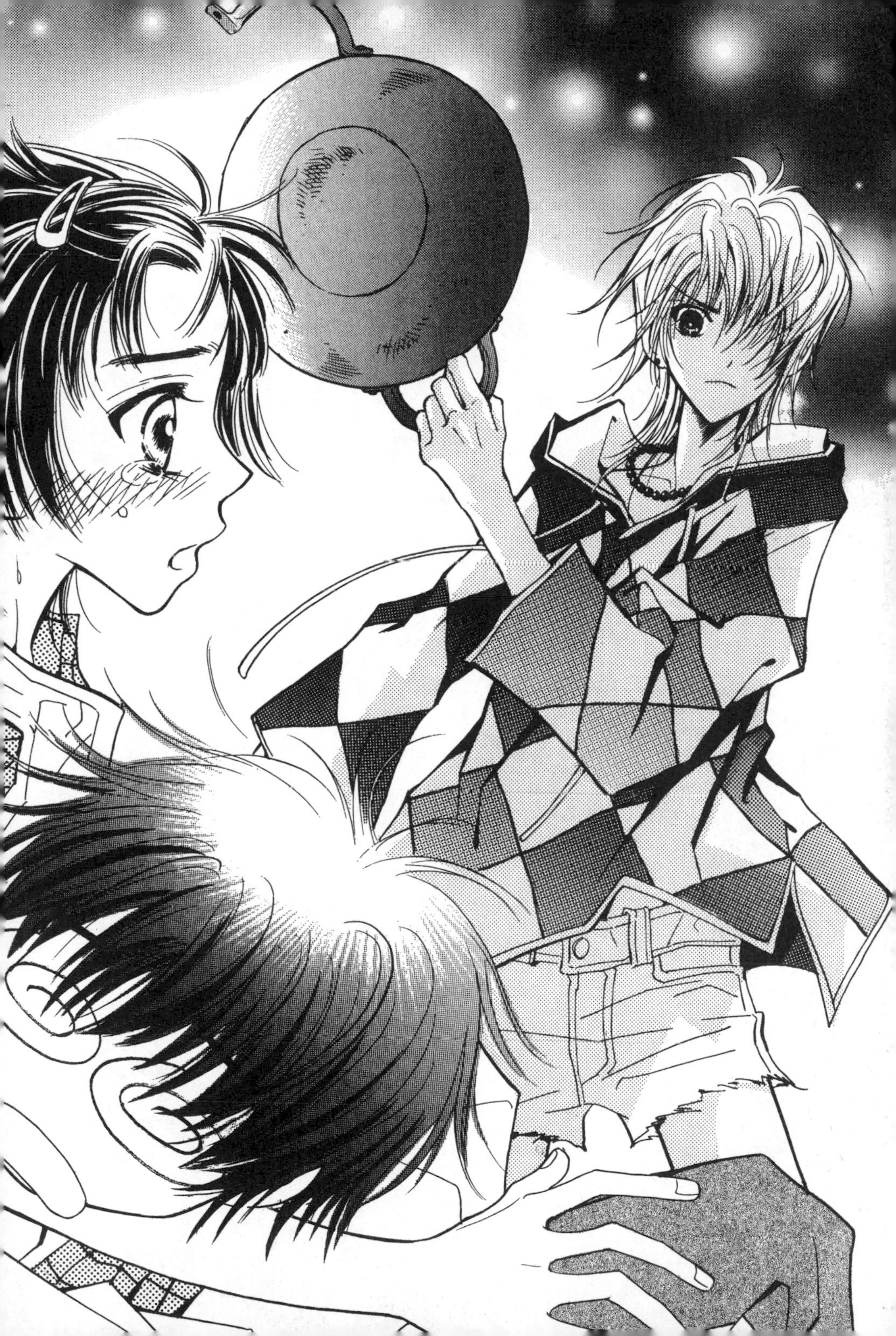

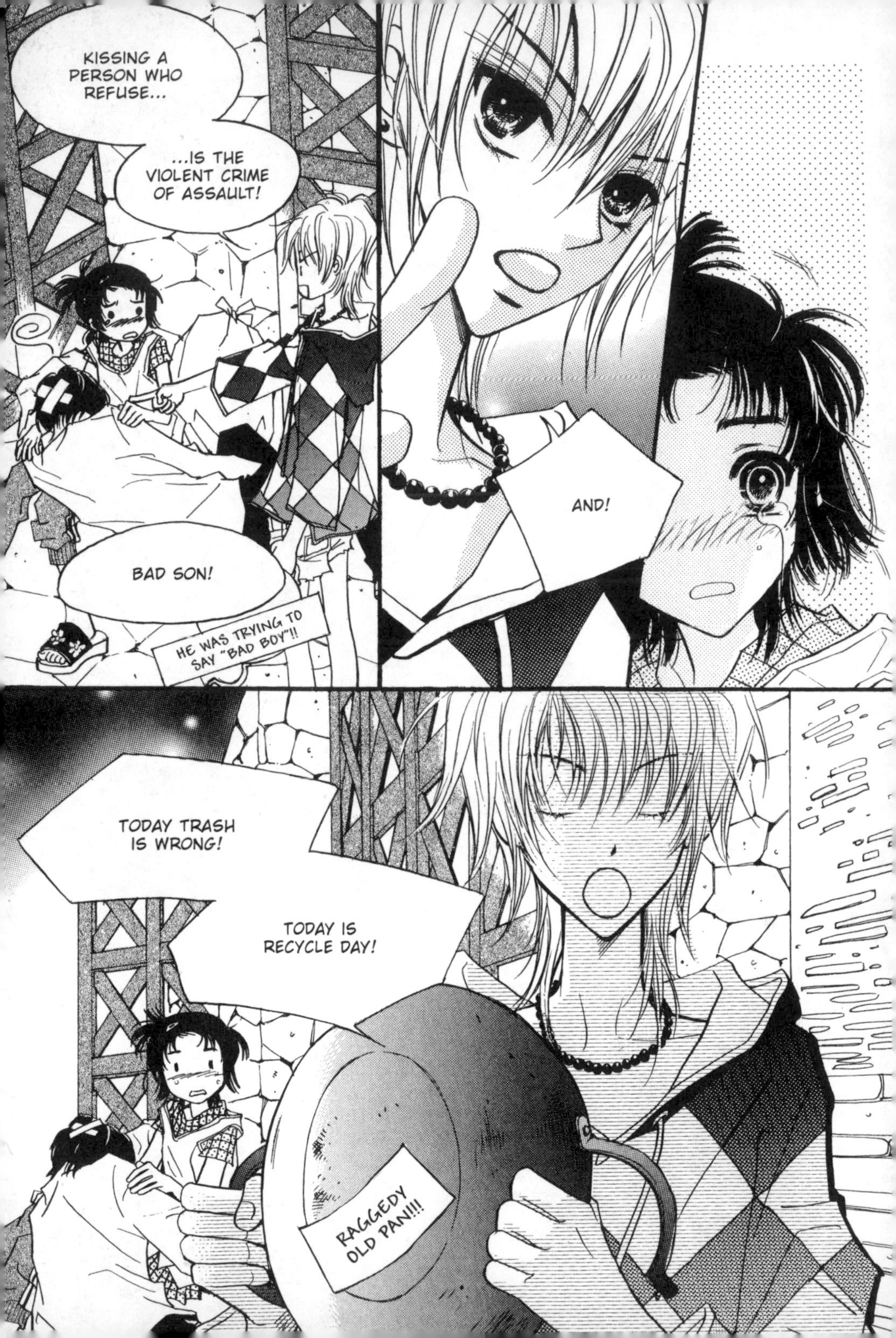
KISSING A PERSON WHO REFUSE...
...IS THE VIOLENT CRIME OF ASSAULT!
BAD SON!
HE WAS TRYING TO SAY "BAD BOY"!!
AND!
TODAY TRASH IS WRONG!
TODAY IS RECYCLE DAY!
RAGGEDY OLD PAN!!!

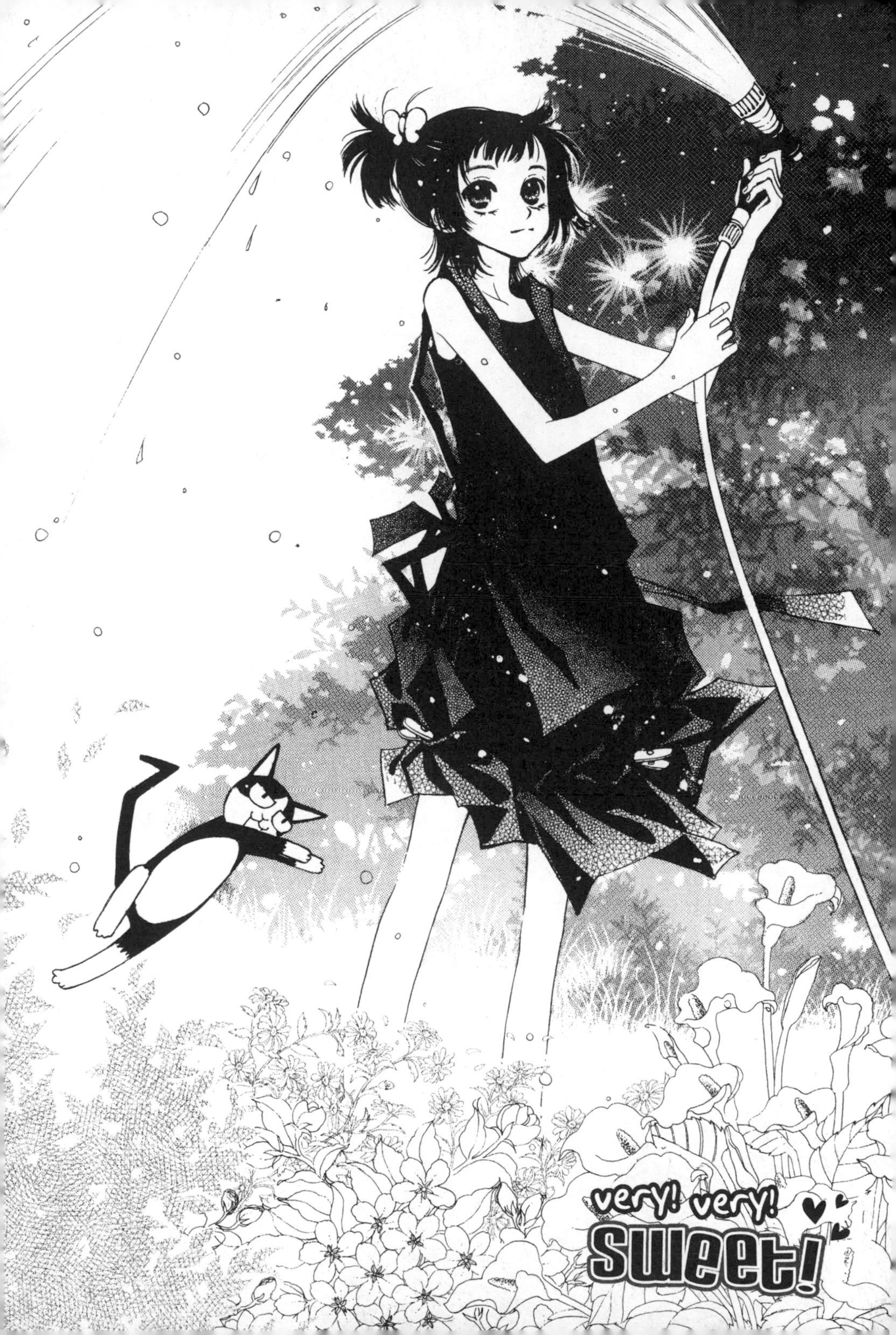
very! very! sweet!

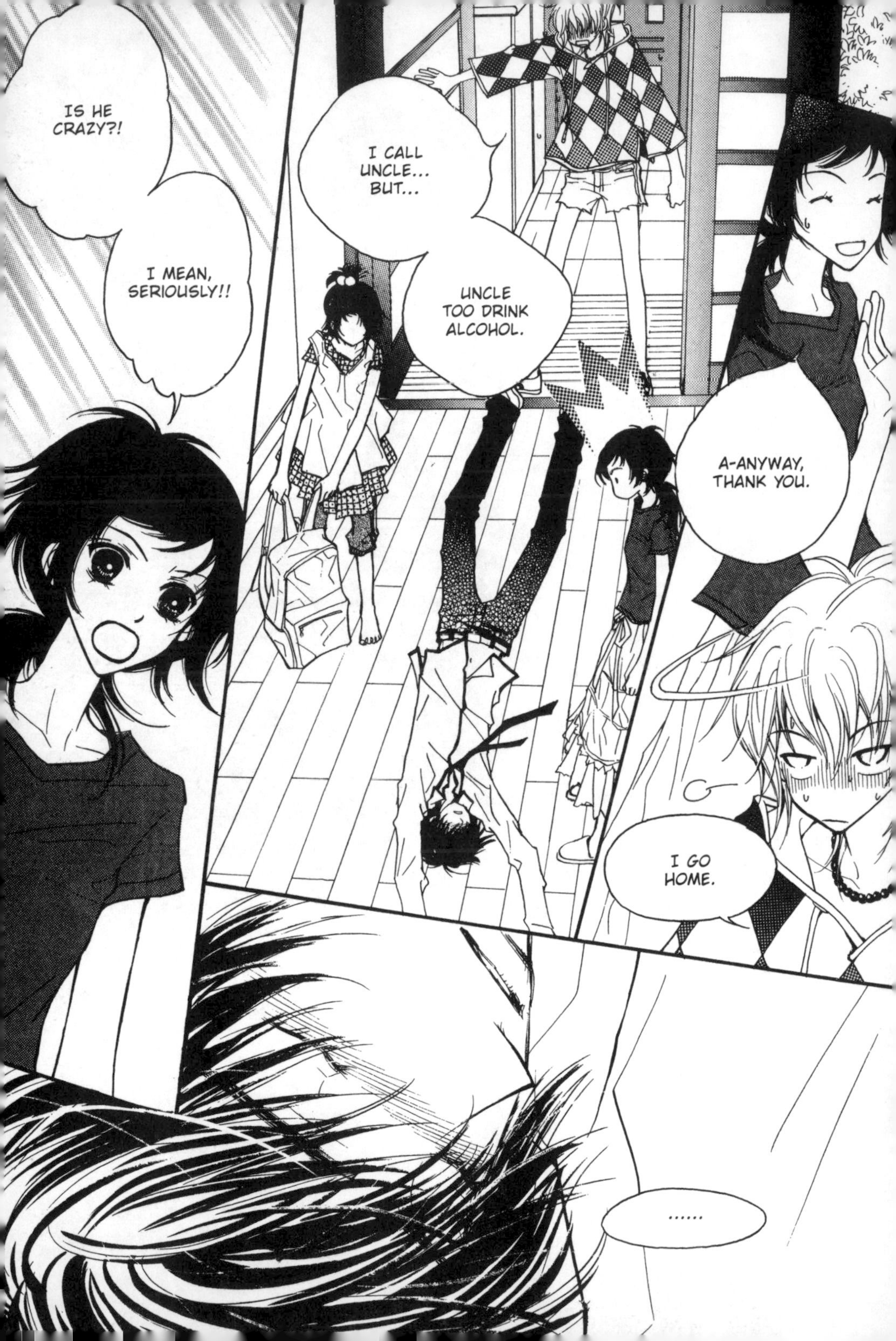
IS HE CRAZY?!
I MEAN, SERIOUSLY!!
I CALL UNCLE... BUT...
UNCLE TOO DRINK ALCOHOL.
A-ANYWAY, THANK YOU.
I GO HOME.
......

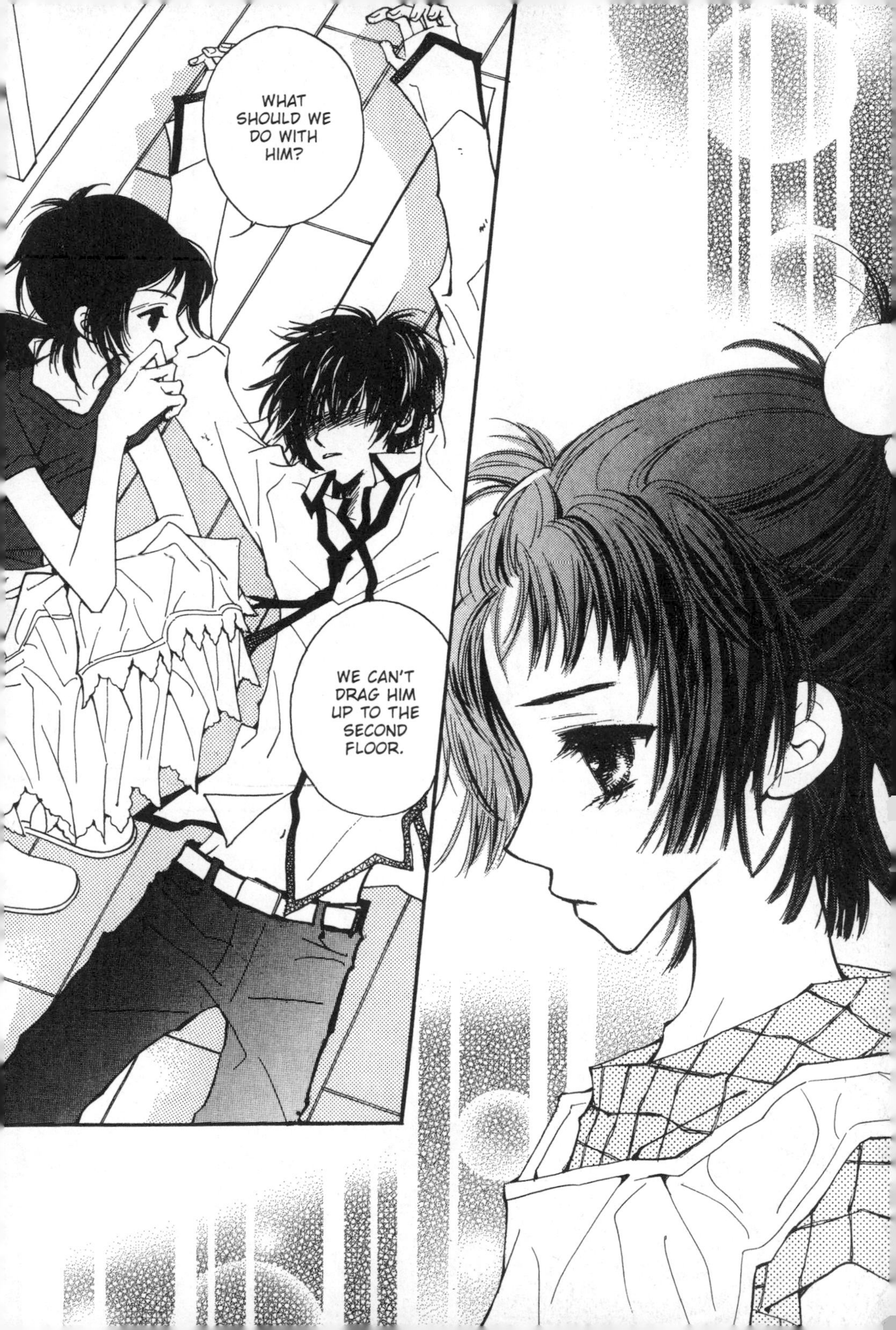
WHAT SHOULD WE DO WITH HIM?
WE CAN'T DRAG HIM UP TO THE SECOND FLOOR.

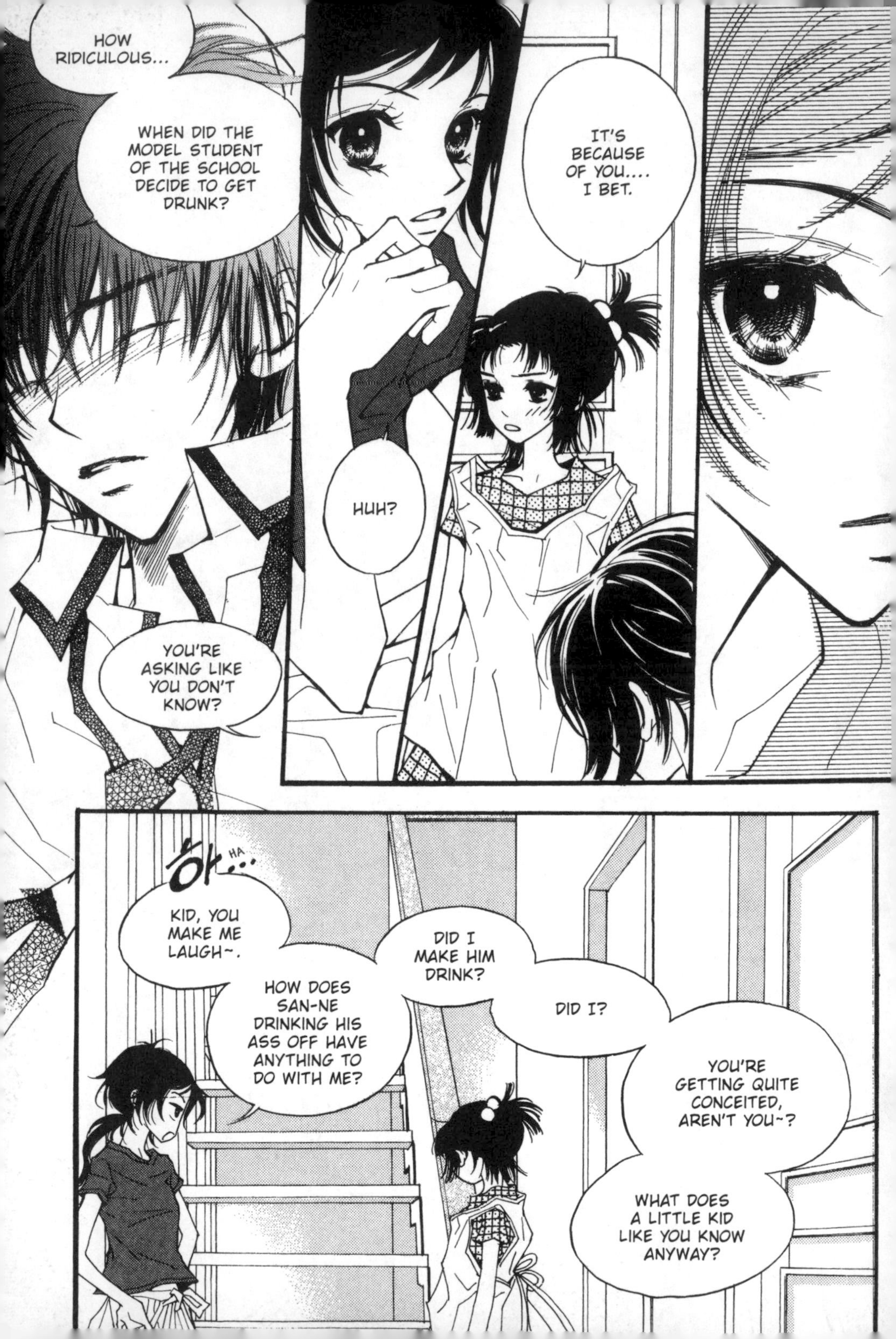
HOW RIDICULOUS...
WHEN DID THE MODEL STUDENT OF THE SCHOOL DECIDE TO GET DRUNK?
YOU'RE ASKING LIKE YOU DON'T KNOW?
HUH?
IT'S BECAUSE OF YOU.... I BET.
하 HA...
KID, YOU MAKE ME LAUGH~.
HOW DOES SAN-NE DRINKING HIS ASS OFF HAVE ANYTHING TO DO WITH ME?
DID I MAKE HIM DRINK?
DID I?
YOU'RE GETTING QUITE CONCEITED, AREN'T YOU~?
WHAT DOES A LITTLE KID LIKE YOU KNOW ANYWAY?

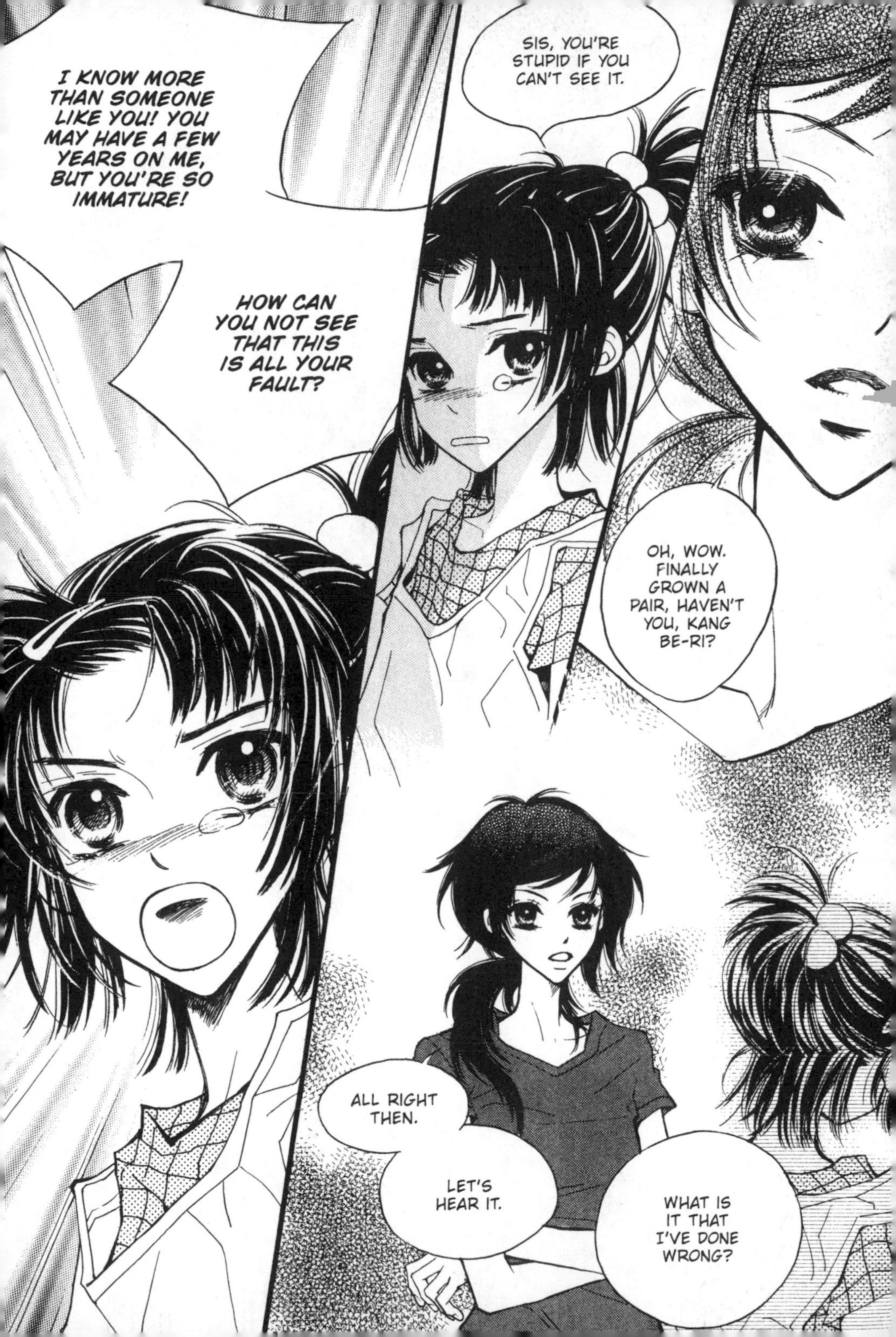
I KNOW MORE THAN SOMEONE LIKE YOU! YOU MAY HAVE A FEW YEARS ON ME, BUT YOU'RE SO IMMATURE!
HOW CAN YOU NOT SEE THAT THIS IS ALL YOUR FAULT?
SIS, YOU'RE STUPID IF YOU CAN'T SEE IT.
OH, WOW. FINALLY GROWN A PAIR, HAVEN'T YOU, KANG BE-RI?
ALL RIGHT THEN.
LET'S HEAR IT.
WHAT IS IT THAT I'VE DONE WRONG?

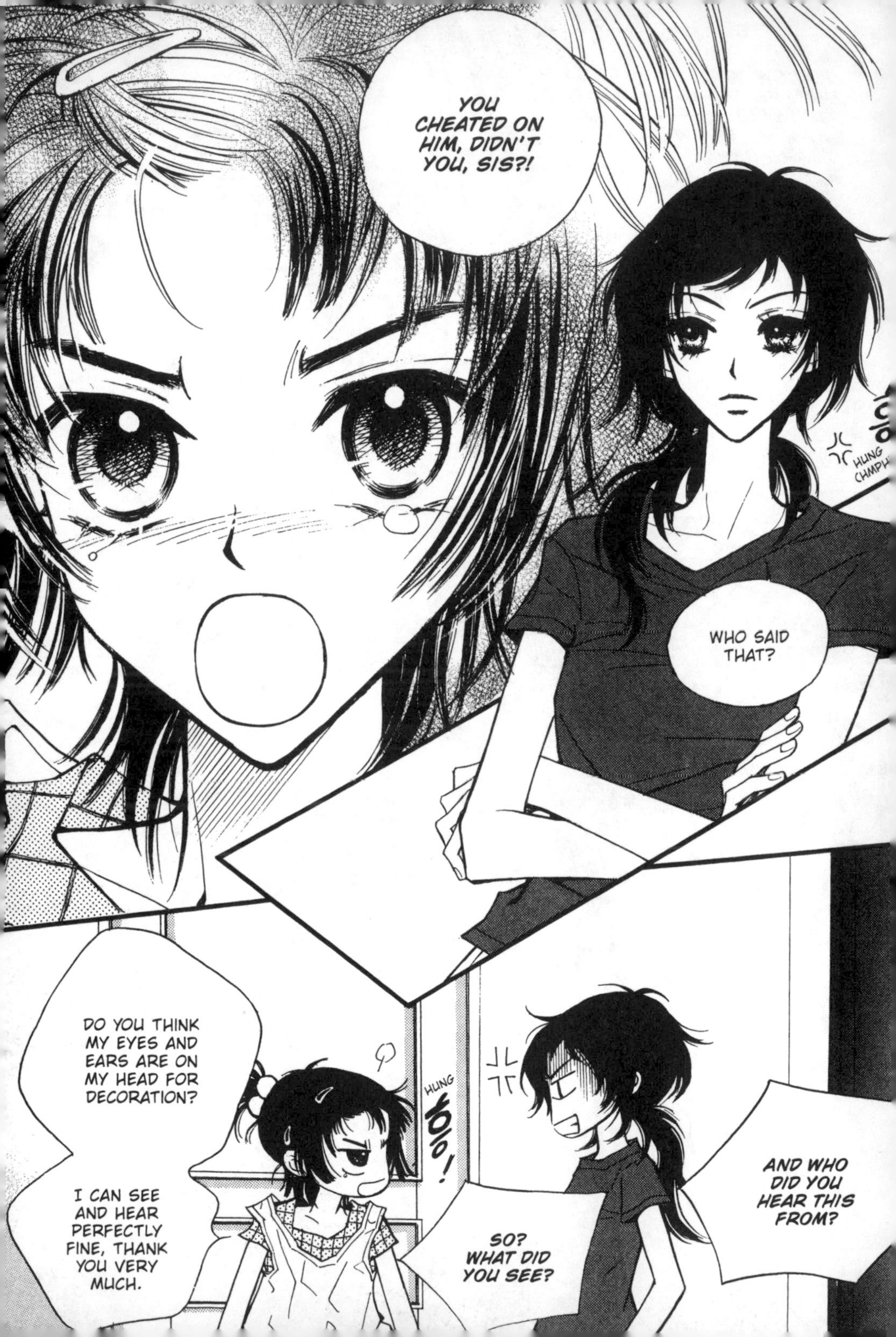
YOU CHEATED ON HIM, DIDN'T YOU, SIS?!
HUNG
CHMPH
WHO SAID THAT?
DO YOU THINK MY EYES AND EARS ARE ON MY HEAD FOR DECORATION?
I CAN SEE AND HEAR PERFECTLY FINE, THANK YOU VERY MUCH.
HUNG
SO? WHAT DID YOU SEE?
AND WHO DID YOU HEAR THIS FROM?

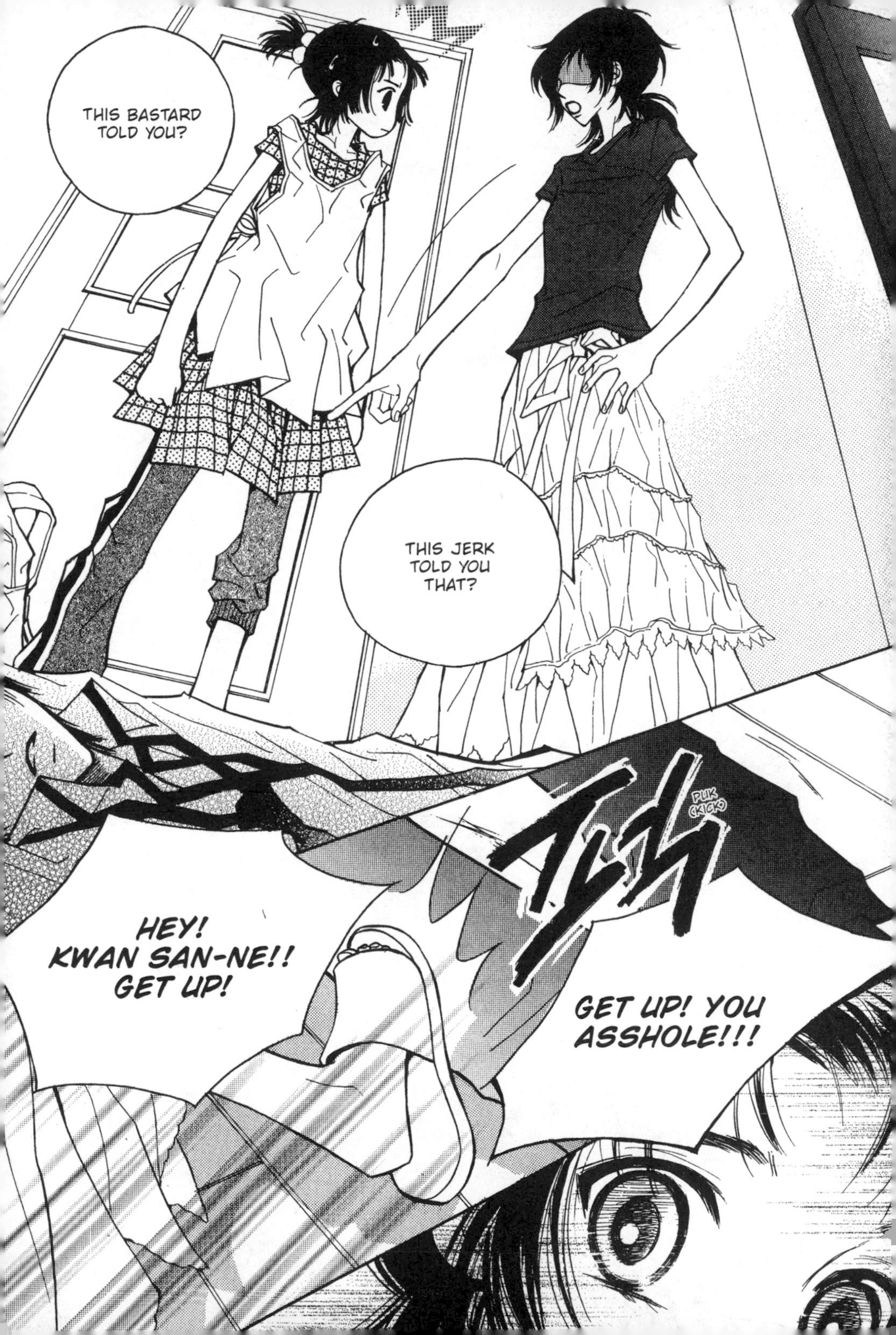
THIS BASTARD TOLD YOU?
THIS JERK TOLD YOU THAT?
PUK (KICK)
HEY! KWAN SAN-NE!! GET UP!
GET UP! YOU ASSHOLE!!!

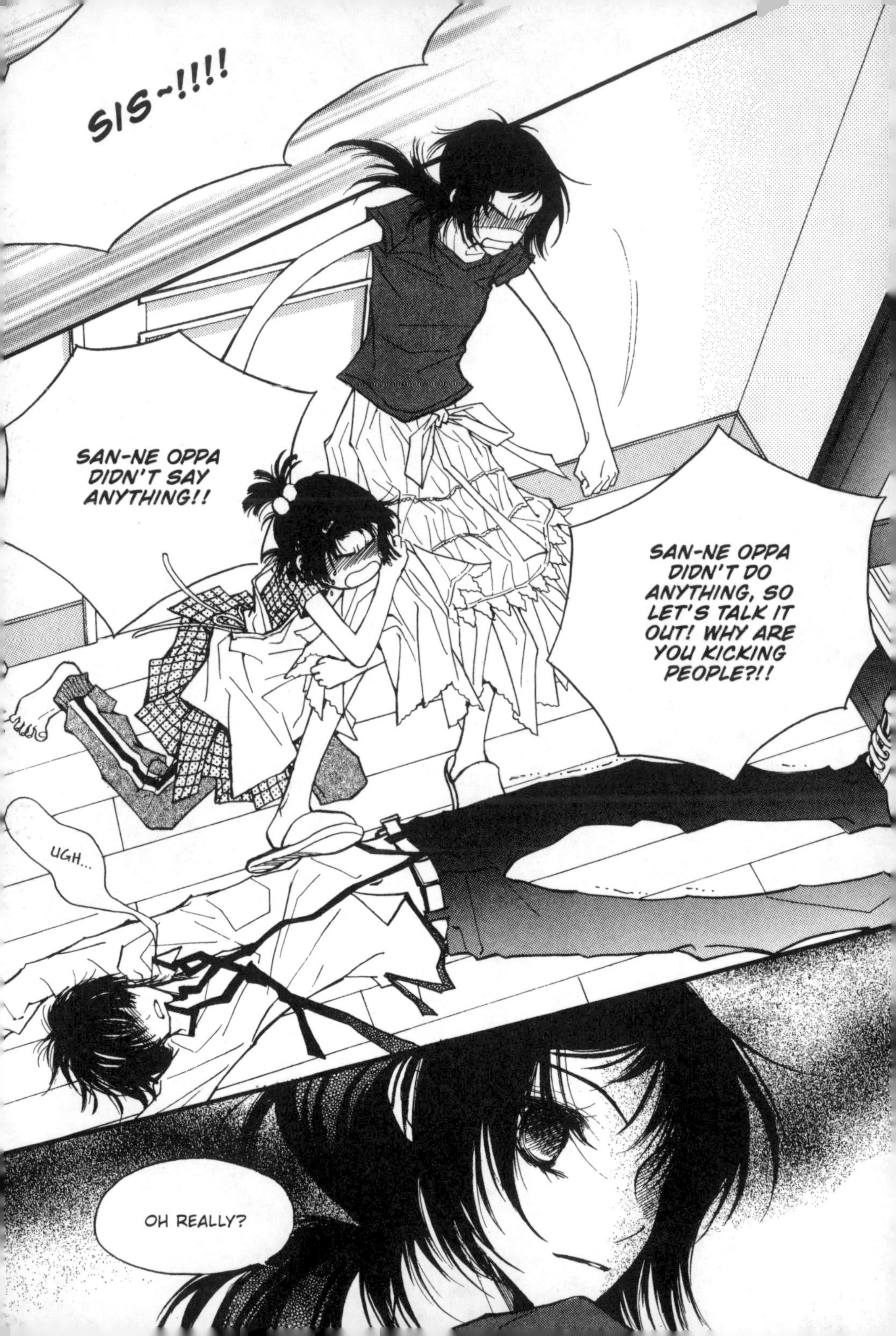
SIS~!!!!
SAN-NE OPPA DIDN'T SAY ANYTHING!!
SAN-NE OPPA DIDN'T DO ANYTHING, SO LET'S TALK IT OUT! WHY ARE YOU KICKING PEOPLE?!!
UGH...
OH REALLY?

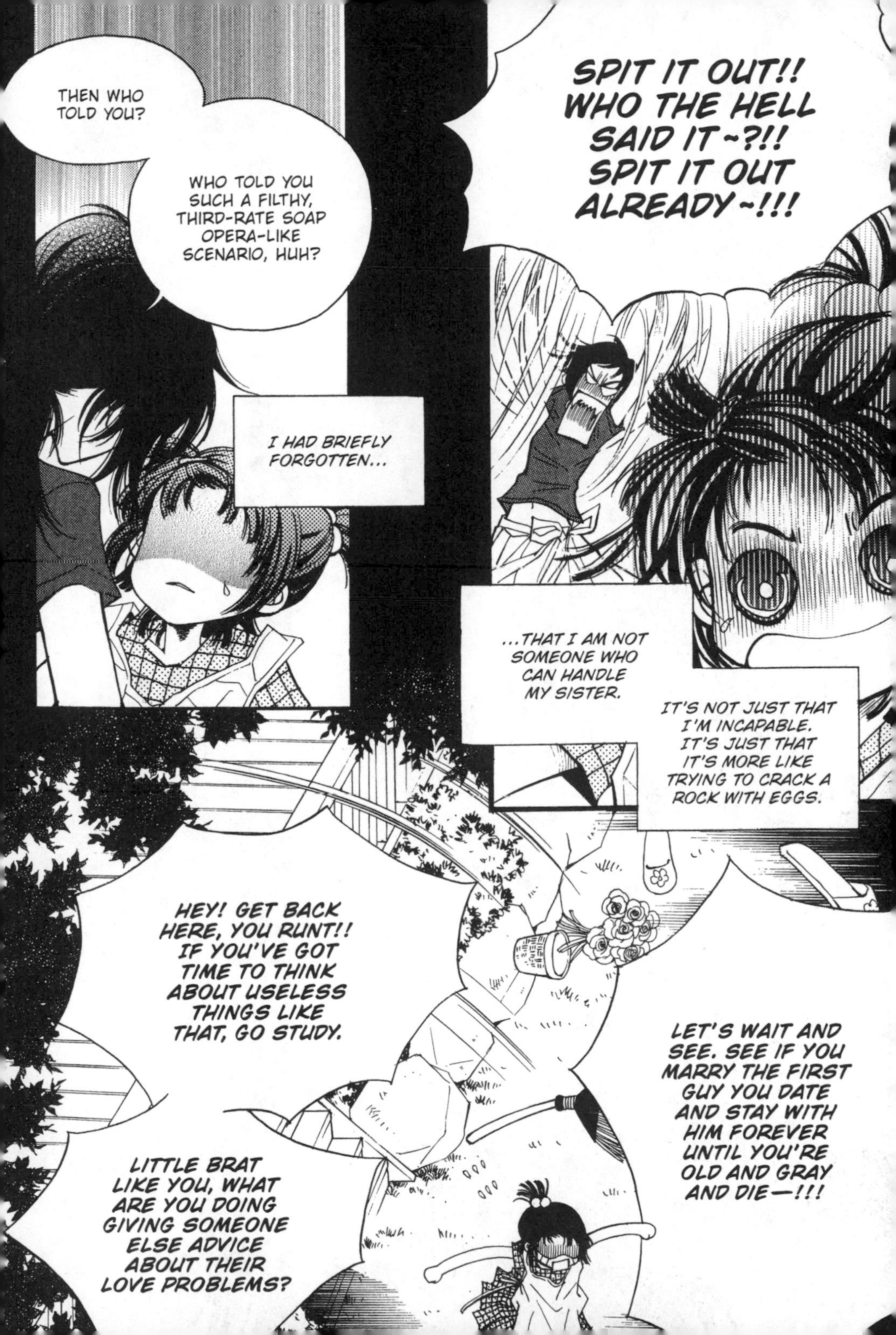
THEN WHO TOLD YOU?
WHO TOLD YOU SUCH A FILTHY, THIRD-RATE SOAP OPERA-LIKE SCENARIO, HUH?
I HAD BRIEFLY FORGOTTEN...
SPIT IT OUT!! WHO THE HELL SAID IT~?!! SPIT IT OUT ALREADY~!!!
...THAT I AM NOT SOMEONE WHO CAN HANDLE MY SISTER.
IT'S NOT JUST THAT I'M INCAPABLE. IT'S JUST THAT IT'S MORE LIKE TRYING TO CRACK A ROCK WITH EGGS.
HEY! GET BACK HERE, YOU RUNT!! IF YOU'VE GOT TIME TO THINK ABOUT USELESS THINGS LIKE THAT, GO STUDY.
LITTLE BRAT LIKE YOU, WHAT ARE YOU DOING GIVING SOMEONE ELSE ADVICE ABOUT THEIR LOVE PROBLEMS?
LET'S WAIT AND SEE. SEE IF YOU MARRY THE FIRST GUY YOU DATE AND STAY WITH HIM FOREVER UNTIL YOU'RE OLD AND GRAY AND DIE—!!!

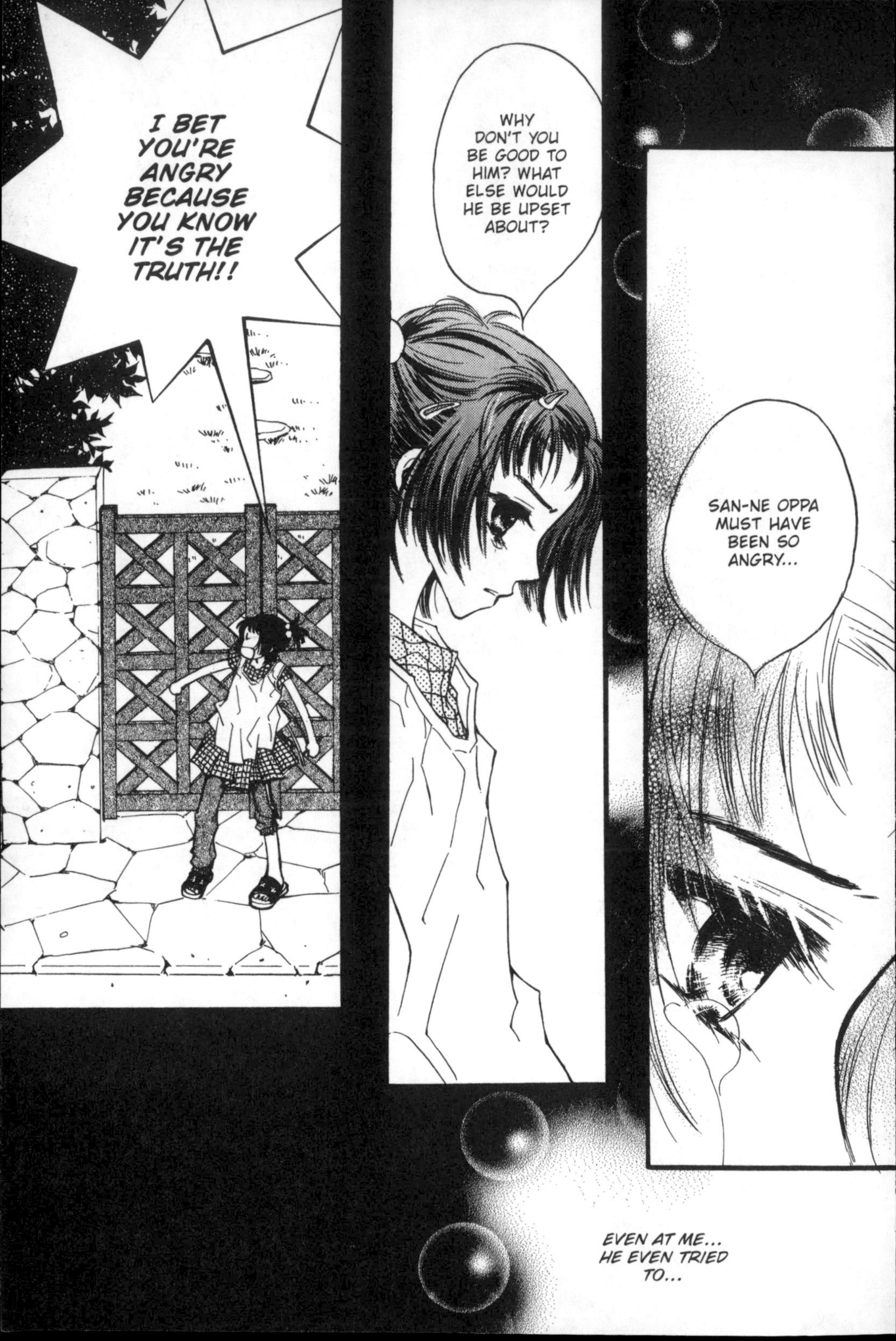
I BET YOU'RE ANGRY BECAUSE YOU KNOW IT'S THE TRUTH!!
WHY DON'T YOU BE GOOD TO HIM? WHAT ELSE WOULD HE BE UPSET ABOUT?
SAN-NE OPPA MUST HAVE BEEN SO ANGRY...
EVEN AT ME... HE EVEN TRIED TO...

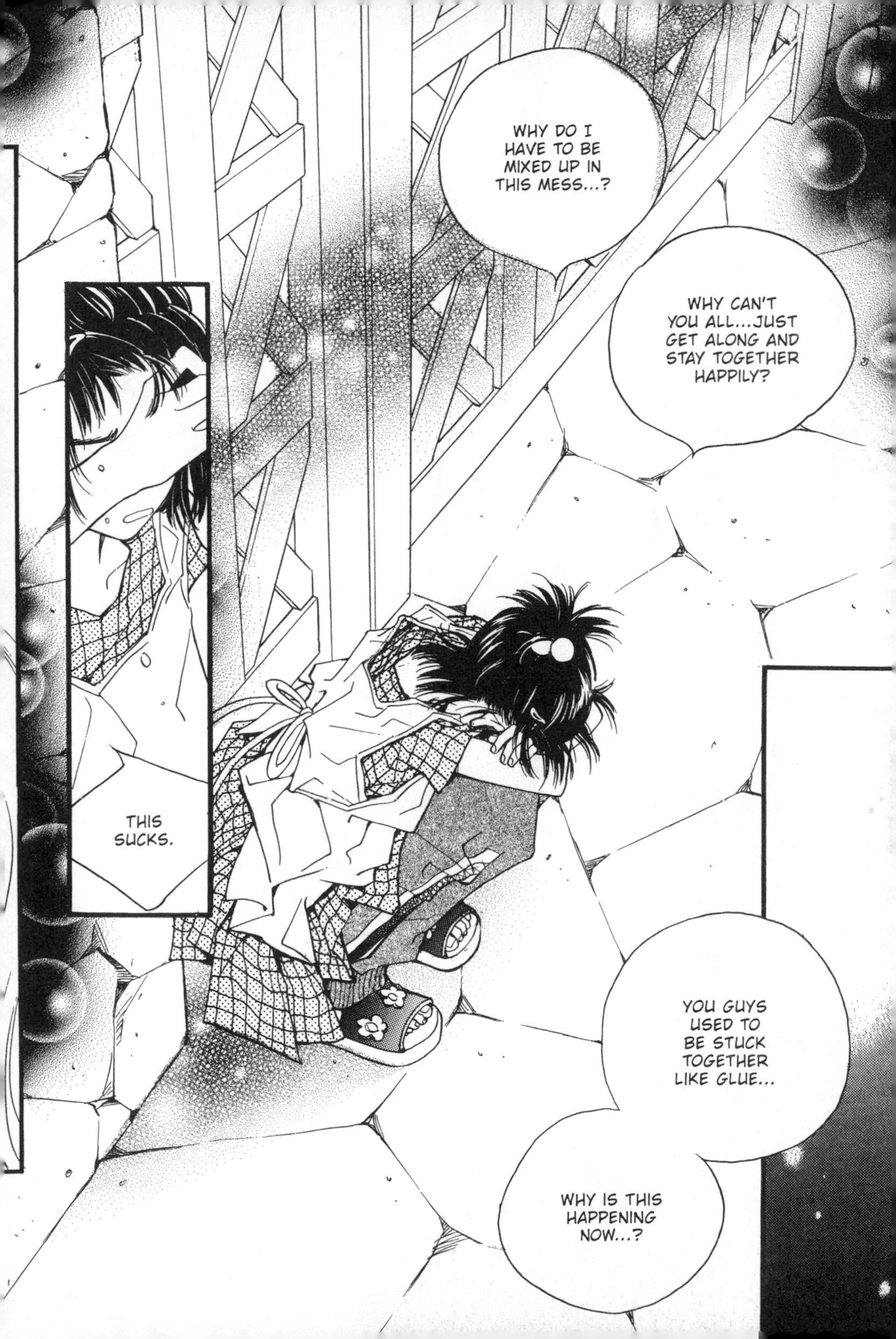
WHY DO I HAVE TO BE MIXED UP IN THIS MESS...?
WHY CAN'T YOU ALL...JUST GET ALONG AND STAY TOGETHER HAPPILY?
THIS SUCKS.
YOU GUYS USED TO BE STUCK TOGETHER LIKE GLUE...
WHY IS THIS HAPPENING NOW...?

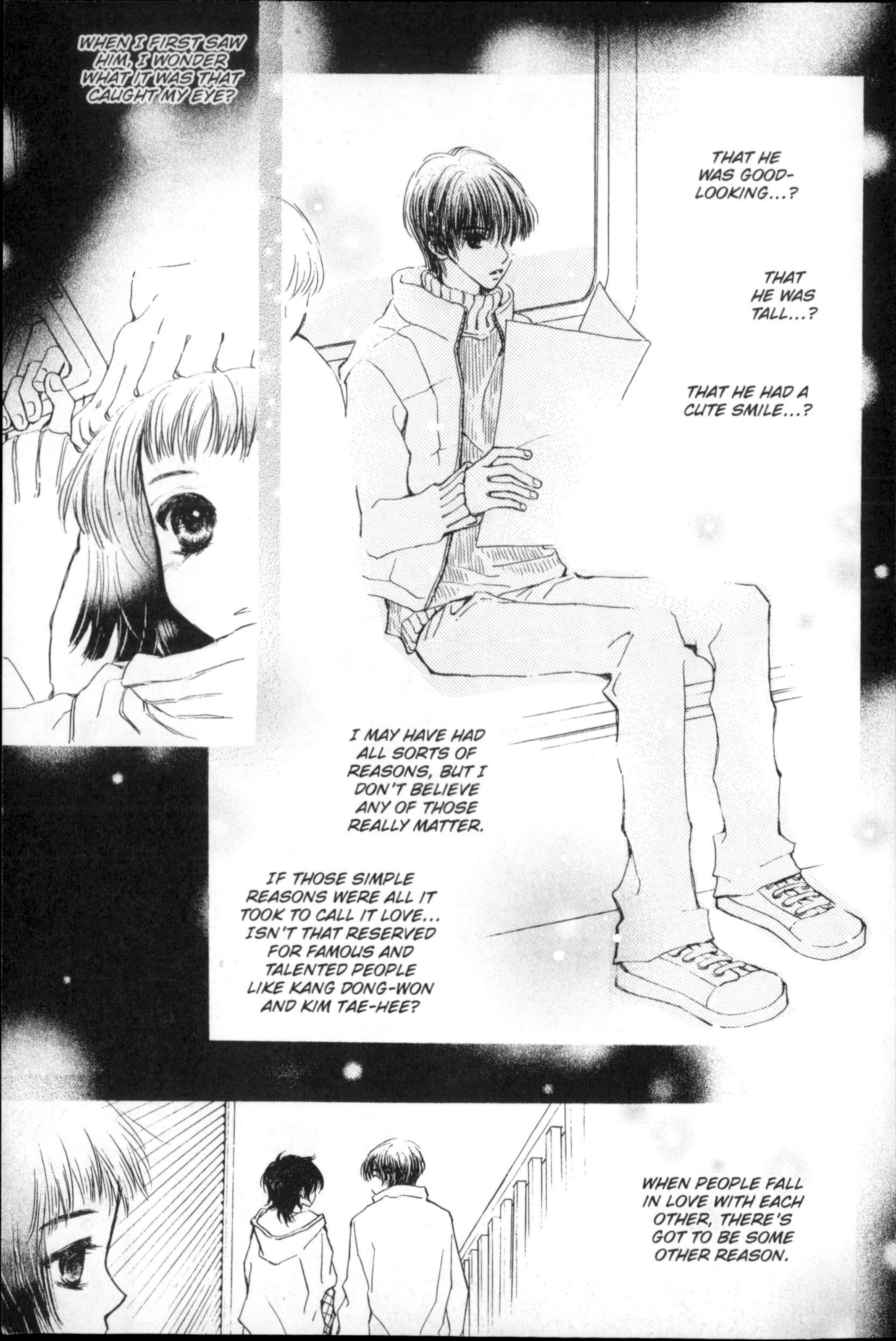
WHEN I FIRST SAW HIM, I WONDER WHAT IT WAS THAT CAUGHT MY EYE?
THAT HE WAS GOOD-LOOKING...?
THAT HE WAS TALL...?
THAT HE HAD A CUTE SMILE...?
I MAY HAVE HAD ALL SORTS OF REASONS, BUT I DON'T BELIEVE ANY OF THOSE REALLY MATTER.
IF THOSE SIMPLE REASONS WERE ALL IT TOOK TO CALL IT LOVE... ISN'T THAT RESERVED FOR FAMOUS AND TALENTED PEOPLE LIKE KANG DONG-WON AND KIM TAE-HEE?
WHEN PEOPLE FALL IN LOVE WITH EACH OTHER, THERE'S GOT TO BE SOME OTHER REASON.

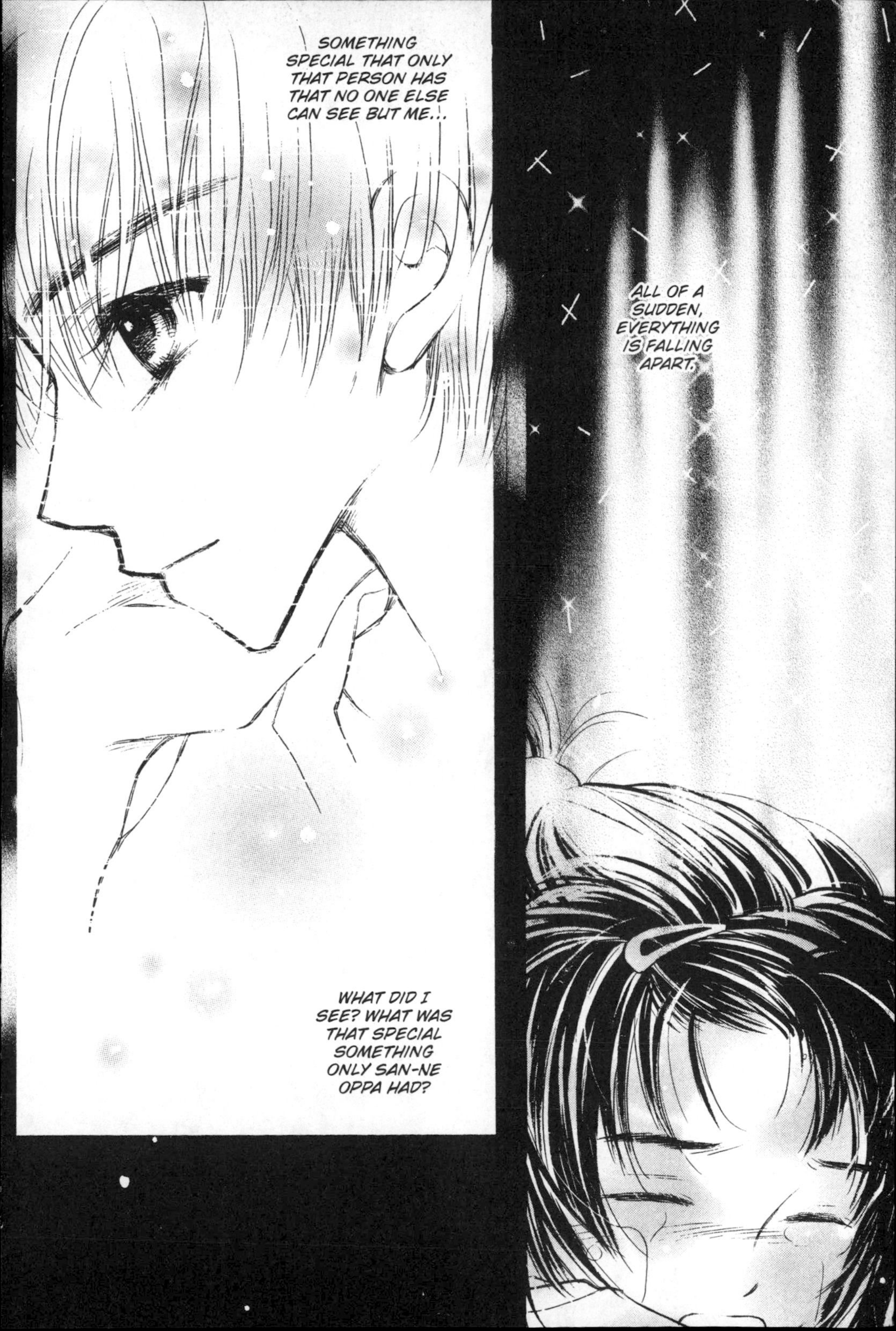
SOMETHING SPECIAL THAT ONLY THAT PERSON HAS THAT NO ONE ELSE CAN SEE BUT ME...
WHAT DID I SEE? WHAT WAS THAT SPECIAL SOMETHING ONLY SAN-NE OPPA HAD?
ALL OF A SUDDEN, EVERYTHING IS FALLING APART.

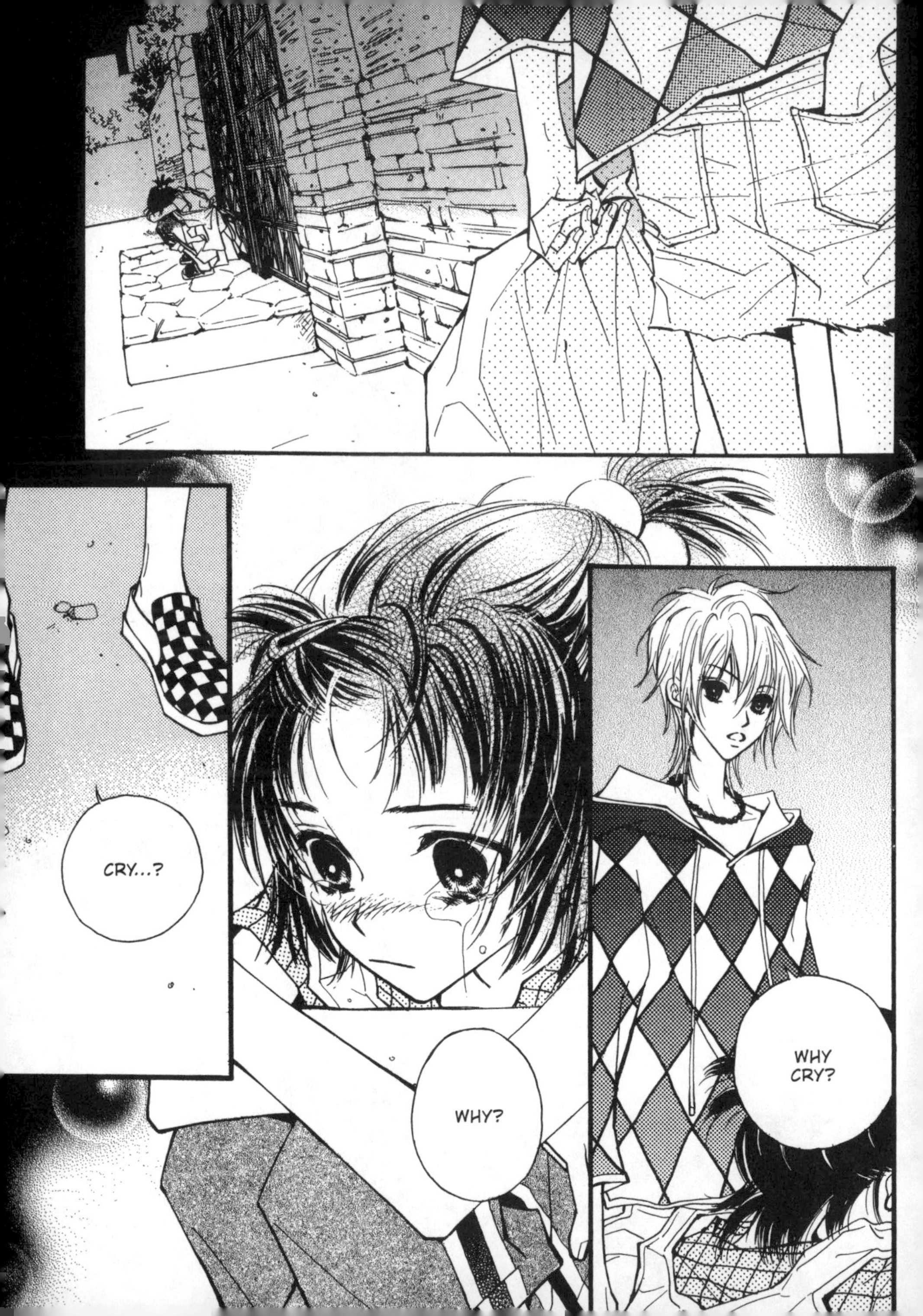
CRY...?
WHY?
WHY CRY?

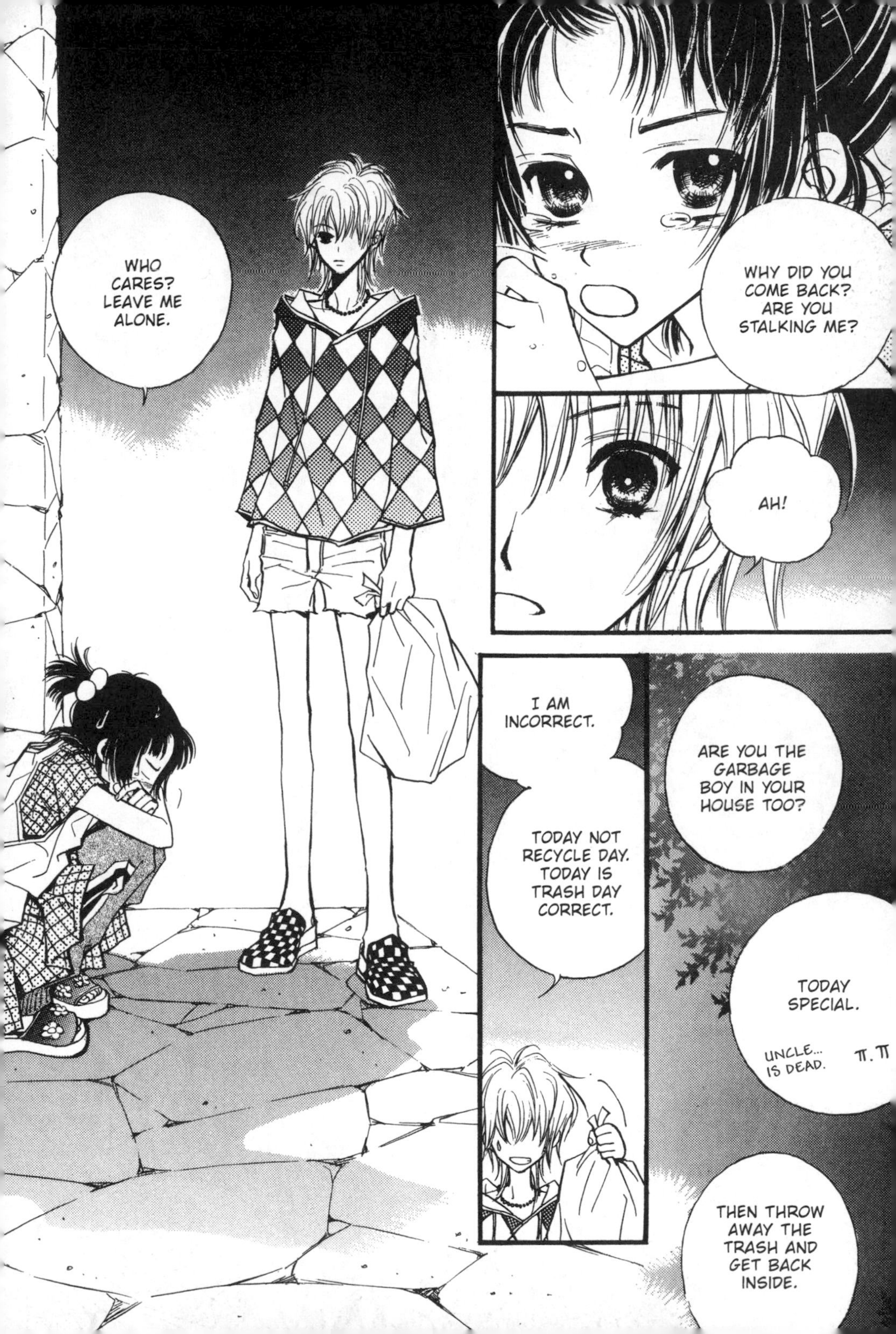
WHO CARES? LEAVE ME ALONE.
WHY DID YOU COME BACK? ARE YOU STALKING ME?
AH!
I AM INCORRECT.
ARE YOU THE GARBAGE BOY IN YOUR HOUSE TOO?
TODAY NOT RECYCLE DAY. TODAY IS TRASH DAY CORRECT.
TODAY SPECIAL.
UNCLE... IS DEAD.
π.π
THEN THROW AWAY THE TRASH AND GET BACK INSIDE.

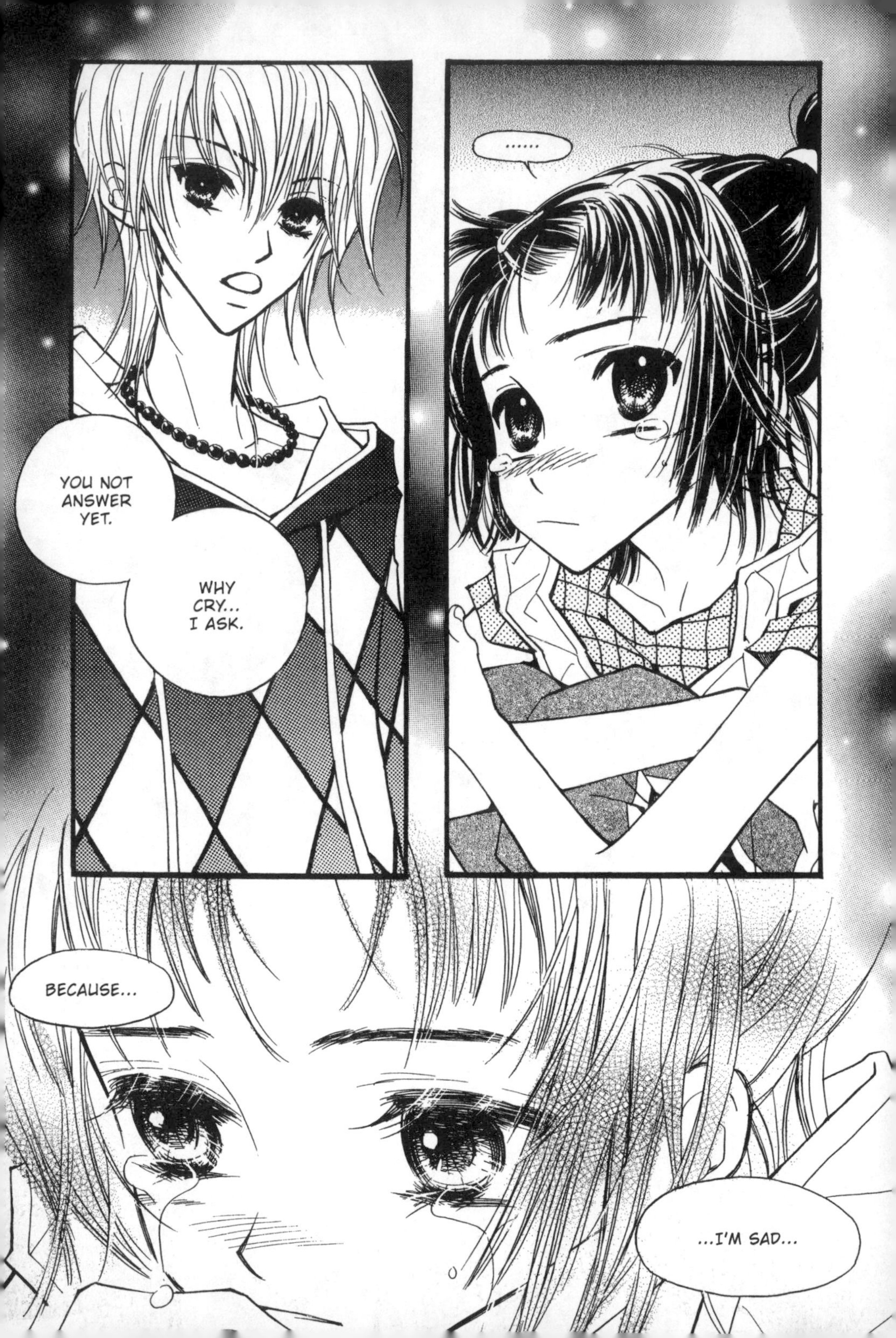
YOU NOT ANSWER YET.
WHY CRY... I ASK.
......
BECAUSE...
...I'M SAD...

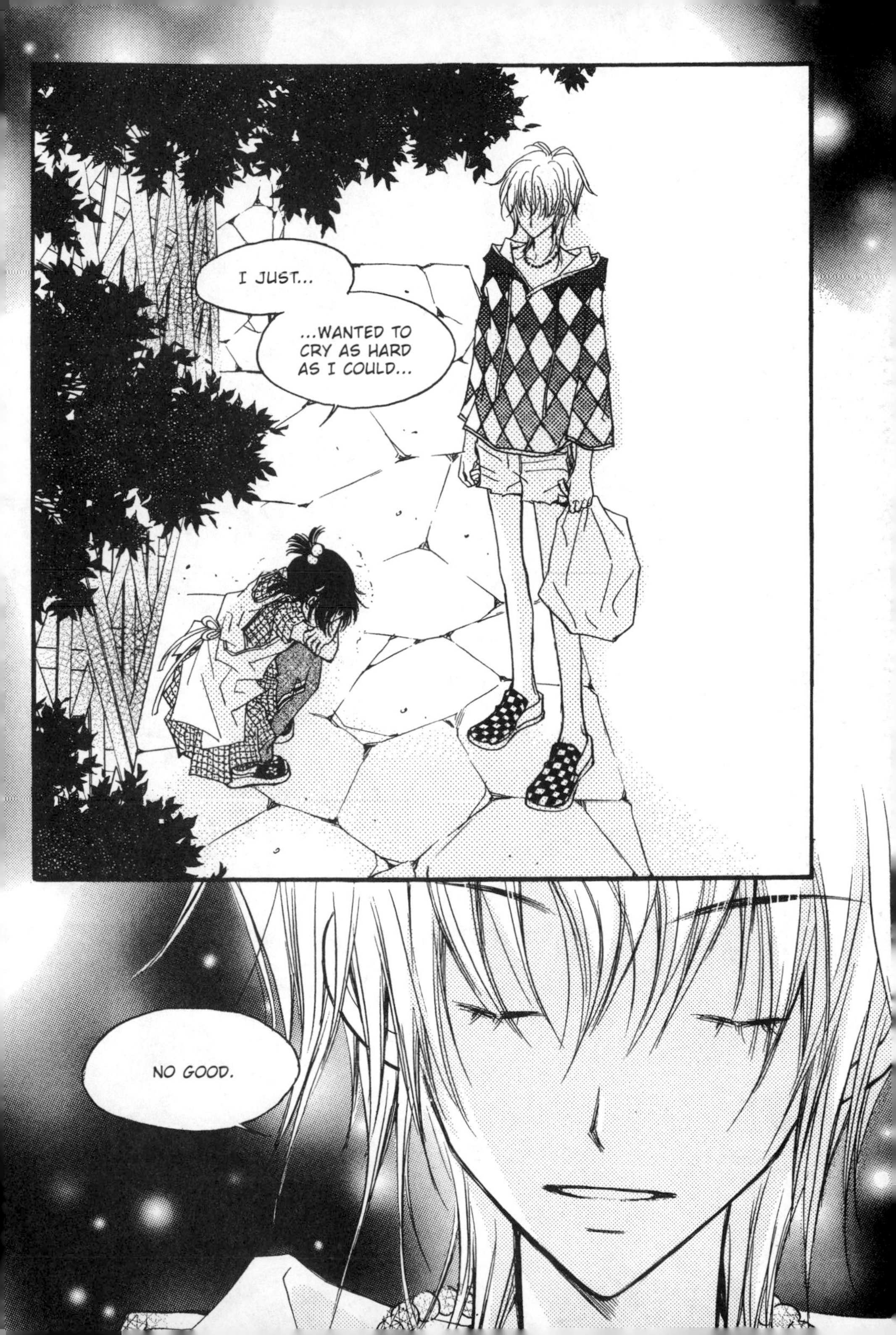
I JUST...
...WANTED TO CRY AS HARD AS I COULD...
NO GOOD.

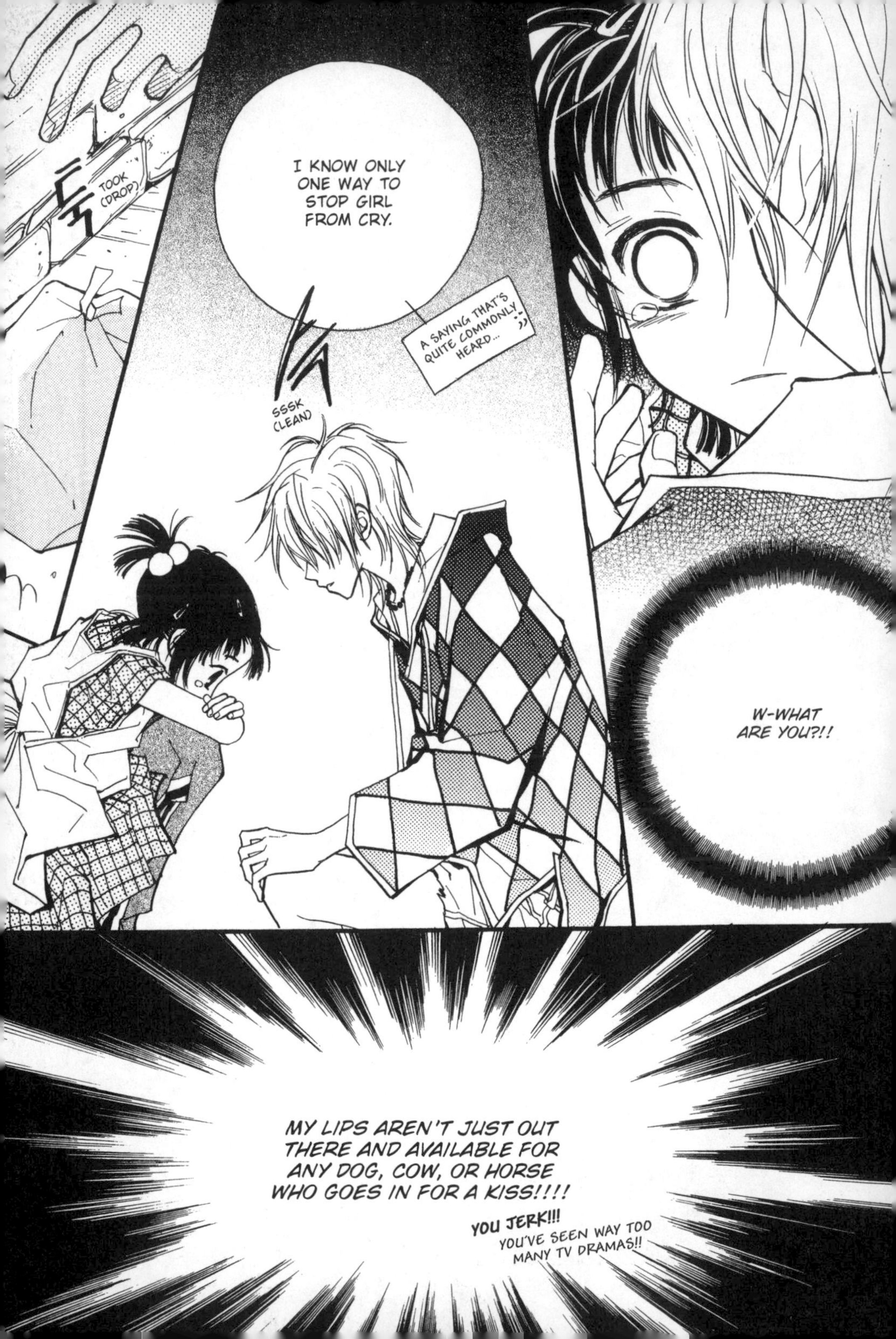
TOOK (DROP)
I KNOW ONLY ONE WAY TO STOP GIRL FROM CRY.
A SAYING THAT'S QUITE COMMONLY HEARD...
SSSK (LEAN)
W-WHAT ARE YOU?!!
MY LIPS AREN'T JUST OUT THERE AND AVAILABLE FOR ANY DOG, COW, OR HORSE WHO GOES IN FOR A KISS!!!!
YOU JERK!!!
YOU'VE SEEN WAY TOO MANY TV DRAMAS!!

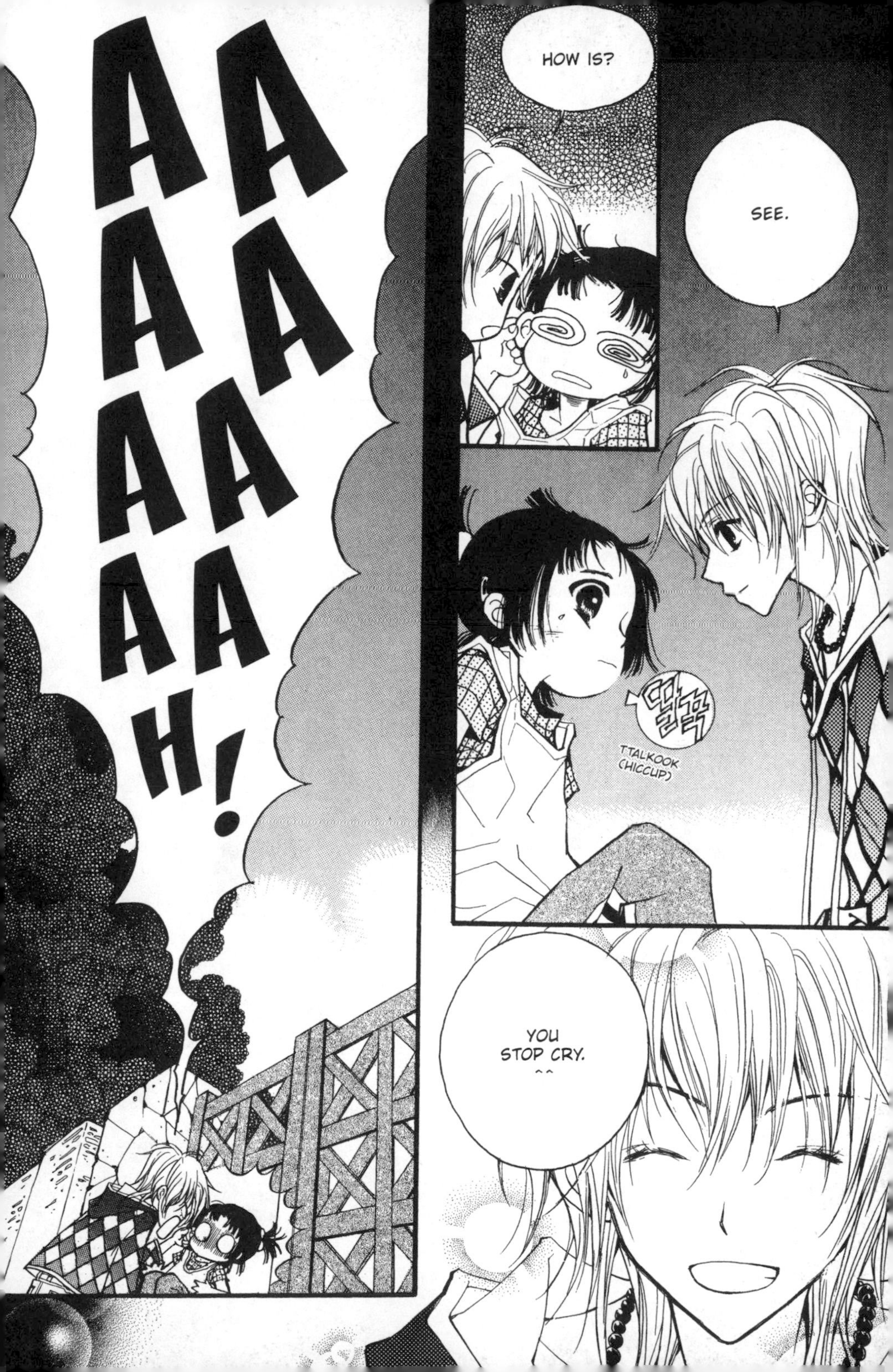
AAAAAAAAAAH!
HOW IS?
SEE.
TTALKOOK (HICCUP)
YOU STOP CRY. ^^

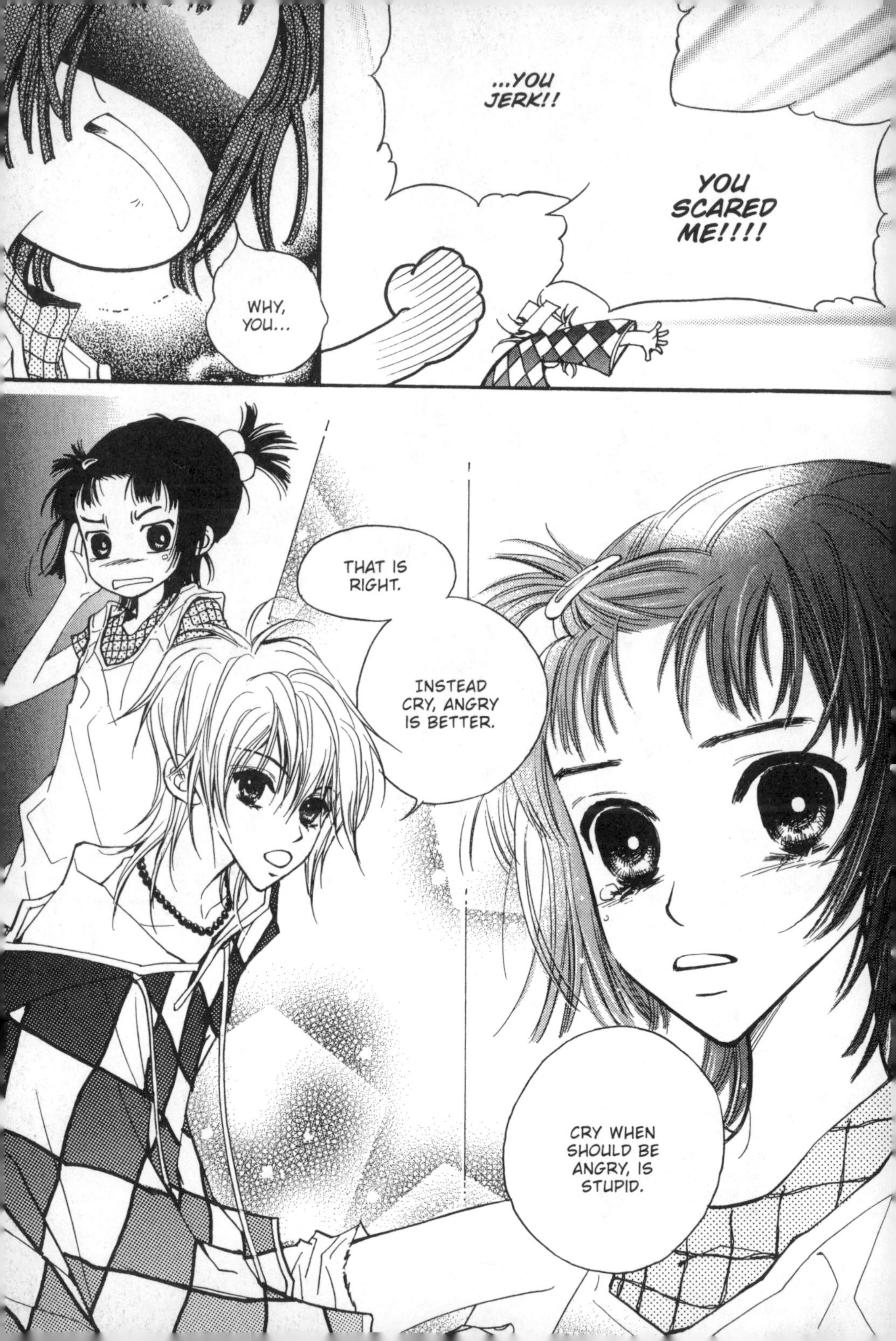
WHY, YOU...
...YOU JERK!!
YOU SCARED ME!!!!
THAT IS RIGHT.
INSTEAD CRY, ANGRY IS BETTER.
CRY WHEN SHOULD BE ANGRY, IS STUPID.

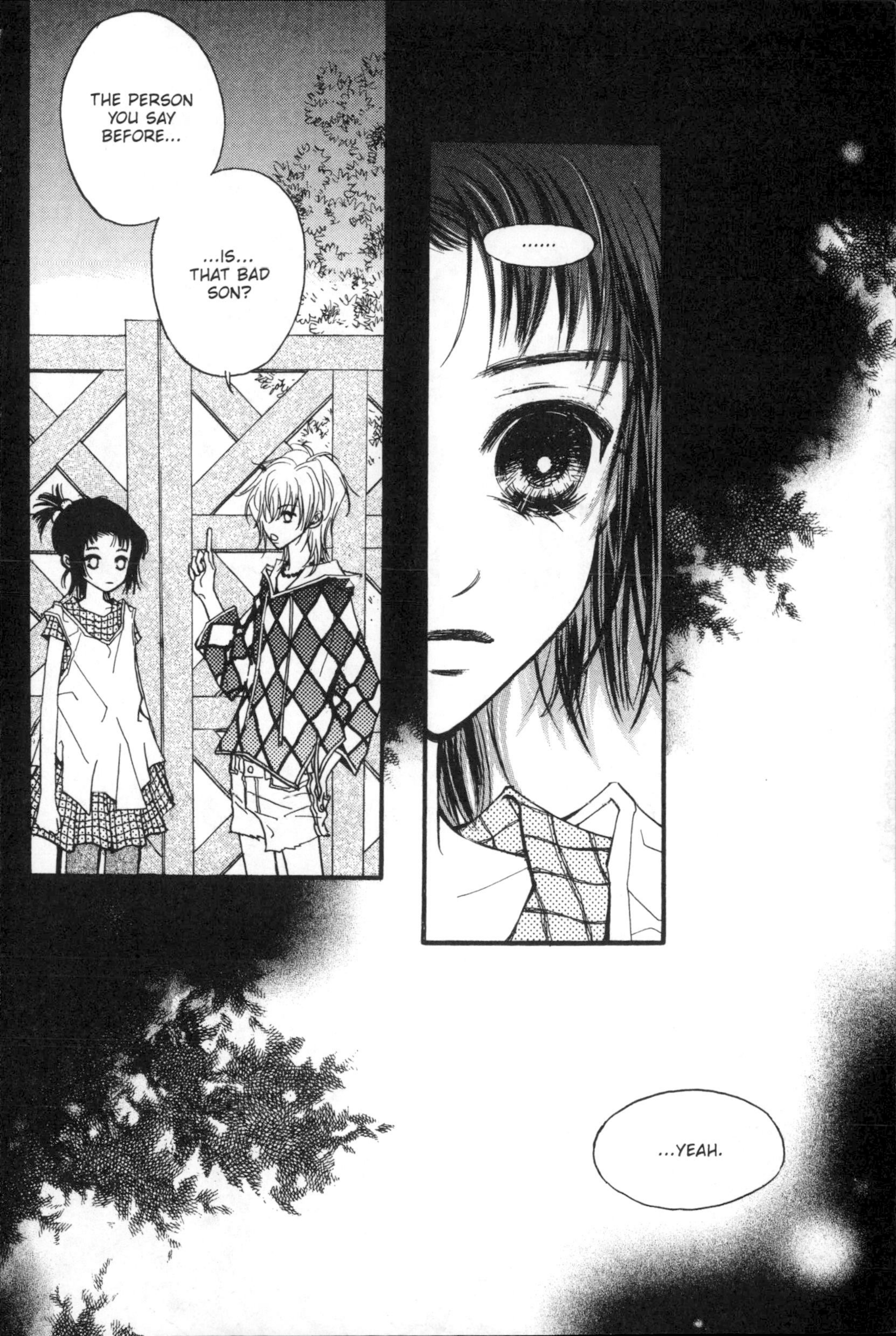
THE PERSON YOU SAY BEFORE...
...IS... THAT BAD SON?
......
...YEAH.

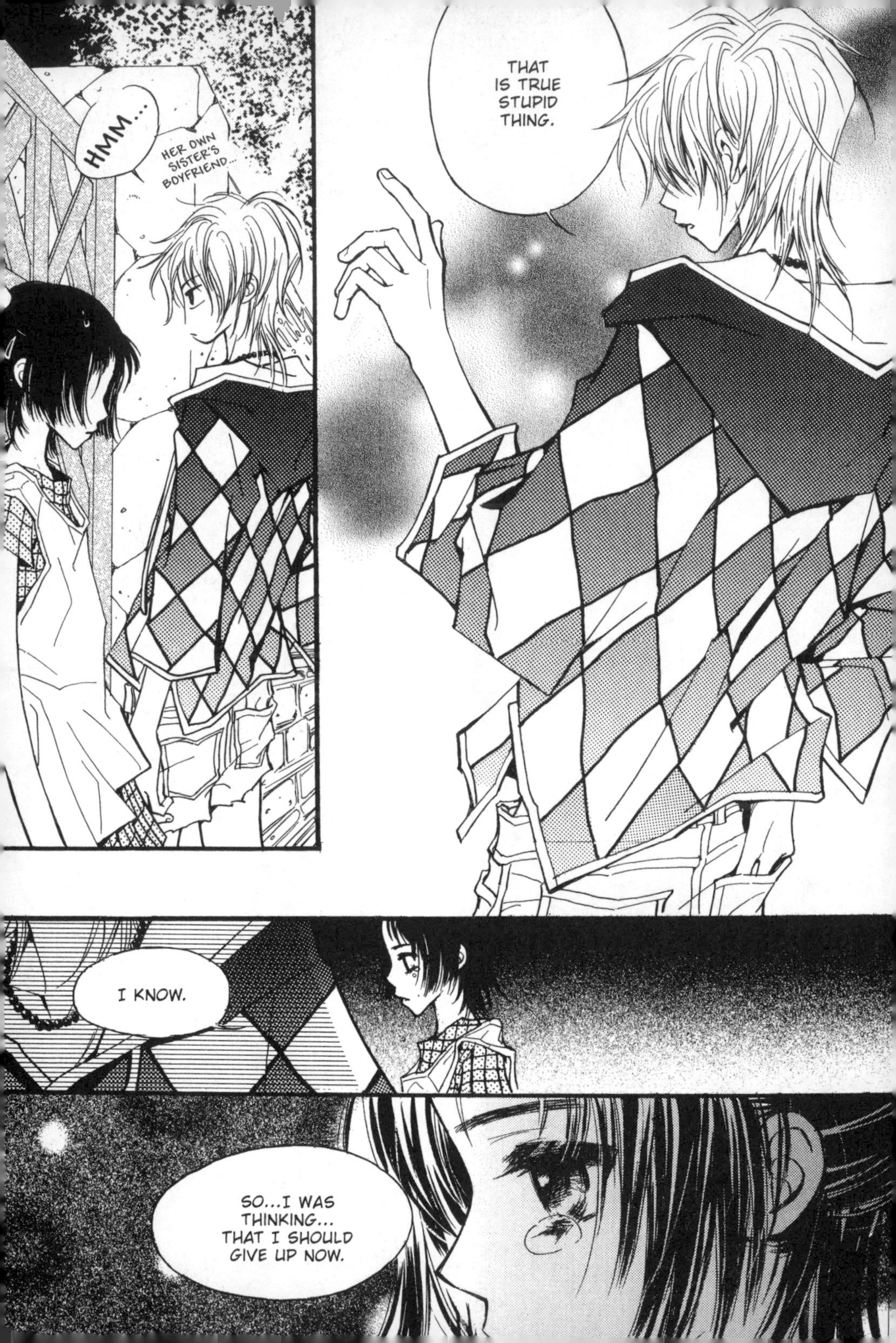

HMM...
HER OWN SISTER'S BOYFRIEND...
THAT IS TRUE STUPID THING.
I KNOW.
SO...I WAS THINKING... THAT I SHOULD GIVE UP NOW.

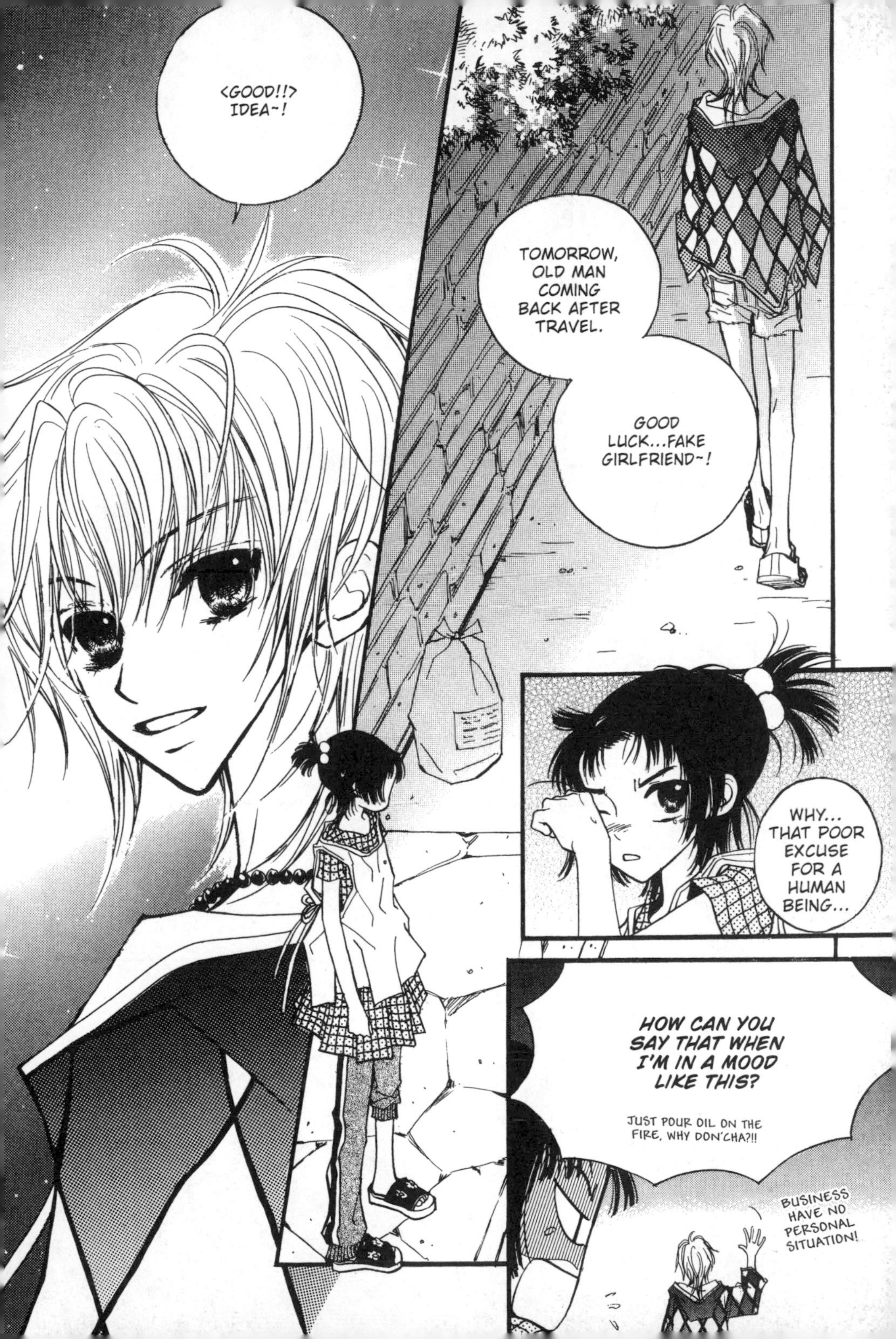
<GOOD!!> IDEA~!
TOMORROW, OLD MAN COMING BACK AFTER TRAVEL.
GOOD LUCK...FAKE GIRLFRIEND~!
WHY... THAT POOR EXCUSE FOR A HUMAN BEING...
HOW CAN YOU SAY THAT WHEN I'M IN A MOOD LIKE THIS?
JUST POUR OIL ON THE FIRE, WHY DON'CHA?!!
BUSINESS HAVE NO PERSONAL SITUATION!

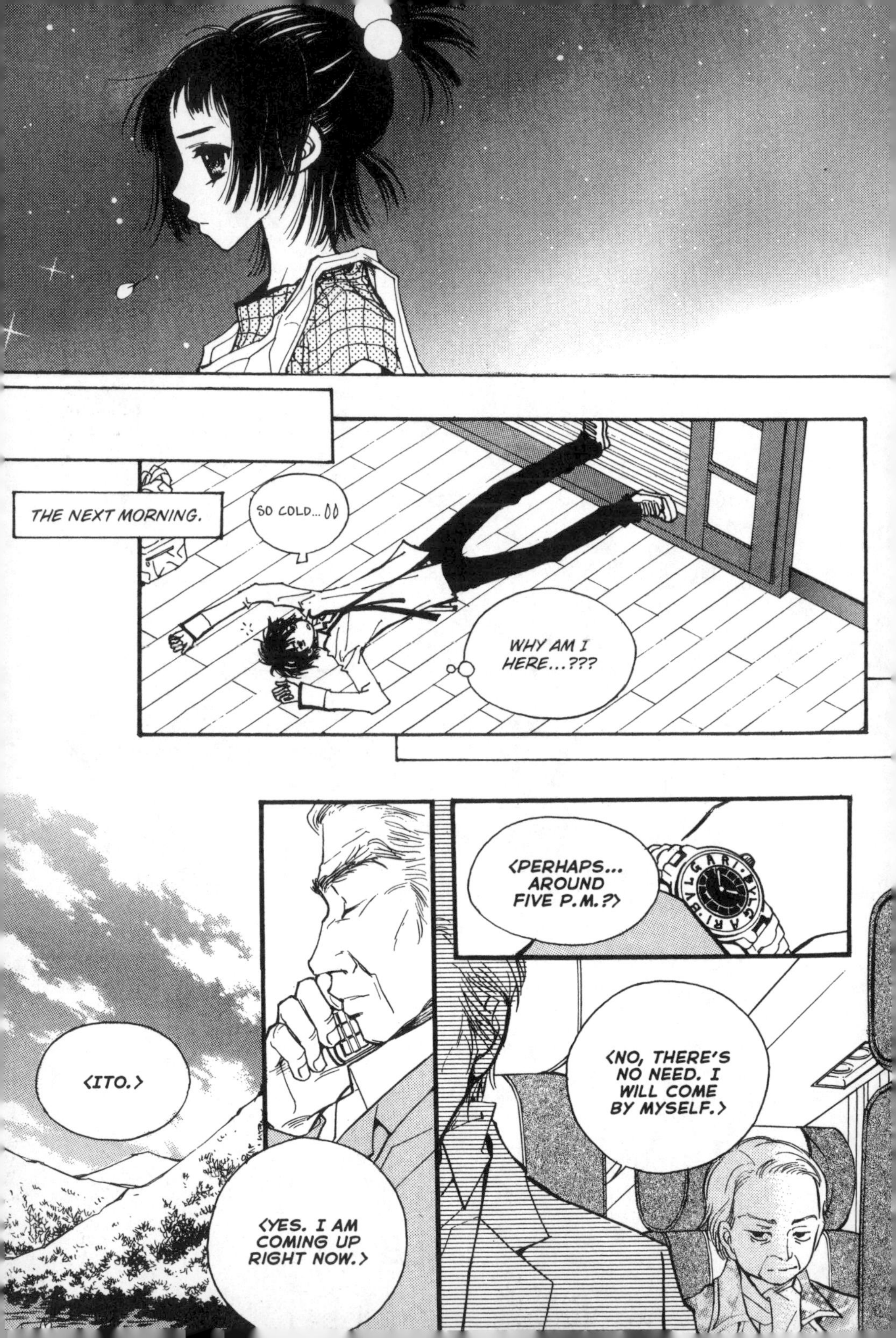
THE NEXT MORNING.
SO COLD...
WHY AM I HERE...???
<ITO.>
<YES. I AM COMING UP RIGHT NOW.>
<PERHAPS... AROUND FIVE P.M.?>
<NO, THERE'S NO NEED. I WILL COME BY MYSELF.>

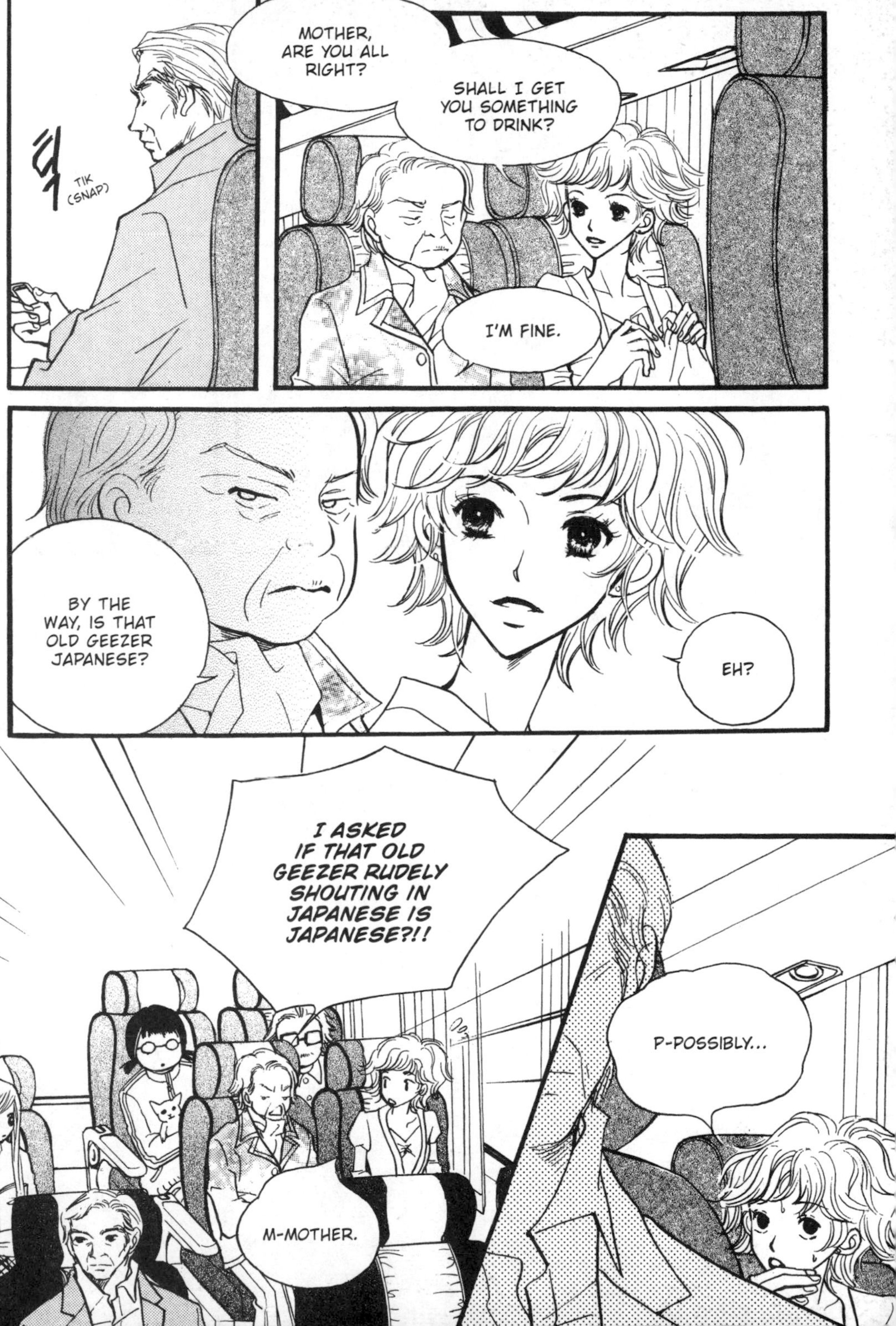
MOTHER, ARE YOU ALL RIGHT?
SHALL I GET YOU SOMETHING TO DRINK?
TIK (SNAP)
I'M FINE.
BY THE WAY, IS THAT OLD GEEZER JAPANESE?
EH?
I ASKED IF THAT OLD GEEZER RUDELY SHOUTING IN JAPANESE IS JAPANESE?!!
P-POSSIBLY...
M-MOTHER.

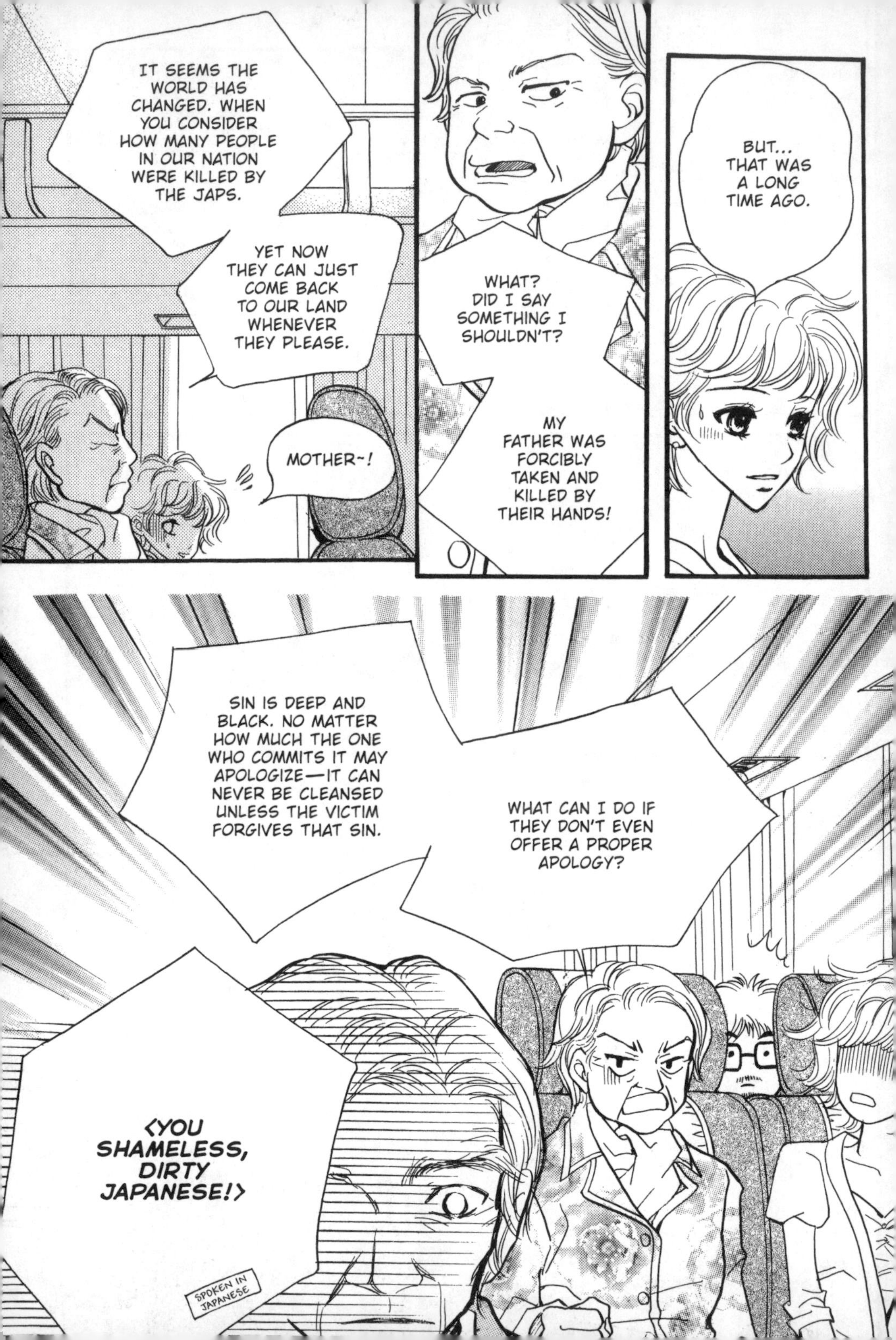
IT SEEMS THE WORLD HAS CHANGED. WHEN YOU CONSIDER HOW MANY PEOPLE IN OUR NATION WERE KILLED BY THE JAPS.
YET NOW THEY CAN JUST COME BACK TO OUR LAND WHENEVER THEY PLEASE.
MOTHER~!
WHAT? DID I SAY SOMETHING I SHOULDN'T?
MY FATHER WAS FORCIBLY TAKEN AND KILLED BY THEIR HANDS!
BUT... THAT WAS A LONG TIME AGO.
SIN IS DEEP AND BLACK. NO MATTER HOW MUCH THE ONE WHO COMMITS IT MAY APOLOGIZE—IT CAN NEVER BE CLEANSED UNLESS THE VICTIM FORGIVES THAT SIN.
WHAT CAN I DO IF THEY DON'T EVEN OFFER A PROPER APOLOGY?
<YOU SHAMELESS, DIRTY JAPANESE!>
SPOKEN IN JAPANESE

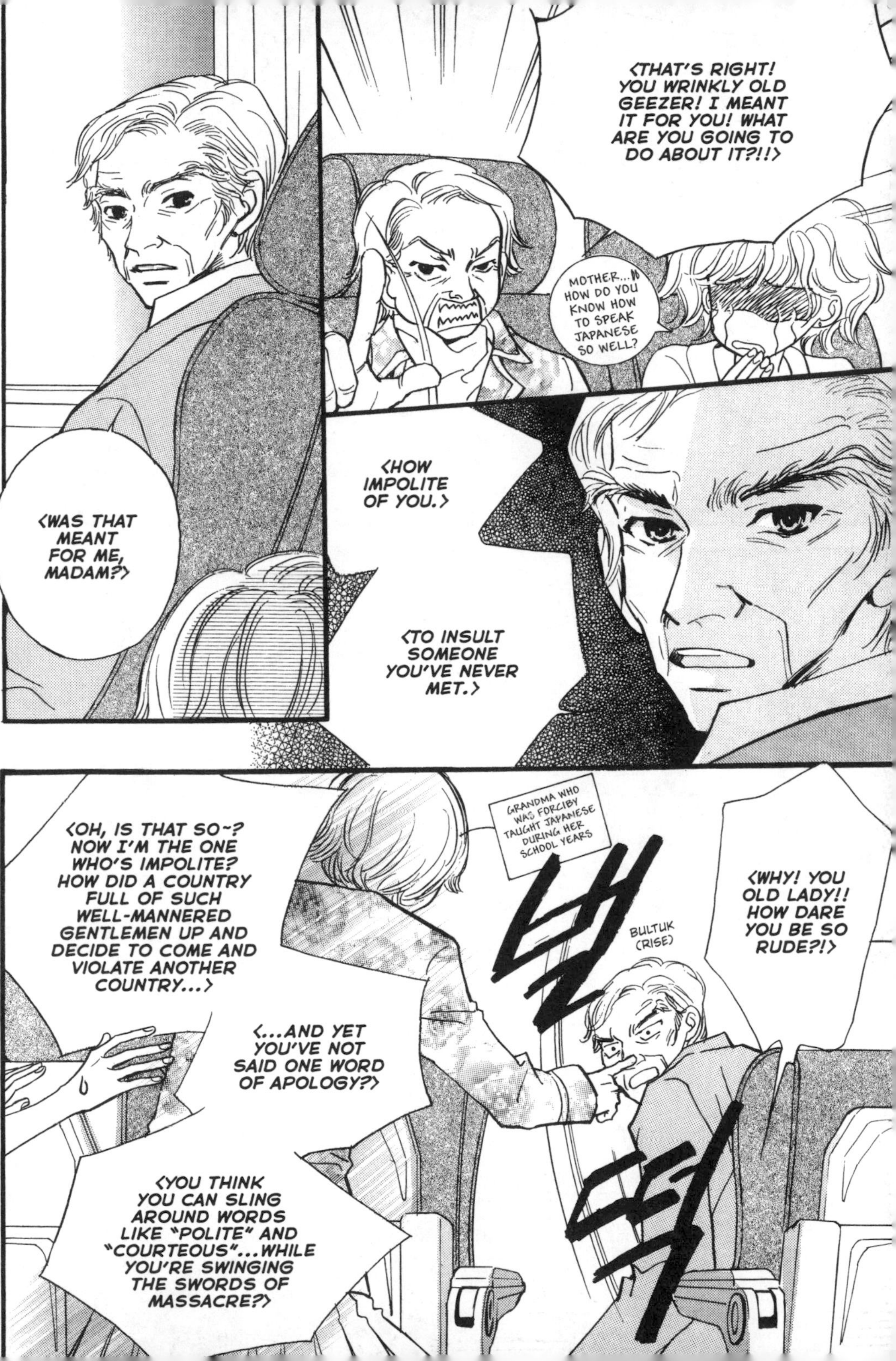
<WAS THAT MEANT FOR ME, MADAM?>
<THAT'S RIGHT! YOU WRINKLY OLD GEEZER! I MEANT IT FOR YOU! WHAT ARE YOU GOING TO DO ABOUT IT?!!>
MOTHER... HOW DO YOU KNOW HOW TO SPEAK JAPANESE SO WELL?
<HOW IMPOLITE OF YOU.>
<TO INSULT SOMEONE YOU'VE NEVER MET.>
<OH, IS THAT SO~? NOW I'M THE ONE WHO'S IMPOLITE? HOW DID A COUNTRY FULL OF SUCH WELL-MANNERED GENTLEMEN UP AND DECIDE TO COME AND VIOLATE ANOTHER COUNTRY...>
GRANDMA WHO WAS FORCIBY TAUGHT JAPANESE DURING HER SCHOOL YEARS
<WHY! YOU OLD LADY!! HOW DARE YOU BE SO RUDE?!>
BULTUK (RISE)
<...AND YET YOU'VE NOT SAID ONE WORD OF APOLOGY?>
<YOU THINK YOU CAN SLING AROUND WORDS LIKE "POLITE" AND "COURTEOUS"...WHILE YOU'RE SWINGING THE SWORDS OF MASSACRE?>

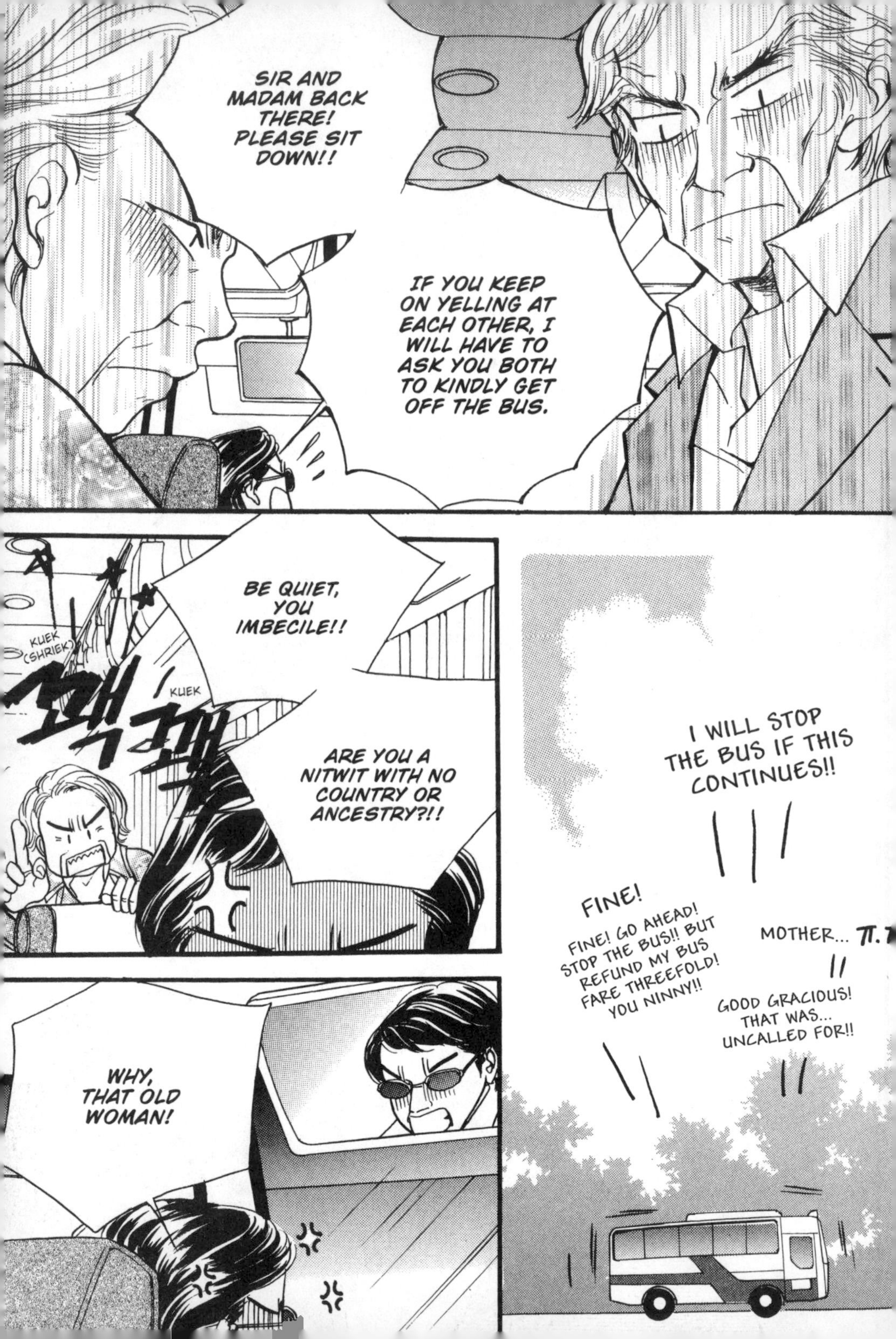
SIR AND MADAM BACK THERE! PLEASE SIT DOWN!!
IF YOU KEEP ON YELLING AT EACH OTHER, I WILL HAVE TO ASK YOU BOTH TO KINDLY GET OFF THE BUS.
KUEK (SHRIEK)
KUEK
BE QUIET, YOU IMBECILE!!
ARE YOU A NITWIT WITH NO COUNTRY OR ANCESTRY?!!
WHY, THAT OLD WOMAN!
I WILL STOP THE BUS IF THIS CONTINUES!!
FINE!
FINE! GO AHEAD! STOP THE BUS!! BUT REFUND MY BUS FARE THREEFOLD! YOU NINNY!!
MOTHER... π.π
GOOD GRACIOUS! THAT WAS... UNCALLED FOR!!

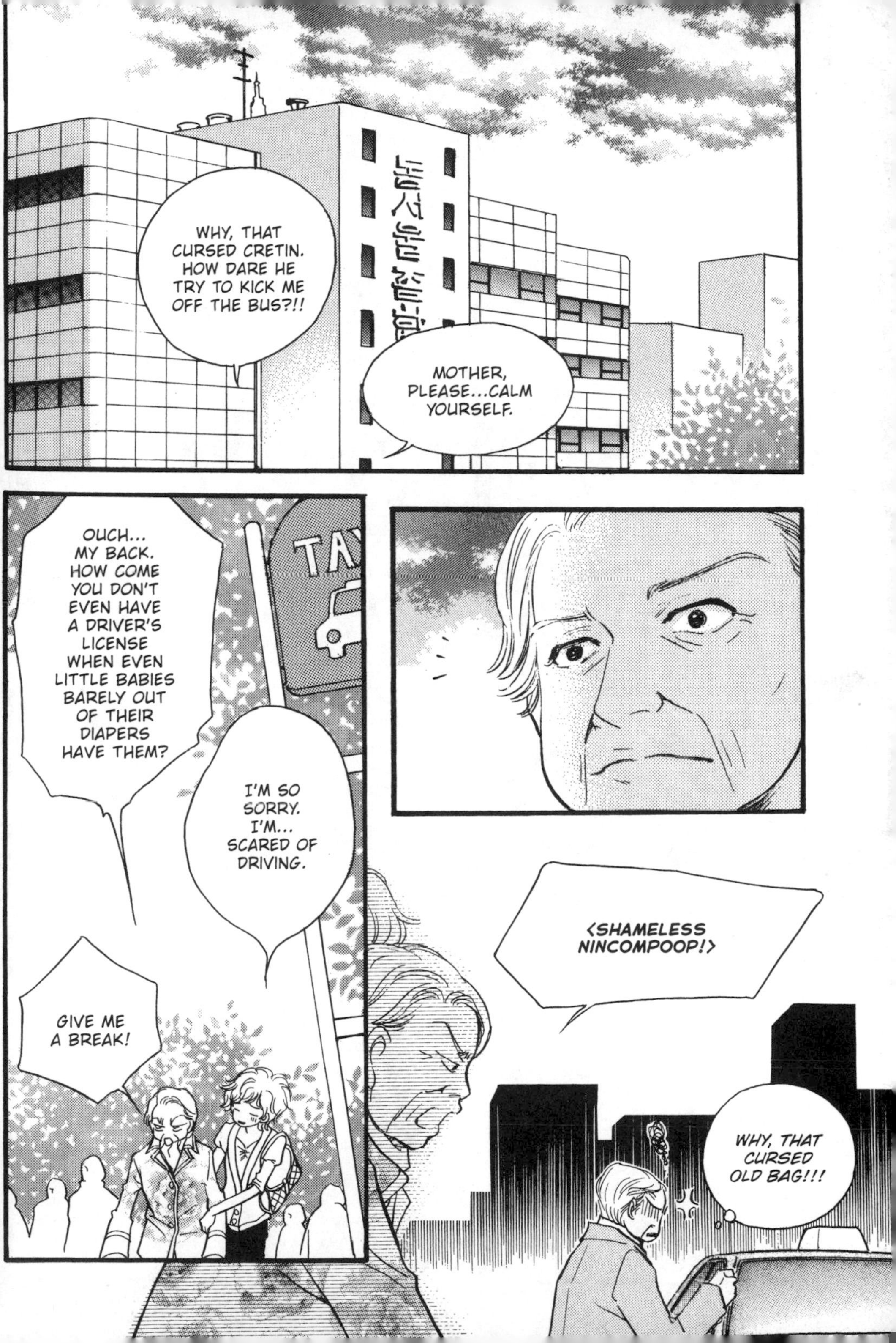
WHY, THAT CURSED CRETIN. HOW DARE HE TRY TO KICK ME OFF THE BUS?!!
MOTHER, PLEASE...CALM YOURSELF.
OUCH... MY BACK. HOW COME YOU DON'T EVEN HAVE A DRIVER'S LICENSE WHEN EVEN LITTLE BABIES BARELY OUT OF THEIR DIAPERS HAVE THEM?
I'M SO SORRY. I'M... SCARED OF DRIVING.
GIVE ME A BREAK!
<SHAMELESS NINCOMPOOP!>
WHY, THAT CURSED OLD BAG!!!

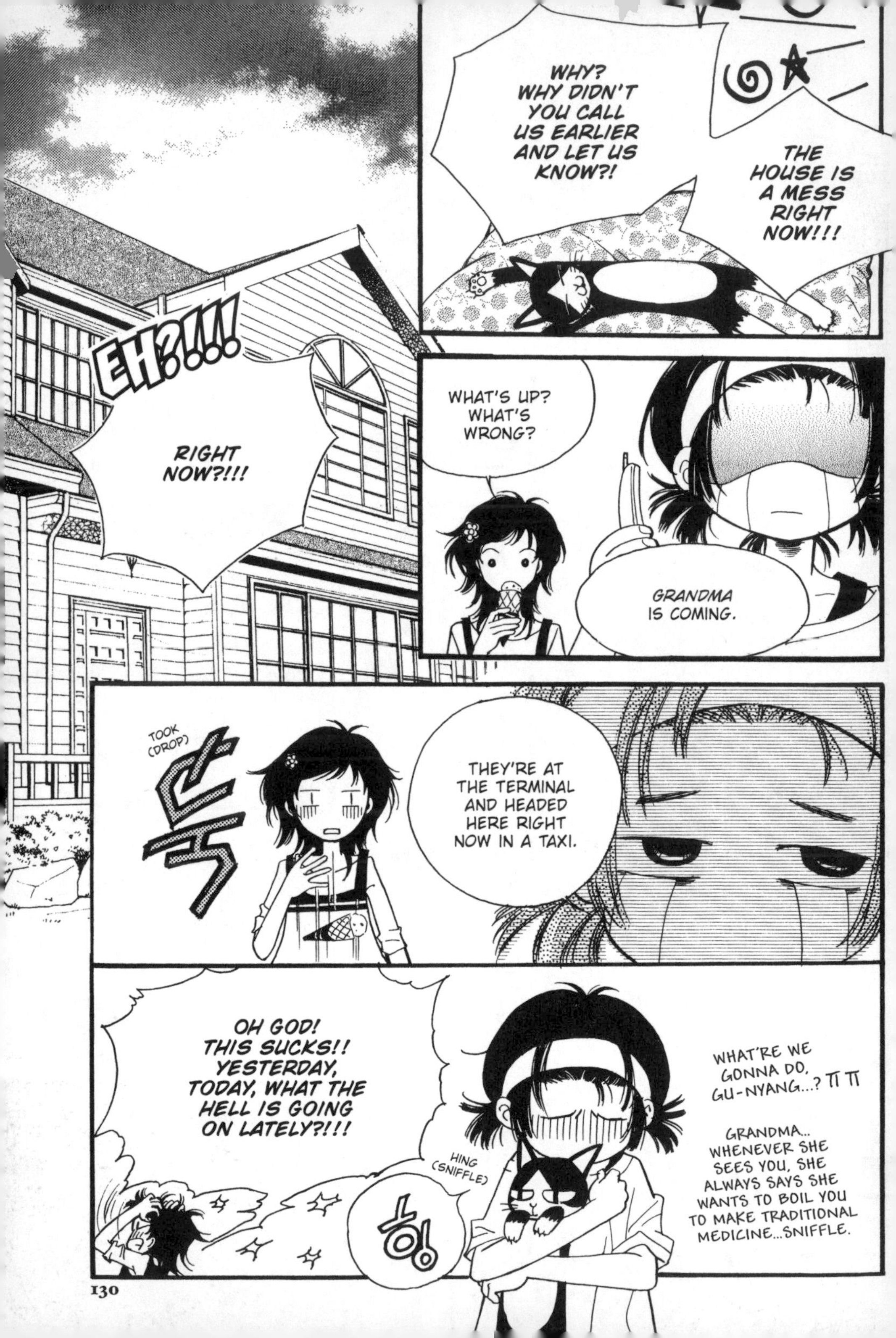
EH?!!!
RIGHT NOW?!!!
WHY? WHY DIDN'T YOU CALL US EARLIER AND LET US KNOW?!
THE HOUSE IS A MESS RIGHT NOW!!!
WHAT'S UP? WHAT'S WRONG?
GRANDMA IS COMING.
TOOK (DROP)
THEY'RE AT THE TERMINAL AND HEADED HERE RIGHT NOW IN A TAXI.
OH GOD! THIS SUCKS!! YESTERDAY, TODAY, WHAT THE HELL IS GOING ON LATELY?!!!
HING (SNIFFLE)
WHAT'RE WE GONNA DO, GU-NYANG...? TT TT
GRANDMA... WHENEVER SHE SEES YOU, SHE ALWAYS SAYS SHE WANTS TO BOIL YOU TO MAKE TRADITIONAL MEDICINE...SNIFFLE.

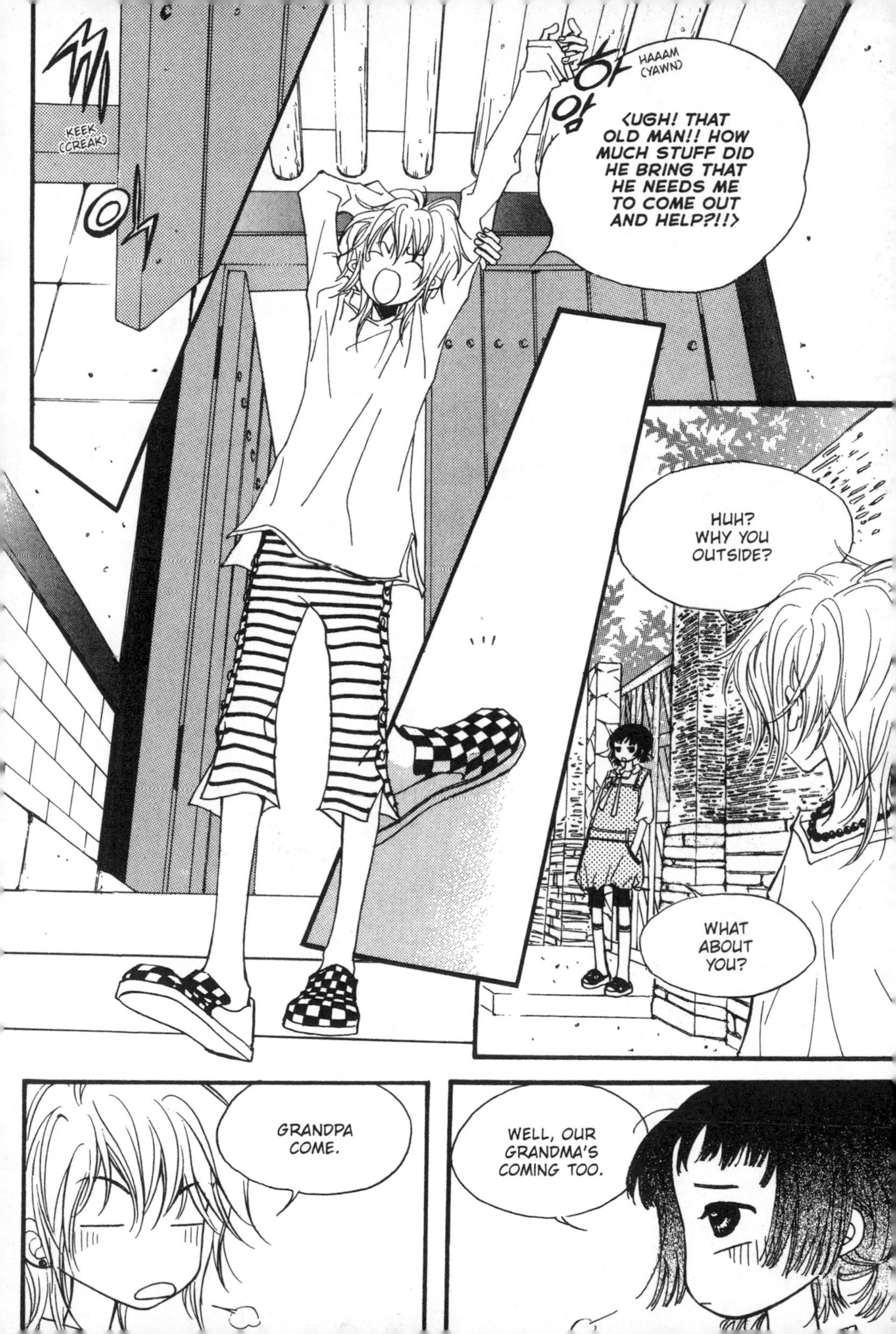
끼익
KEEK (CREAK)
하암
HAAAM (YAWN)
<UGH! THAT OLD MAN!! HOW MUCH STUFF DID HE BRING THAT HE NEEDS ME TO COME OUT AND HELP?!!>
HUH? WHY YOU OUTSIDE?
WHAT ABOUT YOU?
GRANDPA COME.
WELL, OUR GRANDMA'S COMING TOO.

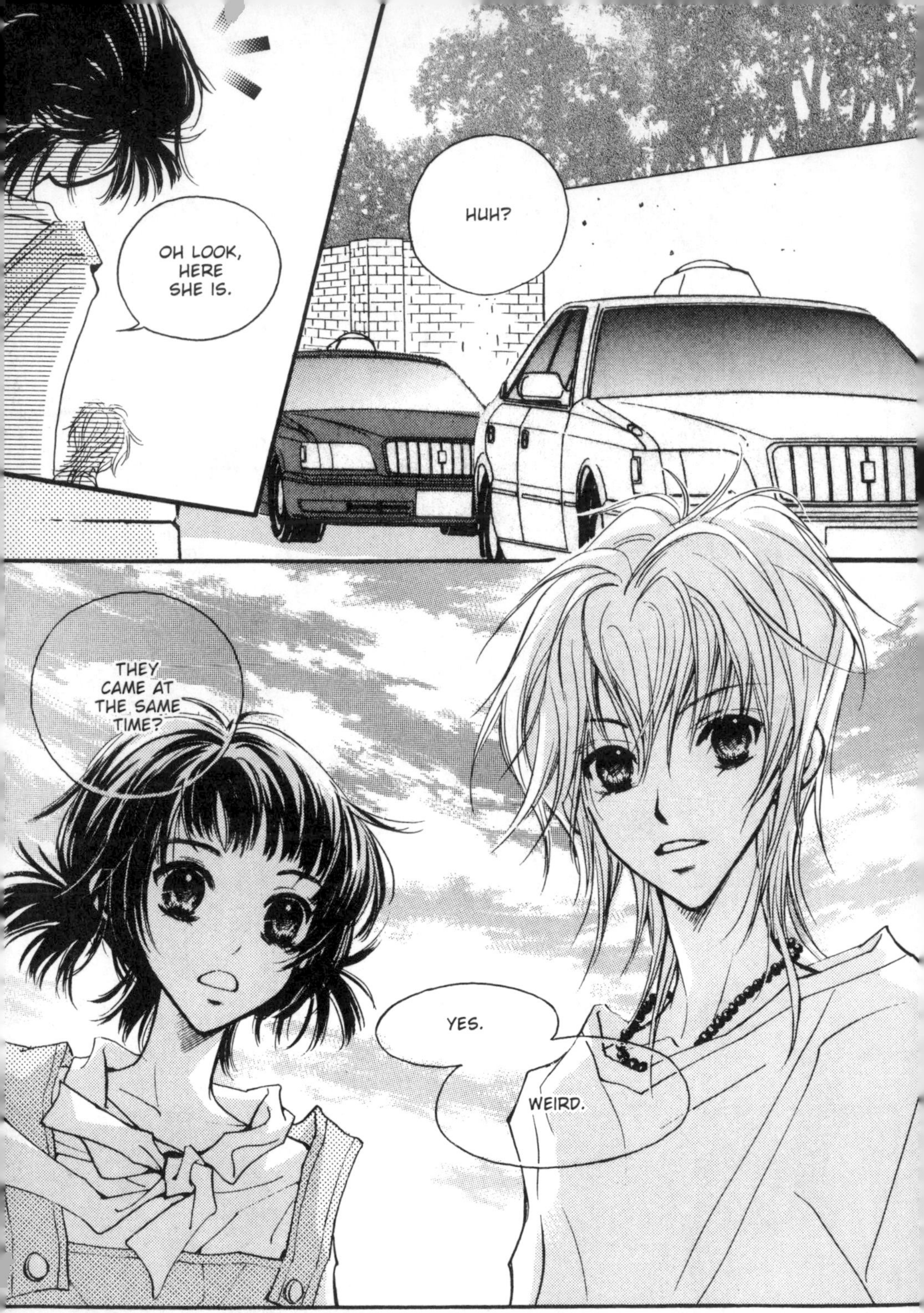
OH LOOK, HERE SHE IS.
HUH?
THEY CAME AT THE SAME TIME?
YES.
WEIRD.

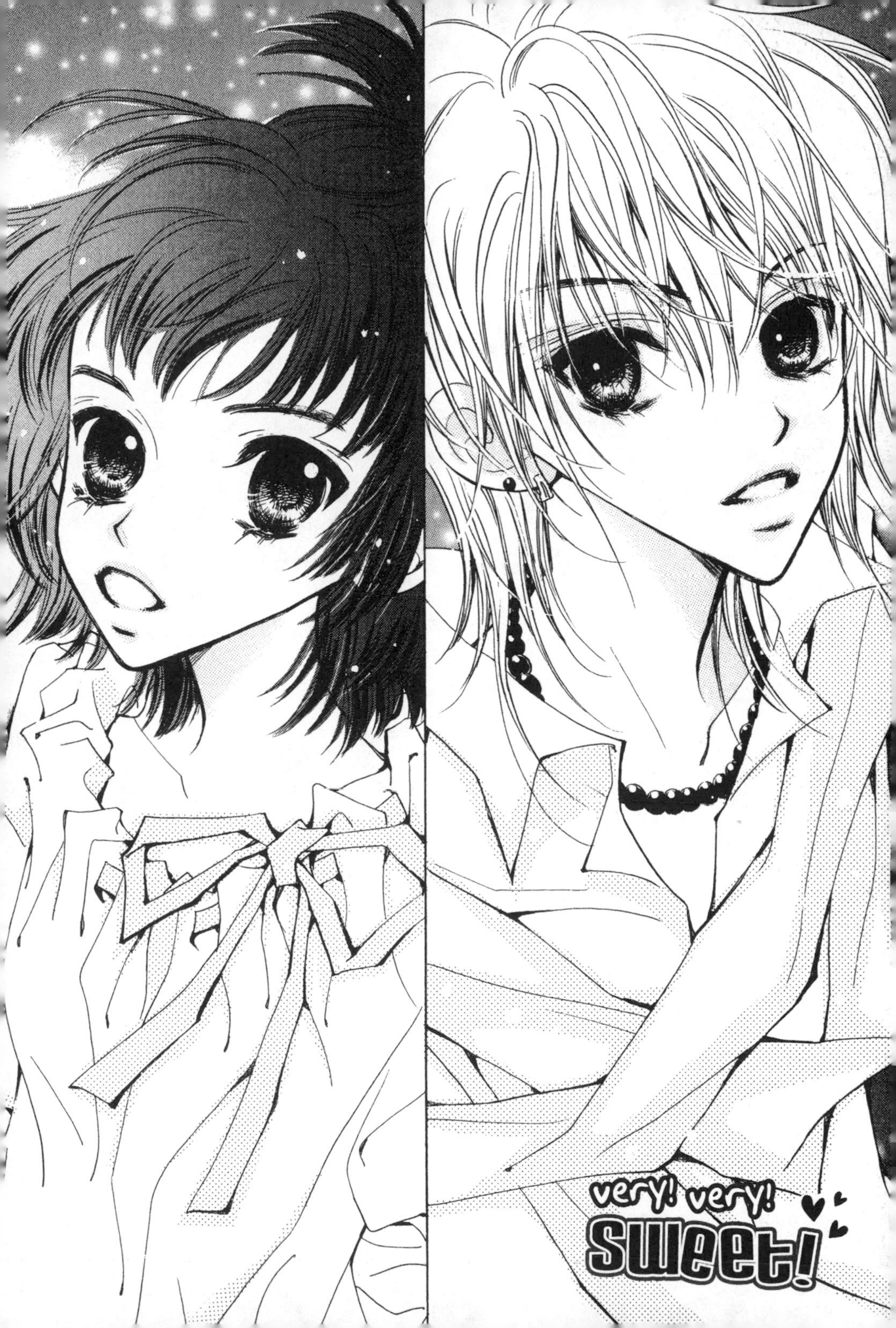
very! very!
sweet!

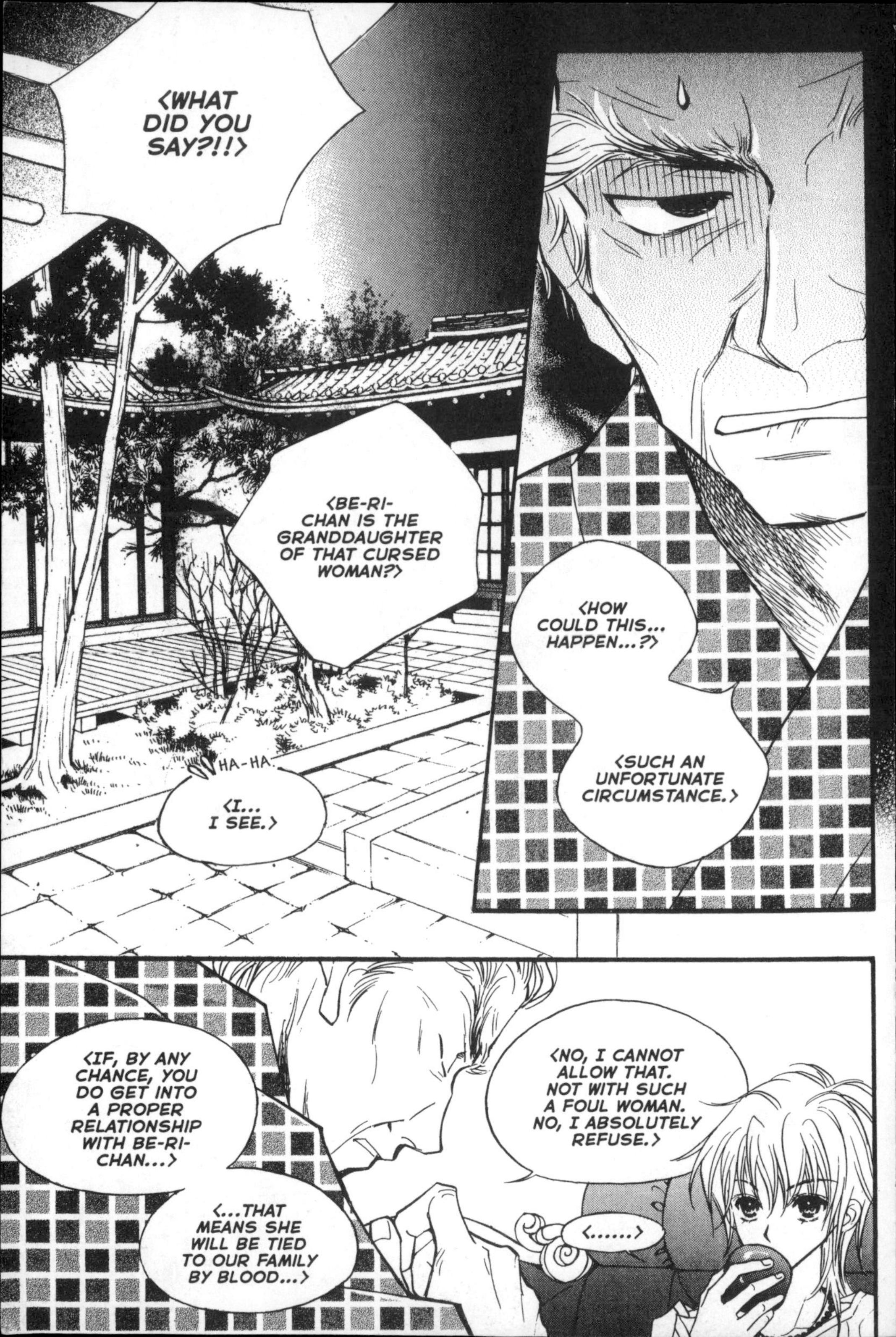

<WHAT DID YOU SAY?!!>
<BE-RI-CHAN IS THE GRANDDAUGHTER OF THAT CURSED WOMAN?>
HA-HA
<I... I SEE.>
<HOW COULD THIS... HAPPEN...?>
<SUCH AN UNFORTUNATE CIRCUMSTANCE.>
<IF, BY ANY CHANCE, YOU DO GET INTO A PROPER RELATIONSHIP WITH BE-RI-CHAN...>
<...THAT MEANS SHE WILL BE TIED TO OUR FAMILY BY BLOOD...>
<NO, I CANNOT ALLOW THAT. NOT WITH SUCH A FOUL WOMAN. NO, I ABSOLUTELY REFUSE.>
<......>

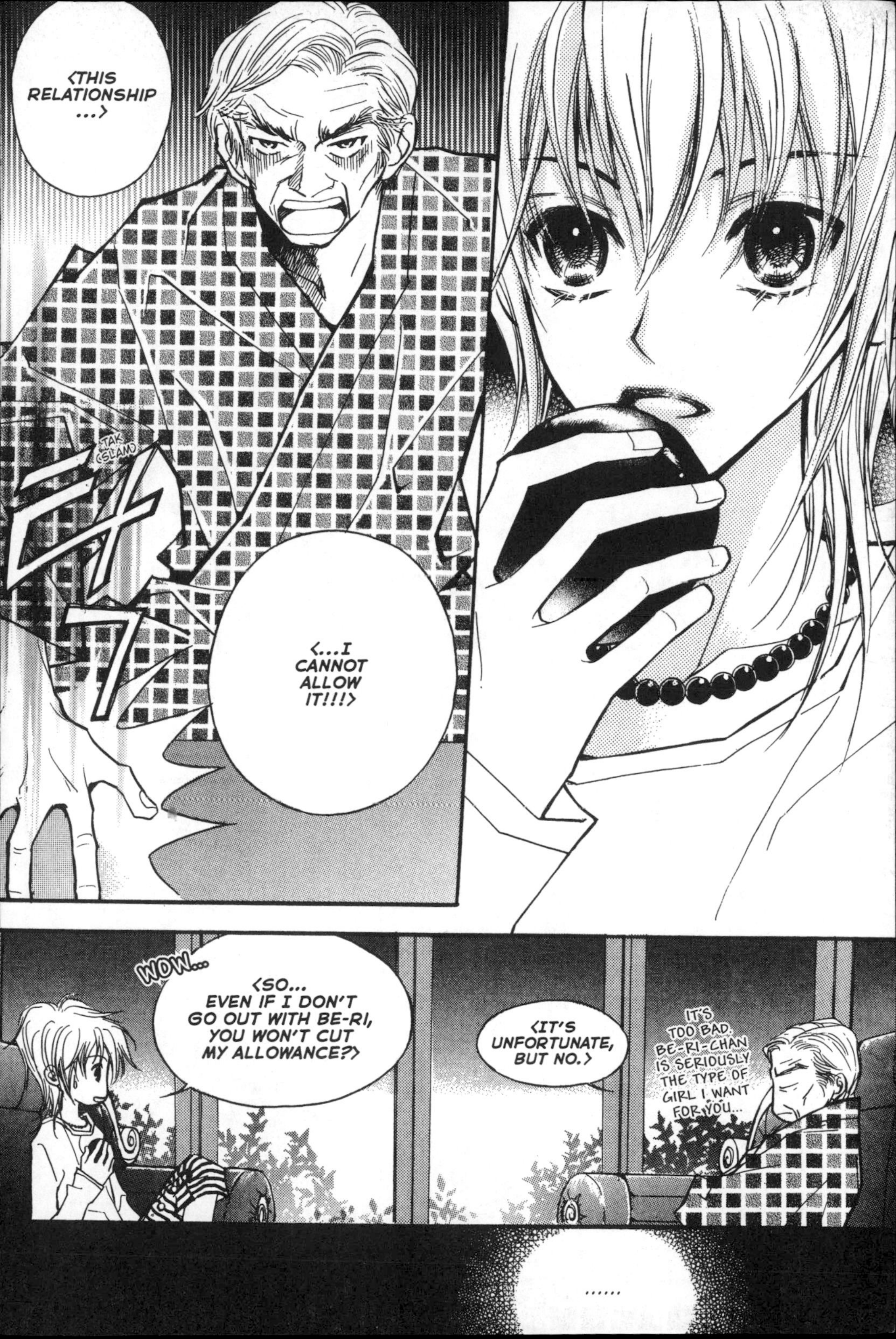
<THIS RELATIONSHIP ...>
TAK (SLAM)
<...I CANNOT ALLOW IT!!!>
WOW...
<SO... EVEN IF I DON'T GO OUT WITH BE-RI, YOU WON'T CUT MY ALLOWANCE?>
<IT'S UNFORTUNATE, BUT NO.>
IT'S TOO BAD. BE-RI-CHAN IS SERIOUSLY THE TYPE OF GIRL I WANT FOR YOU...
......

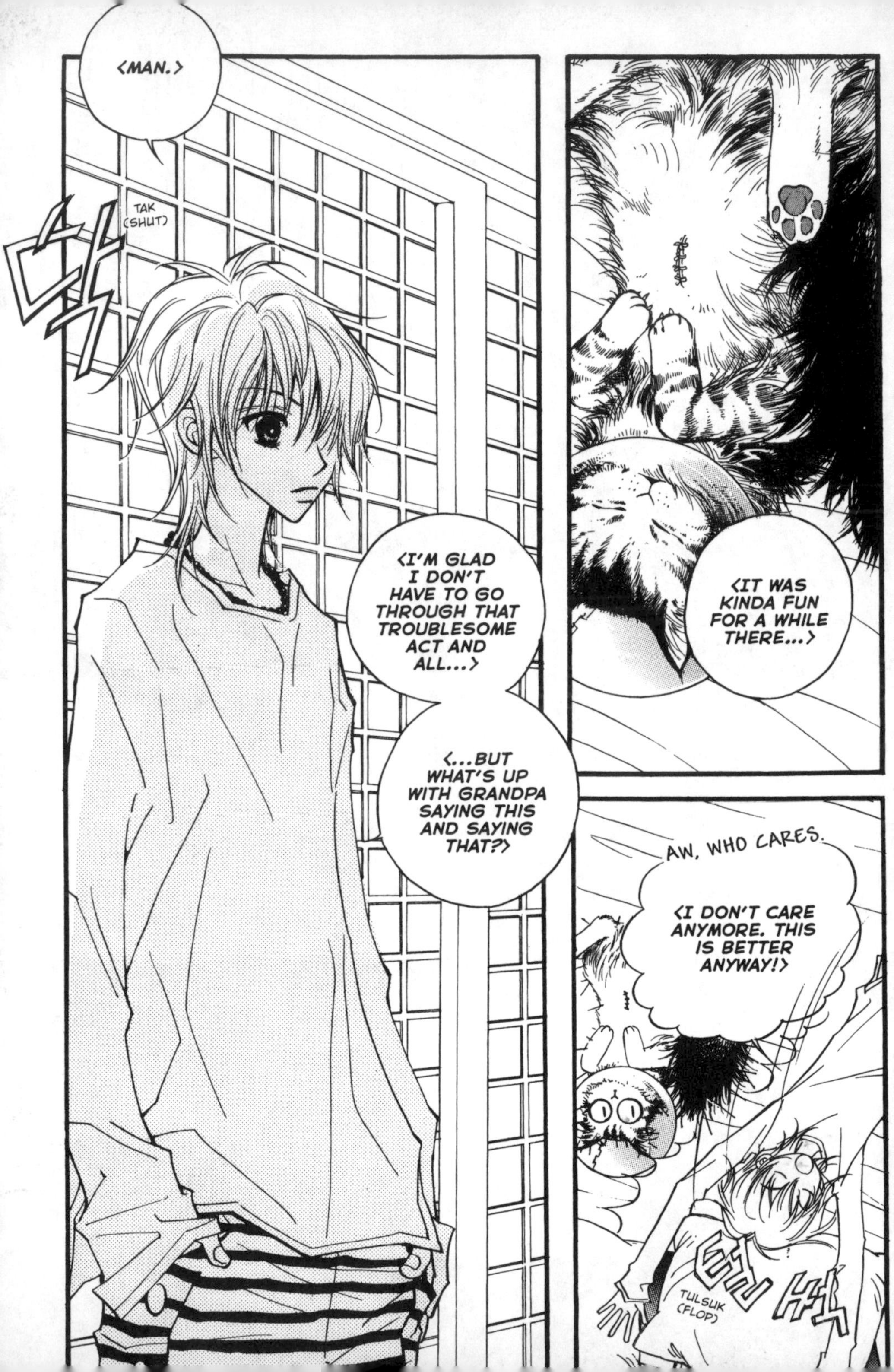
<MAN.>
TAK (SHUT)
<I'M GLAD I DON'T HAVE TO GO THROUGH THAT TROUBLESOME ACT AND ALL...>
<...BUT WHAT'S UP WITH GRANDPA SAYING THIS AND SAYING THAT?>
<IT WAS KINDA FUN FOR A WHILE THERE...>
AW, WHO CARES.
<I DON'T CARE ANYMORE. THIS IS BETTER ANYWAY!>
TULSUK (FLOP)

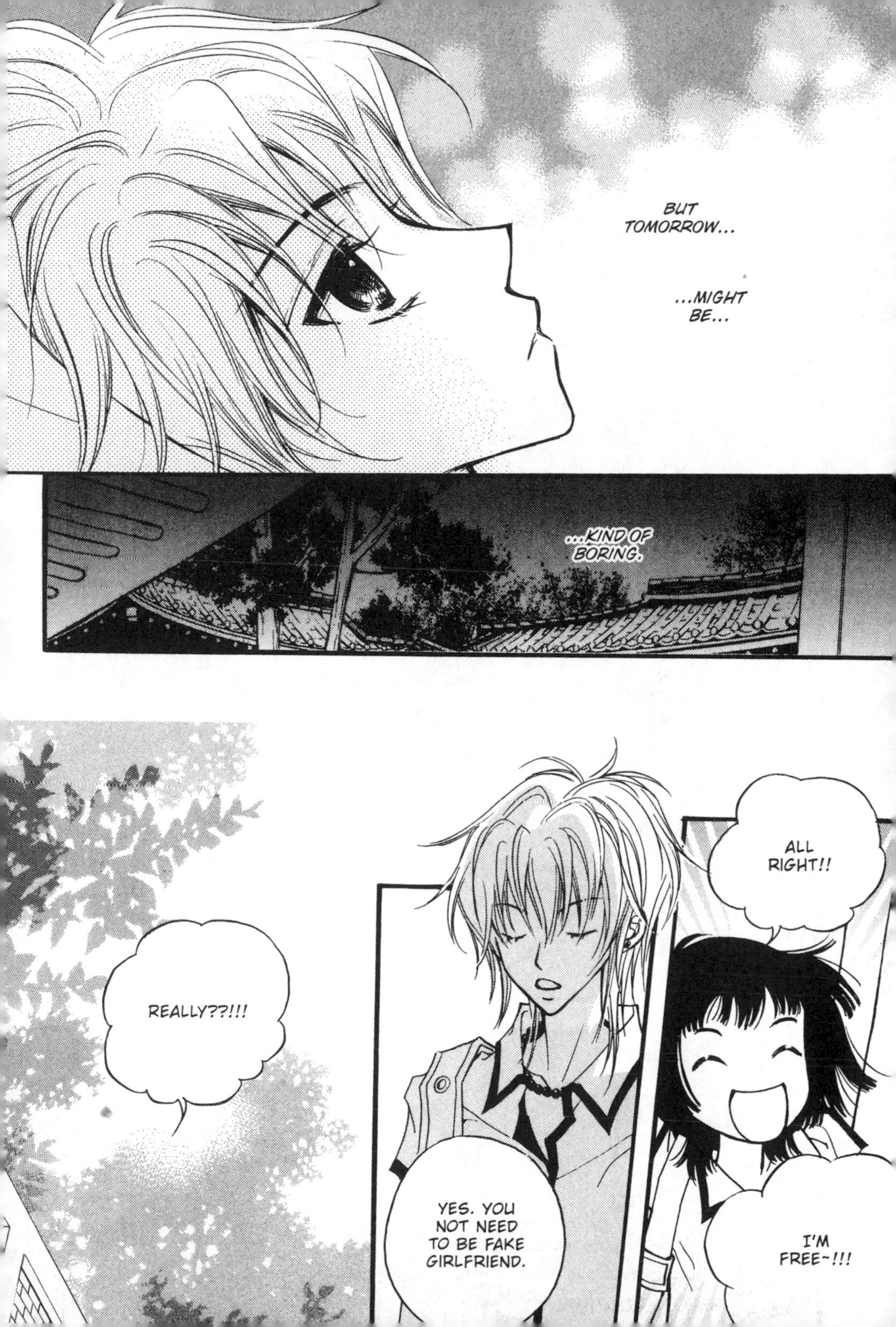
BUT TOMORROW...
...MIGHT BE...
...KIND OF BORING.
REALLY??!!!
ALL RIGHT!!
YES. YOU NOT NEED TO BE FAKE GIRLFRIEND.
I'M FREE~!!!

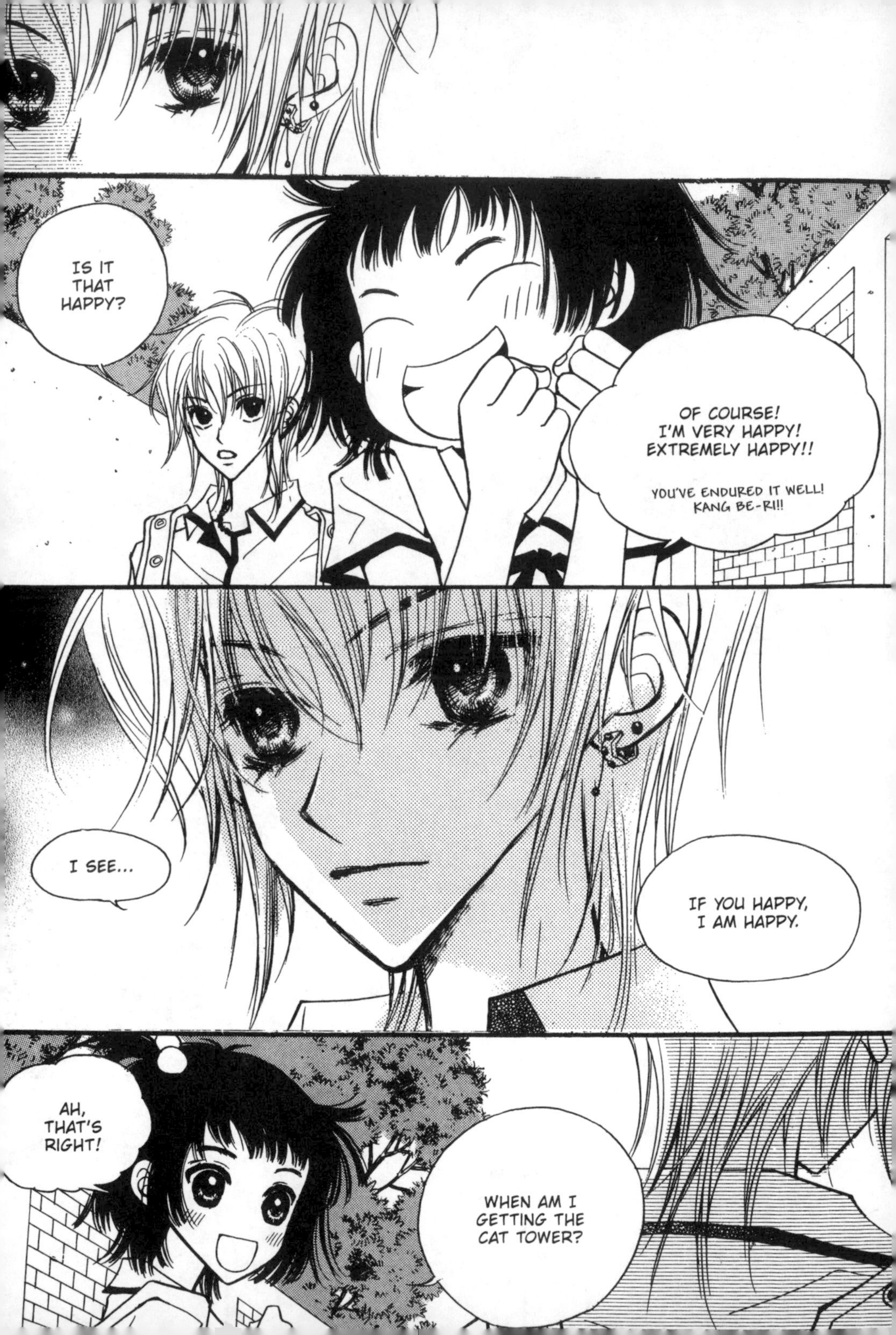

IS IT THAT HAPPY?
OF COURSE! I'M VERY HAPPY! EXTREMELY HAPPY!!
YOU'VE ENDURED IT WELL! KANG BE-RI!!
I SEE...
IF YOU HAPPY, I AM HAPPY.
AH, THAT'S RIGHT!
WHEN AM I GETTING THE CAT TOWER?

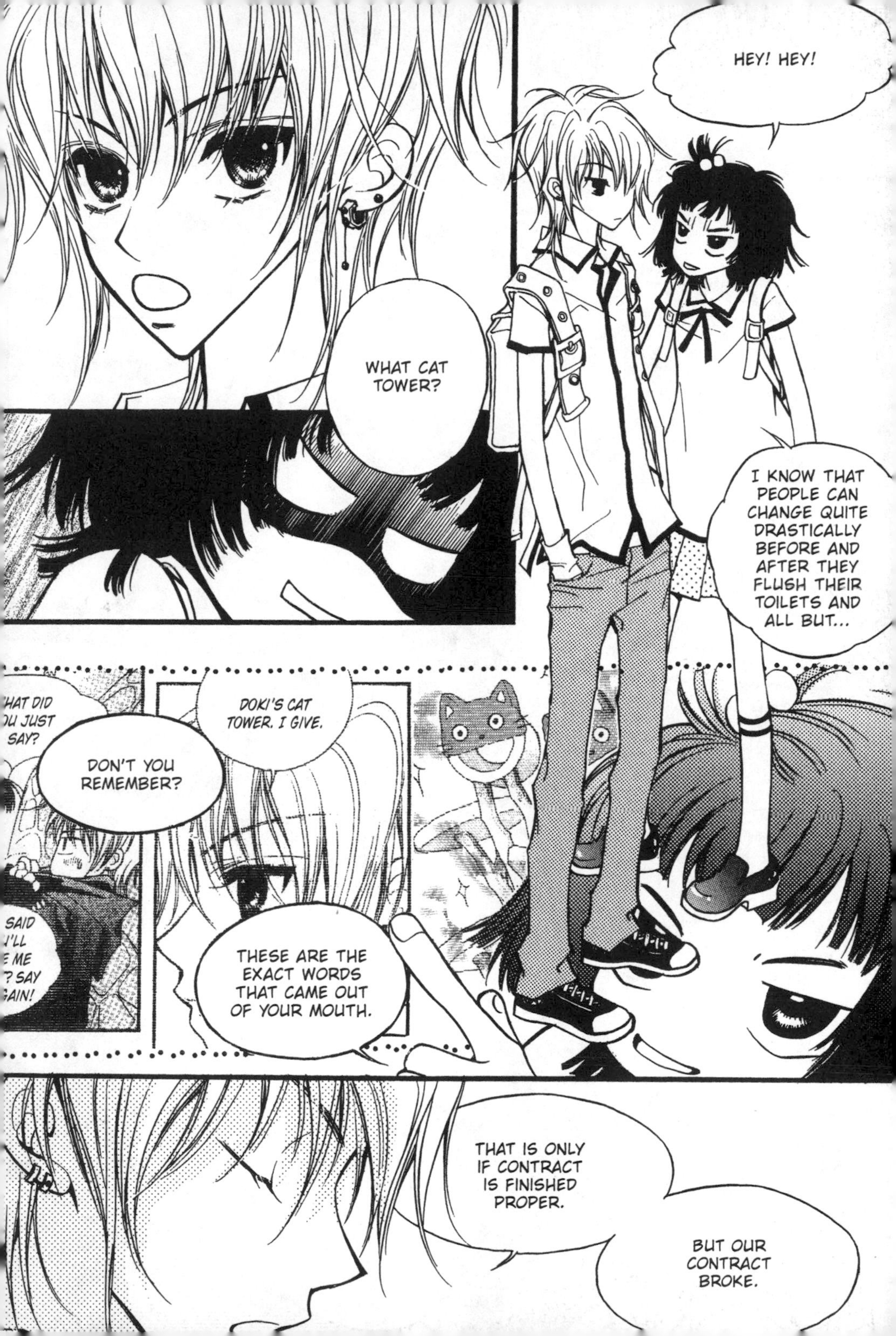
WHAT CAT TOWER?
HEY! HEY!
I KNOW THAT PEOPLE CAN CHANGE QUITE DRASTICALLY BEFORE AND AFTER THEY FLUSH THEIR TOILETS AND ALL BUT...
HAT DID OU JUST SAY?
DOKI'S CAT TOWER. I GIVE.
DON'T YOU REMEMBER?
SAID 'LL E ME ? SAY GAIN!
THESE ARE THE EXACT WORDS THAT CAME OUT OF YOUR MOUTH.
THAT IS ONLY IF CONTRACT IS FINISHED PROPER.
BUT OUR CONTRACT BROKE.

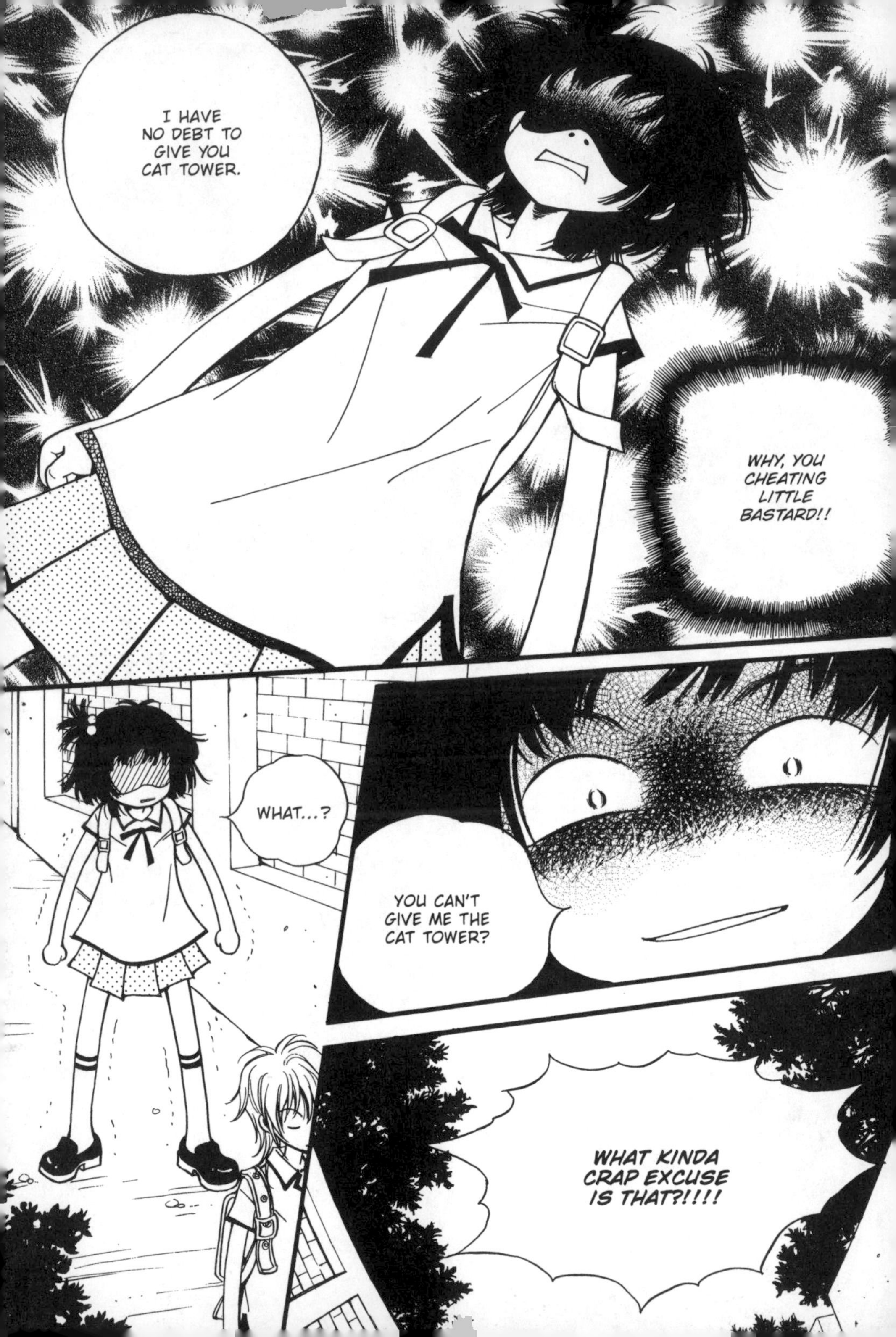

I HAVE NO DEBT TO GIVE YOU CAT TOWER.
WHY, YOU CHEATING LITTLE BASTARD!!
WHAT...?
YOU CAN'T GIVE ME THE CAT TOWER?
WHAT KINDA CRAP EXCUSE IS THAT?!!!!

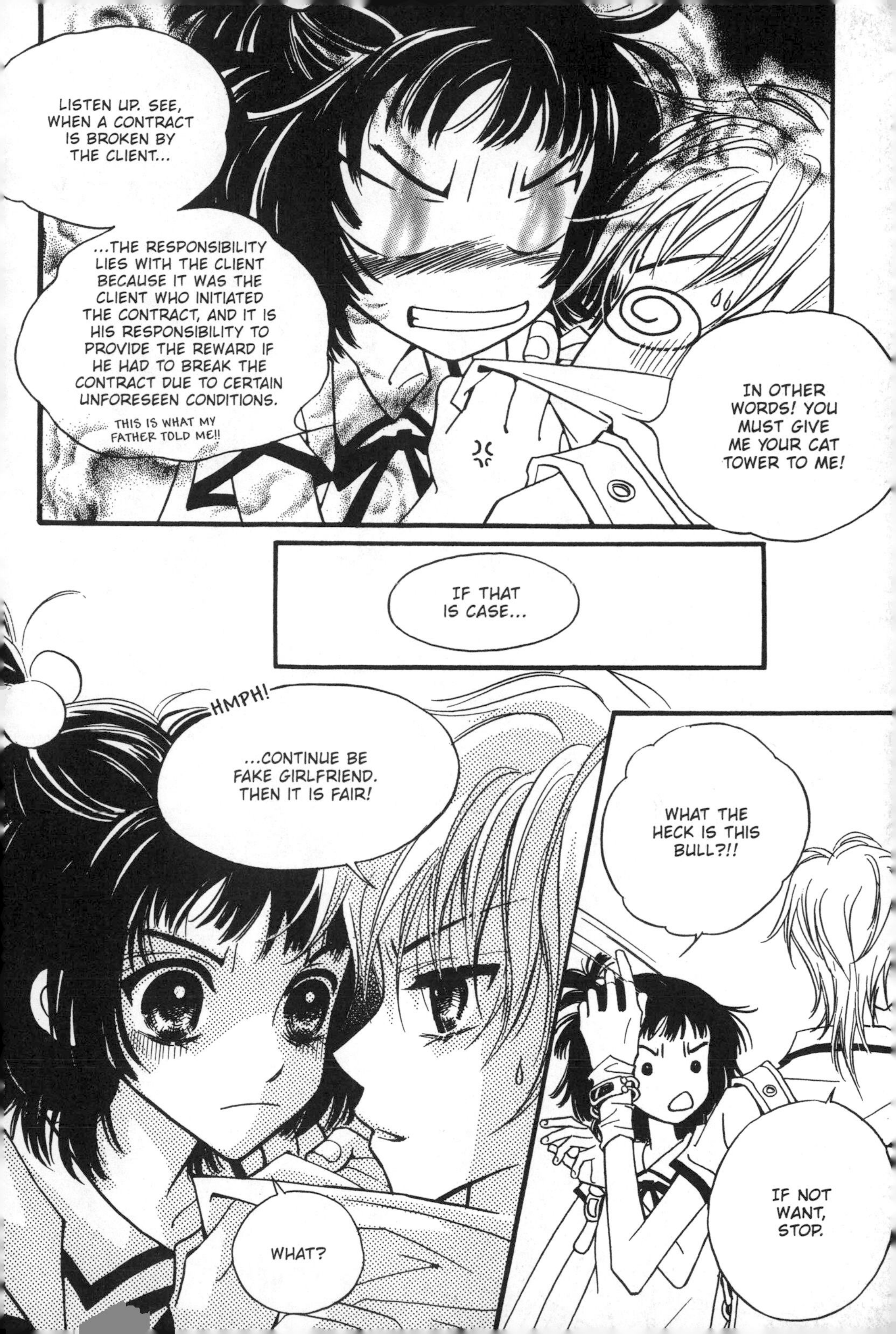

LISTEN UP. SEE, WHEN A CONTRACT IS BROKEN BY THE CLIENT...
...THE RESPONSIBILITY LIES WITH THE CLIENT BECAUSE IT WAS THE CLIENT WHO INITIATED THE CONTRACT, AND IT IS HIS RESPONSIBILITY TO PROVIDE THE REWARD IF HE HAD TO BREAK THE CONTRACT DUE TO CERTAIN UNFORESEEN CONDITIONS.
THIS IS WHAT MY FATHER TOLD ME!!
IN OTHER WORDS! YOU MUST GIVE ME YOUR CAT TOWER TO ME!
IF THAT IS CASE...
HMPH!
...CONTINUE BE FAKE GIRLFRIEND. THEN IT IS FAIR!
WHAT?
WHAT THE HECK IS THIS BULL?!!
IF NOT WANT, STOP.

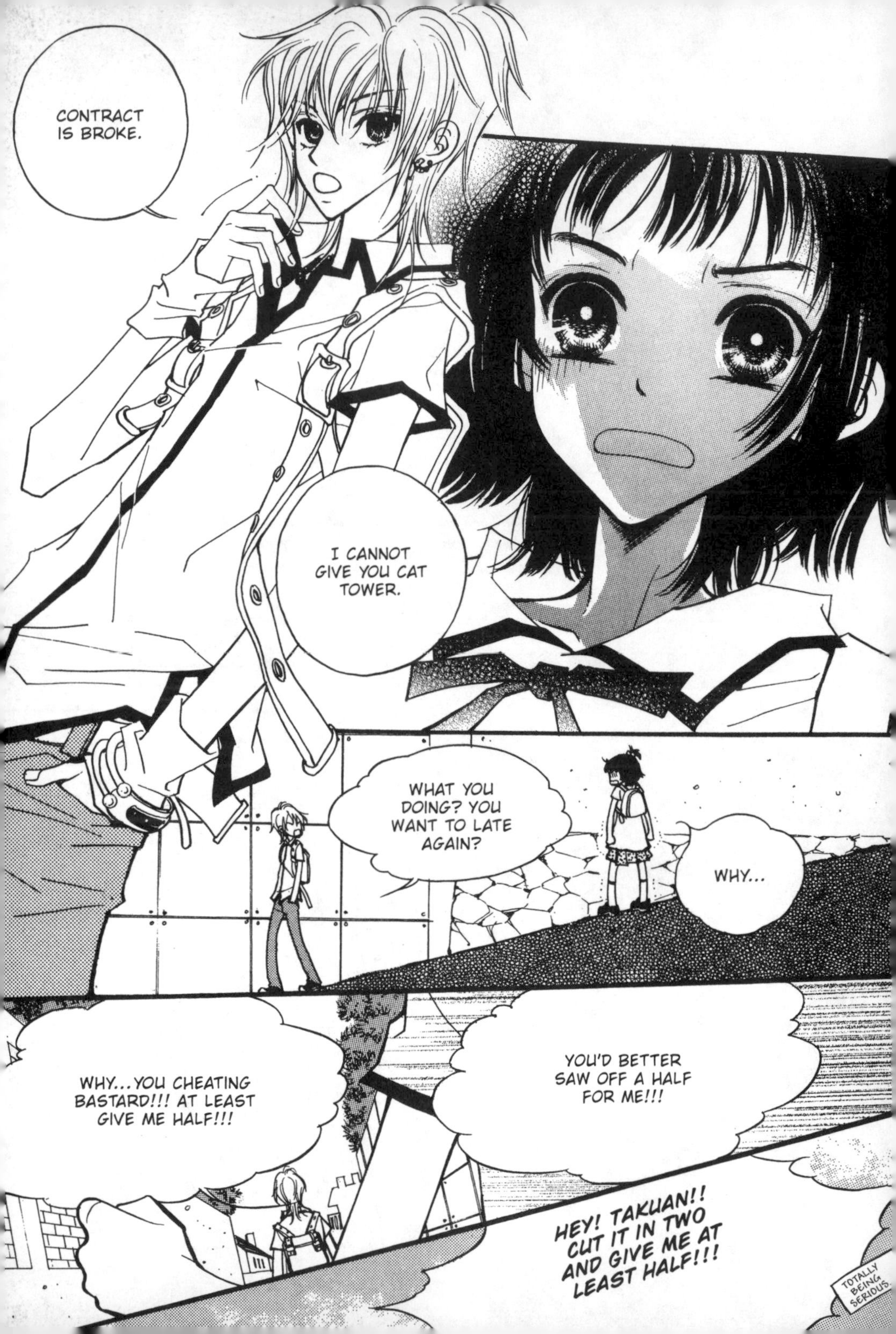
CONTRACT IS BROKE.
I CANNOT GIVE YOU CAT TOWER.
WHAT YOU DOING? YOU WANT TO LATE AGAIN?
WHY...
WHY...YOU CHEATING BASTARD!!! AT LEAST GIVE ME HALF!!!
YOU'D BETTER SAW OFF A HALF FOR ME!!!
HEY! TAKUAN!! CUT IT IN TWO AND GIVE ME AT LEAST HALF!!!
TOTALLY BEING SERIOUS.

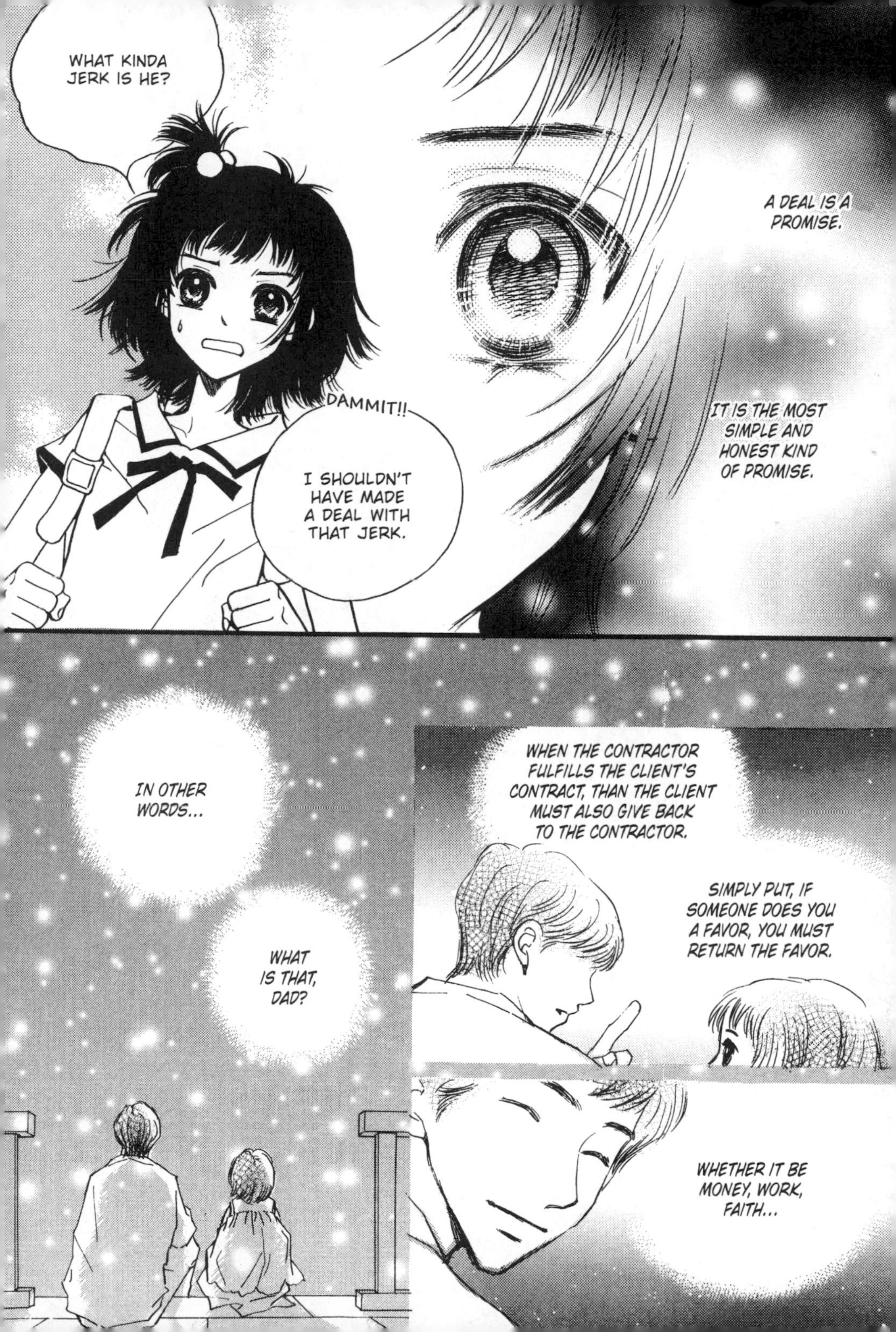
WHAT KINDA JERK IS HE?
DAMMIT!!
I SHOULDN'T HAVE MADE A DEAL WITH THAT JERK.
A DEAL IS A PROMISE.
IT IS THE MOST SIMPLE AND HONEST KIND OF PROMISE.
IN OTHER WORDS...
WHAT IS THAT, DAD?
WHEN THE CONTRACTOR FULFILLS THE CLIENT'S CONTRACT, THAN THE CLIENT MUST ALSO GIVE BACK TO THE CONTRACTOR.
SIMPLY PUT, IF SOMEONE DOES YOU A FAVOR, YOU MUST RETURN THE FAVOR.
WHETHER IT BE MONEY, WORK, FAITH...

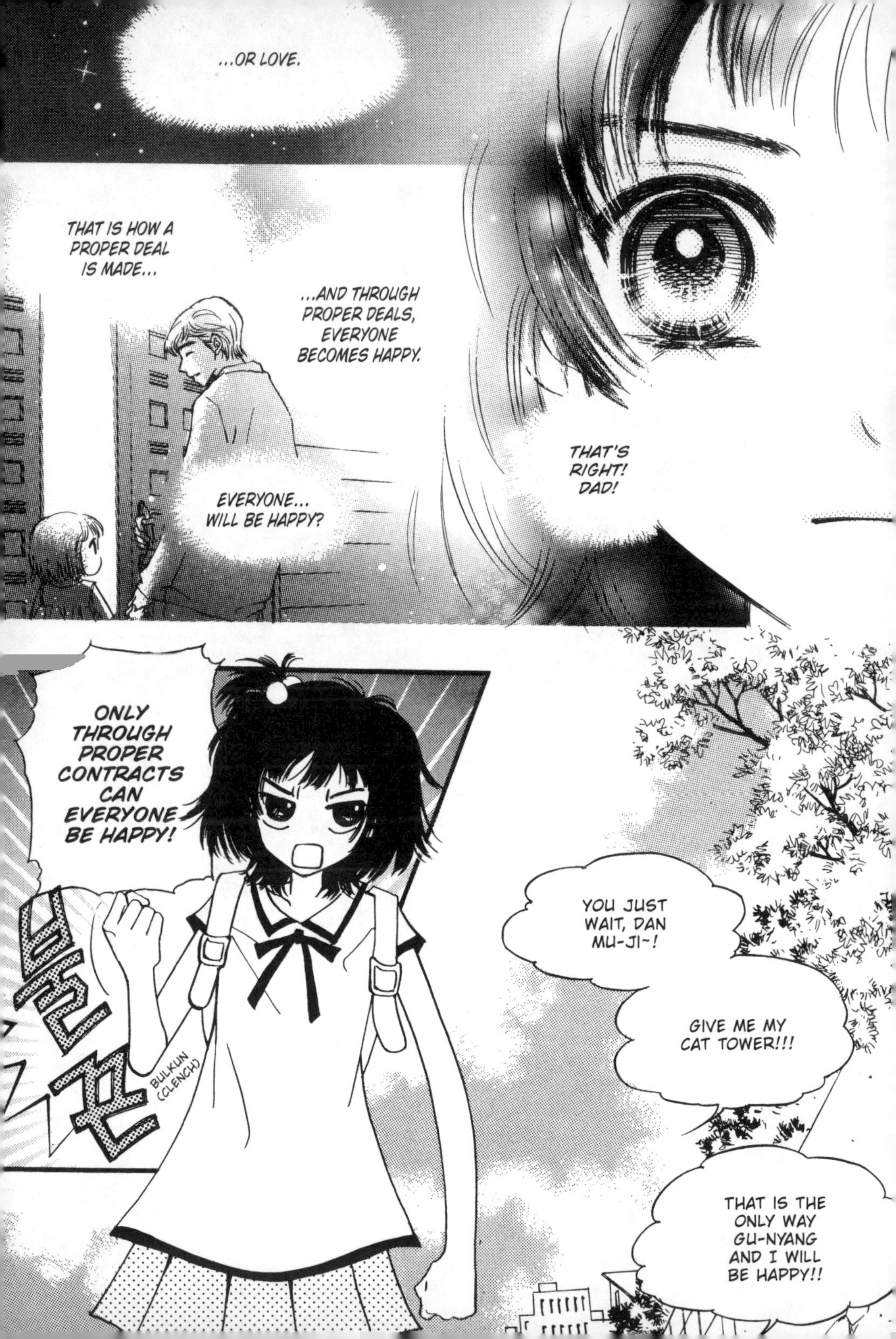
...OR LOVE.
THAT IS HOW A PROPER DEAL IS MADE...
...AND THROUGH PROPER DEALS, EVERYONE BECOMES HAPPY.
EVERYONE... WILL BE HAPPY?
THAT'S RIGHT! DAD!
ONLY THROUGH PROPER CONTRACTS CAN EVERYONE BE HAPPY!
불끈
BULKUN (CLENCH)
YOU JUST WAIT, DAN MU-JI~!
GIVE ME MY CAT TOWER!!!
THAT IS THE ONLY WAY GU-NYANG AND I WILL BE HAPPY!!

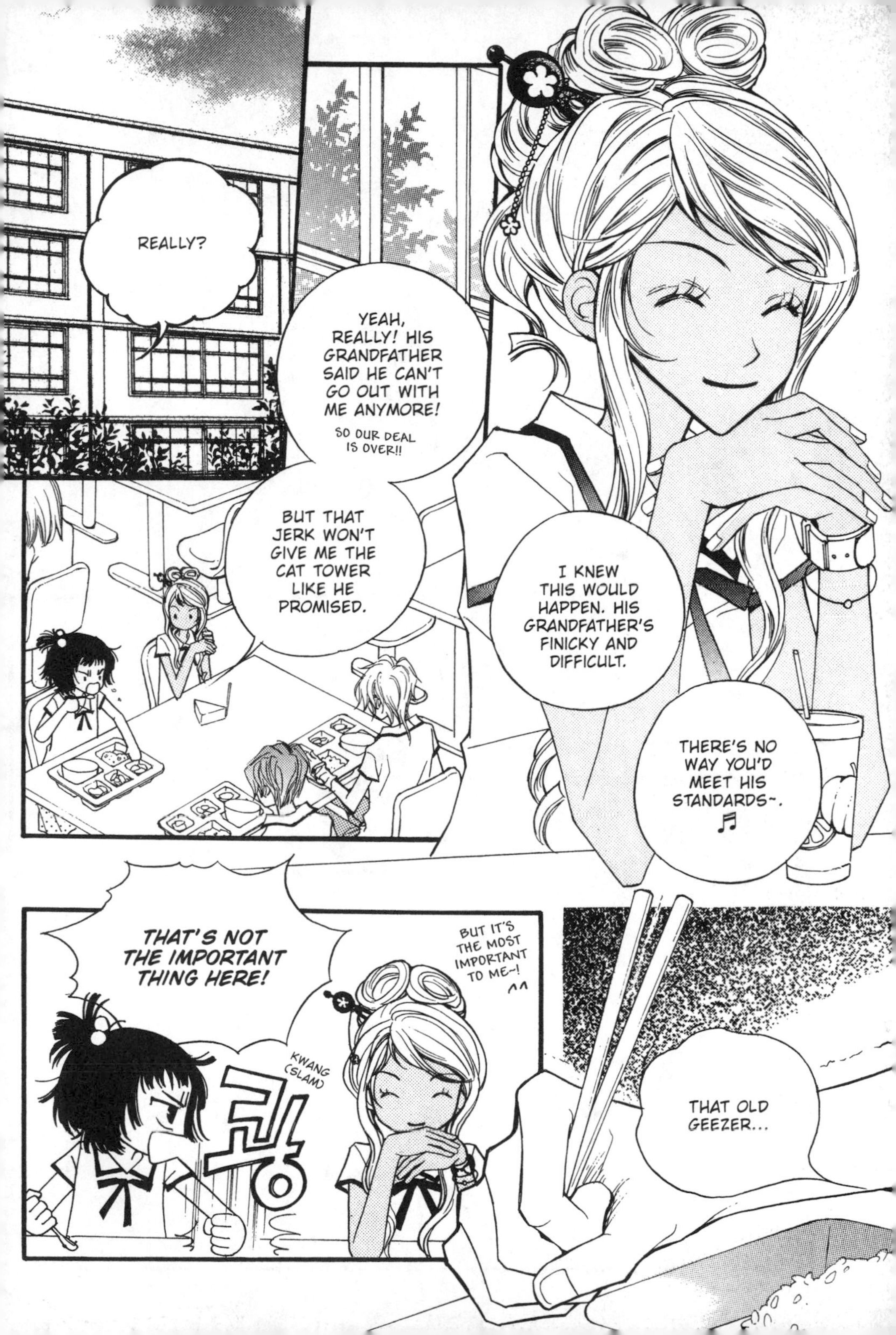
REALLY?
YEAH, REALLY! HIS GRANDFATHER SAID HE CAN'T GO OUT WITH ME ANYMORE!
SO OUR DEAL IS OVER!!
BUT THAT JERK WON'T GIVE ME THE CAT TOWER LIKE HE PROMISED.
I KNEW THIS WOULD HAPPEN. HIS GRANDFATHER'S FINICKY AND DIFFICULT.
THERE'S NO WAY YOU'D MEET HIS STANDARDS~. ♬
THAT'S NOT THE IMPORTANT THING HERE!
KWANG (SLAM)
BUT IT'S THE MOST IMPORTANT TO ME~! ^^
THAT OLD GEEZER...

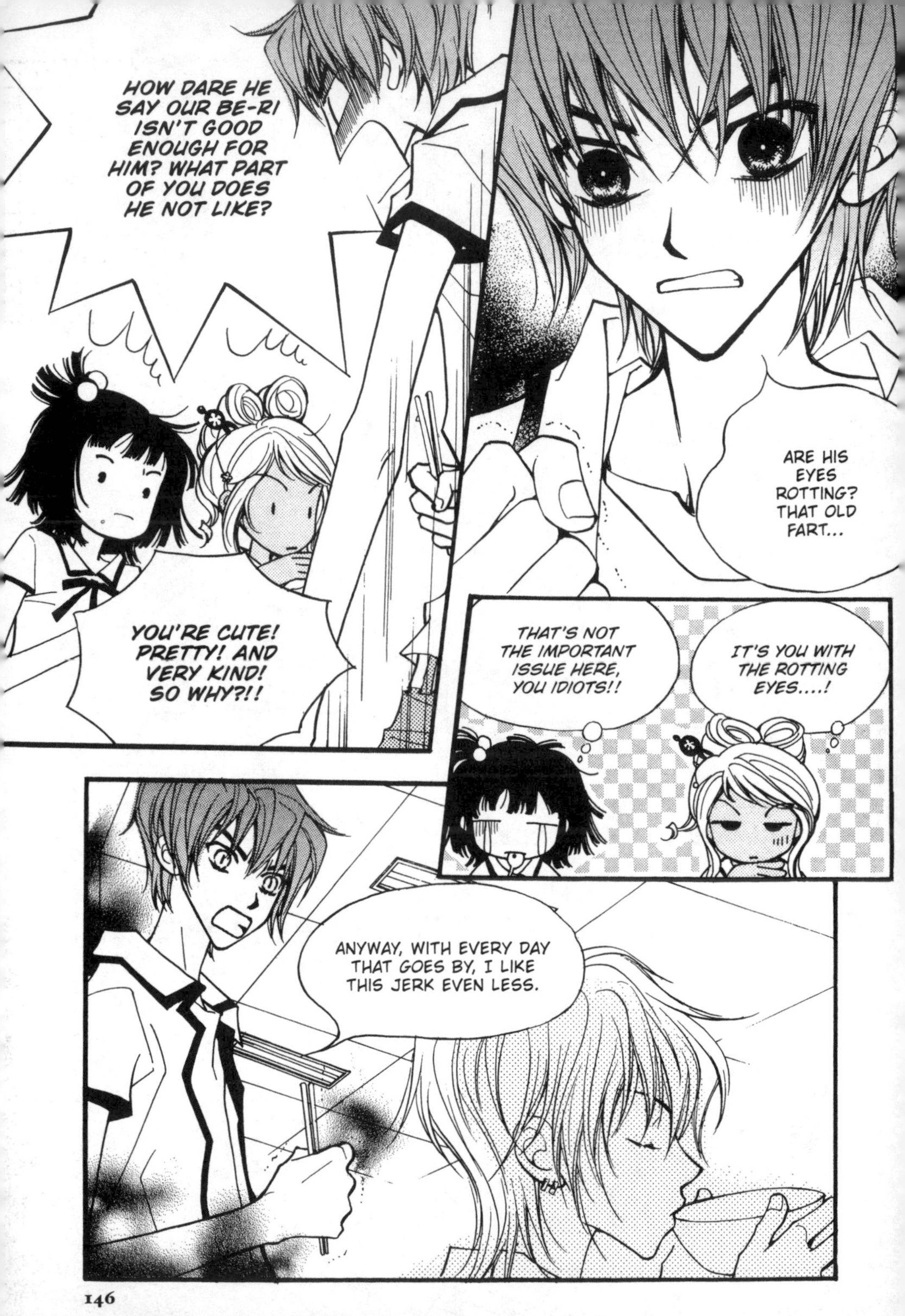
HOW DARE HE SAY OUR BE-RI ISN'T GOOD ENOUGH FOR HIM? WHAT PART OF YOU DOES HE NOT LIKE?
YOU'RE CUTE! PRETTY! AND VERY KIND! SO WHY?!!
ARE HIS EYES ROTTING? THAT OLD FART...
THAT'S NOT THE IMPORTANT ISSUE HERE, YOU IDIOTS!!
IT'S YOU WITH THE ROTTING EYES....!
ANYWAY, WITH EVERY DAY THAT GOES BY, I LIKE THIS JERK EVEN LESS.

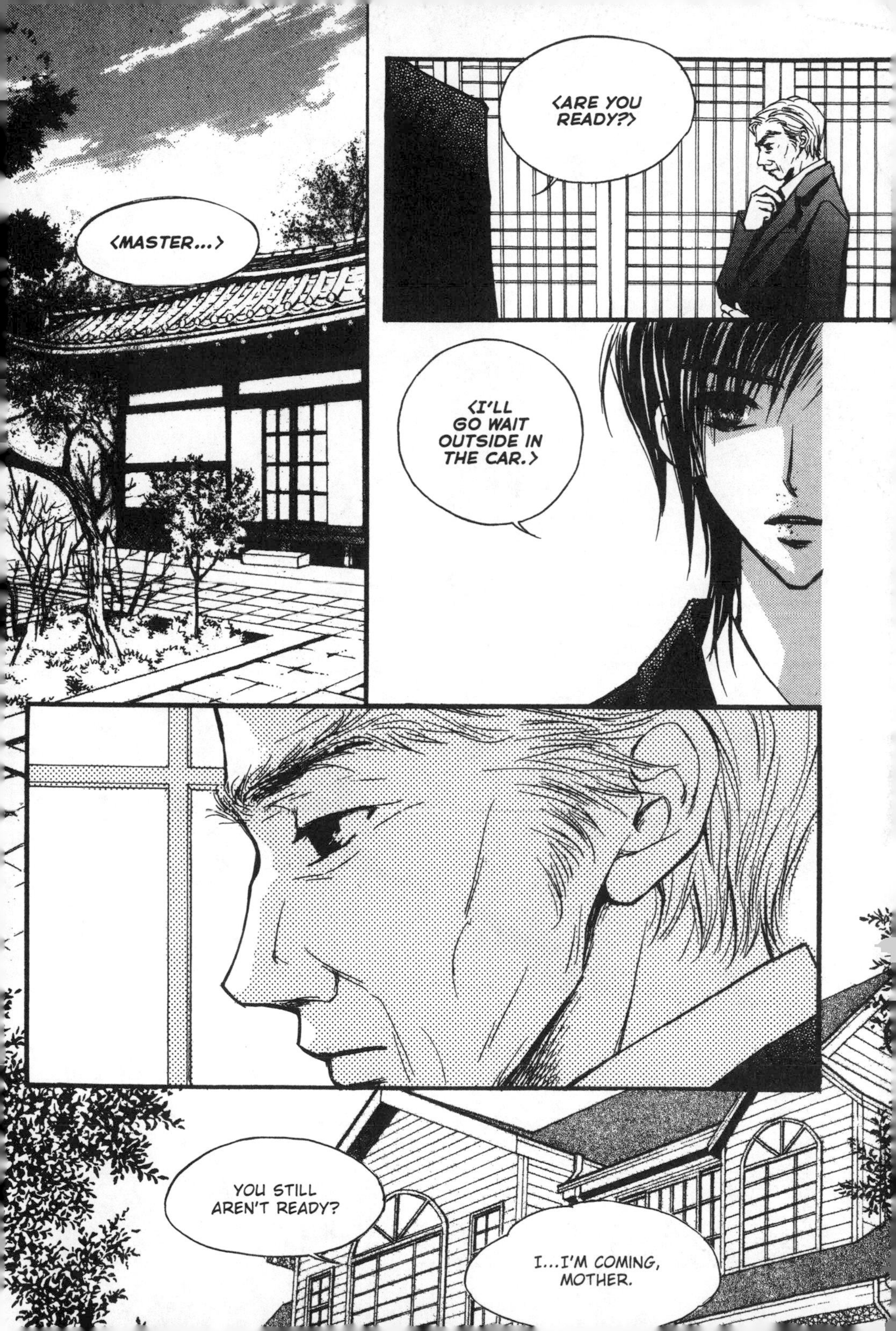
<MASTER...>
<ARE YOU READY?>
<I'LL GO WAIT OUTSIDE IN THE CAR.>
YOU STILL AREN'T READY?
I...I'M COMING, MOTHER.

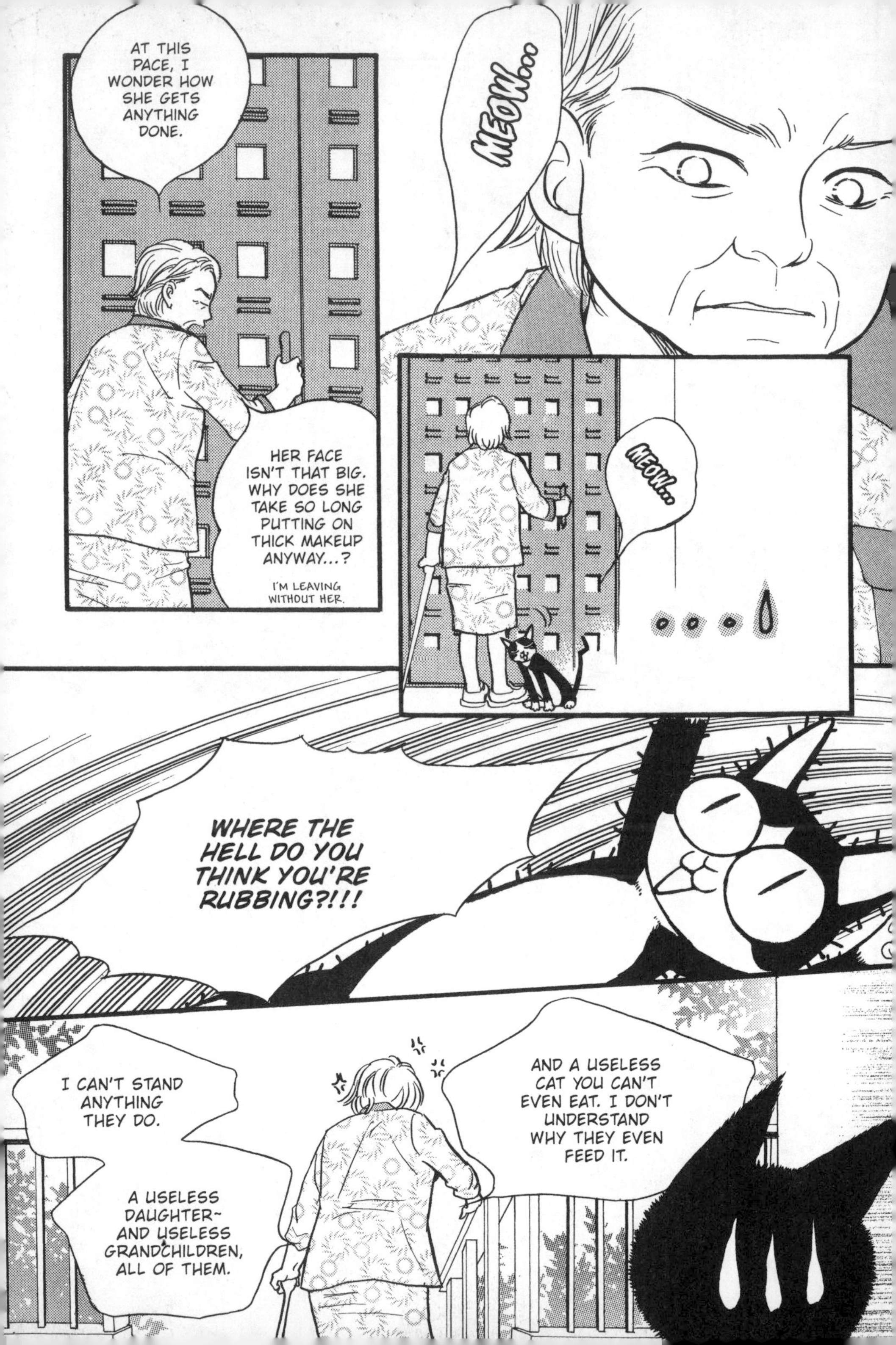
AT THIS PACE, I WONDER HOW SHE GETS ANYTHING DONE.
HER FACE ISN'T THAT BIG. WHY DOES SHE TAKE SO LONG PUTTING ON THICK MAKEUP ANYWAY...?
I'M LEAVING WITHOUT HER.
MEOW...
MEOW...
...
WHERE THE HELL DO YOU THINK YOU'RE RUBBING?!!!
I CAN'T STAND ANYTHING THEY DO.
A USELESS DAUGHTER~ AND USELESS GRANDCHILDREN, ALL OF THEM.
AND A USELESS CAT YOU CAN'T EVEN EAT. I DON'T UNDERSTAND WHY THEY EVEN FEED IT.

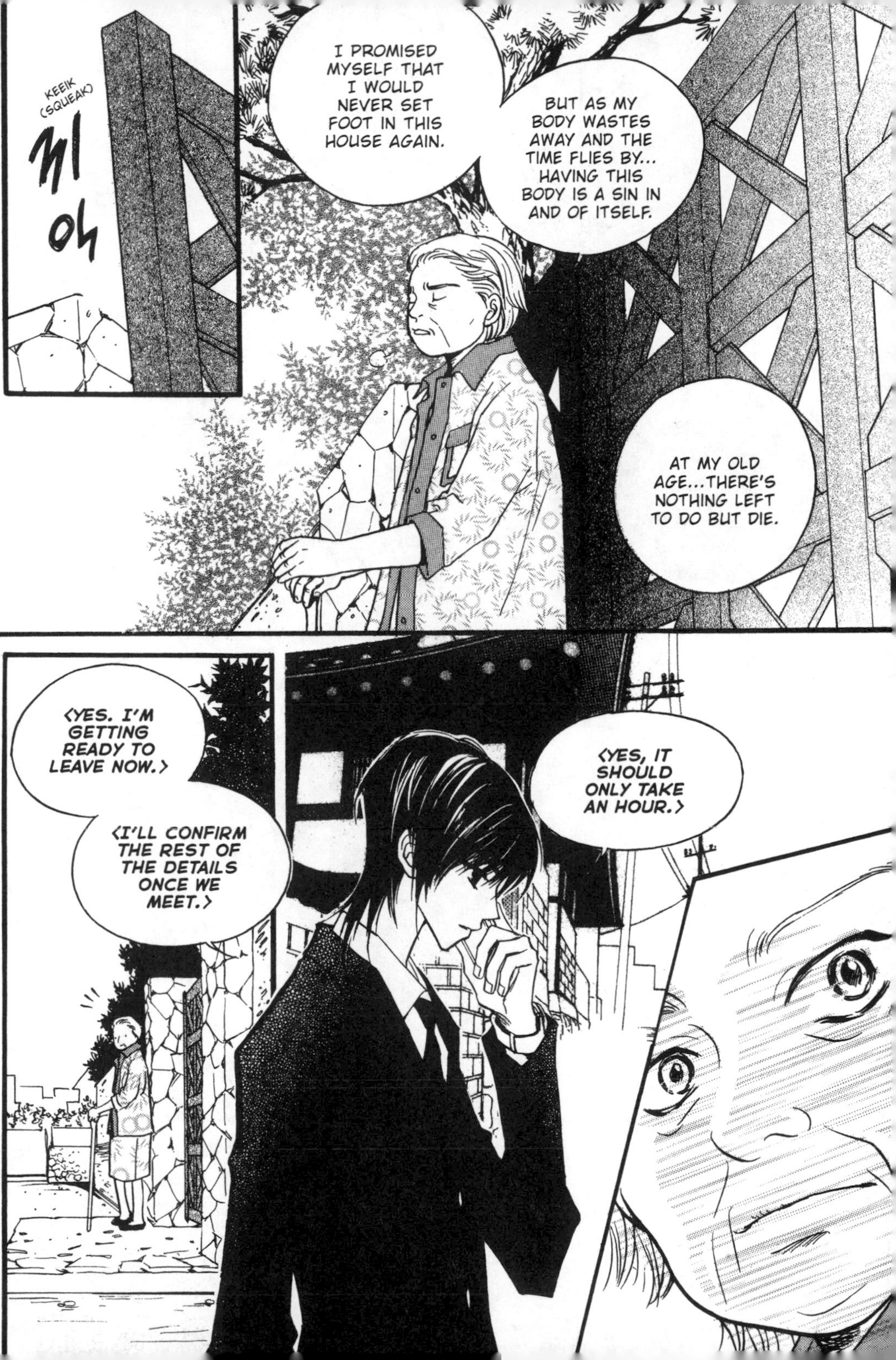
KEEIK (SQUEAK)
끼이
I PROMISED MYSELF THAT I WOULD NEVER SET FOOT IN THIS HOUSE AGAIN.
BUT AS MY BODY WASTES AWAY AND THE TIME FLIES BY... HAVING THIS BODY IS A SIN IN AND OF ITSELF.
AT MY OLD AGE...THERE'S NOTHING LEFT TO DO BUT DIE.
<YES. I'M GETTING READY TO LEAVE NOW.>
<I'LL CONFIRM THE REST OF THE DETAILS ONCE WE MEET.>
<YES, IT SHOULD ONLY TAKE AN HOUR.>

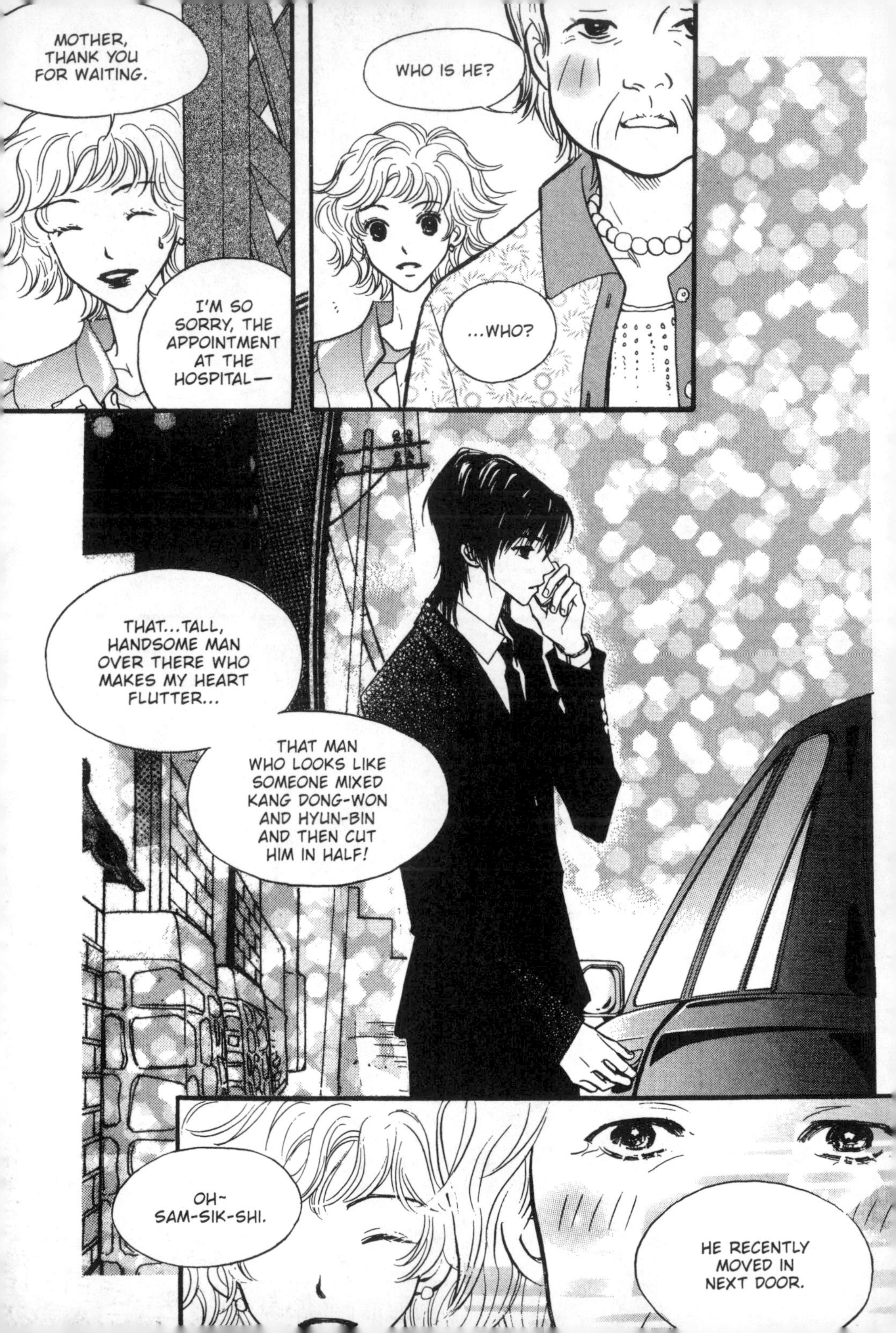
MOTHER, THANK YOU FOR WAITING.
I'M SO SORRY, THE APPOINTMENT AT THE HOSPITAL—
WHO IS HE?
...WHO?
THAT...TALL, HANDSOME MAN OVER THERE WHO MAKES MY HEART FLUTTER...
THAT MAN WHO LOOKS LIKE SOMEONE MIXED KANG DONG-WON AND HYUN-BIN AND THEN CUT HIM IN HALF!
OH~ SAM-SIK-SHI.
HE RECENTLY MOVED IN NEXT DOOR.

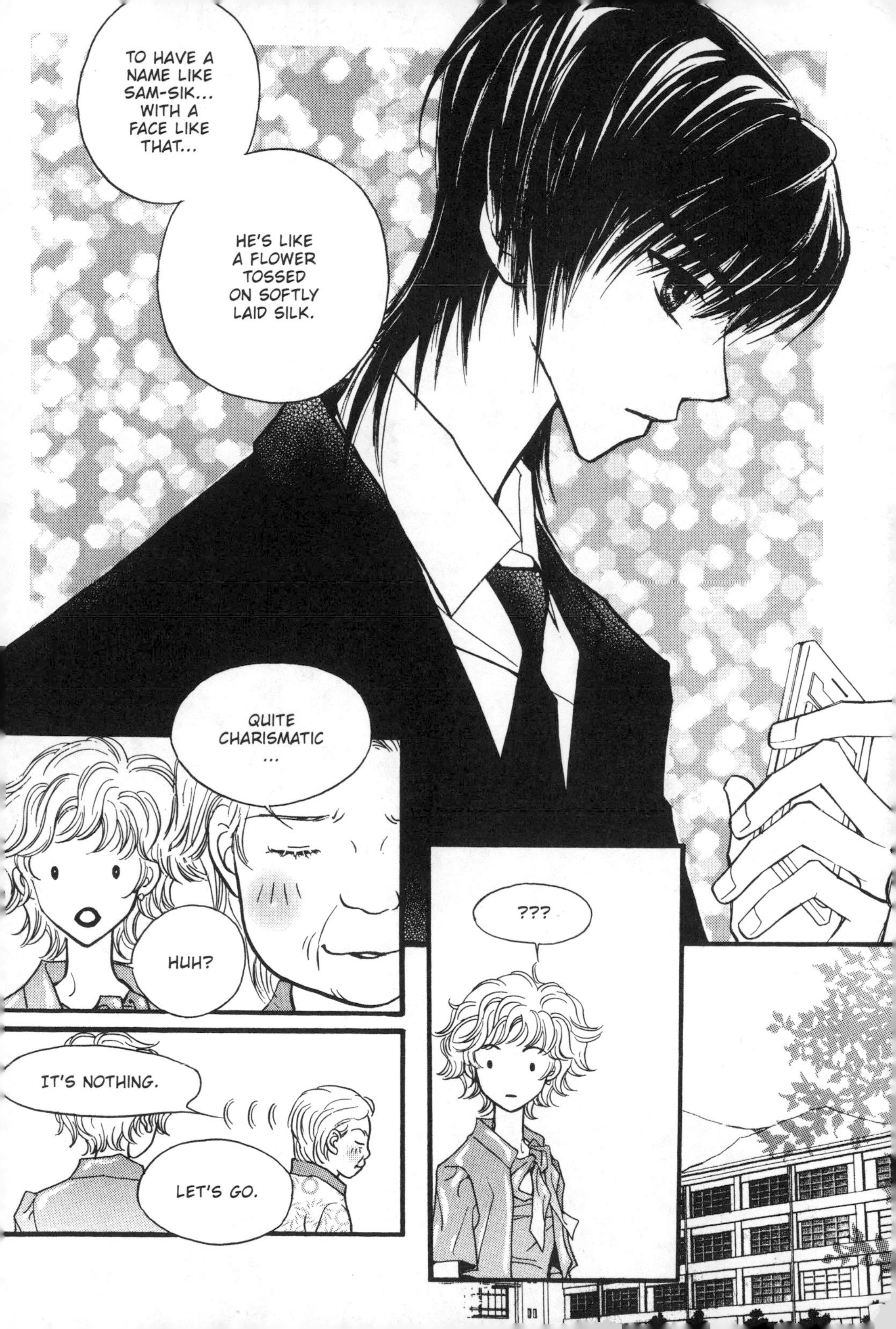
TO HAVE A NAME LIKE SAM-SIK... WITH A FACE LIKE THAT...
HE'S LIKE A FLOWER TOSSED ON SOFTLY LAID SILK.
QUITE CHARISMATIC ...
HUH?
???
IT'S NOTHING.
LET'S GO.

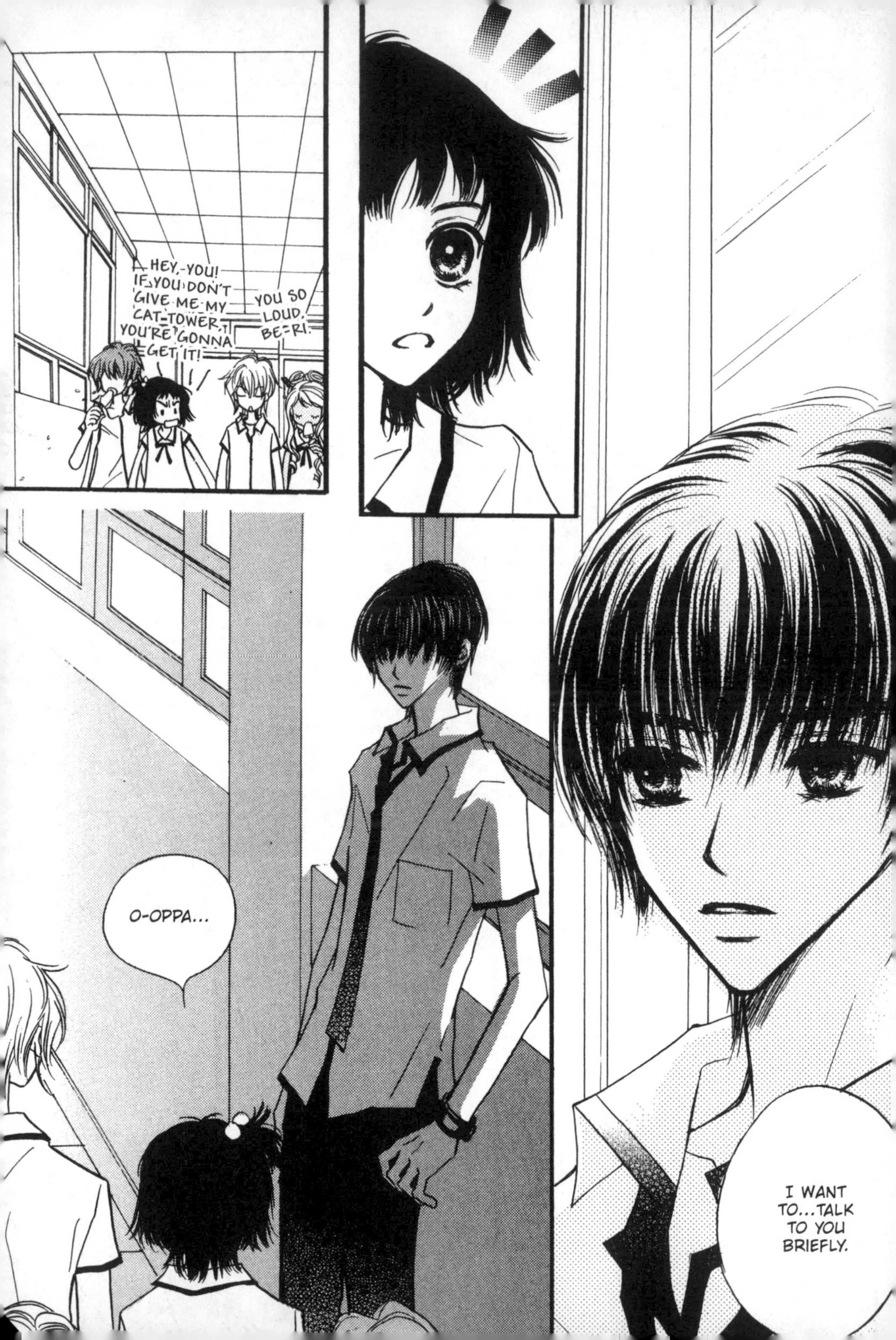
HEY, YOU! IF YOU DON'T GIVE ME MY CAT TOWER, YOU'RE GONNA GET IT!
YOU SO LOUD, BE-RI.
O-OPPA...
I WANT TO...TALK TO YOU BRIEFLY.

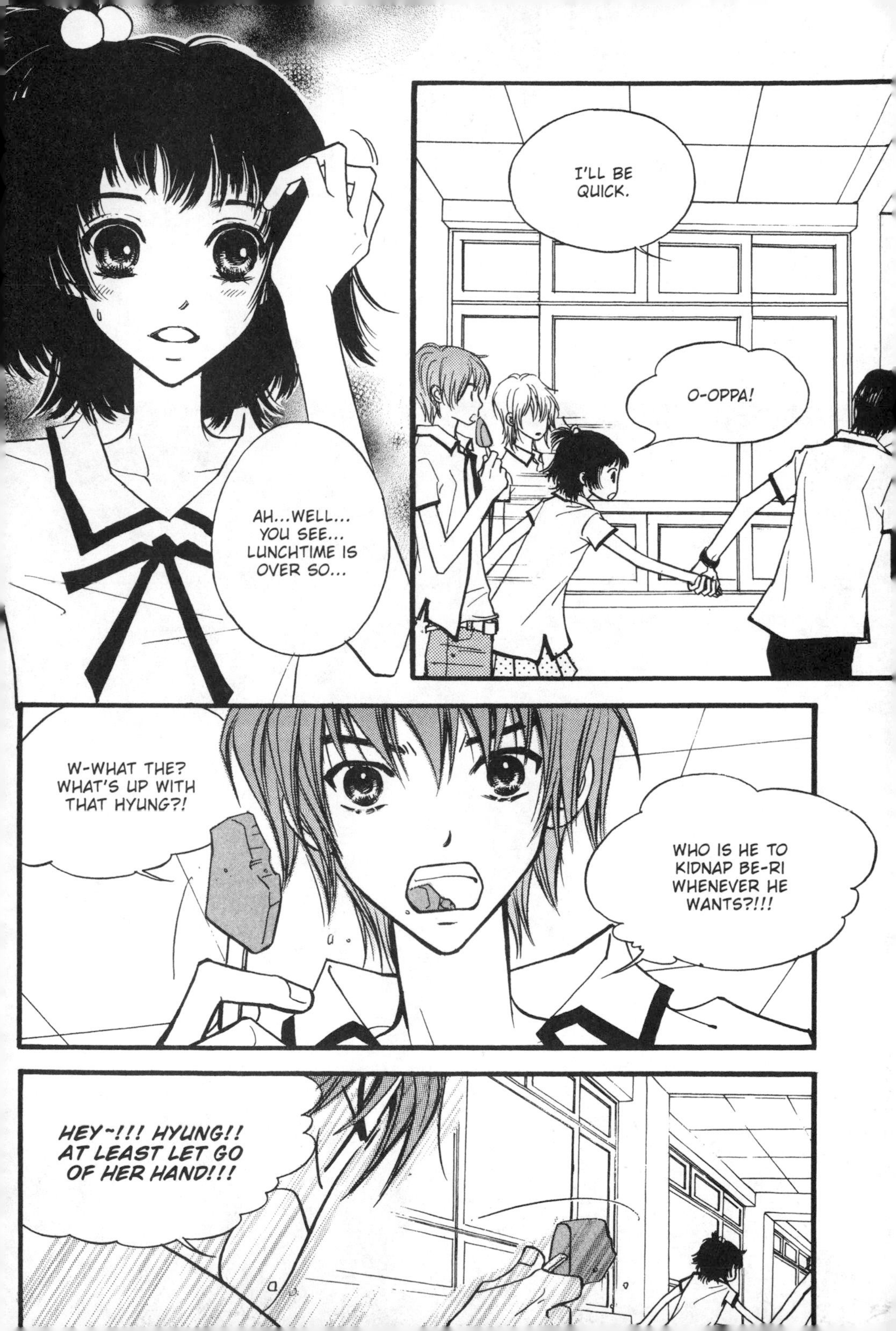
AH...WELL... YOU SEE... LUNCHTIME IS OVER SO...
I'LL BE QUICK.
O-OPPA!
W-WHAT THE? WHAT'S UP WITH THAT HYUNG?!
WHO IS HE TO KIDNAP BE-RI WHENEVER HE WANTS?!!!
HEY~!!! HYUNG!! AT LEAST LET GO OF HER HAND!!!

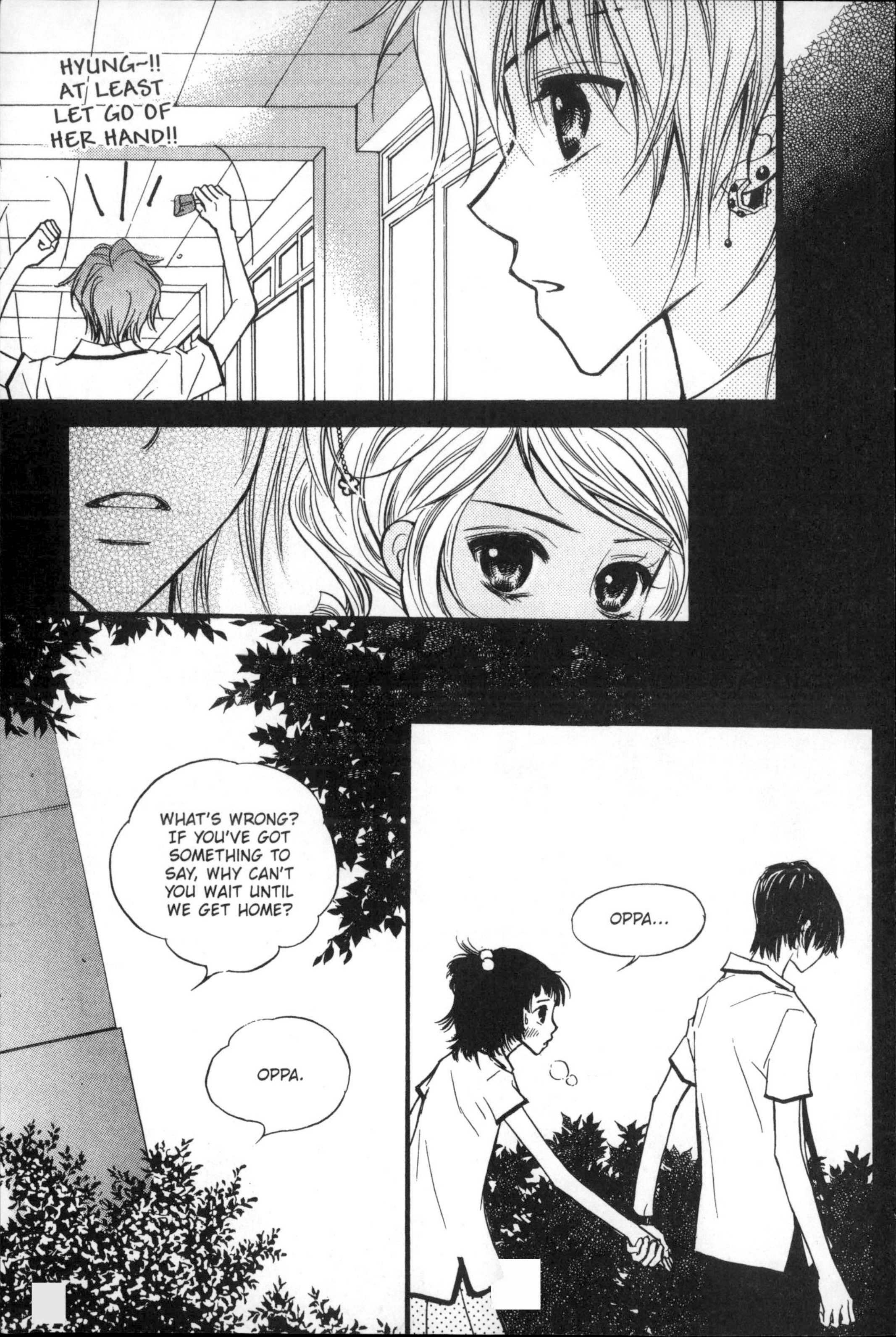
HYUNG~!! AT LEAST LET GO OF HER HAND!!
WHAT'S WRONG? IF YOU'VE GOT SOMETHING TO SAY, WHY CAN'T YOU WAIT UNTIL WE GET HOME?
OPPA.
OPPA...

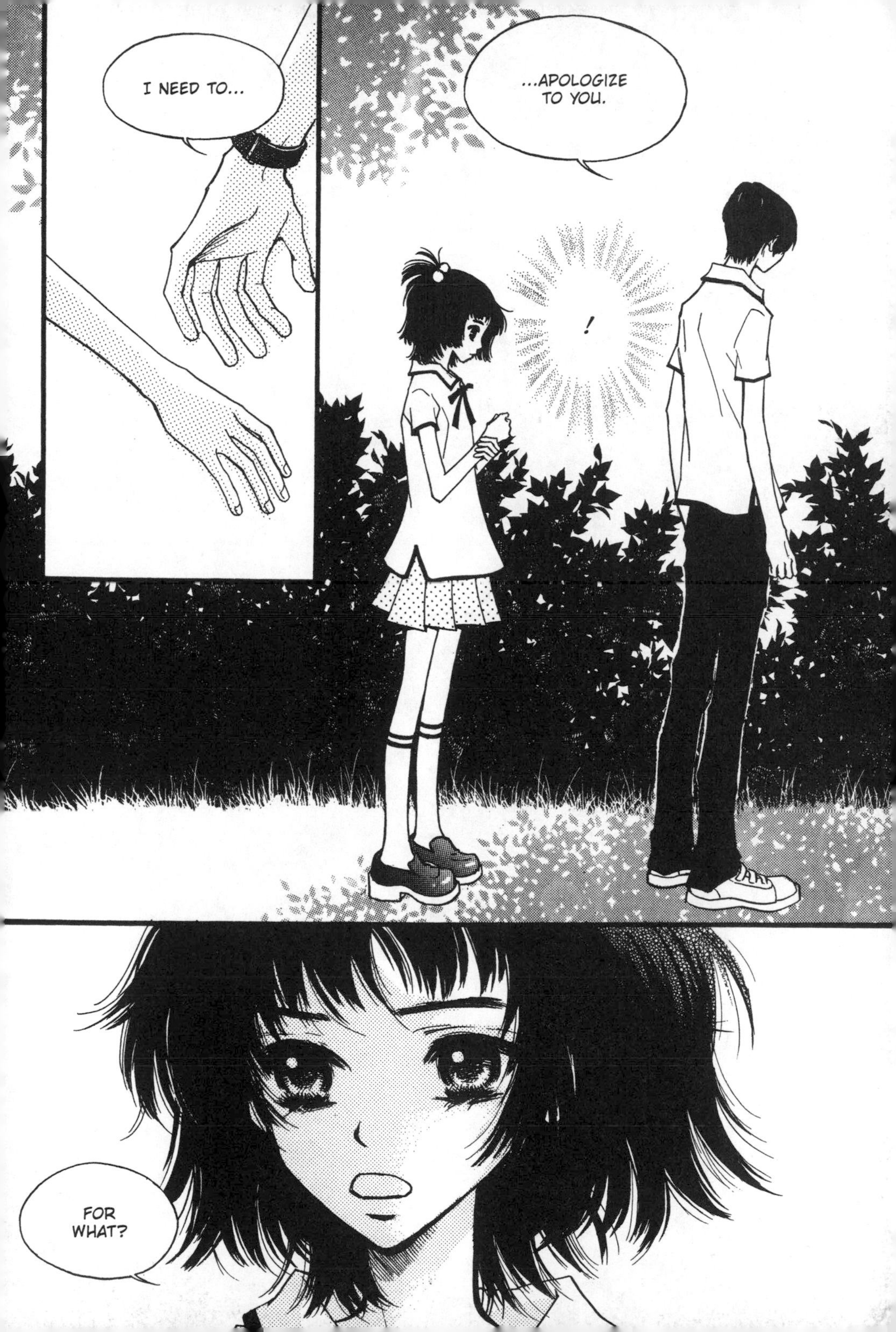
I NEED TO...
...APOLOGIZE TO YOU.
!
FOR WHAT?

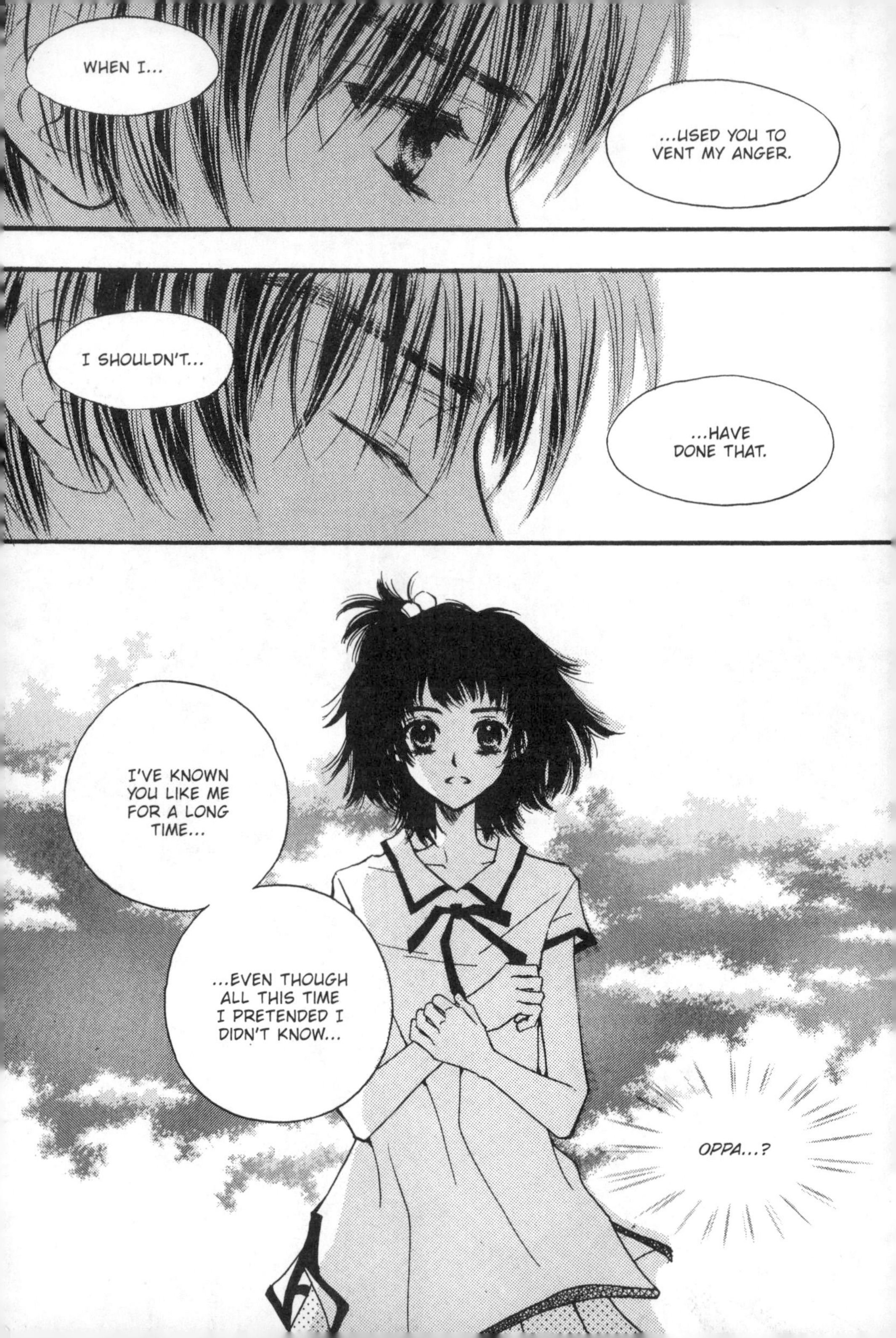
WHEN I...
...USED YOU TO VENT MY ANGER.
I SHOULDN'T...
...HAVE DONE THAT.
I'VE KNOWN YOU LIKE ME FOR A LONG TIME...
...EVEN THOUGH ALL THIS TIME I PRETENDED I DIDN'T KNOW...
OPPA...?

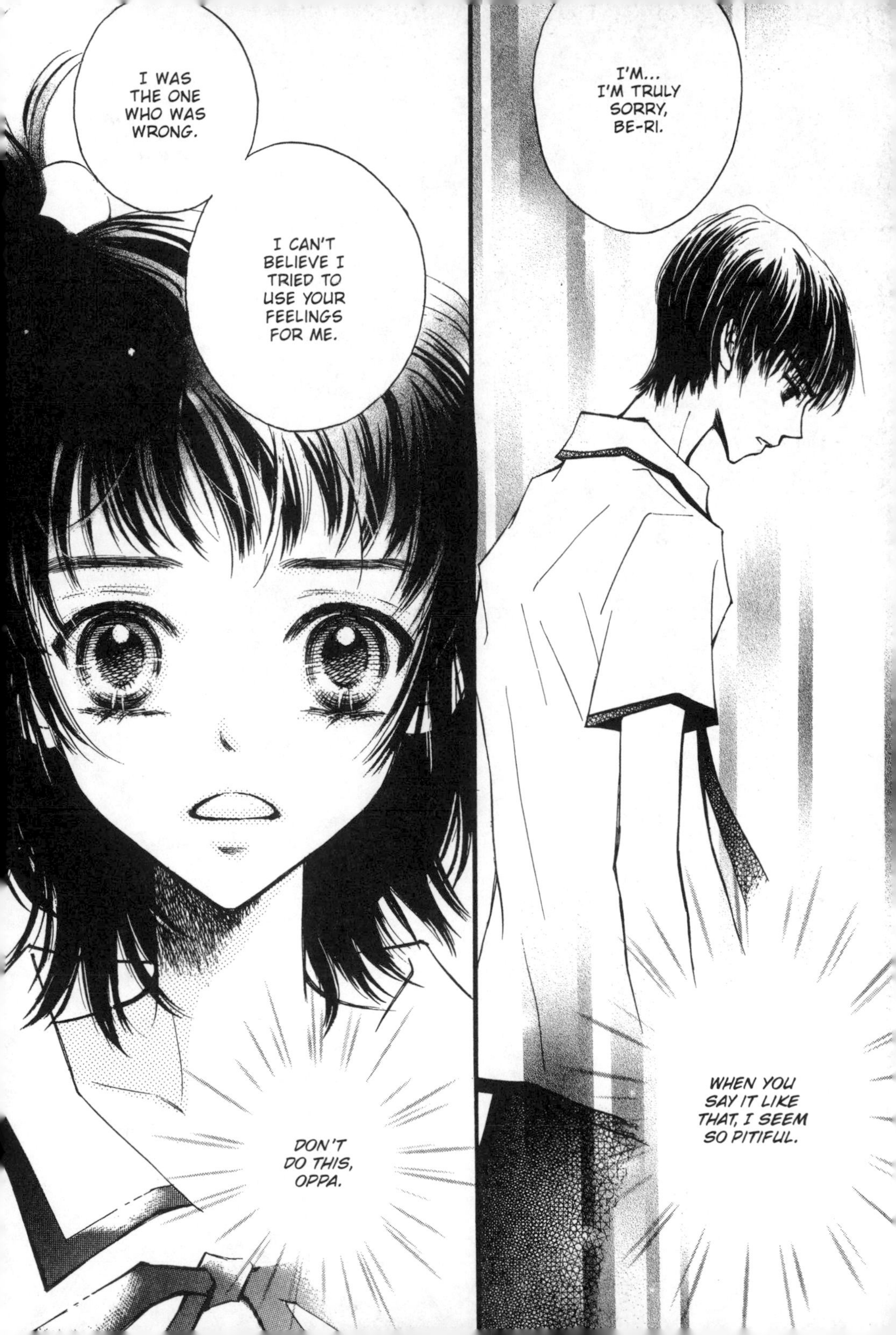
I WAS THE ONE WHO WAS WRONG.
I CAN'T BELIEVE I TRIED TO USE YOUR FEELINGS FOR ME.
DON'T DO THIS, OPPA.
I'M... I'M TRULY SORRY, BE-RI.
WHEN YOU SAY IT LIKE THAT, I SEEM SO PITIFUL.

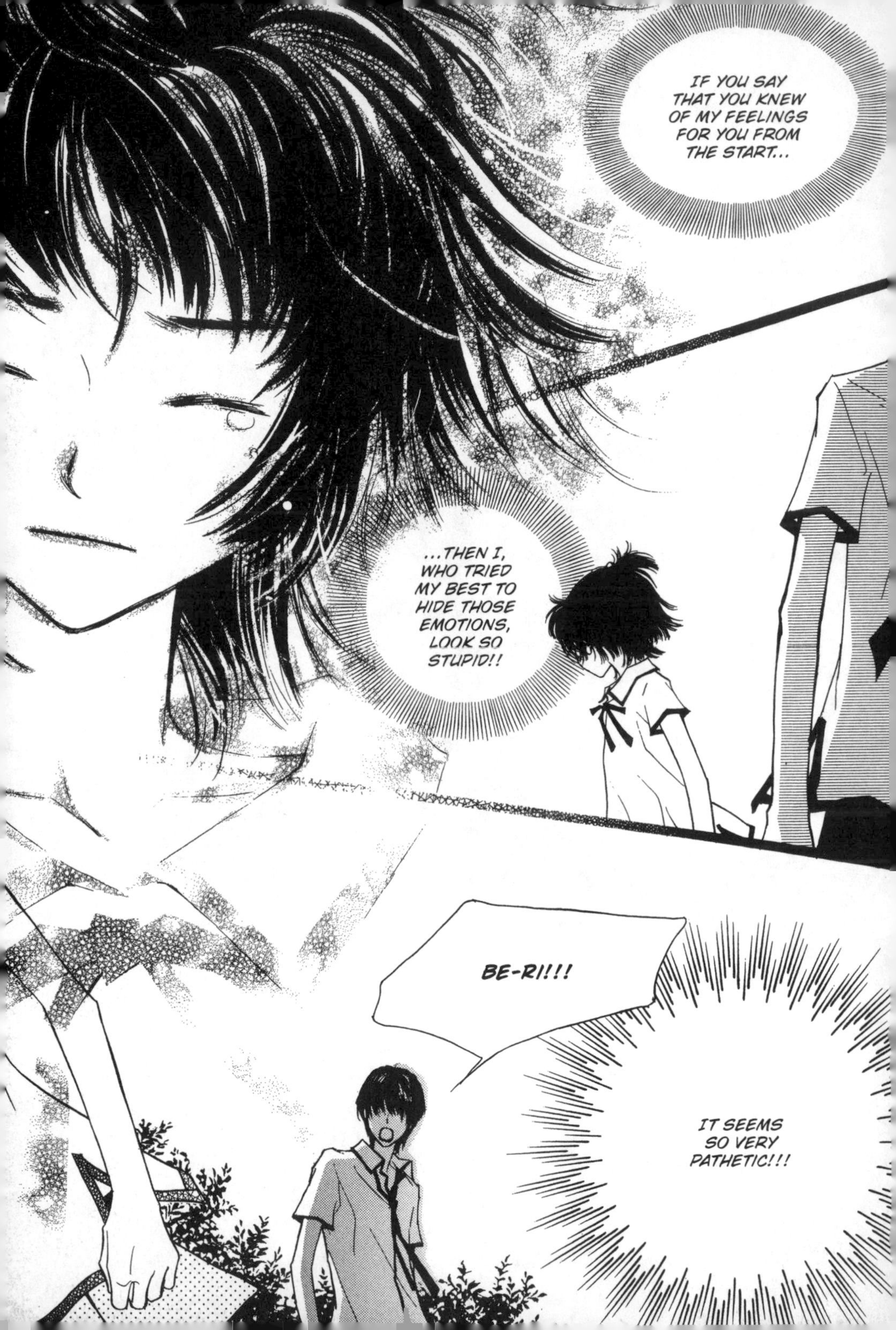
IF YOU SAY THAT YOU KNEW OF MY FEELINGS FOR YOU FROM THE START...
...THEN I, WHO TRIED MY BEST TO HIDE THOSE EMOTIONS, LOOK SO STUPID!!
BE-RI!!!
IT SEEMS SO VERY PATHETIC!!!

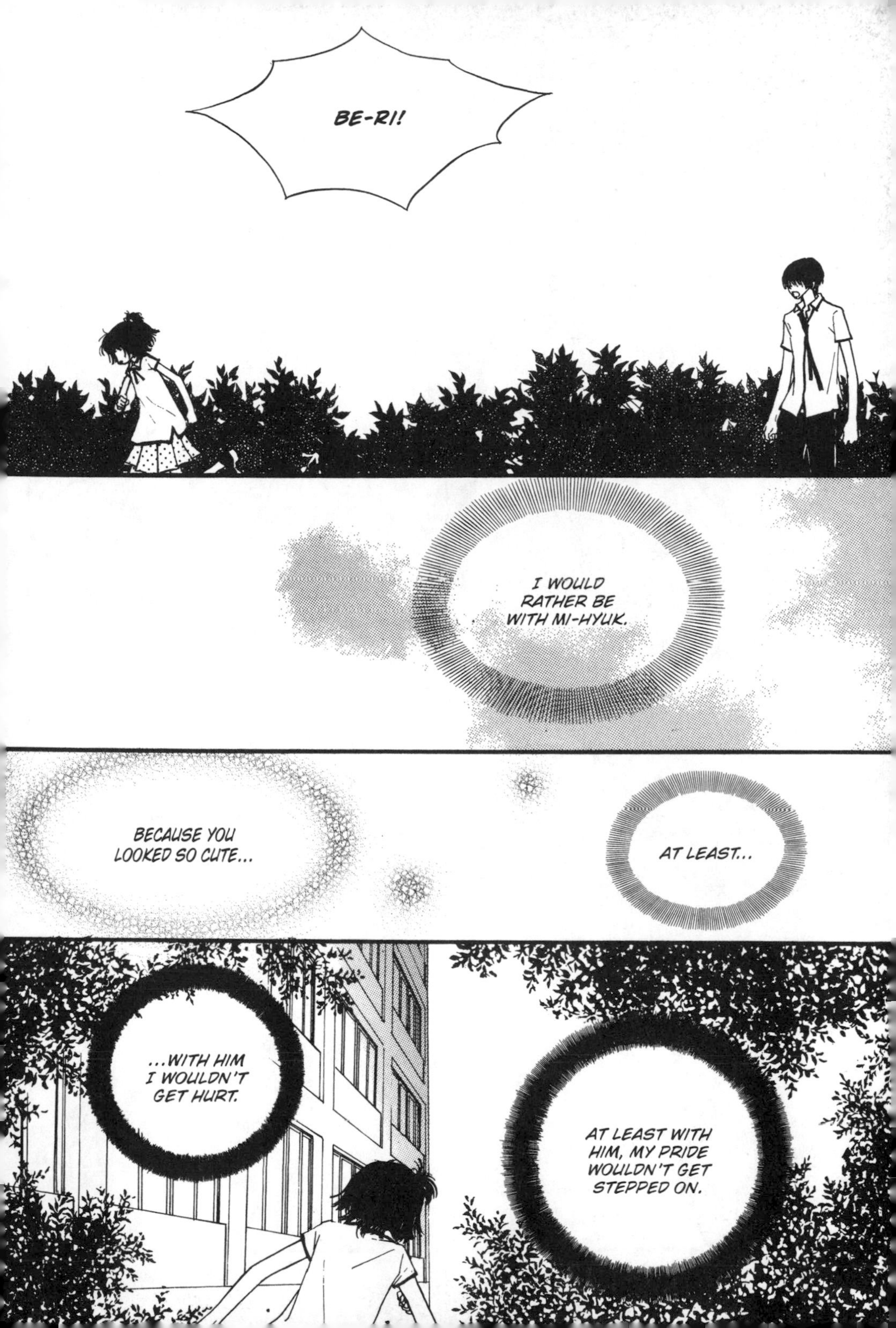
BE-RI!
I WOULD RATHER BE WITH MI-HYUK.
BECAUSE YOU LOOKED SO CUTE...
AT LEAST...
...WITH HIM I WOULDN'T GET HURT.
AT LEAST WITH HIM, MY PRIDE WOULDN'T GET STEPPED ON.

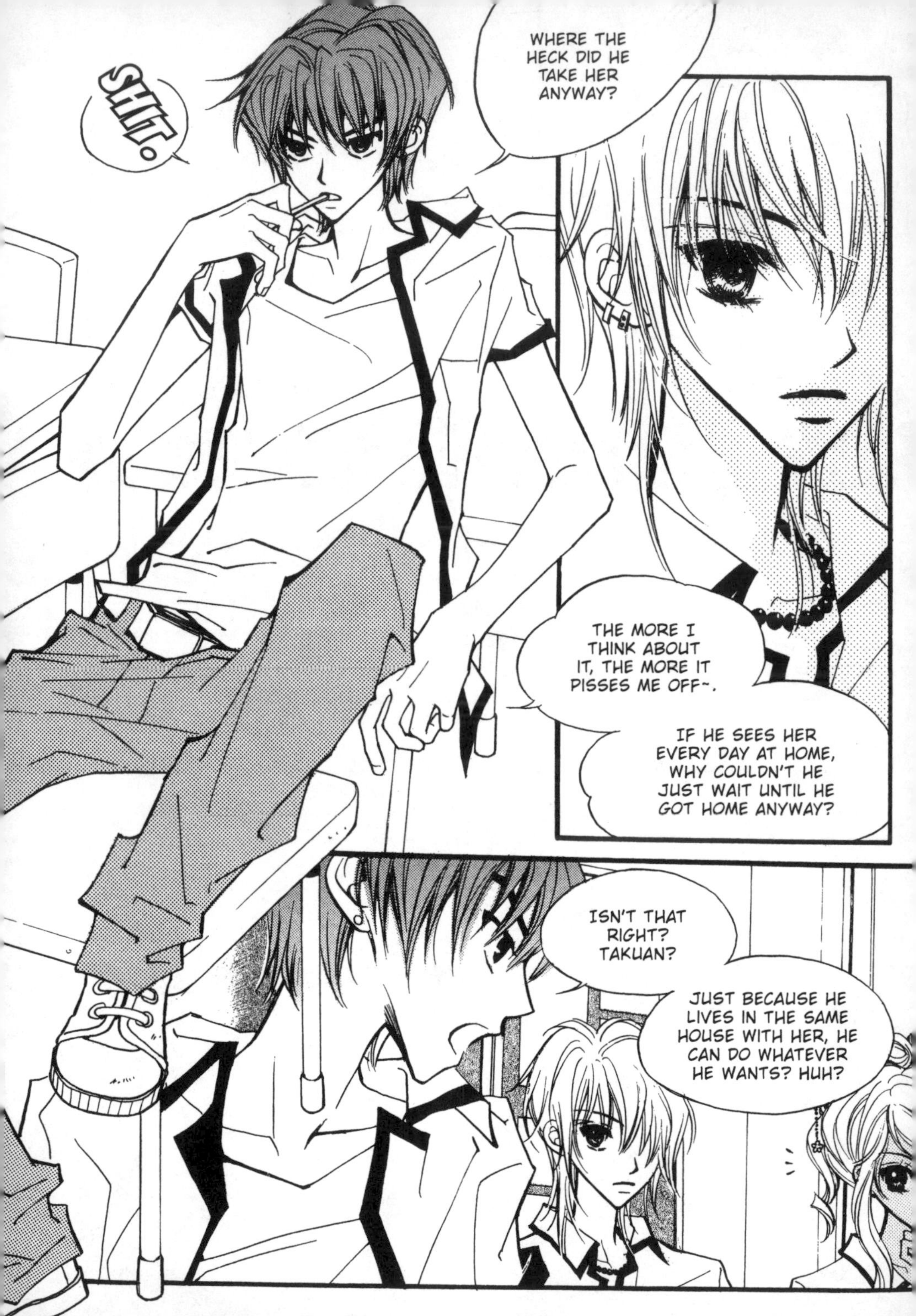
SHIT.
WHERE THE HECK DID HE TAKE HER ANYWAY?
THE MORE I THINK ABOUT IT, THE MORE IT PISSES ME OFF~.
IF HE SEES HER EVERY DAY AT HOME, WHY COULDN'T HE JUST WAIT UNTIL HE GOT HOME ANYWAY?
ISN'T THAT RIGHT? TAKUAN?
JUST BECAUSE HE LIVES IN THE SAME HOUSE WITH HER, HE CAN DO WHATEVER HE WANTS? HUH?

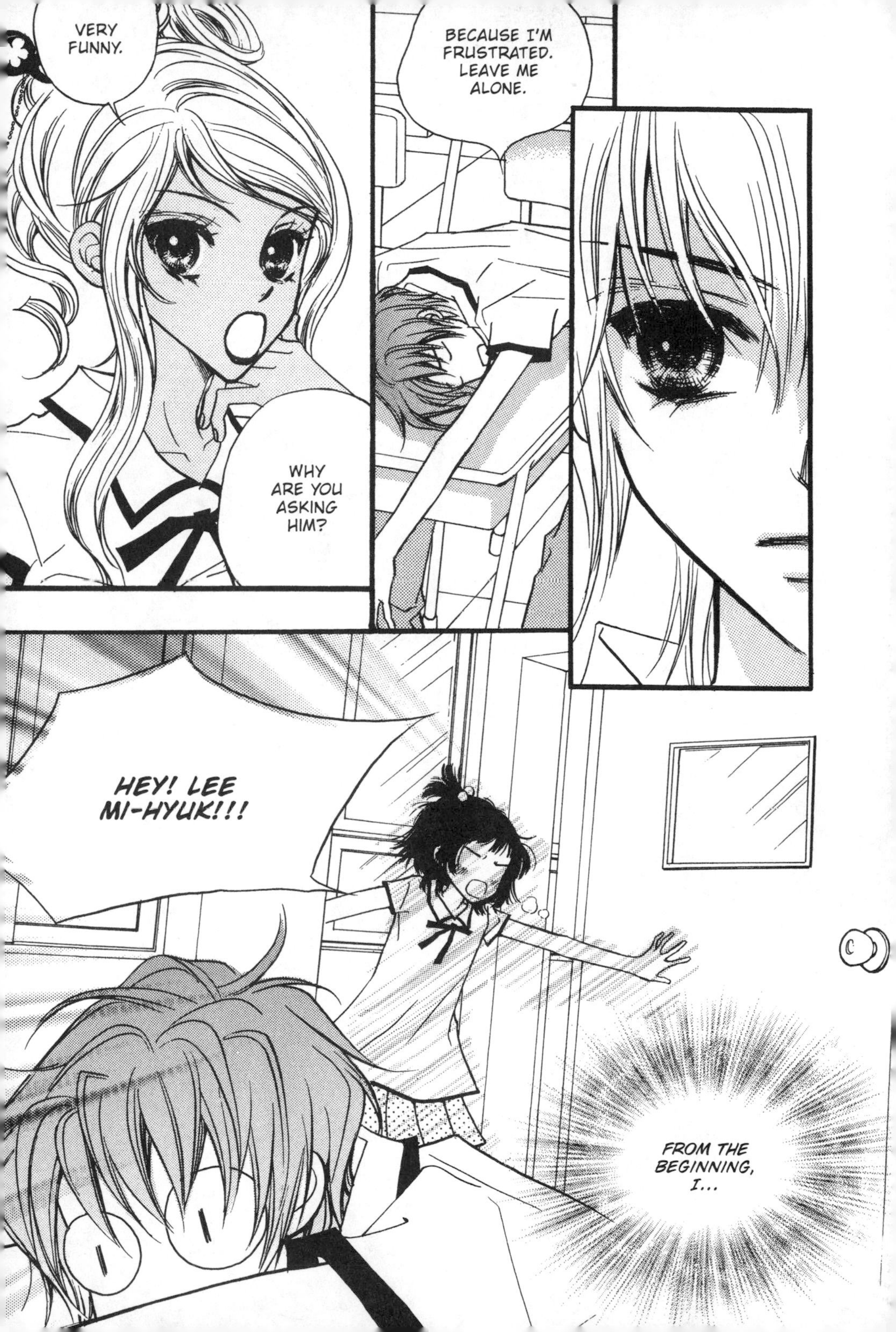
VERY FUNNY.
WHY ARE YOU ASKING HIM?
BECAUSE I'M FRUSTRATED. LEAVE ME ALONE.
HEY! LEE MI-HYUK!!!
FROM THE BEGINNING, I...

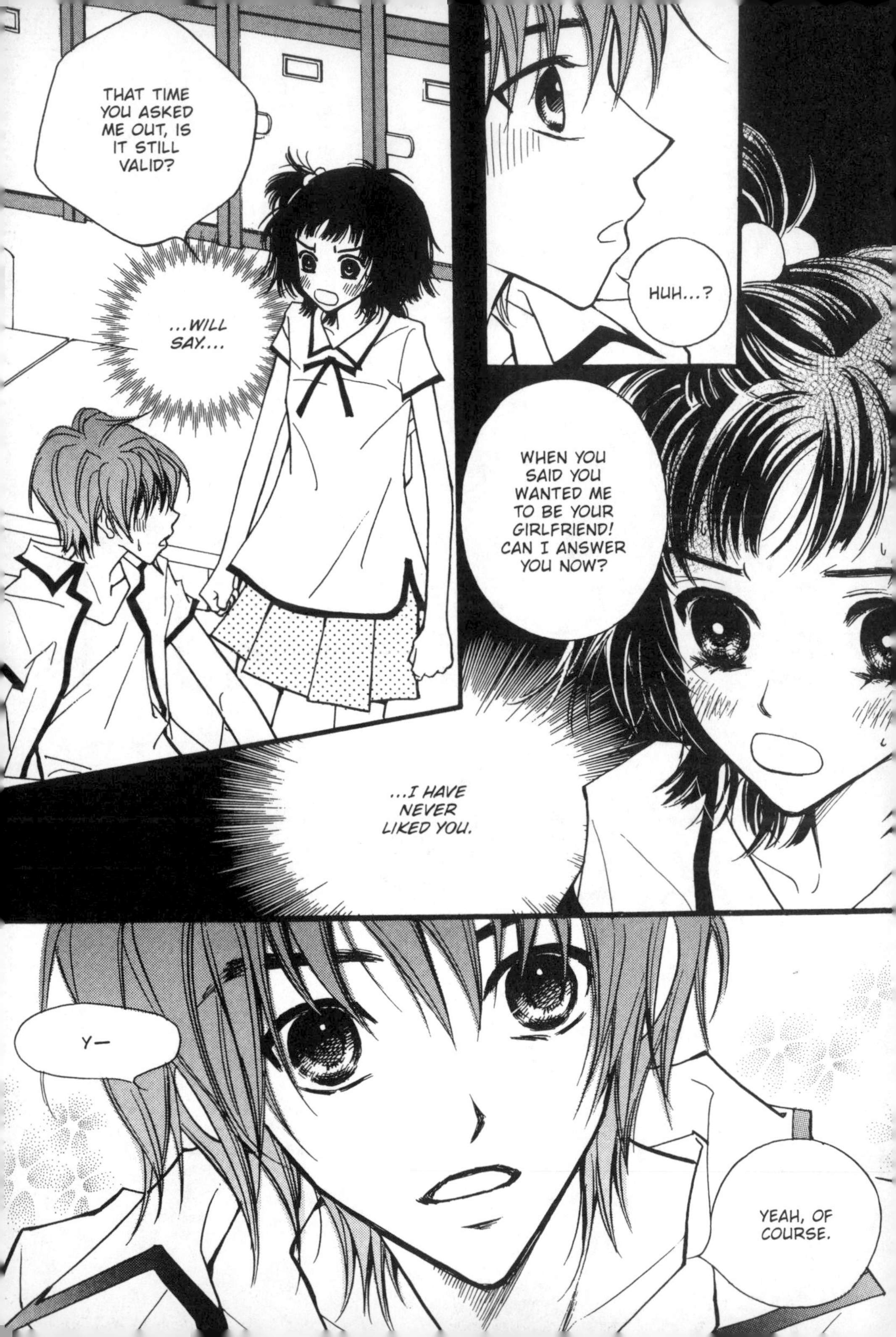
THAT TIME YOU ASKED ME OUT, IS IT STILL VALID?
...WILL SAY....
HUH...?
WHEN YOU SAID YOU WANTED ME TO BE YOUR GIRLFRIEND! CAN I ANSWER YOU NOW?
...I HAVE NEVER LIKED YOU.
Y—
YEAH, OF COURSE.

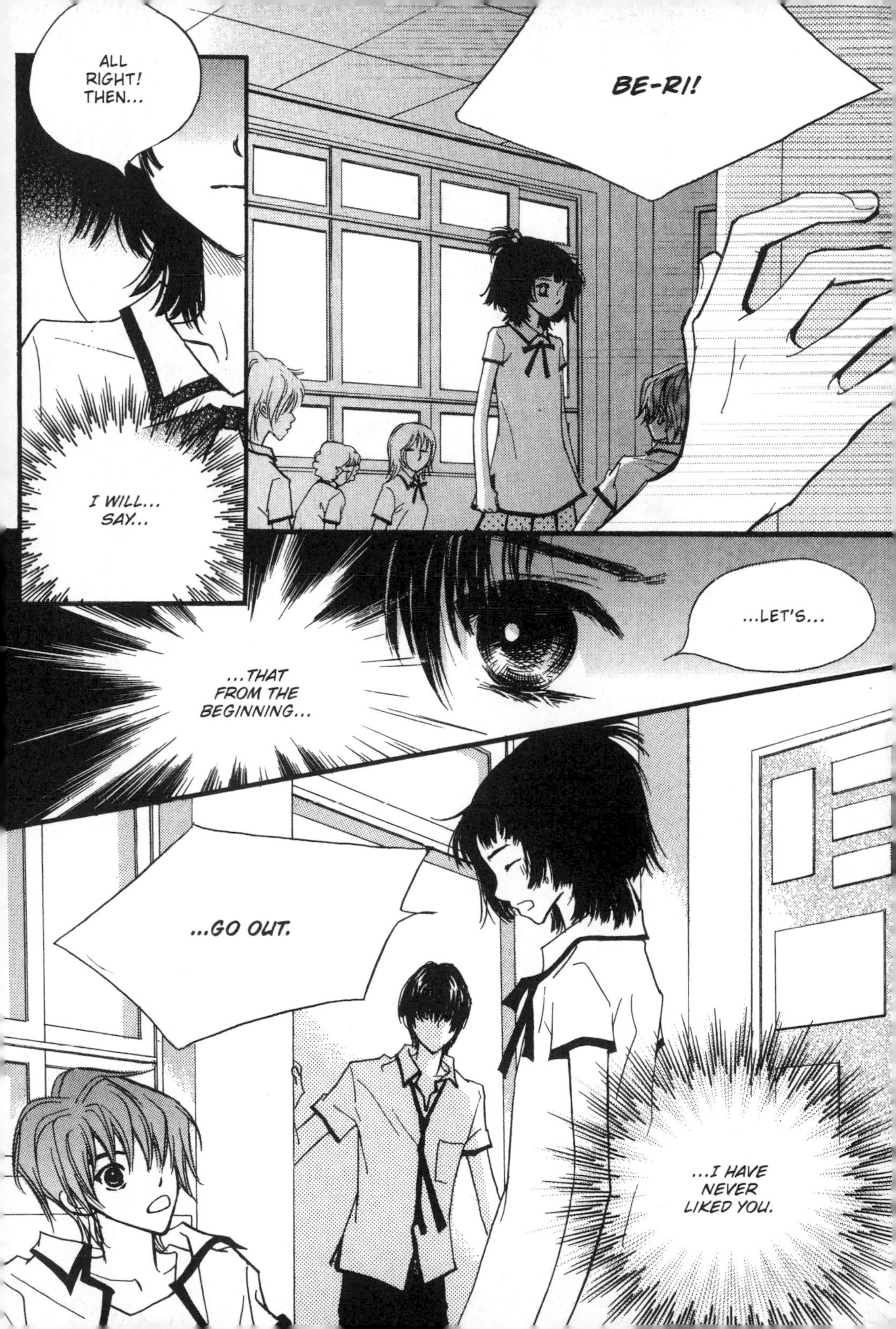
ALL RIGHT! THEN...
I WILL... SAY...
BE-RI!
...THAT FROM THE BEGINNING...
...LET'S...
...GO OUT.
...I HAVE NEVER LIKED YOU.

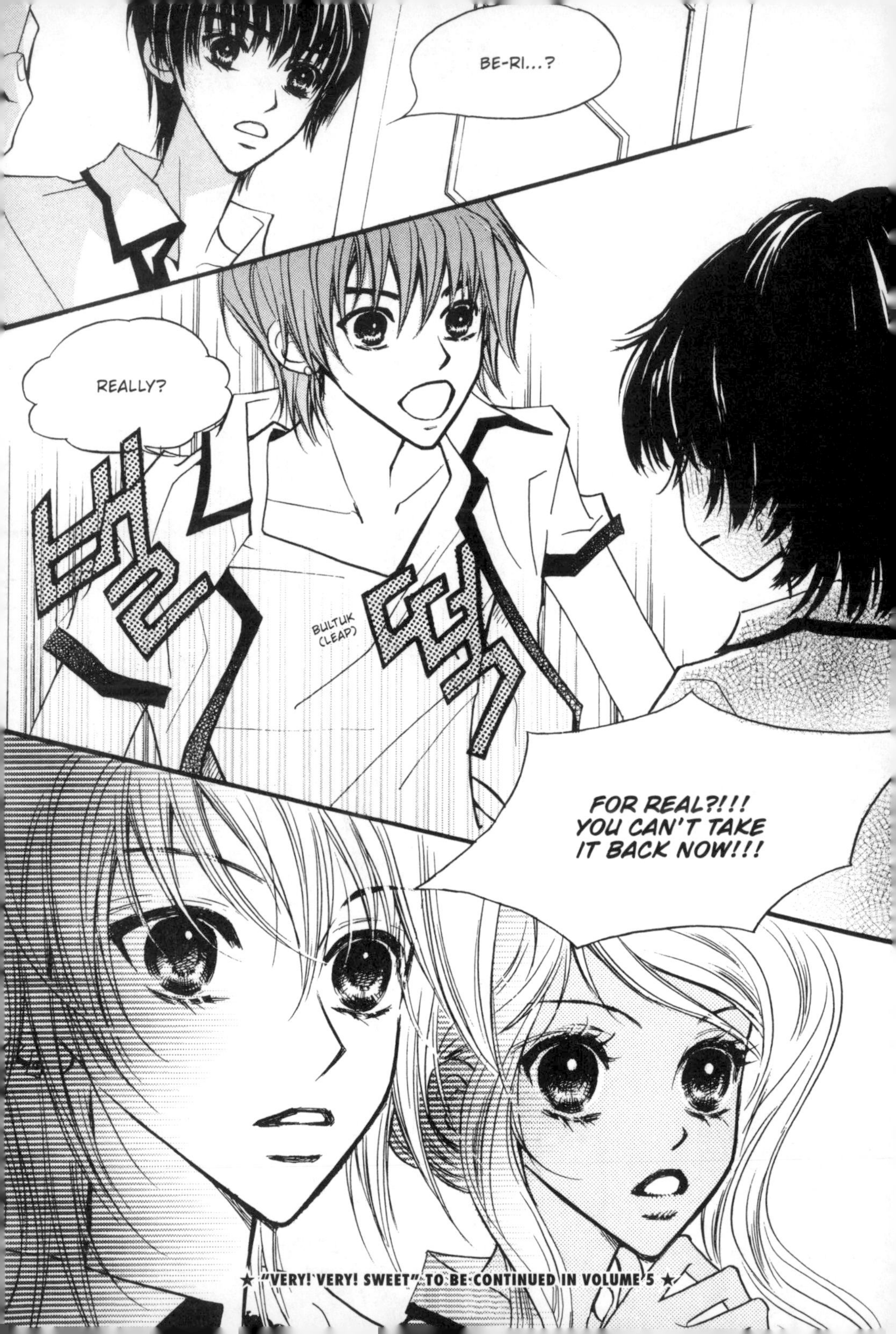
BE-RI...?
REALLY?
BULTUK (LEAP)
FOR REAL?!!! YOU CAN'T TAKE IT BACK NOW!!!
★ "VERY! VERY! SWEET" TO BE CONTINUED IN VOLUME 5 ★

THE FIRST STORY – NOTHING IS FREE.

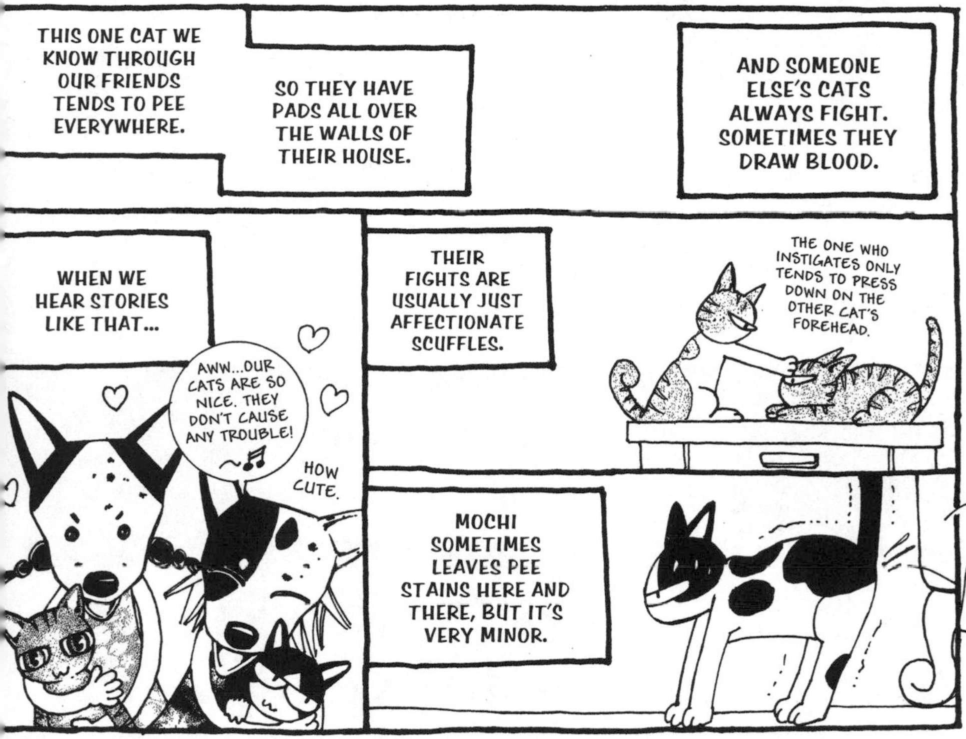

THIS ONE CAT WE KNOW THROUGH OUR FRIENDS TENDS TO PEE EVERYWHERE.
SO THEY HAVE PADS ALL OVER THE WALLS OF THEIR HOUSE.
AND SOMEONE ELSE'S CATS ALWAYS FIGHT. SOMETIMES THEY DRAW BLOOD.
WHEN WE HEAR STORIES LIKE THAT...
AWW...OUR CATS ARE SO NICE. THEY DON'T CAUSE ANY TROUBLE! ~♫
HOW CUTE.
THEIR FIGHTS ARE USUALLY JUST AFFECTIONATE SCUFFLES.
THE ONE WHO INSTIGATES ONLY TENDS TO PRESS DOWN ON THE OTHER CAT'S FOREHEAD.
MOCHI SOMETIMES LEAVES PEE STAINS HERE AND THERE, BUT IT'S VERY MINOR.
SOFA
THE SMELL IS VERY STRONG.

THEN...ONE DAY!

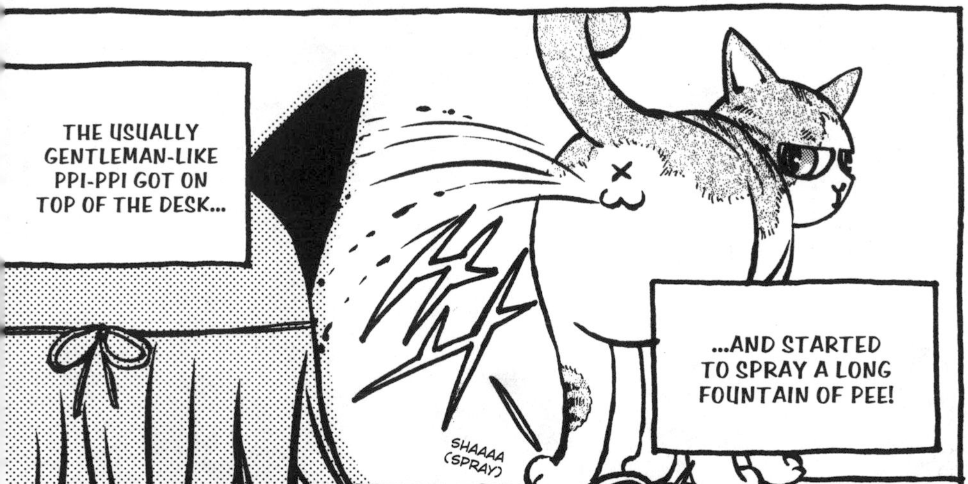

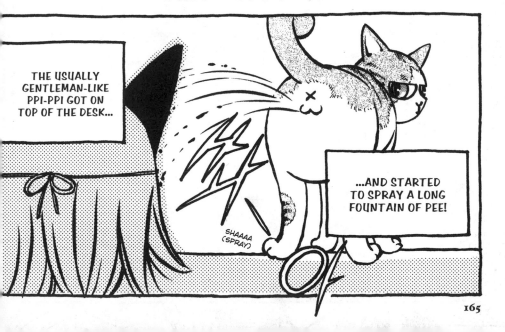

THE USUALLY GENTLEMAN-LIKE PPI-PPI GOT ON TOP OF THE DESK...
...AND STARTED TO SPRAY A LONG FOUNTAIN OF PEE!
SHAAAA (SPRAY)

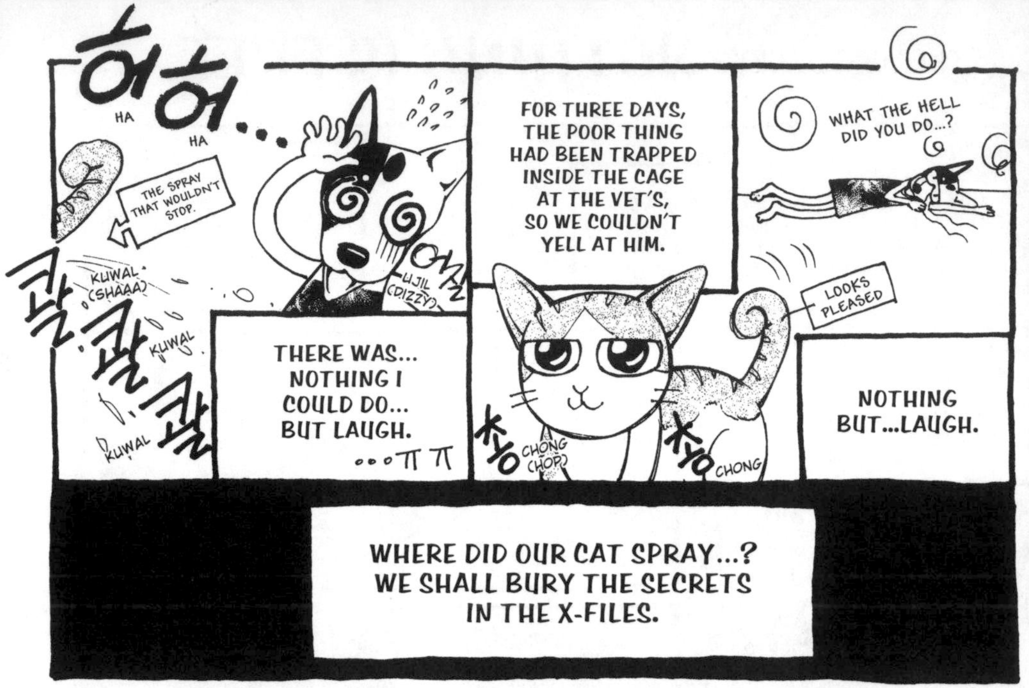
허허...
HA
HA
THE SPRAY THAT WOULDN'T STOP.
콸 콸 콸
KUWAL (SHAAA)
KUWAL
KUWAL
UJIL (DIZZY)
THERE WAS... NOTHING I COULD DO... BUT LAUGH.
...ㅠㅠ
FOR THREE DAYS, THE POOR THING HAD BEEN TRAPPED INSIDE THE CAGE AT THE VET'S, SO WE COULDN'T YELL AT HIM.
LOOKS PLEASED
총
CHONG (HOP)
총
CHONG
WHAT THE HELL DID YOU DO...?
NOTHING BUT...LAUGH.
WHERE DID OUR CAT SPRAY...? WE SHALL BURY THE SECRETS IN THE X-FILES.

THE SECOND STORY – **WHO ORDERED JJA-JANG-MYUN?**

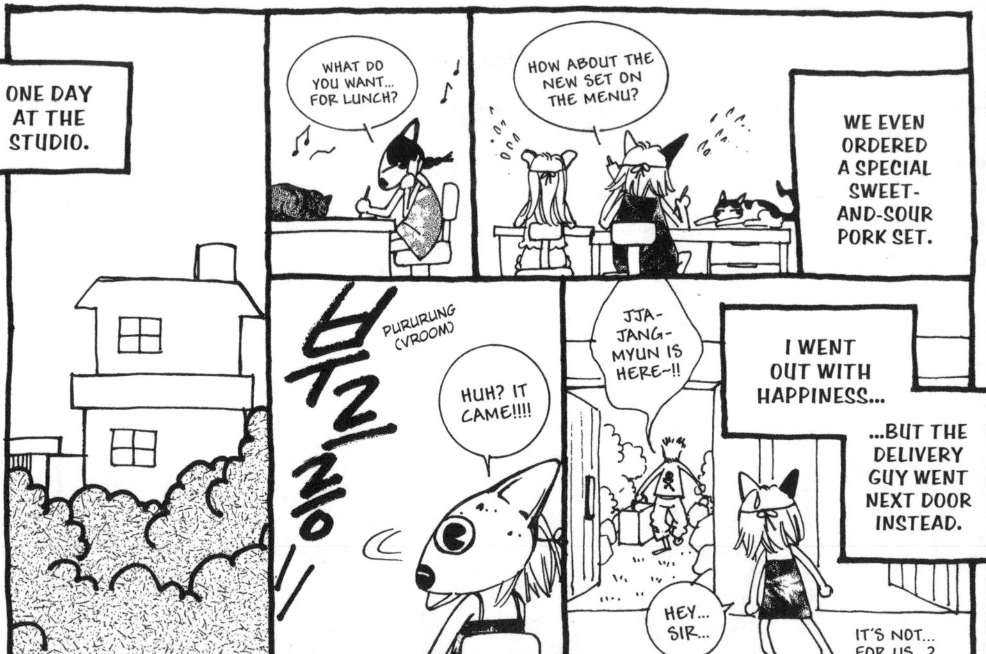
ONE DAY AT THE STUDIO.
WHAT DO YOU WANT... FOR LUNCH?
HOW ABOUT THE NEW SET ON THE MENU?
WE EVEN ORDERED A SPECIAL SWEET-AND-SOUR PORK SET.
부르릉
PURURUNG (VROOM)
HUH? IT CAME!!!!
JJA-JANG-MYUN IS HERE~!!
I WENT OUT WITH HAPPINESS...
...BUT THE DELIVERY GUY WENT NEXT DOOR INSTEAD.
HEY... SIR...
IT'S NOT... FOR US...?

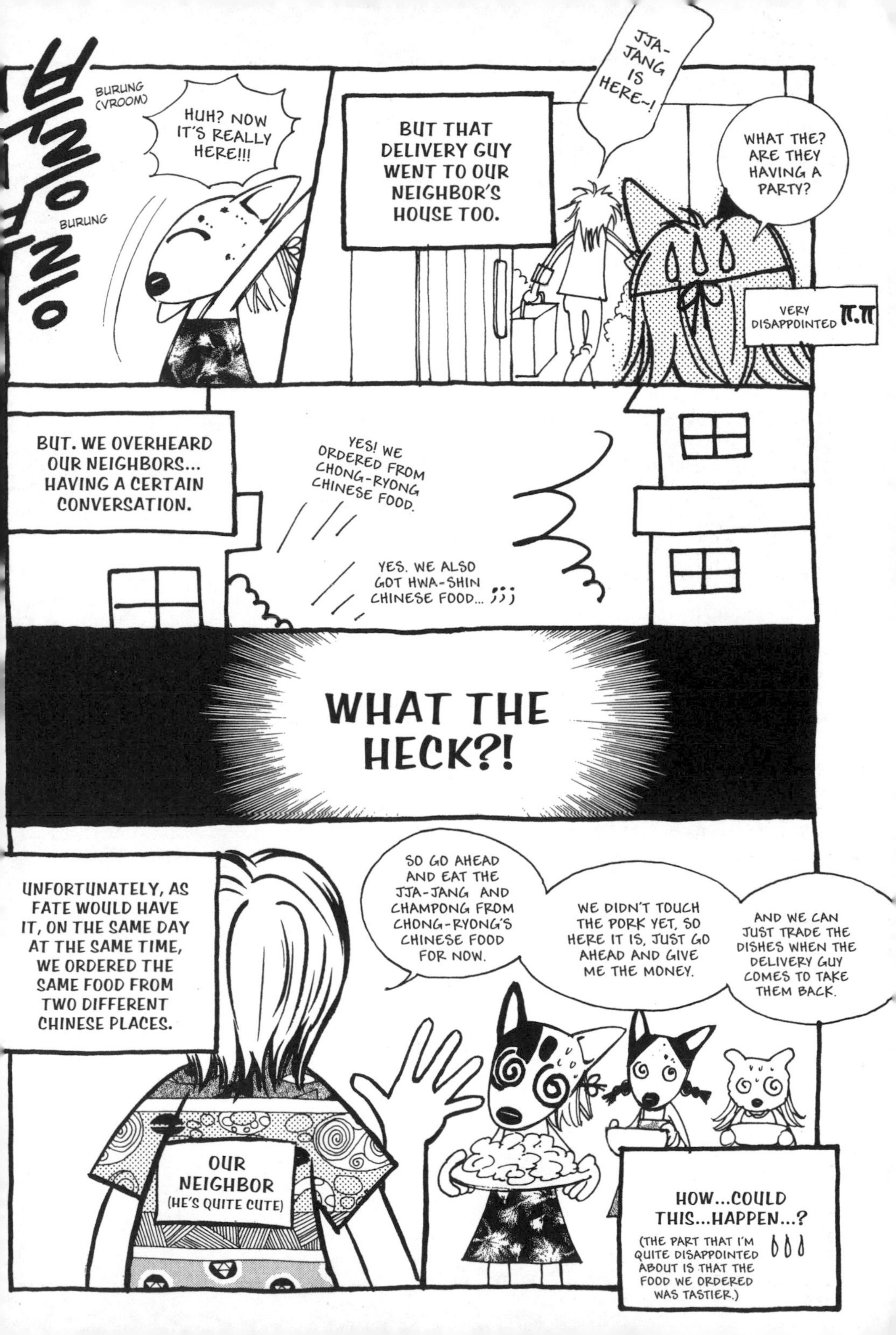
BURUNG (VROOM)
HUH? NOW IT'S REALLY HERE!!!
BURUNG
BUT THAT DELIVERY GUY WENT TO OUR NEIGHBOR'S HOUSE TOO.
JJA-JANG IS HERE~!
WHAT THE? ARE THEY HAVING A PARTY?
VERY DISAPPOINTED π.π
BUT. WE OVERHEARD OUR NEIGHBORS... HAVING A CERTAIN CONVERSATION.
YES! WE ORDERED FROM CHONG-RYONG CHINESE FOOD.
YES. WE ALSO GOT HWA-SHIN CHINESE FOOD... ;;;
WHAT THE HECK?!
UNFORTUNATELY, AS FATE WOULD HAVE IT, ON THE SAME DAY AT THE SAME TIME, WE ORDERED THE SAME FOOD FROM TWO DIFFERENT CHINESE PLACES.
SO GO AHEAD AND EAT THE JJA-JANG AND CHAMPONG FROM CHONG-RYONG'S CHINESE FOOD FOR NOW.
WE DIDN'T TOUCH THE PORK YET, SO HERE IT IS, JUST GO AHEAD AND GIVE ME THE MONEY.
AND WE CAN JUST TRADE THE DISHES WHEN THE DELIVERY GUY COMES TO TAKE THEM BACK.
OUR NEIGHBOR (HE'S QUITE CUTE)
HOW...COULD THIS...HAPPEN...?
(THE PART THAT I'M QUITE DISAPPOINTED ABOUT IS THAT THE FOOD WE ORDERED WAS TASTIER.)

Translation Notes

Common honorifics:
-kun is normally used for boys. (Unlike the *-kun* used in Japanese, it is never used for girls.)
-yang is used for girls.
-shi is a polite way to address another. It is equivalent to *-san* in Japanese.
-chan is an affectionate Japanese honorific used for girls or young children.

Common titles:
Ahjushi is used for an older man of no relation to the speaker.
Ahjumma or *Ahjumuni* is used for older women, normally married women.
Oppa is used to address an elder brother, but also can be used by girls to address an older male that they are close with.
Hyung, like *Oppa*, is used to address an older male, but it is used by boys.

Page 30 – A *kogal* refers to a specific type of Japanese girl who follows the trend of looking very tan and wearing lots of makeup, rather skimpy clothing, and expensive brand-name accessories. It's a subculture comparable to the "Valley Girl" subculture of the 1980s.

Page 42 – 250,000 won is about 163 USD.

Page 123 – Takuan says "Good!!" in English.

Page 126 – The Japanese occupation of Korea from 1910 to1945 is still a very sore subject for those who are old enough to remember the period. There is much controversy over the alleged mistreatment of Korean citizens during that time, but the Japanese government has yet to release an "official" apology for the events that took place, which is what Be-Ri's grandmother is complaining about.

Page 127 – During the Japanese occupation of Korea, Japan wanted to slowly assimilate Korea by erasing Korean culture. Koreans were required to take Japanese names and to read, write, and speak only in Japanese.

Page 150 – *Kang Dong-Won* and *Hyun-Bin* are famous actors who are also well known for their handsome looks.

Page 151 – *Sam-Shik* is a name normally given to manservants and is sometimes considered a generalized name or insult for a slow-learning, homely-looking man.

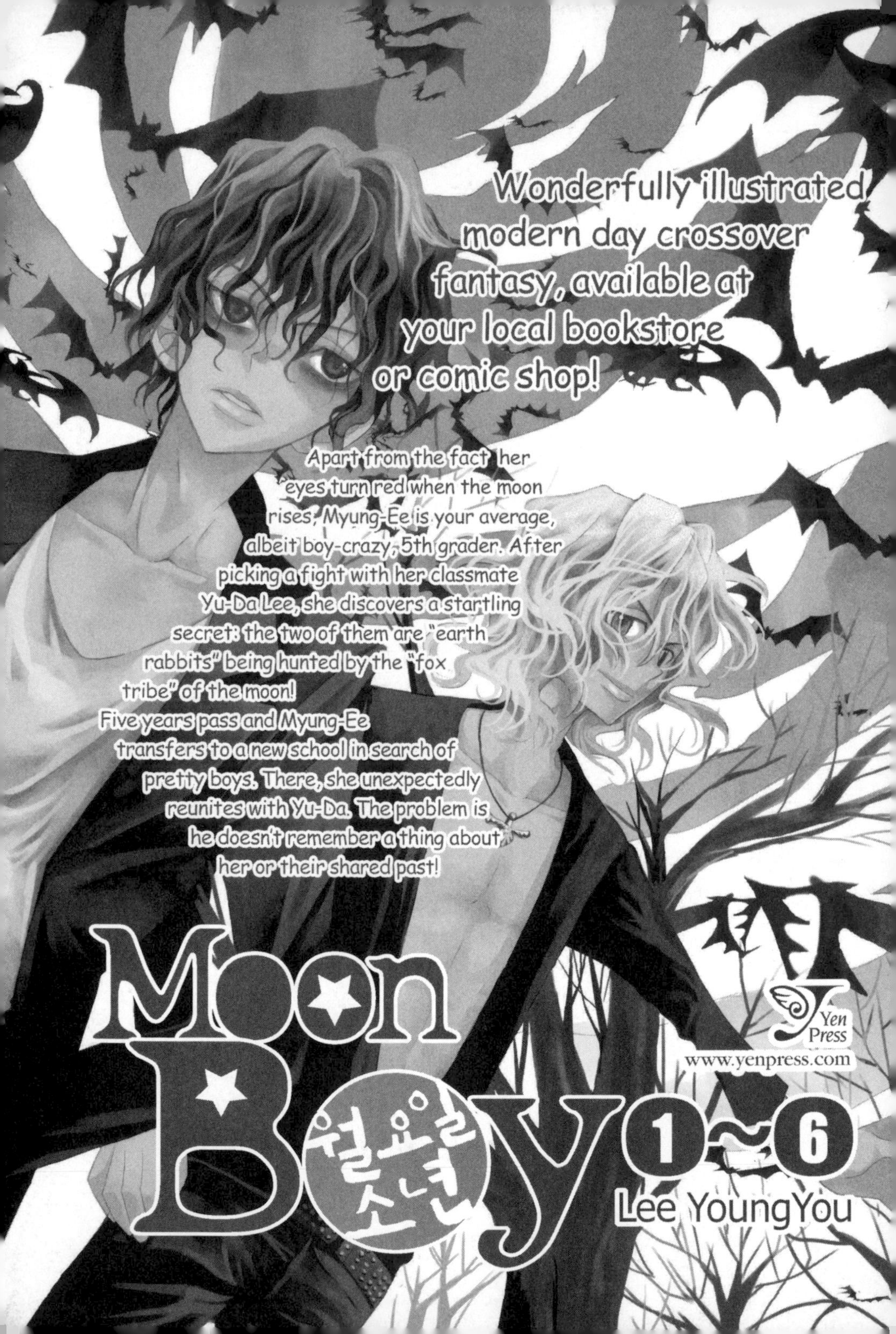
Wonderfully illustrated modern day crossover fantasy, available at your local bookstore or comic shop!
Apart from the fact her eyes turn red when the moon rises, Myung-Ee is your average, albeit boy-crazy, 5th grader. After picking a fight with her classmate Yu-Da Lee, she discovers a startling secret: the two of them are "earth rabbits" being hunted by the "fox tribe" of the moon! Five years pass and Myung-Ee transfers to a new school in search of pretty boys. There, she unexpectedly reunites with Yu-Da. The problem is he doesn't remember a thing about her or their shared past!
Moon Boy
월요일 소년
1~6
Lee YoungYou
Yen Press
www.yenpress.com

Available at bookstores near you!

CHOCOLAT
1~7

Shin JiSang · Geo

Kum-ji was a little late getting under the spell of the chart-topping band, DDL. Unable to join the DDL fan club, she almost gives up on meeting her idols, until she develops a cunning plan–to become a member of a rival fan club for the brand-new boy band Yo-I. This way she can act as Yo-I's fan club member and also be near Yo-I,

How far would you go to meet your favorite boy band?

who always seem to be in the same shows as DDL. Perfect plan...except being a fanatic is a lot more complicated than she expects. Especially when you're actually a fan of someone else. This full-blown love comedy about a fan club will make you laugh, cry, and laugh some more.

Yen
Press
www.yenpress.com

Becoming the princess... Isn't that every girl's dream?!

Monarchy rule ended long ago in Korea, but there are still other countries with kings, queens, princes and princesses. What if Korea had continued monarchism? What if all the beautiful palaces, which are now only historical relics, were actually filled with people? What if the glamorous royal family still maintained the palace customs? Welcome to a world where Korea still has the royal family living in their everyday lives! Only for this one high school girl, Chae-Kyung, is this a tragedy, since she has to marry the prince — who apparently is a total bastard!

THE ROYAL PALACE
Goong

vol.1 ~ 5

Park SoHee

The newest title from the creators of <Demon Diary> and <Angel Diary>!

Once upon a time, a selfish king summoned the monstrous Bulkirin into the real world. The monster killed half of all human beings, leaving the rest helpless as to what to do. That is, until one day when a hero appeared and defeated the Bulkirin with the legendary "Seven Blade Sword." But···what does all this have to do with 8th grader Eun-Gyo Sung?! First, she gets suspended from school for fighting. Then, she runs away from home. The last thing she needed was to be kidnapped—and whisked into the past by a mysterious stranger named No-Ah!

Legend

Available at bookstores near you!

1-5

K a r a · W o o S o o J u n g

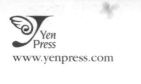

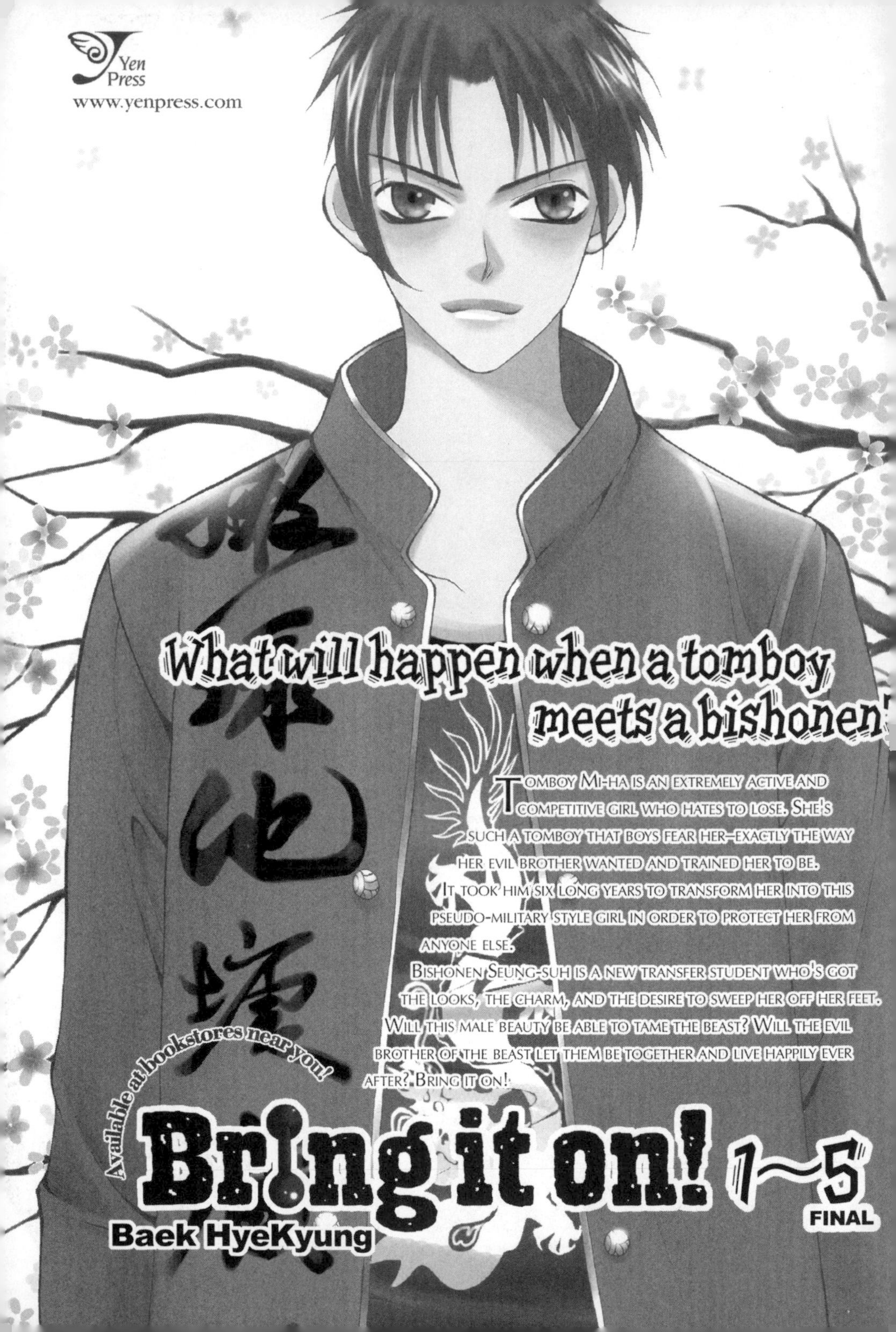
Yen Press
www.yenpress.com
What will happen when a tomboy meets a bishonen?
Tomboy Mi-ha is an extremely active and competitive girl who hates to lose. She's such a tomboy that boys fear her—exactly the way her evil brother wanted and trained her to be. It took him six long years to transform her into this pseudo-military style girl in order to protect her from anyone else.
Bishonen Seung-suh is a new transfer student who's got the looks, the charm, and the desire to sweep her off her feet. Will this male beauty be able to tame the beast? Will the evil brother of the beast let them be together and live happily ever after? Bring it on!
Available at bookstores near you!
Bring it on! 1~5 FINAL
Baek HyeKyung

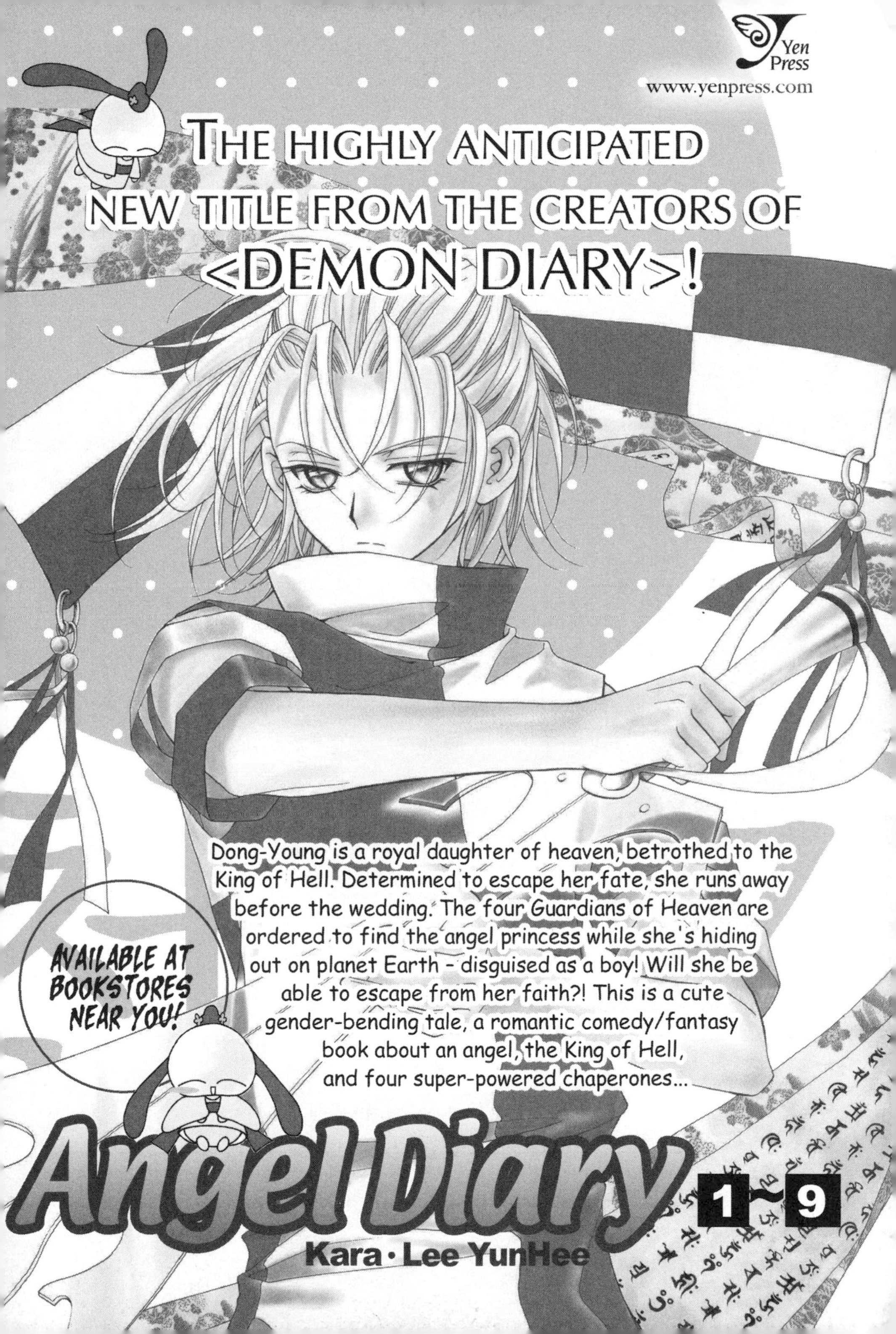
Yen Press
www.yenpress.com
THE HIGHLY ANTICIPATED NEW TITLE FROM THE CREATORS OF <DEMON DIARY>!
Dong-Young is a royal daughter of heaven, betrothed to the King of Hell. Determined to escape her fate, she runs away before the wedding. The four Guardians of Heaven are ordered to find the angel princess while she's hiding out on planet Earth - disguised as a boy! Will she be able to escape from her faith?! This is a cute gender-bending tale, a romantic comedy/fantasy book about an angel, the King of Hell, and four super-powered chaperones...
AVAILABLE AT BOOKSTORES NEAR YOU!
Angel Diary 1~9
Kara · Lee YunHee

THE MOST BEAUTIFUL FACE, THE PERFECT BODY,
AND A SINCERE PERSONALITY... THAT'S WHAT HYE-MIN HWANG HAS.
NATURALLY, SHE'S THE CENTER OF EVERYONE'S ATTENTION.
EVERY BOY IN SCHOOL LOVES HER, WHILE EVERY GIRL HATES HER OUT OF JEALOUSY.
EVERY SINGLE DAY, SHE HAS TO ENDURE TORTURES AND HARDSHIPS FROM THE GIRLS.

A PRETTY FACE COMES WITH A PRICE.

THERE IS NOTHING MORE SATISFYING THAN GETTING THEM BACK.
WELL, EXCEPT FOR ONE PROBLEM... HER SECRET CRUSH, JUNG-YUN.
BECAUSE OF HIM, SHE HAS TO HIDE HER CYNICAL AND DARK SIDE
AND DAILY PUT ON AN INNOCENT FACE. THEN ONE DAY, SHE FINDS OUT
THAT HE DISLIKES HER ANYWAY!! WHAT?! THAT'S IT! NO MORE NICE GIRL!
AND THE FIRST VICTIM OF HER RAGE IS A PLAYBOY SHE JUST MET, MA-HA.

vol.1~7

Cynical Orange
Yun JiUn

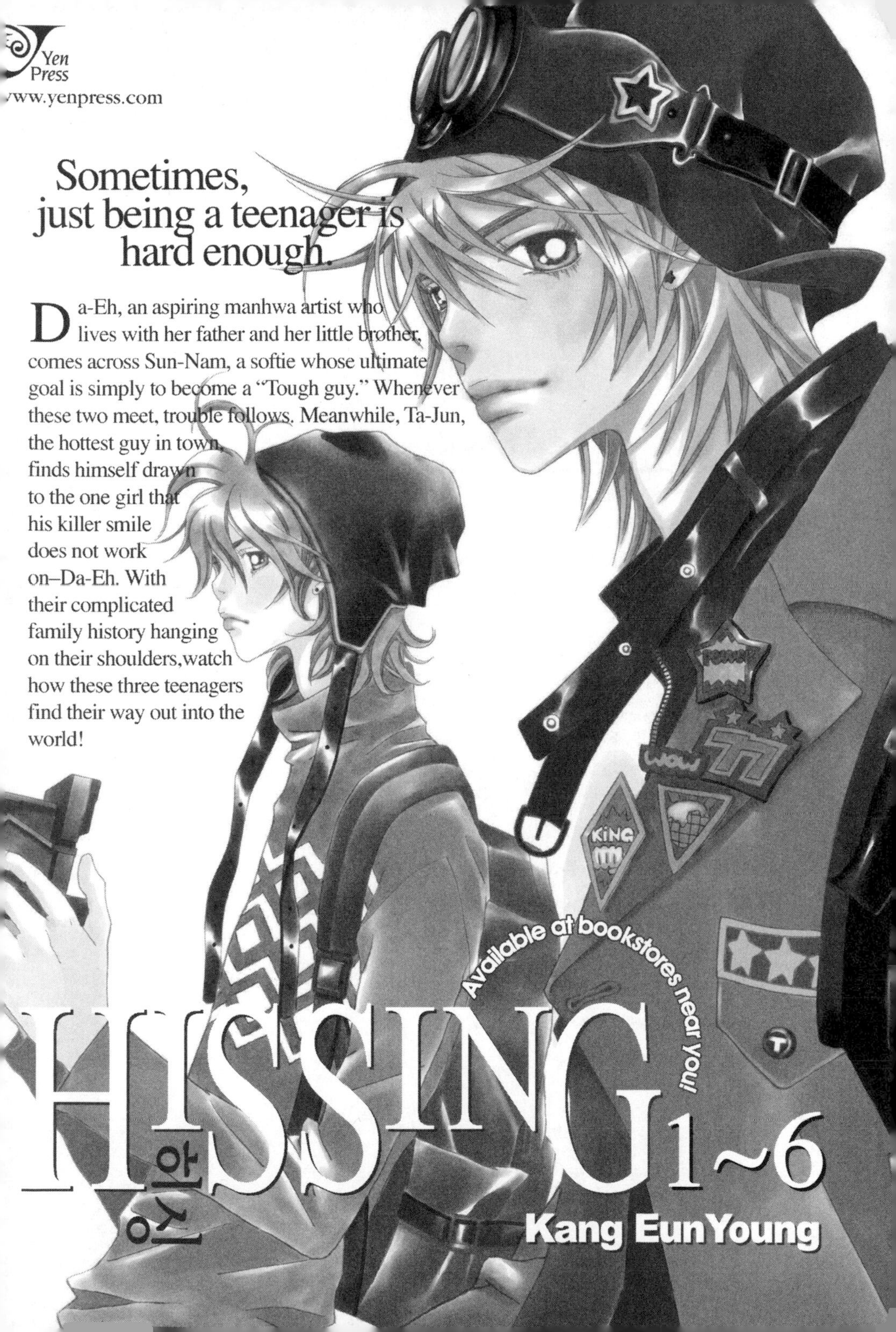
Yen Press
www.yenpress.com
Sometimes, just being a teenager is hard enough.
Da-Eh, an aspiring manhwa artist who lives with her father and her little brother, comes across Sun-Nam, a softie whose ultimate goal is simply to become a "Tough guy." Whenever these two meet, trouble follows. Meanwhile, Ta-Jun, the hottest guy in town, finds himself drawn to the one girl that his killer smile does not work on–Da-Eh. With their complicated family history hanging on their shoulders,watch how these three teenagers find their way out into the world!
Available at bookstores near you!
HISSING 1~6
하이싱
Kang EunYoung

JiSang Shin and Geo

Translation: Jackie Oh   Lettering: Alexis Eckerman

VERY! VERY! SWEET! Vol. 4 © 2007 JiSang Shin and Geo. All rights reserved. First published in Korea in 2007 by Seoul Cultural Publishers, Inc. English translation rights arranged by Seoul Cultural Publishers, Inc.

English translation © 2009 by Hachette Book Group, Inc.

Yen Press
Hachette Book Group
237 Park Avenue, New York, NY 10017

Visit our Web sites at www.HachetteBookGroup.com and www.YenPress.com.

Yen Press is an imprint of Hachette Book Group, Inc. The Yen Press name and logo are trademarks of Hachette Book Group, Inc.

First Edition: July 2009

ISBN: 978-0-7595-3146-8

10 9 8 7 6 5 4 3 2 1

BVG

Printed in the United States of America